Beyond Translation

Beyond Translation

Essays toward a Modern Philology

A. L. Becker

Ann Arbor
THE UNIVERSITY OF MICHIGAN PRESS

Copyright © by the University of Michigan 1995
All rights reserved
Published in the United States of America by
The University of Michigan Press
Manufactured in the United States of America
⊚Printed on acid-free paper
1998   1997   1996   1995   4 3 2 1

A CIP catalogue record for this book is available from the British Library.

Library of Congress Cataloging-in-Publication Data

Becker, Alton L.
   Beyond translation : essays towards a modern philology / A.L.
Becker.
      p.   cm.
   Collection of sixteen previously published essays, 1974–1993.
   Includes bibliographical references and index.
   Partial Contents: pt. 1. Text building in Javanese — pt. 2. Some
Burmese figures — pt. 3. Learning Malay — pt. 4. Translating
Emerson into Old Javanese — pt. 5. Music and language, language and
music — pt. 6. A place for particularity — pt. 7. Afterword.
   ISBN 0-472-10573-6 (alk. paper)
   1. Translating and interpreting. 2. Discourse analysis.
3. Philology. 4. Semantics. 5. Asia, Southeastern—Languages
—Translating. I. Title.
P306.2.B4   1995
418'.02—dc20   94-47089
                                                            CIP

For Richard Emerson Young
pro beneficiis amicitiae diuturnae

Acknowledgments

There is nothing written herein that did not come from someone else, from some prior text, heard or read. As Greg Dening has written, "None of us can plumb the depth of the plagiarism of our general discourse."

People who have made contributions to particular essays are remembered in the notes to those works, but several people have had a more pervasive and direct influence:

The members and staff of the Institute for Advanced Study in Princeton, where many of the essays were written and presented, in particular Clifford Geertz.

The members of the Monday Night Group who have criticized earlier versions of many of these essays and who have become my postretirement university: Rudolf Arnheim, Lee Bollinger, John D'Arms, Kenneth DeWoskin, Bruce Mannheim, the late A. K. Ramanujan, Joseph Vining, James Boyd White, and Christina Whitman.

Fellow humanist-linguists: William Foley, Paul Friederich, James Matisoff, Kenneth Pike, John R. Ross, and Deborah Tannen.

Fellow Southeast Asianists: Judith Becker, Hildred Geertz, Ariel Heryanto, Henk Maier, Mohammed haji Salleh, Amin Sweeney, and Aram Yengoyan.

Teachers in Southeast Asia: U San Htwe, Daw Mi Mi Khaing, Sao Saimong, Soedjati Djatikoesoema, Bambang Kaswanti Purwo, I Gusti Ngurah Oka, L. Mardiwarsito, and Soewojo Wojowasito.

Our contentious family: Judith, Matthew, Andrew, and Margaret. And Rhys Isaac.

❖   ❖   ❖

The author is grateful to the following sources for permission to reprint the material in this book.

Ablex Publishing Corporation for "Text Building, Epistemology, and Aesthetics in Javanese Shadow Theater," in A. L. Becker and Aram Yengoyan, eds., *The Imagination of Reality: Essays in Southeast Asian Coherence Systems* (1979); and "Language in Particular: A Lecture," in Deborah Tannen, ed., *Linguistics in Context: Connecting Observation and Understanding*, Advances in Discourse Processes, vol. 29 (1988).

The Academic Press for "The Figure a Sentence Makes: An Interpretation of a Classical Malay Sentence," in Talmy Givón, ed., *Discourse and Syntax* (1979).

Penerbit Bhratara Karya Aksara, Jakarta, for "Binding Wild Words: Cohesion in Old Javanese Prose" (with Thomas Hunter) in *Pelangi Bahasa* (Kumpulan esai yang dipersembahkan kepada Prof. Dr. J. W. M. Verhaar, S.J.) (1982).

The American Anthropological Association for "Biography of a Sentence: A Burmese Proverb," in Edward M. Bruner, ed., *Text, Play, and Story: The Construction and Reconstruction of Self and Society,* Proceedings of the American Ethnological Society (1983).

Lois Bateson and Mary Catherine Bateson for permission to reproduce the drawing by I Boengklik and Dewa Ketoet Pasek from the Bateson-Mead Collection of Balinese drawings.

The Center for South and Southeast Asian Studies at the University of Michigan for "Aridarma: Framing an Old Javanese Tale" in A. L. Becker, ed., *Writing on the Tongue* (1989); and "Translating the Art of Music" in Judith Becker and Alan Feinstein, eds., *Karawitan: Source Readings in Javanese Gamelan and Vocal Music*, vol. 2 (1987).

DC Heath and Company for "Silence Across Languages" in Claire Kramsch and Sally McConnel-Ginet, eds., *Text and Context: Cross-Disciplinary Perspectives on Language Study* (1992).

Georgetown University Press for "On Emerson on Language," in Deborah Tannen, ed., *Analyzing Discourse: Text and Talk* (1981); and "Beyond Translation: Esthetics and Language Description," in Heidi Byrnes, ed., *Contemporary Perceptions of Language: Interdisciplinary Dimensions* (1982).

John Benjamins Publishing Company for "The Figure a Classifier Makes: Describing a Particular Burmese Classifier," in Colette Craig, ed., *Noun Classes and Categorization* (1986).

Mouton de Gruyter for "The Elusive Figures of Burmese Grammar" in William A. Foley, ed., *The Role of Theory in Language Description* (Trends in Linguistics Studies and Monographs 69) (1993).

The University of California at Los Angeles Department of Anthropology for "Attunement: An Essay on Philology and Logophilia" in Paul Kroskrity, ed., *On the Ethnography of Communication: The Legacy of Sapir* (1988).

The Department of Linguistics, University of California, Berkeley, for "The Linguistics of Particularity: Interpreting Superordination in a Javanese Text," in *Proceedings of the Tenth Annual Meeting of the Berkeley Linguistics Society* (1984).

The University of Hawaii Press for "Person in Kawi: Exploration of an Elementary Semantic Dimension" (with I Gusti Ngurah Oka), *Oceanic Linguistics* 13 (1974).

The University of Texas Press for "A Musical Icon: Power and Meaning in Javanese Gamelan Music" (with Judith Becker), in Wendy Steiner, ed., *The Sign in Music and Literature* (1981).

Contents

Introduction

After a couple of decades spent exploring Southeast Asian languages (beginning in upper Burma in 1958), I came increasingly to wonder what, exactly, I was exploring and why it was so hard. I have taught those languages—Burmese, Thai, Indonesian, Old Javanese, Malay—translated them, tried to speak them, read literature old and new in them, and written about them, but in no sense have I mastered even one. Each remains for me distant and exotic.

After three years' residence in the Shan States of Burma, I could "get along" in Burmese. I spent many hours speaking in Burmese with my neighbors—mostly amusing my neighbors' children and chatting with my own students at the schools where I taught American English to them. At that time many adults in Burma still were easy in English (British English), for it was then only a few years since colonial rule had ended. None of the teachers at the schools where I taught knew no English at all, the way I knew no Burmese at all when I arrived.

I engaged a teacher. The Fulbright Foundation gave me special funds for Burmese lessons. My teacher for the next three years was Saya U San Htwe, who spoke Burmese, Shan, and English (British). From daily lessons at his house I learned to read in Burmese all sorts of stories, popular songs, classical poems, old chronicles, newspapers, Jataka tales, and Buddhist philosophy translated from Pali. There was even a text translated from English (American), Prime Minister U Nu's sincere Buddhistic translation of Dale Carnegie's patently insincere *How to Win Friends and Influence People.* Near the end of the three years, we read together the great dramas of nineteenth-century Burma, the plays by U Po Nya and U Kyin U. I went often to see Burmese theater when a troupe came to perform in or near the town where I lived (Taunggyi), and I traveled a long day's drive down to Mandalay several times to see the venerated marionette artists perform the classics.

My study window in Taunggyi overlooked a Buddhist monastery at the edge of the teak and pine forest. Part of learning Burmese was the considerable time well spent watching the monastic community at various periods of the day while I was at my desk nominally writing. I watched them, young novices and monks of all ages, gather firewood. I watched them in slow walking meditation. I watched them come out of the monastery in the morning with their black lacquer offering bowls. Before that, very early in the morning, the little novices began their lessons, shouting at the tops of their voices the texts their teachers had set, not in unison but each voice separately. It was a loud, thick, pleasant sound.

My reaction then, at least at first, was to discredit this method of learning by rote, but after a few decades of language teaching, here and there, I am convinced of its rightness. It is a way of learning that fit very well the subject, the place, and the time, and, as I was yet to learn, still can. After I got over the annoyance of cacophony at 4 A.M., I learned to pick out words from the noise and later ask my teacher, Saya U San Htwe, what they meant. Slowly, with his patient, wise help, I was learning to hear the noise as languaging.

There were two more lessons to be learned from the cacophony of those predawn lessons, beyond just learning some of the words: I was getting over my alien annoyance, and I was focusing my attention. Maybe there was another: I was getting up early.

Over the duration of the three years I spent in Burma, Burmese emerged for me slowly and in fragments. The best simile I know for that experience of learning a very distant language in situ is that it is like watching a clearer and clearer picture gradually emerge while a photograph develops in a chemical bath. A vast picture, infinitely detailed, and even now it is still developing.

❖   ❖   ❖

What was I learning and why was it so hard? The answer depends on whether one is a philosopher, a linguist, a language teacher, an ethnographer, a translator, a poet, or some other such category of person who does not simply *use* language but is compelled, for one reason or another, to think carefully and repeatedly *about* it.

In our own personal self-consciousness, what are the boundaries, the limits, of our languaging, our inner languaging—what Ernest Becker called *the inner newsreel* in a metaphor that may now be dated? The Spanish philosopher and philologist José Ortega y Gasset called this inner languaging *ensimismamiento*. Where does languaging stop and another kind of "thinking" begin in my own "inoneselfness"? When I study the activity of languaging, what should I focus on? When I learn Burmese, what am I learning? Facts? A skill? A new part in a drama? Or beyond that, beyond translation, a new *ensimismamiento*, a new self-consciousness, not replacing the old one but coming more and more to stand separate beside it. What in me is changing? Where, if anywhere, does languaging leave off and some other aspect of my being begin?

For me, these questions came to the foreground of my *ensimismamiento* when I was getting ready to return to Burma twenty-five years after I had first lived there in the late 1950s. I was getting ready to go back to Burma after a long absence.

I was in a mountain hotel in Central Java, on a balcony in the cool evening air, trying to remember the Burmese I had once known. I remembered knowing Burmese fairly well, but Indonesian and Javanese words were getting in the way now, and I was trying to put them aside and uncover Burmese. I felt that Burmese words were buried deeper in my memory than were the words from these new (for me) languages. Burmese had been my first foreign language studied in situ.

I have always kept field journals about learning languages in various parts of Southeast Asia. That evening I wrote in my journal,

"If you take away grammar and lexicon from a language, what is left?"

Then I wrote, "Answer: Everything!"

At that moment, as I was trying to remember the Burmese I

thought I had once known, grammars and lexicons seemed beside the point, just things we do with languages, not things that are *somehow within* languages, not part of their being as languages. People like me *make* grammars and dictionaries—these artifacts are not in the minds of the users of languages. Grammars and dictionaries were not what was buried in my memory. This came to me with the force of a revelation.

I was by then a professional linguist, and these questions were important in my profession. I wrote them down, then went back to remembering Burmese words. After a while a doorway opened—a curtain parted (there is no nonmetaphoric language for this)—and some of the Burmese I once knew came back to me.

What I remembered were not patterns and definitions, certainly not rules, but particular things. First of all, a children's song—the tune something like "Polly Wolly Doodle": "A poh gyi oh . . . kha khohn khohn . . . m'thay ba hne' ohn . . . nowght hnit ka . . . t'saung mohn . . . pwe kyi ba ohn." I sang it to myself with almost no hesitation, sounding it in my mind. I remembered memorizing it many years before in my study in Burma, during the first months I was there. One of the other teachers had written it out awkwardly in English letters as I have done here. U San Htwe told me what the words meant and the story that went with them: "Old man, bent back, don't die yet. Come back next year, month of Tazaungmon, see the play." The old man was the heir to the Peacock throne in Mandalay, the lost king of Burma who had been deposed and exiled to India by the British in 1886. The schoolchildren were calling him back, next year, in the cool dry months, during the season of the plays when famous groups of actors toured the towns and villages. The familiar "Polly Wolly Doodle" tune and the covert references were crafted to sound innocent to colonial ears. By the time I was there Independence had come, and to these children the song was not, I think, political. To older people it still was.

I got the words for 'back' (*kha*), 'bent, convex' (*khohn khohn*), 'old' (*oh*), and 'year' (*hnit*) not separately but together. The tune helped me remember. I am sure everyone has a story like this to tell, some old remnant of learning a language.

I think the particularity of it made it memorable. It came with so much particular context: the other teachers, the written words, the children singing, the familiar tune, the rhymes, the story. The particularity made a unique place in my memory for "it," the little text.

❖   ❖   ❖

Those first few months in Burma had been awkward, full of common, everyday misunderstandings. Part of the awkwardness was not knowing how to cope with those misunderstandings, except to smile foolishly and switch to English (American). Most people switched too quickly, before I wanted them to, and so I sought out some monolinguals, all but one of them children. The one who was not a child was a woodchopper saint, the gentlest man I ever met, who would hold the block of wood he was chopping in his lap before every stroke of his axe and carefully brush off the bugs. He answered every question I ever asked him.

Everyday misunderstandings in languaging come down to a paradox, according again to Ortega:

> Two apparently contradictory laws are involved in all uttering. One says, "Every utterance is deficient"—it says less than it wishes to say. The other law, the opposite, declares, "Every utterance is exuberant"—it conveys more than it plans and includes not a few things we would wish left silent.

These two apparently antithetical laws, which are involved in every utterance we make, spoken or written—that all languaging is deficient and says less than we wish it to, and that at the same time all languaging is exuberant and says more than we know—are Ortega's first two axioms for a new philology: *una nueva filología*.

They are not conditions first to be understood and then overcome but a basic necessity of all human languaging. In Burma, unlike at home, the scale of misunderstanding was vast, and coping with it seemed to require very complex rhetorical moves of repair, politeness, and explanation. Everything was wildly and unforeseeably deficient and exuberant at the same time.

Across two languages, there are many silences, and these amplify the deficiencies and exuberances. To quote Ortega once more,

> The stupendous reality that is language cannot be understood unless we begin by observing that speech consists above all in silences. A being who could not renounce saying many things would be incapable of speaking. And each language represents a different equation between manifestations and silences. Each people leaves some things unsaid *in order* to be able to say others. Because *everything* would be unsayable. Hence the immense difficulty of translation: translation is a matter of saying in a language precisely what that language tends to pass over in silence.

A simple example of this might be number or gender. English marks distinctions we call *singular* and *plural* on many nouns and pronouns: other languages may be silent about this distinction. It is not that this distinction is necessarily manifest in some other formal way in those languages: it is that number is not used to sort out the roles and references of discourse, the way it is used in English. Linguists might say of such languages that in them number is not grammaticized, that you aren't constrained by demands of understandability and coherence to make number distinctions. The same might be said of gender—a common Indo-European grammatical instrument for sorting out in our utterances the things of the world (and outside it: gods, abstractions, planets). But gender is an instrument that is not used this way everywhere. In learning English from within languages without number or gender (like Burmese, or Javanese, or Malay, the languages of those I was teaching), we can appear obsessed with quantities or full of built-in sexism. I have talked for many hours about these things with Burmese, Javanese, Balinese, Malays, in their languages and in English, with gradual, unfolding awareness of silences across languages. Number and gender are but simple examples of silences. There are many, many more to be discovered in comparing and translating even the simplest acts of languaging. A few of the more important silences are discussed in the essays that follow.

❖   ❖   ❖

In considering these silences, we come to some of the limiting factors of languaging—whether we are languaging in our own native language or translating across languages. If Ortega is right, then not everything sayable is sayable in English, and furthermore, not everything is sayable.

❖   ❖   ❖

Silence, as Ortega thinks of it, is clearly a term of comparison. Silences emerge when one looks across two or more languages, and silences are products of that looking. All language description is thereby comparative: one language in terms of another. There is no neutral language to use in describing other languages. There are silences across all languages.

Between English and Burmese there are many silences—things in English that have no counterpart in Burmese and things in Burmese that have no counterpart in English. I can say with real assurance that if we compare any sentence of Burmese and a translation of it in English, at least half of what is there in English will have no counterpart in the Burmese original and at least half of what is conveyed by the original won't make it into English. A simple sentence like "I am" in English is not easily translatable into a language that has no neutral first-person pronoun, no tense, and no copula. (For amplification, see "Biography of a Sentence," one of the essays that follows.) Translation is no respecter of silences. It works because it ignores almost all of them.

One thing that makes learning Burmese hard is that we usually come to it with the false expectation that we can translate most of it into English.

Our general tendency is to "read into" our experience of a distant language the familiar things that are missing, all the silences, and then we claim that all these things are "understood," "implied," or "part of the underlying logical structure" of those languages. We do this because that is the way we learn to treat silences in our own language. We are used to filling them in when necessary. We practice all day long. Someone says "Super!" and we understand, without anyone saying it, what was super and, drawing on our experiences with the word *super,* we give it a meaningful past by which to understand the present use. If necessary, for example, to repair a misunderstanding, we can fill in many of the silences. But our everyday filling in of silences often doesn't work across languages where the silences may well have new meanings, involving new distinctions that are silent in English.

It takes a while to learn that things like tenses, and articles, and the copula are not "understood" in Burmese, Javanese, or Malay. I mean *understood* as language teachers often use the term, to mean something not uttered but implied. In Burmese these things aren't implied; they just aren't there. And all the rhetorical acts that we perform with grammatical elements like tense and articles and the copula (among the most common elements of our own language, the things that the coherence of our discourse is built around) are things you can't do in Burmese. I will come back to this later.

First, however, it is important to discuss a second reason why our image of language itself disguises the difficulty of learning Burmese. It is not just that our understanding is in English and that there are many profound silences between Burmese and English. It is that our common image of language rather radically separates language and thought. We tend to assume that language is a means of expressing thought. We commonly speak of language as a code, with thoughts as the "input," the stuff that is encoded. But what if language extends down into the very ways we shape our experiences, store them, and retrieve them, and is not only a means of communicating them? The code metaphor seems to limit languaging unduly.

A *language,* as we commonly speak of it, is not what Burmese (out of Pali) calls a *batha.* A *language* is a *batha* that has been reduced to rules of grammar and a lexicon. A *language* is a *batha* abstracted from its content and its context.

Language and Languaging

In order to distinguish this image of *batha* from the dominant code image of *language,* I have been following the practice of John Dewey and, more recently, Humberto Maturana, in trying to use two different words: *language* for the code image, *languaging* for the view that combines shaping, storing, retrieving, and communicating knowledge into one open-ended process.

A *language*, then, is a system of rules or structures, which, in the Saussurian view, relates meanings and sounds, both of which are outside it. A language is essentially a dictionary and a grammar.

Languaging, on the other hand, is context shaping. Languaging both shapes and is shaped by context. It is a kind of attunement between a person and a context. Languaging can be understood as taking old texts from memory and reshaping them into present contexts. This is the basic way languaging contrasts with language. Most current theories of language have no place for memory. But building a new memory, a new past, a new *ensimismamiento*, is, it seems to me, the hardest part of learning a new way of languaging.

It is in this way that an image of language gets in the way of learning Burmese and makes it hard.

Languaging is shaping old texts into new contexts. It is done at the level of particularity.

My own early understanding of context in this sense came to me in the 1950s, before I went to Burma, in reading a new book written by one of my professors at Michigan, Kenneth Boulding. It is called *The Image*. It was written while Boulding was away from Michigan at the Center for Advanced Study at Stanford. In the book, Boulding lays the groundwork for a new science he calls *eiconics*, the study, in other words, of the shaping, storing, retrieval, and communication of knowledge as images of context.

The book begins like this.

> As I sit at my desk, I know where I am. I see before me a window; beyond that some trees; beyond that the red roofs of the campus of Stanford University; beyond them the trees and roof tops which mark the town of Palo Alto; beyond them the bare golden hills of the Hamilton Range . . .

After moving out in concentric circles, he comes to the edges of his space.

Looking still further I see our star the sun as a member of millions upon millions of others in the Galaxy. Looking still further, I visualize the Galaxy as one of millions upon millions of others in the universe.

I am not only located in space, I am located in time. . . . Certain dates are meaningful: 1776, 1620, 1066. . . . Many of the images are vague, but Greece follows Crete, Rome follows Assyria.

I am not only located in space and time, I am located in a field of personal relations. . . . There are places into which I go, and it will be recognized that I am expected to behave in a certain manner. I may sit down to worship, I may make a speech, I may listen to a concert, . . .

I am not only located in space and in time and in personal relationships, I am also located in the world of nature, in a world of how things operate. I know that when I get into my car there are some things I must do to start it; some things I must do to back out of the parking lot; some things I must do to drive home. . . .

Finally, I am located in the midst of a world of subtle intimations and emotions. I am sometimes elated, sometimes a little depressed, sometimes happy, sometimes sad, sometimes inspired, sometimes pedantic. I am open to subtle intimations of a presence beyond the world of space and time and sense.

What I have been talking about is . . . my *Image* of the world.

And a page later Boulding says, in italics, *"The meaning of a message is the change which it produces in the image."*

Languaging is involved in all these kinds of context—space, time, social relations, nature, emotions, and subtle transcendental intimations. Boulding's image is a web of languaging. This is not to say that it is only languaging, but rather that languaging pervades it and binds it.

A few years later, in Burma learning Burmese, I began to learn how entering upon a new way of languaging entailed not so much profound changes in my image of the world—I had expected that— but new images.

Things silent now were articulated, and important distinctions fell silent:

> Pitch contours changed words in ways I had not experienced before in English. (A missionary in Burma gave me a book from which I learned that Burmese is a tone language. It was also my first awareness of Kenneth Pike, who had written the book, and who was the linguist I wanted to study with when I returned to America.)

> When I tried to tell a story in Burmese, I put in past time markers in imitation of English tense—and totally confused people. Time took on new distinctions, lost old ones.

> Writing was no longer alphabetic. The Burmese image of a word was very different, even though they, too, wrote from left to right, as we do. I remember in Burma asking a student to point to the front of a word written on the blackboard. He pointed to the right side of it, and everybody in class agreed that that was the front. One of the tone markers on a Burmese word, looking like our colon in place and shape, is called *dots-in-front*. For me the front was where the "first" letter was, on the left. Space took on new distinctions, lost old ones.

> People over and over said they were *"ah nah deh,"* which might translate as '(my) strength hurts (me)'. It was a reluctance to put themselves forward—their own power made them uneasy—a signal that more persistent inviting was needed, a positive emotion of "shame" that I learned very slowly to value. And I began to understand a new set of metaphors involving new pains and with them a new set of emotions.

An ethnolinguist can fill pages with these little stories of the exotic. They have a particular esthetic that is one of the genuine pleasures of learning new ways of languaging: the delight of defamiliarization.

Like a rain of fresh new poetic metaphors, Burmese defamiliarized the image of the world I took for granted.

That it was exotic at all is, of course, only a measure of how much of an outsider I was. And yet, that is also what good poems do— defamiliarize the world I take for granted. Exoticism is a positive thing, a source of energy in fieldwork. I do not see how anyone learning a new way of languaging can escape a pervading sense of exotic pleasure.

Restocking Memory

Languages differ in the silences they practice, in the way they make your face look, in the images of context they shape. But beyond those things, the biggest reasons Burmese is hard have to do with memory.

Burmese seems exotic because I lack the stock of remembered prior texts, the lingual memory, to make it seem familiar. I seldom know if what someone says is new and original or old and familiar. I do not "get" jokes. Ever. I have almost no lingual memory in Burmese.

Grammar rules and dictionaries are our foreign substitutes for lingual memories, but they are poor ones. They lack the richness of prior texts, the particularity and special memorability that come only with languaging in context.

Learning Burmese is learning Burmese ways to reshape Burmese memories into new Burmese contexts. The old prince is alive, is invited to come back next year after the rainy season when the magical plays and nighttime festivals begin again. Burmese is a web of words and silences that shapes a context, in space, in time, in social relations, in nature, and in emotions and subtle intimations. What could be harder to learn than that?

❖   ❖   ❖

After the three years in Burma and graduate study in linguistics (with Kenneth Pike at Michigan), which had grown out of my years there, I taught and studied in East Java for two years. For the first time I visited Bali and Lombok, Sulawesi and Jogjakarta. I had teachers in all those places with whom I read, in Old Balinese, Sasak, Bugis, and Old Javanese. I translated and wrote essays about pronouns, deixis, the complexity of person, and the absence of tense. And I studied every day with a shadow puppeteer, Soedjati Djatikoesoemo, sitting cross-legged at a wayang screen we set up in my house. I wrote about his lessons.

By then I had learned from Gregory Bateson to be concerned with cultural epistemology, the study of how people know what they know, their "way of knowing." Studying distant, unrelated ways of languaging can make you newly aware that your own languaging is just one possibility among many, that English, like Burmese or Javanese, is an artifact created over time from the materials at hand, like a style of dwelling, a traditional cuisine, or a way of dressing.

Looking outside of my own languaging helped me to see that much of my way of knowing the world—and acting in it—is shaped by the texts I was born into. This self-consciousness is not a new experience in human history—rhetoricians, poets, philosophers, and Buddhist monks have described it for eons, but it always seems to come personally with a shock, a revelation, an intimation of epistemological mortality.

Our own languaging is such an elusive thing. "It" is the most personal thing we possess, in the sense that the particularities of our repertoire of acts, and voices, and all our lingual memories are unique to each of us, yet "it" is in large part inherited and shaped in interaction with others. It fills our *ensimismamiento* with what Ernest Becker called an *inner newsreel*, and Buddhists sometimes call *gossip*—that personal, unuttered commentary on the present mixed with replays of the past and preplays of the future. It is the world each of us lives in, the individual *lebenswelt*, the personal noosphere, consciousness, the arena of meditation . . . there are many, many names for "it." Not so long ago "it" was called by Emerson *the soul*, and before that *psykhe*, that which most Christians believe is eternal and most Buddhists insist is the ultimate illusion. The question that formed over my years of studying Southeast Asian languages is: how does "it" change when one learns a distant language? In other words, how do we become, internally and in our relations to the rest of the world, different persons in Burmese?

It became clear in those years that learning a language in situ could be profoundly transforming for an individual. Burmese requires a new voice, and because a voice is made with the face, learning Burmese requires a new face. You stand differently in Burmese—nearer to another man than you usually would for American English, often face-to-face and holding hands with the person you are talking to. Eye contact is different. Silence is different. Few words are easily translated, and sentences connect in funny ways. I learned that, although an Anglophone could make passably good sentences in Burmese, Malay, or Javanese, it took no more than two or three sentences in sequence for any native hearer to recognize in the disconnectedness the foreignness of the speaker.

An "episteme"—a way of knowing—seems not to be an abstract thing, although, like a grammar, it can and usually has been represented abstractly. An episteme has its full being in individual persons, in their minds and bodies, not in some abstract realm of Platonic ideas. Constrained as we are by the many dimensions of the contexts we live in, it still seems to me that the transactions of consciousness *happen* particularly in particular individuals.

Furthermore, to lay another belief on the table right here at the start of this book, an episteme seems to me to be pervaded by languaging. Memory certainly evokes more than words, but it just as certainly evokes words along with sensory images. We forget particular words, even the socially accepted names of things, but names are not the only words evoked. In my own consciousness, I find it impossible to separate words from other images. I have been told that this is a peculiarity of my own, that I am a "verbal person." I am told that painters think visually, entirely in voiceless shapes. On the other hand, seriously meditating Buddhist monks in Burma (and in America) have told me that separating words from experience is the hardest thing for a meditator to do. Very few individuals ever achieve it, they say. I believe them.

Two things became clear to me about epistemes: they are fully realized only in their particularity, in individuals; and they are pervaded by languaging. The individuality of their occurrence is balanced by the communality of their medium, prior texts, which are in large part inherited. Languaging is inherited not as grammatical rules or patterned lexicons but particularly, in particular memories of particular instances of languaging, what I have called *prior texts*. Knowing a way of languaging means having a repertoire of prior texts—all the particular instances of languaging any one of us remembers, always imperfectly. When we speak or write, we take those imperfectly remembered prior texts and reshape them into new contexts.

After many years it became clear to me that distant languages are difficult because there are no shared prior texts: one has to build a new memory in Burmese, Javanese, or Malay. It won't do to speak these languages out of an English memory.

Thus, the term *episteme* came to make sense to me as describing a repertoire of prior texts, acquired over a lifetime, to be reshaped and used in making sense of experience. This, too, is not a new way of thinking. It has long been a theme in American pragmatism, strongly rooted in the work of Ralph Waldo Emerson, William James, Charles Santiago Peirce, John Dewey, and Gertrude Stein, to mention only the more famous names.

❖   ❖   ❖

After studying Southeast Asian languages for a while, I began to look back into my own philological tradition, to the prior texts I had inherited and accumulated in English, to see whether I could go back far enough to find in them, in my own tradition, the same sorts of strangeness, silence, and opacity that I had found in Southeast Asia.

I searched in my own philological past for that opacity, that sense of philological distance I still feel with Burmese. I found it in Ralph Waldo Emerson's words on language in the book *Nature*, published in 1836. It seemed at first superficial, excessive in style, and full of generalizations that were too vague and almost entirely irrelevant to the concerns of a modern linguist. This had also been my initial reaction to most Southeast Asian writing about languaging.

On the title page of the revised 1849 edition of Emerson's *Nature* one finds a poem in lieu of a subtitle, a poem printed in small caps, each line centered.

A SUBTLE CHAIN OF COUNTLESS RINGS
THE NEXT UNTO THE FARTHEST BRINGS;
THE EYE READS OMENS WHERE IT GOES,
AND SPEAKS ALL LANGUAGES THE ROSE;
AND, STRIVING TO BE MAN, THE WORM
MOUNTS THROUGH ALL THE SPIRES OF FORM.

The central question of Emerson's chapter on language is also the central question of the whole work, *Nature*. It is an epistemological question: how is a Soul, an individual observing person, related to Nature? Two very distant, archaic words, *soul* and *nature*.

As for *nature*, Emerson defines it as "all that is separate from us, all which philosophically distinguishes as the *not me*, that is, both nature and art, all other men and my own body." How does an individual observer, a live being, "relate to its environment" (to use Dewey's terms)? We might now call Nature *context*.

But to read a word like *soul* in a way that is fair to Emerson (who told us to remember George Fox's admonition that "Every scripture is to be interpreted by the same spirit which gave it forth") means to make an effort to erase at least a few of the things *soul* has come to mean since 1836 and to learn at least a few of the things it might have meant then, in 1836, before it was displaced in most of our everyday language and even in the serious discourse of philosophy. That effort to read a word fairly—to set aside exuberances of meaning and to fill in deficiencies—was what my work with Southeast Asian languages and literatures had been all about. *Soul* for Emerson was a metonymy for an individual being, a term shared at that time by science and religion. We don't have a word nowadays quite like *soul* in that same range. Since Emerson's day whole continents of prior text have drifted away.

After several years of reading Emerson, I learned, with some effort, to make use of him, to appropriate him to help me understand my own experiences, including my experiences in Southeast Asia. I learned to see, as he wrote in that essay, that "parts of speech are metaphors," and that because of languaging "the whole of nature is a metaphor of the human mind." I began to understand Emerson when I began to find him useful in describing my own experience. Burmese words seemed to me powerfully metaphoric, unlike English, until, in learning Burmese, English began to seem metaphoric, too.

On my return from Burma in 1961, I came to Michigan to study with Kenneth Pike. That missionary in Burma had loaned me Pike's book on tone languages, and I had learned a great deal from it, particularly what it meant to say that the language I was learning was a tone language. Pike gave me, among many terms, the word *emic*. As he often said to his students, the observer is always part of the data, and we should strive for an emic perspective, an empathy with the perspective of the engaged user not just that of the detached observer. The term came from the word *phonemic*. Phonemics (in contrast to phonetics) is the study of the sound distinctions that make a difference in a particular language. We all can make and hear different sounds, but only some are used to distinguish the words of our language. Many forms of writing are based on the representation of "differences that make a difference." In his classes, Pike taught us, using subtle problems from Native American languages, methods of distinguishing the emic from the etic. He extended this idea beyond sounds to encompass all of the distinctions a language makes.

Few outsiders, maybe none, ever achieve a wholly emic view of any Southeast Asian language, any text in Burmese, or Javanese, or Malay. We never overcome all of the exuberances and deficiencies of our outsider's understanding. There is often a lack of candor about this, a kind of philological machismo. Traditional philologists sometimes come to feel just as sure of their definitions of words and translations of texts in distant languages as of their understanding of something they heard at home, something, say, a friend said just yesterday. The difference is that the distant word or text comes to us without a negotiator to insist that our reading is not what was meant, not what was meant at all. The distant text doesn't say, like a spouse, "You just don't understand!" Open-ended negotiation of meaning, the sorting out of exuberances and deficiencies, is part of our experience of languaging with those with whom we normally exchange utterances, but such things are not normally in the foreground of a translation of a Burmese song or a Javanese shadow play. Here, in these essays, I want them to be.

The essays center on a few translations of different bits of Southeast Asian languaging. I attempt to describe how the text of a Javanese shadow play is built, what some of the past life of a Burmese proverb has been, how a sentence of Emerson might sound in Old Javanese, what the difficulty is in translating a line from a Malay epic, how a scene in a shadow play is coherent in different ways in Javanese and English, and how a well-known Sanskrit story is recontextualized and used in Old Javanese.

Beyond Translation

A final word about the title of this book, *Beyond Translation*. What I am attempting here is beyond translation in a simple sense. Translation is not the end point, the final outcome of a philological endeavor. Rather, it is a starting point, the beginning of moving back, looking back, toward the source of the translation.

In a more complex sense, moving beyond translation is also an attempt at restitution for the careless aggression and violent appropriation involved in any act of translation—a restoration of the balance, a making visible of our failures. It is a new sense of what fidelity in translation means.

A translator's need for restitution is richly described by George Steiner in *After Babel*. He suggests adding to our usual understanding of the acts of translation this compensatory "move," this new fidelity, which takes us beyond translation in the traditional sense, the sense in which this move is not usually made.

The need for restitution came to me strongly a few years ago when I discussed before a Malay audience, in a stranger's version of their language, my experiences in translating the opening lines of the great Malay classic, the *Hikayat Hang Tuah*, which remains only partially translated into English. When I was finished, and the last polite questions appeared to have been asked, a respected Malay scholar stood up and said he hoped I would not translate *Hang Tuah* into English.

I was nonplussed. Why not? He explained that if it were available in English, no one would read the Malay. He seemed to state this as a matter of obvious fact, not as an accusation. I did not make a good response. I suspect he knew I wouldn't and had politely waited until the end of the questioning. I had not thought that a translation might come to represent the Malay original. I had seen it, naively, only as giving access to the original. I had no sense of the responsibility of it or even of being entitled to . . . translate.

Silly foreigner's sensitivities? People I have talked to about this come down on both sides. Does translation need to happen to great works? All of them? Walter Benjamin suggests it is a possible stage in the life of any work that it be translated. Carrying that image further, we can think of translation itself as happening in stages. It begins before the first word is replaced and continues after the last one has been. Before translation there is anticipation, getting the prior texts in mind, and then, in George Steiner's words, "We venture a leap: we grant ab initio that there is 'something there' to be understood." And beyond the last word of the translation is this need for retribution. Translation has not been a neutral, painless act. It has been necessarily full of politics and semi-intended errors of exuberance and deficiency. Steiner saw very clearly that herein is "the crux of the metier and morals of translation."

Some reciprocity is called for, not out of silly sensitivities and politeness alone but because translation is not a neutral act. Translation fidelity itself demands reciprocity, a sorting out of exuberances and deficiencies, a confession of failures and sleights of hand. It is the only way I know of by which to make restitution to those who, in old Malay words, *mpunya carita* 'wrought the words and in that sense own them'.

Beyond translation, then, an explorer of languages faces a demand for fidelity and restitution around which a new philology can be shaped. Full restitution lies well beyond these essays, but it is a goal toward which they have been written.

With regard to the other part of this book title, *Modern Philology*, a friendly Javanese translator once asked me why anyone would want to be moving toward something modern in a postmodern time (*pascamoderen*, he said, a nice blend of a word out of Sanskrit-Javanese and Romance). So much for stages. The only answer I could think of was that maybe, in philology, we haven't become modern yet.

ACKNOWLEDGMENTS

Footnotes in a personal essay seem inappropriate, but proper respect demands acknowledging sources. Furthermore, lessons of the sort I recount above can seldom be brought down to single page references. So I will mention just the particular works I referred to or quoted from. All are identified with full page references in the essays that follow. From John Dewey I draw on *Art as Experience* (New York: G. P. Putnam, 1934). From Humberto Maturana and Francisco Varela, *The Tree of Knowledge: The Biological Roots of Human Understanding* (Boston: New Science Library, 1987). From Ernest Becker, *The Birth and Death of Meaning: An Interdisciplinary Perspective on the Problem of Man* (New York: Free Press, 1962). From José Ortega y Gasset, *Man and People [El Hombre y La Gente]*, translated by Willard R. Trask (New York: Norton, 1957). From Ralph Waldo Emerson, *Nature*, new edition (Boston and Cambridge: James Munroe and Company, 1849). From Kenneth Boulding, *The Image* (Ann Arbor: University of Michigan Press, 1956). From Gregory Bateson, *Mind and Nature: A Necessary Unity* (New York: Dutton, 1979). From Kenneth Pike, *Tone Languages: A Technique for Determining the Number and Type of Pitch Contrasts in a Language, with Studies in Tonemic Substitution and Fusion* (Ann Arbor: University of Michigan Publications, 1948). And from George Steiner, *After Babel: Aspects of Language and Translation* (New York: Oxford University Press, 1975).

PART 1
TEXT BUILDING IN JAVANESE

Text Building, Epistemology, and Aesthetics in Javanese Shadow Theater

This essay was written just after I had spent two years learning how to perform (not too well) the wayang kulit, *the Javanese shadow play, in Malang, East Java, in 1969 and 1970. Although it came in the middle of my study of Southeast Asian languages (which started with Burmese in 1958), this essay marks a beginning of an approach that I have used and developed ever since in describing lingual artifacts of Southeast Asia. Therefore, it makes an appropriate beginning.*

I studied wayang kulit *not to perform it—at least not until my teacher convinced me that one performance is worth a year of lessons—but rather to see how it was made, how a particular language "game" was put together. I called it text building. I think of myself as an observer, one who "likes to watch," but I learned early, perhaps while playing jazz in school, that you become a better observer after you have tried to perform.*

This developing approach of mine has been called a theory—mistakenly, I think—since it grew from a very practical problem of writing and represents a solution to that problem. The problem was how best to convey to an outsider the many, many things I had been learning about wayang from lessons and from performances. The solution was to describe how the shadow play was put together—what the choices were and what constrained them. Text building.

My teacher, Soedjathi Djathikoesoemo, was one of the most popular young puppeteers, or dalangs, *in East Java. A dalang is a hero in Java. He gets fame and money for sustaining an all-night performance, and holding an audience, without a text. In the performance a dalang builds a unique, very complex, oral text.*

He taught me many things in our daily lessons in the back room of my house, like how to move puppets slightly off the beat and sing slightly off the pitch of the accompanying instruments—right-on was ugly, he said, give it a little edge; or like how I was not to try to interest everyone in the audience at the same time, for they were of all sorts and conditions. Our daily audience was a small and changing group of pedicab drivers, street people, and neigh-borhood children who watched from the open door. They laughed freely at my mistakes.

I remember after my last performance I asked my teacher how it was, and he said if it were a little better it would be bad.

This essay is an account of one foreigner's trying to learn to perform a shadow play, in Java, over a period of about two years. I was not, as a hostile critic recently said, trying to be an Aristotle for Java, but in looking back at it now I think I should have tried harder to make sure that that kind of reading didn't happen.

❖   ❖   ❖

Speaking the Past and Speaking the Present

If aesthetics is ever to be more than a speculative play, of the genus philosophical, it will have to get down to the very arduous business of studying the concrete process of artistic production and appreciation.

—Edward Sapir

In this essay I would like to describe some of the constraints on text building in a language quite different from our own. The language is Javanese, the kind of text the Javanese shadow play, *wayang kulit*, as I learned to perform it from an East Javanese puppeteer, or *dalang*, Soedjathi Djathikoesoemo, in daily lessons and in watching performances and discussing them together over a period of two years, 1969–71. My goal there was not to become a dalang myself—though that was necessary in order to discover what *not* to do—but to discover how to build a text in Javanese, to explore what text building revealed about Javanese epistemology, and to learn how to respond aesthetically to a very different artistic medium. I have studied these things and shall describe them within a particular, evolving set of assumptions about what a text is and how it can be said to be meaningful. These assumptions have their roots in traditional philology, modified and expanded by the insights of modern linguistics, ethnography, psychology, and Javanese aesthetic theory itself into what might be called a *modern philology*. These assumptions form a partial epistemography[1]—a specification of *what* it is important to write about concerning Javanese shadow theater, and how one achieves coherence and completeness in writing about it.

As an intellectual discipline, *philology* can be defined as the text-centered study of language. Philologists have traditionally set themselves the task of making ancient and foreign texts readable. Only part of this task is simple translation, since any careful philologist knows that few foreign words have translations. Words and phrases must be described, often in great detail, not merely mapped onto a foreign term. This description traditionally takes the form of masses of footnotes, which explain the contextual relations of words, phrases, sentences, and larger units of the text. These relations ideally include the following.

1. The relations of textual units to each other within the text, which establishes hierarchy and coherence in the text.
2. The relations of textual units to other texts, since part of the context of any text is, more or less, all previous texts in a particular culture, especially texts considered to be in the same genre; readable literature is structurally coherent with its own ancestors.
3. The relations of the units in the text to the intention of the creators of the text, with *intention* defined as the relations of the creator to the content of the text, the medium, and to the hearers or readers.
4. The relation of textual units to nonliterary events with which units in the text establish relations of the sort usually called *reference*.

The *meaning* of a text, then, is a set of relations, by no means all of which are listed above. The information necessary to describe the kinds of relations just listed must be known, discovered, or reconstructed before one can know the essential meaning of a text, any text. For contemporary English works—except for the most esoteric or specialized literature—contextual relations have been presumed not to require philological explication for English-speaking readers. However, texts whose contexts (or epistemologies) are distant from the best-trained readers require philological notes as an essential foundation for interpretation. In a multicultured world, a world of multiple epistemologies, there is need for a new philologist—a specialist in contextual relations—in all areas of knowledge in which text building (written or oral) is a central activity: literature, history, law, music, politics, psychology, trade, even war and peace.

The specific activity of the philologist is contextualizing conceptually distant texts. For many philologists in the past that was the only goal, an annotated edition of a written or oral text. Some philologists, however, in the course of this activity and based upon it, have sought generalizations about the major constraints on text building itself, the laws of grammar, poetics, narration, etc. Nowadays philology has been partitioned and distributed among various specialists. In the study of literature, there has developed a gulf between those who study particular texts (especially written texts) and those who study constraints[2] on the activity of creating texts: the former is usually part of the humanities (literary scholarship), the latter a science (linguistics).

In the study of texts, however, these two activities correct each other, since any meaningful activity is a conjunction of preexisting constraints (or rules, or structures, or laws, or myths) with the present, the unpredictable, particular *now*. In this way a text always—but to varying degrees—contextualizes the present in the past.[3]

One can roughly specify for any language activity the degree to which the speaker/writer is speaking the past or the present. Repeating is almost entirely speaking the past, whether it be repeating something said a moment ago or written a millennium ago—a repeated remark, a prayer, a song. Yet in these activities there is always something of the present, some variable of the communicative act that is free to express the *now*, be it only the voice quality of the speaker, the variations of tempo and pitch and resonance that express the repeater's attitude about what he is repeating. Furthermore, each repetition of a text (or bit of a text) is in a new context and takes new meaning from its context.

One can never wholly speak the past.[4] Even in those ritual repetitions when we speak the past as intently as possible in a kind of temporary trance, there is always something of the present communicated.

Likewise, one can never wholly speak the present. Even every-day language is highly conventional, far more constrained than we normally recognize. Consider how small talk varies from language to language in both content and form. Most conversations begin with repeated conventional content that is not meant to be discussed truthfully (i.e., in the present): How are you? (English); Where are you going? (Javanese); Have you eaten yet? (Burmese), etc. At this point in a conversation relationships are being established, between speaker and hearer first, then between speaker and other—the people or things referred to. Some conversations never get beyond this stage, and the pace at which one moves conversationally from the conventional, predictable past to the present varies widely from language to language.

Notice that language, in these instances and always, communicates on at least two levels, the actual surface content of the message (the proposition being asserted, requested, questioned, etc.) and the relational statements that are conveyed simultaneously, more often by intonation, posture, facial expression, and the like, than by direct statement. This relational communication has been called *metacommunication* by Gregory Bateson and others—communication about relationships, about the context of the message.[5] Hence, in speaking the past, in prayer or small talk, too, we are communicating our relations to the hearer and the people or things referred to in the lexically expressed message. Ritual language speaks the past on the surface but conveys the present at the metalinguistic level.[6]

How, then, does one most fully express the present? Only by decreasing the redundancy (the predictability) at either the lexical level of the message (L), or at the metalinguistic level (Lm), or at both. In short, by spontaneity. *Completely* spontaneous linguistic activity is impossible. Rather, other people could not understand it—or even recognize it as language: the uncompromising position of the schizophrenic, the lonely alienated poet, and the foreign-language learner. As Wittgenstein put the paradox: "if lions could talk, we couldn't understand them."[7] One can increase, however, the spontaneous, the *here and now*, in communication. One way is to speak directly what is in your mind right at the time you are speaking, speak right from what Ernest Becker calls the "inner newsreel," the impressions, observations, musing, and rehearsing of embarrassing moments in the past or yet to come that constantly occupy the idling, otherwise not preoccupied mind, the background noise of living—an area of linguistic activity studied at present mostly by Freudians and Buddhists (E. Becker 1962:77–79; Lacan 1973; Waldo 1975). We might revive an old term and call this the *imagination*. Many (e.g., Croce, Sapir, Freud, Lacan, Ernest Becker, Emile Benveniste) have argued that the imagination is an aspect of language, or at least "structured like a language" (Croce 1970; Lacan 1973; Benveniste 1971; Wilden 1972:29). It is obvious to us all that we *imagine* constantly, waking or sleeping, yet it is very difficult to get at our imagining and examine it, and it takes considerable skill and confidence or wildness or naïveté to brush aside enough of the conventional to speak from the imagination. Literary conventions create situations in which it is possible.

All language activity, including literature, involves, then, variation between spontaneity (present) and repetition (past) and communicates on at least two levels, the lexically expressed message (L) and the relational message (Lm). Of course, the lexically expressed message may be about the relationship, in which case a new relational communication is conveyed, leading, if repeated, to the sorts of linguistic involutions exposed by R. D. Laing (1970).

Various forms of indirect speech complicate the act of communication further by at least doubling every variable. Take a statement like the following.

" 'You sound nervous,' she said, ironically."

This statement involves at least two speakers ("she" and the writer), two hearers ("you" and the reader), *two lexical communications* ("You sound nervous" and " 'You sound nervous' she said, ironically"), and at least *four metacommunications* ("she" relating to "you"; "she" relating to the statement "you sound nervous"; the writer relating to the reader, pointing out the irony; and the writer relating to his statement: does the irony refer to "she" or to the whole statement, or, was she ironic or is the writer being ironic?). The writer here is speaking the past or only pretending to speak the past (it may be either fiction or reporting—or fiction disguised as reporting—present disguised as past—or vice versa). The ambiguous term *ironically* may be a comment from the present in which the writer is writing, or a reported fact about "she." If "she" is being intentionally ironic, then "her" statement is probably not a spontaneous remark to "you" but perhaps a re-peating of something said to her by "you" ("You" may have told "she" she sounded nervous a few days before, and "she" is now ironically repeating the remark back to "you"). Fuller context is necessary to resolve *some* of the ambiguities; others are resolvable only in the imagi-nation of the reader. As complex as this seems, all these relations and many more are necessarily part of the understanding of the statement.

To summarize, then, the analysis of a text requires, minimally, that the modern philologist describe several kinds of relations in order to recreate a conceptually distant context. A minimal set of these relations includes:

1. The relation of words, phrases, sentences, and larger units of the text to each other (i.e., the coherence of the text)
2. The relation of this text to other texts; the extent that it is repetition or new (speaking the present or the past)
3. The relation of the author to both the text and the hearers/readers of the text—seen from the point of view of the author or from the points of view of the hearers/readers (i.e., the intent of the text builder)
4. The relation of units in the text to nonliterary events (i.e., reference)

Context, then, includes coherence, degree of repetition/sponta-neity, intent, and reference. Sorting out the *sources* of constraints on all these relations is a further task for the modern philologist: to what extent are the constraints on these relations human (i.e., universal to all texts)? Or are they operative only within a single language family or cultural tradition, or within a single language, or only in a specific genre, or only in the works of one author? Any work is constrained at all these levels.

The methodology of this essay will be to describe, in the order just stated, the various sorts of relations a particular kind of text, the Javanese shadow play, has with its context. I have been able to isolate some of the generic constraints on contextual relations, and some of these above the generic, particularly at the level of the Javanese language itself. By implication, too, I reveal something of that area of variation constrained only by the individual performer (the dalang) in a particular place and time (A. Becker 1974; Young, Becker, and Pike 1971).

Textual Coherence in a Wayang:
Plot as Symbolic Action

Textual coherence can be examined at any level of structure in the hierarchy of structures that make up the text. One might examine the structure and categories of words in a wayang, isolating the special vocabulary and distinctive phonology of the language of the puppeteer (*basa padalangan*). At the level of sentences, and across sentences, there are kinds of coherence unexploited in most Western languages, coherence based not on tense (which is the basis of Western narrative coherence) but upon a system of person (in its grammatical sense) elaborated far beyond similar systems in other languages. I have described this system elsewhere in relation to Old Javanese (Kawi) literature (A. Becker and Oka 1976; Zurbuchen 1976). These are constraints that are used in building many other kinds of Javanese texts as well. Here I would like to focus on a higher-level system of constraints, a level intermediate between the usual sentential (i.e., sentence-based) concerns of the linguist and the global concerns of the literary scholar, the level of plot.

The plot of a story or a play is a set of constraints on the selection and sequencing of dramatic episodes or motifs.[8] These constraints are like the rules of a game, say tennis, which constrain the selection of possible acts in the game (i.e., defining illegal acts) and the arrangement of acts in the game (i.e., defining what may not be done at certain times within the context of the game). Plots, like tennis rules, do not allow one to predict—except in very general terms—what will happen in a play. Rather, plots tell us what cannot be done appropriately. They also, like scientific theories, tell us one other important thing, what the relevant variables are in the things one can do in the play. There is no rule in tennis against scratching my head as much as I want to in the course of a game. There is a rule, however, against serving with my feet across the baseline. Head scratching is, by implication, an irrelevant variable, but foot faulting is a constraint on position: it tells me where I may not stand not where I must stand. Likewise, a set of constraints on a plot specifies what areas of variation are particularly relevant and what are insignificant. If I may borrow from a closely related medium, music, we may note that melodic variation is highly relevant to some kinds of Western music but rather insignificant in some kinds of Javanese music.[9] An American who is looking for melodic variation in gamelan music will be bored; a Javanese looking for dense musical texture in a symphony will also be bored. Likewise in drama, an American who seeks character development in wayang is going to be disappointed in all but a very few wayang stories, and a Javanese who seeks complex coincidences in all but a few American movies (those few being comedies, like the Marx Brothers' *Animal Crackers*) is also going to be disappointed. Plot (i.e., constraints on the selection and arrangement of dramatic episodes) includes constraints on the *kinds* of variation that are relevant.

For the most part, in most cultures, knowledge of plot constraints is unstated background knowledge, like the knowledge of grammar and syntax. It is learned indirectly, first through fairy tales and nursery rhymes (and their equivalents in other cultures), and then from the various media that have access to children. Some Greeks, however, were self-conscious about plots. Aristotle's *Poetics* includes a description of plot that still holds for most Western drama and narrative.[10]

Aristotle calls plot *fable:* "The imitation of the action is the fable," he writes. "By fable I now mean the contexture of incidents, or the plot." He lists the six major variables in a drama:

1. fable or plot
2. manners or character
3. diction or metrical composition
4. sentiments or speeches
5. decoration
6. music

Aristotle continues, "Of all these parts the most important is the combination of incidents or the fable." Fable or plot is most important because it imitates what Aristotle held was the most important referential content of the drama, action (or imitation of action).

Among the constraints on plot that Aristotle lists are the following. Note that they are all phrased negatively—i.e., as constraints.

1. A proper fable must not be incomplete: "The poet who would construct his fable properly is not at liberty to begin and end where he pleases. . . ." A fable should, he explains, suppose nothing to precede it and require nothing to follow it (book 2, chapter IV). Completeness here is completeness of linear (i.e., temporal) causality, a powerful constraint on selection *and* arrangement.
2. Coincidences are to be avoided. Sequences should follow as probable and necessary consequences. Nothing improbable should be admitted, or, if necessary, it should arise out of the fable. Perhaps Aristotle's most famous comment on plot makes just this point: "Impossibilities, rendered probable, are preferable to improbable, though possible" (book 2, chapter VI; book 4, chapter VI).
3. No part of a proper fable may be transposed or omitted without destroying the whole. Anything that can be left out,

should be (book 2, chapter V). Again there is emphasis on linear (temporal-causal) sequence.

4. The time in the text should not be more than a single day (book 1, chapter IX).

These basic constraints all have to do with unity and causality, above all with temporal unity and linear causality—two aspects of the same thing. All of them are rooted in the simple fact that intersentence coherence in Indo-European languages is achieved primarily by *tense*. Clarity and coherence *means* to speakers of these languages linear temporal/causal sequencing. Tense is seen as iconic: that is, past, present, and future are taken as facts about the world rather than facts about language. Tense is not iconic in all language-cultures and hence temporal-causal linearity is not the major constraint on textual coherence in all languages.[11]

The linearity of Aristotle's constraints can be stated in another way. If meaning comes from temporal-causal sequences, then epistemologies do not, and cannot, change from episode to episode, or, as stated in a recent study of plot, "Semantically standard universes always have consistency in the interpretation of several connected ambiguous episodes" (Hahn 1973:8). That is, Jay Gatsby, Godzilla, Agamemnon, John Wayne, and Charlie Chaplin do not and may not appear in the same plot.

What emerges in the episodes of Western serious drama are the disambiguating causes of actions. These causes are at base represented as character defects, often minor ones. The episodes lead to a catastrophe and a climax, a reversal of expectations, all of which leads on to the end of the causal chain.

Nearly all these constraints are violated by wayang plot structure. It is not that wayang plots may not have temporal unity, causal linear sequences, catastrophes, reversals, and all the rest. These do appear in wayang plots, particularly in those plots most admired by Western viewers such as the plot of *Dewa Ruci*, a linear search for the water of immortality, or the plot of the simplified and shortened versions of the *Ramayana*, a search for a stolen wife. These Aristotelian constraints, however, are not *necessary* to a good wayang plot, and to focus on, for instance, causal sequences and character development is to miss the area of relevant variation in wayang theater and to miss the subtlety and depth of good wayang.

Wayang plots are built primarily around *coincidence*, a word that we in the West use to explain away things of no meaning. "A mere coincidence" cannot, in the West, sustain prolonged scrutiny and analysis. In wayang theater coincidence motivates actions. There is no causal reason that Arjuna, the frail wayang hero, meets Cakil, a small demon, in the forest, as he (or a counterpart) does in each wayang. It is a coincidence; it happens (*jadi*), and because they are who they are, they fight and Cakil dies, but not forever; he will be killed over and over again in each wayang. When Arjuna and Cakil meet, two worlds, two epistemologies coincide for a moment. Cakil is purely physical. He attacks Arjuna because Arjuna makes him uncomfortable. Arjuna's meditation has raised the heat of the forest higher than the creatures who live there can bear. Cakil responds instinctively to this thermal pollution. On the other hand, Arjuna attacks Cakil because he recognizes him as evil (i.e., other), not because of anything he has done, but because he knows—by thought, not instinct—that it is his duty (*dharma*) to combat evil. He kills coolly, dispassionately, the passionate Cakil, who is defending his forest home against the intruder. Arjuna controls nature by killing it, but it renews itself again and again. There are other interpretations of this motif. Not every observer of wayang will agree with this interpretation of it. It does seem evident, however, that Arjuna and Cakil live in different conceptual worlds and that their meeting is not caused but is rather an accident, a coincidence of these worlds. Nothing in the prior events of the text nor in the succeeding events made it a necessary part of the plot in Aristotle's terms. Yet this motif is necessary (obligatory) within the constraints of wayang plot.

This is but one coincidence, one intersection in the interwoven, cyclic actions that inform a wayang plot—unmotivated, unresolved, meaningless within a chain of causes and effects, but symbolically very rich.

The name for a wayang plot derives from the root *laku* 'step or act' plus the suffix -*an*, which nominalizes the root, giving us, by vowel sandhi, *lakon* 'an action, a way, an event, a plot'. A *lakon* includes three major divisions, within each of which a certain range of voice pitches and a valuing of particular pitches is maintained, and within each of which there is a prescribed internal structure. These divisions, called *pathet*, include combinations of scenes called *jejer* (audience scenes, before a ruler or holy man), *adegan* (scenes outside the audience hall, e.g., *adegan wana* 'forest adegan', *adegan gapuran* 'gate adegan', *adegan gara-gara* 'turmoil adegan', etc.), and *perang* (battle). The meanings of these names for the parts of a wayang are richly metaphoric. Understanding them as words helps to contextualize them within the Javanese semantic world. *Jejer* also means 'what exists', 'the subject of a sentence', and 'the handle of a *kris*', as well as 'an audience before the king'. *Adegan*, the scenes outside the audience hall, means also 'propped up', 'standing', 'door frame', and 'the punctuation of a sentence' (two vertical, parallel lines). The linguistic metaphors suggest a paradigmatic, associational link between sentences and plays, within whose structures experience is shaped and expressed.[12]

A wayang plot, then, is built hierarchically in structures made up of three basic units. A *lakon* (event) is divided into three *pathetan*, or acts, each with the same internal structure. Each *pathet* is made of three basic scenes: (1) the *jejer* (static audience in a court or a hermitage where a problem arises and a plan is formed); followed by (2) two or more *adegan* derived from that audience and always involving a journey away from the audience place; and (3) a *perang* (battle) at the end of the journey.

Each scene, in turn, has three basic components: (1) description of a situation (either *janturan* 'description of a place' or *carios* 'description of prior action'); (2) dialogue (*ginem*); and (3) action (*sabetan*). The *minimal* structure of a play—or an event—is shown in figure 1. Any given wayang allows for three basic operations on this minimal structure: permutation (reordering units below the level of *pathet*), conjunction (repeating units below *pathet*), and embedding (putting units within units below the level of *pathet*). *Pathet* structure was fixed in the tradition I studied.[13]

(1 = description, 2 = dialogue, 3 = action or motion)

Fig. 1.   Structure of a wayang

The only permutation regularly evident is in *pathet sanga,* within which the *adegan gara-gara* 'turmoil scene' (a clown scene during the world turmoil created by the power of the meditation of the hero) *may* precede the *jejer* (the *jejer pertapan* 'meditation audience' or *jejer pandita* 'audience with a holy man, usually Abiasa'). This inversion is perhaps constrained by dramatic rhythm, particularly impatience among the viewers for the clown scene.

Conjunction may be the repeating of a scene or a whole sequence. That is, there may be more than one *adegan,* or *perang,* or the whole sequence *jejer + adegan + perang* may be repeated. *Jejer* are not repeated unless the whole sequence is repeated. In the first *pathet* (act), called *pathet nem,* there are frequently, not always, two or three complete sequences, though each succeeding sequence is shorter in time and complexity than the one preceding it. Seldom does this occur in the other two *pathet.* There are often up to three *adegan* in a sequence, however, and two *perang.* This may occur anywhere in the play. This derived structure might look like the following.

> *jejer + adegan + adegan + adegan + perang + perang*

These different *adegan* and *perang* are given special names, as are the various *jejer,* and the contents of each is constrained by its place in the entire *lakon.* In the repertoire of a puppeteer are at least the following scenes.

A Basic Repertoire of Scenes

1. Kinds of Jejer (Audience Scene)

jejer kraton	'palace jejer'
jejer sabrangan	'foreign jejer'
jejer sabrangan rangkep	'second foreign jejer'
jejer pertapan	'jejer before a meditating person'
jejer pandita	'jejer before a holy man'
jejer tancep kayon	'closing scene in which the Tree of Life (*kayon*) is stabbed (*tanceb*) into the banana log with the other puppets arranged around it'

2. Kinds of Adegan (Outside Scene)

adegan gapuran	'gate adegan'
adegan kedatonan	'inner-palace adegan'
adegan paseban jawi	'outer-court adegan'
adegan kareta	'chariot adegan, i.e., assembling the army'
adegan gara-gara	'turmoil adegan'
adegan wana	'forest adegan'
etc.	

3. Kinds of Perang (Battle)

perang ampyak	'gang rumble'
perang gagal	'unsuccessful battle'
perang simpangan	'crossroads battle'
perang kembang	'flower battle, i.e., forest battle between small, refined hero and small demon'
perang gridan	'slow-motion, very refined battle'
perang tanggung	'middle battle'
perang tandang	'everyone-rallies-together battle'
perang amuk	'wild, frenzied battle'

Each of these scenes involves certain kinds of characters and characteristic choreography. One could not present a shadow play without knowing how to do these basic scenes, though the list is not by any means exhaustive. Individual dalangs may invent additional scenes (usually scenes involving newly invented demons, one of the most common areas of innovation over the past three hundred years) and are frequently known for the kinds of scenes they do best. For instance, a dalang may be famous for his monkey battles, for his *adegan gara-gara* (clown scenes), or for the depth and pathos of his meditation scenes (*adegan pertapan*).

Within any given scene (*jejer, adegan,* or *perang*) the structure is, as stated: (1) description, (2) dialogue, (3) action. There are two kinds of description, *janturan,* the description of a place and the people there, and *carios,* the description of a prior action. Only the *janturan* is accompanied by music. After the description, one or more *suluk* (described later) are sung and the dialogue begins. When the mood changes or a new character enters, other *suluk* are sung. Finally the dialogue ends and an action occurs, a movement of the puppets—for example, a journey or a battle (there is different music for each, *srepegan* for journeys, *srepegan* or *sampak* for battles). All of this follows specific rules for the speech and movement of each different puppet, and for each puppet in relation to each other puppet.[14]

The *suluks*—sung poetic passages in Old Javanese—are of three kinds: *pathetan* (descriptive verses accompanied by several instruments including the *rebab, gender, gambang,* and *suling*); *sendon* (lyric emotional verses accompanied only by a few instruments, usually *gender, suling,* and *gambang*); and *ada-ada*—verses that build excitement accompanied by *gender* and the knocking of a small mallet against the puppet box or a set of metal plates (Probohardjono 1966, in J. Becker, forthcoming). There are, in turn, three possible versions of *pathetan* and *ada-ada*: a short version (*jugag*), a long version (*agung*), and a normal version (*wantah*). The pitch center, or mode, of the *suluks* changes (i.e., gets higher in pitch) in each succeeding *pathet* (*nem, sanga, manyura*).

Within scenes, as well as between them, there are variations in structure; however, no permutation is possible in scenes and conjoining is rare. Embedding is the common practice. For instance, during the dialogue of a scene, a new character may enter, in which case there will be an embedded description + dialogue + action, after which we return to the previously interrupted dialogue. This produces structures of the following type.

Scene/*Adegan*

Description (with *suluk*) + Dialogue [description (*suluk*)
+ dialogue + action]   + Dialogue (continued) + Action

Here the bracketed sequence is an embedded scene.

As night goes on, different parts of the scenes are foregrounded, that is, some parts are shortened, others prolonged. In the first act (*pathet nem*) description usually takes more time than dialogue and action combined. In the second act, dialogue—mostly jokes but also very heavy spiritual instruction from a holy man—is foregrounded. In the third and final act (*pathet manyura*), action—usually battle—predominates. When one part of a scene is dominant, however, the other two always appear, albeit often briefly.

One may notice that in describing the structure of a dramatic event, the words used are all Javanese not Sanskrit. Though stories are often imported into wayang, chiefly from Sanskrit epics, plots appear to be uniquely Javanese.

Having seen something of the sequencing of events or motifs in a wayang play, let us turn now to the paradigm of events themselves and the kinds of coherence that appear within the structure that has been described. It is often very difficult for the viewer, foreign or Javanese, to know just where he is in the story being presented, that is, in knowing that polarities between protagonists and antagonists are being established. One always knows, however, where one is in the plot—the structure defined earlier. The story may be very obscure, much of the action may take place off the screen or be assumed by the dalang to be well known, and there may be all sorts of loose ends left after the plot cycle has finished. It is primarily the clowns who try to tell the audience what is happening. Certainly little of the *motivation* for action appears in the plot. The clowns, using modern language, modern ideas, and modern behavior, step among the heroes and demons and gods like wide-awake men in a dream world.

They bring the present into the story (i.e., they always speak the present), and, with the paradox of forethought, contextualize the present within the tradition, changing both, as usually seems to happen when epistemologies are allowed to coincide.

In the coincidence of epistemologies, as just noted, the real subtlety of wayang appears. The major epistemologies are (1) that of the demons, the direct sensual epistemology of raw nature; (2) that of the ancestor heroes, the stratified, feudal epistemology of traditional Java; (3) that of the ancient gods, a distant cosmological epistemology of pure power; (4) that of the clowns, a modern, pragmatic epistemology of personal survival. All these epistemologies coexist in a single wayang, and others may be added (most often the epistemology of the Islamic saints, that of the modern military, or that of some strange foreign land where one of the clowns goes to be king, like Gulliver among the Lilliputians). Between each of these epistemologies there may be—and usually is—a confrontation and a *perang*, a battle. No one ever wins conclusively, but rather a proper balance is restored. Each epistemology, each category of being, exists within a different concept of time, and all the times occur simultaneously. That is, nature time, ancestor time, god time, and the present are all equally relevant in an event, though for each the scope of an event is different. Throughout the wayang, each is kept distinct, even in language (which will be discussed later). The constraints on wayang plot sustain the notion of multiple time and multiple epistemology.

The differences with the Aristotelian notion of plot should now be apparent. What in the wayang plot are significant coincidences, in the Aristotelian plot are crudities, violations of the basic notions of unity and causality. In wayang, we might say that Gatsby, Godzilla, Agamemnon, John Wayne, and Charlie Chaplin—or their counterparts—do appear in the same plot, and that is what causes the excitement; that clash of conceptual universes is what impels the action.

As far as I know, the wayang tradition has no Aristotle, no one who has attempted to articulate the set of constraints that underlie the tradition. I cannot, as an outsider, do this with any depth or hope of adequacy. I am not even sure that in Javanese eyes it is worth doing, but the symmetry of this essay, the plot we are caught within at this moment, seems to demand it. A wayang plot, then, seems to be constrained in the following ways, all stated *by contrast* to Aristotelian constraints.

1. A wayang plot can begin at any point in a story. It has no temporal beginning, middle, or end. Indeed, a wayang plot is very similar to a piece of traditional Javanese music, in which a musical pattern is expanded from within, producing layer upon layer of pattern moving at different times.

A wayang plot, however, must begin and end in certain *places;* it cannot begin and end anywhere, though it can begin and end anytime. It must also pass through a certain place in the middle. Thus wayang plot has a spatial, rather than temporal, beginning, middle, and end. It must begin and end in a court, the first the court of the antagonists, the last the court of the protagonists (to use the Greek *agon* terminology, which seems appropriate here). The middle section must be in nature, usually in the forest on a mountain, but sometimes, too, in or beside the sea. It is movement out and back, a trip. This structure may well reflect the origin of wayang as an instrument of communication with the dead via trance (Rassers 1959).

Like an Aristotelian plot, a wayang must not be incomplete, but incompleteness is not temporal or causal, but rather spatial.

2. Coincidences, far from being avoided, impel action, for they induce cognitive puzzles or paradoxes. Coincidences are the way things happen, and the way communication between unlikes occurs. In Javanese and Indonesian, the word used to describe what we call a coincidence (a causeless interaction) is *kebetulan* (or *kebenaran*), literally a 'truth' (an abstract noun derived from the adjective *betul/benar* meaning 'true'). There are many related terms (e.g., *dadi* 'happen, become', *cocok* 'come together, fit'), which make up a semantic set used to describe events none of which imply linear causality. Likewise, a piece of music is structured by the coincidence of gongs occurring

together, and a holy day by the coincidence of simultaneous calendrical cycles.[15]

3. Any scene in a wayang plot may be transposed or omitted, except for the constraint that the plot begin in a court, have its center in nature, and return to a court. Transpositions and omissions of story material do not destroy or even change the whole. Almost anything can be left out or brought in.

   When something is brought in, however, it must follow the paradigmatic and syntagmatic constraints of the *lakon* structure described above. This structure defines an event (*lakon*) as made of three acts (*pathetan*), which we can now on the basis of the spatial constraint just discussed call the *pathet* of the antagonists (because the first scene is located in the antagonists' court, the antagonists dominate the action and win the battles), the *pathet* in nature, and the *pathet* of the protagonists (because the final scene is located in the protagonists' court and the protagonists dominate the action and win the battles). Each act, in turn, is made up of three scenes (*jejer, adegan, perang*), which may be permuted and conjoined in limited ways. Each scene, in its turn, is made up of three parts (description, dialogue, and action) and scenes are frequently embedded one within another. There are further constraints on the sets of characters (demons, heroes, gods, clowns) in relation to one another (e.g., how they speak and how they move), which will be described later. All of this makes up what might be called the *grammar* of a wayang plot.

4. Aristotle suggests that the time of a serious drama should not be more than a single day. He meant the time enacted within the plot on stage, not the whole story. Here is his most stringent constraint on temporal unity, one not always followed by Western playwrights but rather held as an ideal, even by such modern American dramatists as O'Neill, Miller, and Albee. Indeed, it may be one of the reasons for identifying these as good, serious playwrights in the Western tradition.

   The *time* enacted within wayang is unconstrained, except

that it must be multiple. Coincidences are timeless. But the *performance* time of a wayang is *symbolically* a single day. It is necessary to explain this rather strange phenomenon. The division of scenes is marked by a large image of a tree (or a mountain) called a *kayon* (or *gunungan*). During the play, which is usually performed at night, the *kayon* marks the imaginary progression of the sun from east to west by the angle at which it is set against the screen (which is properly set up on an east-west axis, or, if necessary, north-south, in which case north substitutes for east).[16] The *kayon* is a dramatic clock that marks only the progression of the *plot* not the times in the story or the time on the wristwatches of the viewers.

These are but a few of the features that define the coherence of a wayang plot, particularly those few that contrast most sharply with Aristotle, whose writings about plot well define the unconscious constraints on plot that most of us in the West have absorbed since childhood. I now turn from discussion of the structure or coherence of a wayang to consideration of the relations of the text with its context, from inner to outer relations, with a full awareness that there is much more to be said, particularly at more technically linguistic levels of focus, about Javanese textual coherence in general and wayang coherence in particular.

Text within Text: The Javanese Art of Invention

The distinction between story and plot is very important in studying the structure and development of a wayang text. The *plot* has been defined as a set of constraints on the selecting and ordering of episodes or motifs. The story is a prior text, fictitious or factual or both, which is the source of these episodes or motifs; it is a prior text to some degree known by the audience. Literature, in this sense, is mostly about prior literature. For example, in our own tradition any cowboy movie tells the story of the past more in the sense that it repeats episodes and characters of previous cowboy movies and novels than that it recounts "real" events that occurred in the American West. The "truth" of a cowboy movie is much more a matter of its correspondence with a mythology (a body of prior literature) than with any events recognizable by nonfiction cowboys in their own experiences.[17]

Wayang has reference to a mythology accessible to us in Old Javanese or Sanskrit literature, primarily the two great epics, the Ramayana and the Mahabharata. Javanese, of course, have access to this mythology in many less literary ways: in names of people and places, in other theatrical performances and oral literature, in comics, in the very language itself (Resink 1975; Anderson 1965; Emmerson, forthcoming). A wayang plot, however, *need* not draw on this mythology, though it almost always does. That is, a dalang may well turn to Islamic or Christian or autochthonous Javanese mythology, wholly or in part, as a source of the motifs and characters for his performance, and he can do so without violating any of the plot constraints discussed earlier.

The story, whatever its source, provides *content* and *context* for the plot. To introduce Arjuna, the hero of the Mahabharata, as a character into a particular plot establishes as a context for that particular plot all the prior texts (mythology), oral or written, related to Arjuna. Arjuna has done certain things, relates in certain ways to other characters, and is associated with many details of appearance, dress, behavior, speech, etc., which have been established in prior texts (Anderson 1965; Hardjowirogo 1968; Kats 1923).

What happens to Arjuna in a particular plot may either repeat episodes from prior texts or it may be new, although consistent with prior texts. The new creation fills in more details of the growing text or mythology related to Arjuna, new episodes in his life, only hinted at previously, or a return to the world by Arjuna across time, into, for instance, an ancient Javanese court. The Arjuna mythology (or Rama mythology, or Hanuman mythology, etc.) is a living expanding text in Java. Two examples of this sort of text expansion may help to make this process of invention clearer.

During the Indonesian national elections in 1971, one dalang who supported the incumbent military government created a wayang in which Krishna, when he realizes that he must direct the Pandawa armies (the armies of Arjuna and his brothers Yudistira, Bima, Nakula, Sadewa, and their allies) in the great war of the Bharata, seeks out the old clown-servant Semar. Krishna asks Semar what he should do and how he should behave as a military leader. Then, in the center of the play, in the forest, Semar instructs Krishna in his duty, the common man in an era of democracy instructing the ruler. The text for these instructions was the *Sapta Marga*, the official Code of Behavior for modern Indonesian soldiers. This brilliant new story, *Bagawan Ismojo Sandi*, conceived by Ki Hari Puribadi, very deftly contextualizes past in present and present in past simultaneously; the *Sapta Marga* is sanctified as a modern Bhagavad Gita, and the ancient mythology is given rich current relevance.

Another kind of invention involves no overt innovation at all but rather lets the audience infer the connection with current events. This second example was performed in 1971, too, but this time by a dalang opposed to the military government, a supporter of the PNI, the political party associated with former President Soekarno. This dalang performed the old text nearly without change, except that the clowns did say they were volunteer workers at the PNI party headquarters and made several jokes about campaign activities on a day-to-day level. The story was *Kangsa Adu Jago*, a traditional Sanskrit story of a powerful villain (Kangsa/Kamsa) who usurps Krishna's kingdom and drives Krishna into the forest. Krishna seeks the aid of his cousins, the Pandawas, particularly Bima, in defeating and driving out the powerful Kangsa. No one missed the political statement.

It is interesting to note that in those national elections the most powerful public statements against the government were made by dalangs using just this technique. Every other medium of communication, including other forms of theater, was noncritical. It is also interesting that two sides, the government and the PNI, recognized the same mythological context; the difference lay in whether Krishna represented the modern Ksatria or the deposed king.

One of the most important differences between traditional artistic expression and modern individualistic artistic expression is that in a traditional medium the artist is consciously expanding a prior text, an open corpus of literature, art, or music, whereas an artist whose intent is self-expression creates and develops his own text, his own mythology, so far as he can and still communicate. When an artist can no longer work within the inherited mythology and plot constraints, he seeks new mythology and constraints, often from his own imagination, and he works in alienation from his own society. This same distinction appears to have been made by Lévi-Strauss, this time in distinguishing the shaman and the psychoanalyst:

> the shamanistic cure seems to be the exact counterpart to the psychoanalytic cure, but with an inversion of all the elements. Both cures aim at inducing an experience, and both succeed by recreating a myth which the patient has to live or relive. But in one case, the patient constructs an individual myth with elements drawn from his past; in the other case, the patient receives from the outside a social myth which does not correspond to a former personal state. To prepare for the abreaction, which then becomes an "adreaction," the psychoanalyst listens, whereas the shaman speaks. Better still: When a transference is established, the patient puts words into the mouth of the psychoanalyst by attributing to him alleged feelings and intentions; in the incantation, the shaman speaks for his patient. (Lévi-Strauss 1963)[18]

No dalang is in this sense a modern artist (or psychoanalyst). It is as if he were performing a new act of Hamlet, or relating a new episode from the Gospels, working on an expanding text, which extends through space and time far beyond his own imagination. In this kind of traditional creation, the skill of the dalang is revealed in his ability to recreate the past, which he must do at the beginning of each wayang and at certain points throughout the performance, most particularly in singing short descriptive passages from Old Javanese (Kawi) texts. Here he speaks directly *to* the past of his own culture in words almost entirely unintelligible to the dalang or his audience.

These *suluk* occur at dramatic transitions in the plot, at any point where there is a descriptive passage (one of the three requisite components of a scene, description + dialogue + movement). The content of these Old Javanese quotations is usually unrelated in any easily discernible a priori way to the particular plot, except that the dalang can substitute relevant names, if he wishes. A bit of another story is recited, and it coincides mysteriously with the evolving plot, linking old text with new. Here is part of the first *suluk* in most performances:

> Leng leng ramyanikang, sasangka kumenyar, O. . . .
> Mangrengga rumning puri, O. . . .
> Mangkin tanpa siring, halep ikang, umah,
> Mas Iwir murub ring langit, O. . . .
> Tekwam sarwa manik, O. . . .
> Tawingnya sinawung, O. . . . , O. . . .
> Saksat sekarning suji, unggwan Bhanuwati, O. . . .
> Ywan amrem alangen, mwang Nata Duryuddana, O. . . .
> Mwang Nata Duryuddana, O. . . .

Very few dalangs are aware of the erotic nature of this quotation from section V, verse 1 of the Old Javanese *Bharatayuddha*, composed in Kediri (Daha) by Mpu Seddah in approximately 1157. Krishna has come to the palace of the Kurawas, enemies of the Pandawas, in order to try to avert war; at least on the surface that is what is happening. After the initial audience with Krishna, King Duryuddana retires to the inner palace. It is early night, and the moon has risen. Then comes the passage quoted:

> Beautiful was the moon that shone over the palace where the women lived. More and more it grew golden, an incomparable golden house against the sky. And so too its curtain of gems, like flowers on an embroidered fabric. And here was the chamber of Queen Bhanuwati where she slept with King Duryuddana. . . .

Here prior text is being quoted directly, the history of the genre is being displayed, and the Javanese art of invention exemplified. One must interpret the actions of the present in the mysterious context of this scantily understood passage.

The art of invention for the dalang, working within the plot constraints of his medium, involves selection of motifs and characters from the body of mythology he believes in. This is not unlike the Aristotelian art of invention, which was primarily the selection of quotations and ideas from the classics—a kind of information retrieval—in order to interpret the present (Young and A. Becker 1966).

A political change in Indonesia can be reflected in wayang as a change in mythology, as it has been described in the penetrating studies of Donald Emmerson (forthcoming), Benedict Anderson (1965), and G. J. Resink (1975). One generation of heroes may replace another, or one set of gods may replace another, as was the case in a village wayang I saw in Lombok in which the Hindu gods were the villains who were defeated by Moslem heroes. This is, however, essentially new wine in old bottles, or what we might call *surface change*. Deep change, in terms of this essay, would be change in the plot, change in the constraints on selecting and ordering the characters and motifs. Deep change would be change in the Javanese conception of time and event, change of epistemology.[19]

Intentionality in a Text: The Uses of Texture

One of the first things a dalang learns is that not everyone will respond to a wayang in the same way. There is no assumption that everyone will be interested in the same things at the same time; someone will always be dozing. The setting for a wayang is noncompulsive, more like a Western sports event than serious theater. It is not shameful or embarrassing to sleep through what someone else is enjoying. Jokes, philosophy, action, poetic language, each has different appeal to different people, depending on their own mental makeup, which is often described in a way parallel to the Indian theory of *rasa* and *guna* (Coomaraswamy 1957), a theory parallel, in turn, to the archaic theory of humors in the West. One responds according to his makeup. There can be no single, intended correct response to a play, no one complete interpretation. This multiplicity of events and perspectives builds the kind of thick texture that Javanese favor. As an old man responded when asked why he liked wayang,[20] "Asalnya ramai!" ('Above all because it is bustling/complex/busy/beautiful!') *Ramai* < Old Javanese *ramia* < Sanskrit *ramya* 'pleasing, beautiful'. Notice the semantic change in Java from 'beautiful' to 'beautiful because bustling and complex'. Sanskrit words, like Sanskrit stories, are recontextualized in Java.

Within the variety of responses—too thick to be untangled here—there are always two separate audiences at every wayang, an essential audience, without whom the play is pointless, and a nonessential audience, who may or may not be present and who in some sense overhear much of the drama. It is the nonessential audience that we have described so far, the various people who have various responses to a noncompulsive event, which is noncompulsive precisely because they are the nonessential audience.

The essential audience of a wayang is normally unseen: spirits, demons and creatures, gods, and ancestors. To whom does the dalang speak in Old Javanese and Sanskrit if not to those who understand these languages, which are unintelligible to the nonessential audience? Archaic language is not merely embellishment or mystification, else it would have been lost long ago. Rather it is essential language addressed to the essential audience, the ancients, the dead. All drama, as we have noted, speaks from the past, the unseen sources of power that are the widest context of the play.

The first words of a wayang—prior even to the *lakon* itself—are uttered softly to unseen hearers, "prayers" or mantra to the sources of power. Before the puppeteer arrives at the place of performance he establishes relations with this wider spiritual context, including his own, nonhuman brothers (*kanda empat*) who guard and extend his senses and provide buffers in an unpredictable, often hostile environment (Hooykaas 1974).

There are several prayers uttered by the dalang between his home and the place of performance, all seeking safety and support. The words of these prayers are not repeated exactly each time, but they are highly constrained variants of the Javanese-Sanskrit phrase that begins literary works.

Awighnam Astu 'Be there no hindrance'.

This initial phrase of a wayang text is called the *manggala* in Old Javanese (Kawi) written literature. A *manggala* is anything—word, god, or person—that has the power to support the poet. The *manggala* is invoked, praised, and then relied upon to sustain the poet/dalang in his effort. Here is a point of choice, then, for the puppeteer, who is likely to turn his mind to several sources of support. For the dalang, unlike the poet in the *kakawin* (poetic literature of the Old Javanese period), it is a private act, invoking the widest context of the shadow play, the earth, the light, the wind, the mountains.

The language of the *manggala*-prayers is usually a single expanded sentence, which includes a descriptive subject and an imperative predicate. The sentence is preceded by the original syllable, *Om*, which establishes the parameters of all language sounds in Sanskrit linguistics. In structure, the *manggala* is very similar to a Vedic hymn.

Om. O' (insert name of the *manggala* and phrases describing him/ her/it) + imperative predicate.

For example, as he adjusts the lamp (kerosene or oil), the dalang may softly say:

Om. Be there no hindrance. God of spirit, center of all, God of light—let the flame of this lamp illumine the world.

The phrases of the prayer linguistically are parallel. All prayers follow the general pattern just given, except that the phrase "Be there no hindrance" is not always stated. The language is a blend of Sanskrit and Javanese, the subject in Sanskrit (the language of the gods, the remote past) and the predicate in modern Javanese (the language of the dalang himself, the immediate present). The words bridge past and present and must be uttered with full attention.[21]

Perhaps here is the place to note an extraordinary fact about the language of the wayang, a fact of great importance in understanding what is happening at any given moment. A wayang includes within it, in each performance, the entire history of the literary language, from Old Javanese, pre-Hindu incantation and mythology to the era of the Sanskrit gods and their language, blending with Javanese in the works of ancient poets (the *suluk*), adding Arabic and colonial elements, changing with the power of Java to new locations and dialects, up to the present Bahasa Indonesia and even a bit of American English (in which one clown often instructs another). I do not just mean here what might be said of English, that it reflects its history in vocabulary, syntax, and phonological variation. That is also true of modern Javanese. The difference is that in the shadow play, the language of each of these different eras is separate in function from the others; certain *voices* speak only one or the other of these languages and dialects, and they are continually kept almost entirely separate from each other. One could even say that the content of the wayang is the languages of the past and the present, a means for contextualizing the past in the present, and the present in the past, hence preserving the expanding text that is the culture. I shall point out these different kinds of language as they appear, though we have already seen that the prayers (mantra) to the gods and other sources of power use Sanskrit and modern Javanese, the *suluk* use Old Javanese (Kawi), and the clowns use all modern languages, Javanese, Indonesian, Dutch, English, Japanese, French, neatly reflecting the context of modern Indonesia. Clowns speak the older languages only to mock them.

Like the *manggala*-prayers, the *suluk* speak to the ancients (not the gods but the Javanese ancestors) in their own language at the beginning of each scene. In many cases the chanted *suluk* are addressed to the individual characters represented by the puppets in the wayang. Like Vedic hymns they invoke the character in his own language by a kind of word magic in which to state a thing properly and effectively, even without intent (as in a casual Brahmin's curse, which cannot be revoked), is to effect power in the world, bridging time and space.

It is here that wayang becomes an education in power. Wayang teaches men about their widest, most complete context, and it is itself the most effective way to learn about that context. There has been much written about the mystical communication in wayang, and its details are best left to Javanese themselves to write about. For us in the West it might be called *trance-communication*. The dalang is above all a man who can be "entered," a "medium," though to use our own terminology is to invoke all the wrong associations. *Trance speaking* can be defined as communication in which one of the variables of the speech act (I am speaking to you about x at time y in place z with intent a) is denied, most frequently the variable I is paradoxically both speaking and not speaking, or speaking involuntarily or nonintentionally. Trance is a kind of incongruence between statement and intent (I/not I am speaking to you/not you . . .), and covers a wide spectrum of linguistic experiences from the minor trance of singing the national anthem—or any song you *believe*—to the major trance of hypnosis and schizophrenia (Haley 1963).

In any case, it is as trance communication as a means of relationship with an unseen, essential audience that wayang can be linked to the Barong drama of Bali, the autochthonous trance ritual of the other islands (e.g., the *ma'bugi* in Sulawesi),[22] and the use of puppets and dolls as spirit media throughout Southeast Asia.

What is the use of communication with the ancients besides preserving the text of the culture, which is probably not a primary goal but a constant effect of this communication? Two uses are implied in the instruction books for the dalang: to exorcise danger or potential danger, and to contextualize the present in the past. There are many well-known myths about the origin of wayang as a way of subduing or at least calming down dangerous power, the power of Siva amuck or the power of his demon son Kala (time) who formerly dealt out death indiscriminately.[23]

How does wayang *control* power gone amuck, madness, demons, disease, and stupidity? By nature all these are sources of chain-reacting, linear power, which accelerates by repeating more and more of the same. Someone who is amuck kills and kills *without intent* until he in turn is killed. Likewise disease or madness feeds upon itself. The closest answer to the question of how wayang subdues power gone amuck came to me from a Balinese friend, who answered, "You know, it's like the doors in Bali." (Note: an entrance in Bali and traditional Java is backed by a flat wall or screen [Javanese *wrana*] a few feet behind the entrance gap in the outer wall, so that one cannot go straight in but must pass right or left. Demons and people possessed or amuck move in straight lines not in curves like normal human beings.) My friend continued, after I looked mystified, "The demons can't get in. The music and shadow play move round and round and keep the demons out." Then he paused and laughed heartily, and added, "As you might say, demons think in straight lines!"

Clearly, from this point of view, it is not the story or the archaic words or the puppets but the whole thing, the *texture* itself, the maze of relations, that is most important. The structure of the medium itself subdues power gone amuck, inducing paradox and coincidence, anathema to those who think in straight lines.[24]

In summary, then, the dalang speaks as himself and as the past through himself to an unseen, essential audience and to the immediate, nonessential audience, each containing a wide variety of perspectives on the action being performed. And he is playing with fire. If, for the immediate audience, the event is noncompulsive, for him it is powerfully compulsive. Once begun, he may not for any reason (illness, storm, violence, power failure) stop until the play has finished. Hence he must be careful not to begin anything he cannot end.[25]

Reference: On Language and Things of This World

The first sentence of Hardjowirogo's *Sedjarah Wajang Purwa* (*History of Traditional Shadow Theater*, 1968), like the book itself a subtle blend of Javanese and Indonesian, sets the perspective of the book: "Wajang purwa adalah sebagai perlambang kehidupan manusia didunia ini" ('Traditional shadow theater is a signification of the life of man in this world'). Part of the statement is that it is our present life as men in this world, not our ancestors in the ancient world, nor a spiritual world, nor an imaginary literary world, but this world, that *wayang* signifies. To understand how that can be so is to understand the referential meaning of wayang, the relation of the text to the present-day nonwayang world. This aspect of the meaning of wayang is both the easiest and the most difficult to describe. It is easy because interpreting the present relevance of shadow theater is a ubiquitous kind of discourse, oral and written, in Java; hence there are countless examples of wayang hermeneutics. It is difficult because the linguistics of wayang commentary—the constraints on it as a language activity or speech art—are as yet unexamined. And it is difficult, too, because there are major epistemological differences in the way people of different cultures relate language to nonlinguistic phenomena. That is, we all too frequently apply our own current Western assumptions about how linguistic reference works—particularly how reference works in *fictional* literature—to a non-Western text. A study of the way a wayang text relates to "this world" ought to begin, then, with a study of *how* words are thought to refer in Javanese. Once again, as with Aristotle and the notion of plot, the strategy will be to begin with some features of the dominant Western notion of reference and then try to show how wayang epistemology differs.

In the dominant Western notion of reference (the one assumed in introductory and popular books about linguistics), there are three categories, which can be labeled roughly *words* (language), *thoughts* (or concepts), and *things* (objects in the sensible world). These are assumed to be separable (though slightly overlapping) categories of being, since concepts appear to be stateable in different languages, and there appear to be different, unrelated names for the same things in different languages. The relations of language to concepts and things are therefore felt to be fundamentally arbitrary. If anything, natural language gets in the way of clearly seeing things as they *are* (Bacon's "idols of the market") and gets in the way of clear, logical thought (based as it is for us now on measurable identities and differences). Thinkers in the West tend to give priority to concepts or things and treat language as a "tool" to be shaped to our ends or discarded and replaced. Not for many centuries in the West (until recently in the works of Foucault and Lacan and with the development of modern linguistics) has language itself been given priority as a source of highly valued knowledge.

Opposed to this notion of the arbitrary nature of reference is one familiar in American thought in the work of Emerson, particularly in his essay "Language." In this earlier view, the relation of words, thoughts, and things is not arbitrary, though it has been confused by the multiplicity of languages. The laws of Nature govern thoughts, words, and things alike. Emerson could, therefore, make his essay "Language" a subsection of his larger work, *Nature*. *Signified* and *signifier* are constrained by the same laws. To know is to interpret either words, or things, or concepts. All three—signifier (words), signified (things), and the relations between them (concepts)—offer themselves to men to be deciphered in order to discover the "text" of the world. As Emerson wrote, "The world is emblematic. Parts of speech are metaphors, because the whole of nature is a metaphor of the human mind" (Emerson 1948:18; A. Becker 1975).

A favored form of discourse in this epistemology is the commentary or the essay, a decipherment or interpretation of language and nature. In commentary, etymology is an important strategy, not as an attempt to discover the original meaning of words but rather as an attempt to discover the "intrinsic 'properties' of the letters, syllables, and, finally, whole words." One of the things that strikes us about the text of a Javanese shadow play is the pervasiveness of etymologizing as an explanatory strategy. Javanese call this etymologizing *djarwa dhosok* or "forced" (imposed) interpretation.[26] My own first impulse was to dismiss etymological commentary in wayang as "folk" linguistics, rooted in ignorance about the true history of the words explained, for many of which I knew the Sanskrit etymons. I dismissed etymologizing, in spite of its frequency and obvious importance as a text-building strategy, since it did not give the "true" origin of words. Even more, it appeared to me as an embarrassing and silly aspect of wayang. What I failed to see then was that, since the meanings of words constantly change, etymologies must be reformulated (like genealogies) based upon what one now, in the present, sees as the "intrinsic" meaning of the word under consideration. A brief example: etymology A of the word *history* traces it to French *histoire*, then to Latin *historia* 'a narrative of past events', to Greek *istoria* 'learning by inquiry', and back to *istor* 'arbiter, judge', and hence back in time to a possible Indo-European root. Etymology B of the same word divides it into *his* and *story* and interprets the elements of the word in the present. "His-story" is also an account of past events but an account relating primarily to men, with women in a secondary role. Which etymology is correct? It is impossible to answer, for the question is wrong in insisting that we reject one or the other conceptual strategy, etymology A or etymology B. Certainly etymology B tells us more that is relevant and true to current thought than etymology A. In traditional Javanese discourse, including wayang but also including history and commentary, the strategy we have called *etymology B* is held to be serious and an important part of a text, a basic way of deciphering this world.

Etymologizing of this second sort is known to us, in part, as *explicating*, and the object to be explicated is usually a text clearly recognized as literary, or religious, or legal, and we have specialists who explicate each of these kinds of text. What they do is relate the words of the text (and the phrases and sentences, etc.) to the current context. Precisely in this sense, though less specialized, the dalang relates the old words to the current context. What differentiates the dalang from the explicators of texts in our society is that he explicates primarily proper nouns, names for things, whereas we tend to feel that names are the most arbitrary words of all, given to people and places before they really "are." Etymologizing about names is not unknown in our culture, of course, but it is not particularly highly valued as a way of understanding people and places. What can we know by explaining the name Detroit via etymological strategy A or B?

There are two structural points in a *lakon* when etymologizing, as a text-building strategy, is appropriate: in description or dialogue. (It never occurs in *suluk*s, where it is most needed.) Etymologizing is the descriptive part of a scene (either *janturan* 'description of a place', or *carios* 'description of prior action'), is done by the dalang directly, and is serious. Etymologizing in a dialogue is done by one of the characters and may be serious and "academic," if spoken by Krishna or Abiasa, or only half-serious, if spoken by a clown. A major skill in puppetry is the ability to etymologize in all these ways. Let us examine a few instances.

After the mantra and a set musical interlude, the dalang brings out the puppets for the first scene, and begins the description of the first scene of the first *pathet* of the *lakon*, using fixed phrases.

Once there was a land. Many are god's creatures that walk the earth or fly the air or swim in the water. Many are the beauties of the world. Yet none can equal those of this land, Manikmantaka [here the name of the particular place in the particular story is inserted]. Among a hundred there are not two, among a thousand not ten like Manikmantaka.

Then the dalang describes the kingdom following the strategy of moving from widest physical context to narrowest, from the place of the kingdom among all kingdoms, the mountains around it, the sea, the town itself; the houses, the people, narrowing to a specific person, the king, and those about him. All this is set language, though phrases can be left out or reordered slightly. In these passages, the skill of the dalang in controlling the rhythm and pitch contours of his voice in relation to the gamelan is established (or not).[27] In speaking the past almost entirely his legitimacy as a dalang is being proved in one area. At some point in the description, usually as a transition from the description of the kingdom to the description of the king, the dalang begins his first etymology, either on the name of the country or on the name of the king, or both. Here another skill is brought to the foreground, for the etymologies are not set, although one may borrow them from wayang promptbooks called *pakem* (at the risk of being known, condescendingly, as a "book" dalang).[28] The dalang displays his skill at explication; he must be authoritative and informative. He does not, however, explain words by consulting a dictionary of Sanskrit roots but interprets the elements of the words as Javanese words.

The king who ruled this land is called Maha Prabu Niwata Kawaca. And his name means 'one who wears armor that may never be pierced', which, in our time, means 'one who could not be defeated', for he and all his people believed that, and acted as if that were true. His name is made of three words: *Ni, Wata,* and *Kawaca. Ni,* or *nir,* is from the word *nirwana. Nirwana* means 'freedom from desires, freedom from the past, freedom from the future', something that cannot be likened to anything. In other words, the Great God. *Wata* means 'blind', without vision. *Kawaca* comes from *kaca*, which means 'mirror'. Hence, his name, Niwatakawaca, means 'a mirror that is broken, a mirror that has lost its ability to reflect the truth', the Great God. When he was young he was called Nirbito, which comes from *nir* and *bito*. *Nir* is, as was said, from *nirwana*. *Bito* means afraid. For, although all feared him, he was himself a coward and turned away from the Great God.

This is a version of the first etymology from the story, *Arjuna Wiwaha*, as I learned it. Notice that the name is explicated more than once, and that the meaning as a whole ('one who could not be defeated') is not the same as the meaning of the parts ('a mirror blind to *nirwana*'). Both are true, and both, along with the childhood name of the king, tell us about him. If he had other names they would be interpreted here, too. Clearly, words here are not arbitrarily related to people and things.[29]

I do not intend here to go into the ritual and magical potentialities of this language, chiefly because I only very dimly understand them.[30] It is enough to say that the shadow play is a text nonarbitrarily related to the world outside the play, and that explication of the language is a means to cut through the hidden nature of things. The dalang is a skilled explicator who demonstrates that complexity and obscurity can be unmasked and, hence, provides a model for understanding the world.

Others (Anderson, Resink, Emmerson) have described how the present world looks within this model. Events in Indonesia really are interpreted by some Javanese as *lakon*, the *lakon* plot does have psychological reality as a kind of meditation, names of political leaders are taken as revealing character and role, and changes in stories or mythologies from which motifs are drawn do parallel social and religious changes. That is, each way that the text relates to its context (see the first section) is emblematic of the world and defines a way of interpreting the world, once one believes, knows, or pretends that reference is nonarbitrary.[31]

Conclusion: Toward an Aesthetic Understanding of Communication

The methodology of this essay has been to describe the various sorts of relations a text (or a part of a text, a word, a sentence, a passage, an episode) has with its context. Parts of a text relate to the whole under the constraints of what we called *plot coherence*. The motifs or episodes of a text relate to their source in a cultural mythology under the constraints of invention. The text and its parts relate to the participants in the linguistic act (direct or indirect speaker, direct or indirect hearer, direct or indirect beneficiary, etc.) under the constraints of intentionality. The text and its parts relate to the nontext world under the constraints of what we have called *reference* (either naming or metaphoric reference). In the previous sections of this commentary, these relations have been examined, not in terms of their specific content but at the more general level of constraints on specific content.

By no means have all the relations of text to context been explored here. The complex grammatical and phonological constraints on wayang language have so far only been hinted at. The semiotics of voice qualities and typologies of dialect and style, for example, relate a character to particular attributes. The dalang learns to reshape his mouth and alter his entire vocal mechanism systematically to distinguish certain characters and types of characters. Pushing the points of the articulation of sounds forward in the mouth suggests refinement and culture, pushing them back toward the throat suggests roughness and raw nature. Between these two extremes is an unmarked area where characters most like the "us" defined by the dalang speak. Steady, even pitch and rhythm suggest control; wide pitch and rhythm variation suggest impulsiveness, a dimension of character very important to Javanese. It is interesting that gods speak outside the system of evenness versus irregularity; in wayang they have their own semiotics. Nasality is tied to cleverness, and *latah*, a version of the speech pathology echolalia,[32] is related to a wild and powerful inspiration in both gods and men. Each character speaks in a certain way, in a certain range: taken together, the voices of the set of characters reveal the semiotic polarities of Javanese phonological variation.

Nor have the visual constraints, the constraints on the shape and color of the puppets (called *wanda*) and their movements (called *sabetan*) been explored here (Mellema 1954; Hardjowirogo 1968). The voice qualities of the puppets are supplemented (or contradicted for humor) by labeled, recognized variations of eye shape, head angle, ornamentation and clothing, stance, arm and body movement, speed, etc. Furthermore, certain puppets and styles of puppets are attributed to particular people in history,[33] and keen observers of wayang can recognize the different *wanda* of, for instance, Siva as *Bartara Guru wanda Karna*, attributed to Senapaten Mataram I in the Javanese year 1541 (A.D. 1619), or *Batara Guru wanda artja*, attributed to Susuhunan Mangkurat in 1578 (A.D. 1656). The fire-haired demon (Kala Dahana) is attributed to Sultan Agung Hanjakrakusuma of Mataram in 1563, and the eggplant demon (Buta Terong) is attributed to Susuhunan Paku Buwana II at Kartasura in 1655. This lore adds further kinds of meaning to the total text, relating it to particular people, places, and things in the history of Java. And beyond sound and vision are the other perceptions of the wayang night, the smells, tastes, and feelings that add further layers of meaning, more and more particular, to the context of the wayang text.

Commentary here approaches closer and closer to the performance itself and the total responsiveness of the ideal Javanese audience.

The goal of the philologist is to guide outsiders (here non-Javanese) to what might be called an *aesthetic* understanding of a text. To achieve an aesthetic understanding it seems reasonable to say that in interpreting a text, the outsider must be aware of his own differences—particularly those most "natural" to him—and must learn to use new conventions of coherence, invention, intentionality, and reference. For an aesthetic response to be possible, a text must appear to be more or less coherent; the mythology it draws upon and presupposes must be more or less known; the conventional intent of the creator or speaker of the text in relation to one's own role as hearer/reader/interpreter must be relatively well understood; even the more basic assumptions about how words relate to thoughts and the things of the world need to be more or less shared. If any of these kinds of meaning is not understood, then one's responses to wayang are either incomplete or contradictory. Never fully to understand and constantly to misunderstand are linguistic pathologies that characterize a wide range of phenomena from the strategic understanding of the schizophrenic to the persistent confusion and uneasiness of one who is learning to use a foreign language; all these pathologies subject one to a world in which language and metalanguage are incoherent, where, to take an extreme case, people say "I love you" and at the same time reveal contradictory messages, even "I hate you," in a look or a slap.

The universal source of language pathology is that people appear to say one thing and "mean" another. It drives people mad (the closer it gets to home). An aesthetic response is quite simply the opposite of this pathology. It is opposite in the sense that the same constraints are relevant to both, but there is one difference. That is, opposites are things that are in the same class but differ in one feature (Hale 1974). Schizophrenia, foreign-language learning, and artistic expression in language all operate under the same set of linguistic variables, constraints on coherence, invention, intentionality, and reference. The difference is that in madness (and in the temporary madness of learning a new language or a new text) these constraints are misunderstood and often appear contradictory; whereas in an aesthetic response they are understood as a coherent integrated whole. Shadow theater, like any live art, presents a vision of the world and one's place in it that is whole and hale, where meaning is possible. The integration of communication (art) is, hence, as essential to a sane community as clean air, good food, and, to cure errors, medicine. In all its multiplicity of meaning, a well-performed wayang is a vision of sanity.[34]

ACKNOWLEDGMENTS

I wish to acknowledge the important contributions of several people with whom I discussed this essay or parts of it: Gregory Bateson, Judith Becker, Maurice Bloch, Vern Carroll, Soedjathi Djathikoesoemo, Donald Emmerson, Shelly Errington, William Foley, Patricia Henry, Peter Hook, Robin and

George Lakoff, James and Susan Matisoff, I Gusti Ngurah Oka, Kenneth Pike, Charles Pyle, Soewojo Wojowasito, Richard Wallis, Susan Walton, Aram Yengoyan, and Mary Zurbuchen.

NOTES

1. I owe this term, and much of my understanding of it, to Vern Carroll.
2. I am using the term *constraint* here in a special way that may puzzle some readers. The basic notion is from information theory. It is given wider relevance in Gregory Bateson's essay, "Cybernetic Explanation" (1972:399–410). There Bateson uses the term *restraints*. I use the term *constraints* since it is current in linguistics and appears perfectly compatible with Bateson's term. The linguistic term first appeared to me in the work of John R. Ross and George Lakoff where linguistic variables were not subject to rules but constraints with differing scope and force. Bateson writes (p. 399): "In cybernetic language, the course of events is said to be subject to *restraints*, and it is assumed that, apart from such restraints, the pathways of change would be governed only by equality of probability. In fact, the 'restraints' upon which cybernetic explanation depends can in all cases be regarded as factors which determine inequality of probability." Later, "Restraints of many different kinds may combine to generate this unique determination. For example, the selection of a piece for a given position in a jigsaw puzzle is 'restrained' by many factors. Its shape must conform to that of its several neighbors and possibly that of the boundary of the puzzle; its color must conform to the color pattern of its region; the orientation of its edges must obey the topological regularities set by the cutting machine in which the puzzle was made; and so on. From the point of view of the man who is trying to solve the puzzle, these are all clues, i.e., sources of information which will guide him in his selection. From the point of view of the cybernetic observer, they are *restraints*" (p. 400). In a text, or any unit of artistic expression, "constraints" are different in different languages and in different cultures. That is, the area of significant variation is not the same in all languages, in all cultures, but it can be discovered by finding what the constraints on the text are, which is what this essay endeavors to do for wayang.
3. The notion of speaking the present and speaking the past came to me from Maurice Bloch. Speaking the past is a particular kind of speech act or mode of communication, which Bloch defines for the Merina of Madagascar, who themselves describe certain ritual speech making as "speaking

the words of the ancestors" (Bloch 1974). Bloch is wrong, I think, in contrasting formalized speech acts and everyday speech acts, on a scale of most-to-least formalized language. Everyday speech acts are also highly formalized. I feel that the poles of this scale range from repetition (most formal, speaking the past) to imagination or internal discourse (least formal, speaking the present), and I argue that neither pole is ultimately attainable. For an early view of wayang as "speaking the words of the ancestors," see W. H. Rassers (1959).

4. The implications of this notion are explored in Jorge Luis Borges's short story, "Pierre Menard, Author of Don Quixote" (1962). Menard, by copying Cervantes' novel word for word in the twentieth century (i.e., by changing the context of the text act), produces a very different work (brought to my attention by Susan Walton).

5. A similar, multichanneled view of language has been developed by Kenneth L. Pike (see especially Pike 1963).

6. This is most apparent in trance communication and hypnosis. The latter is described in these terms in Jay Haley, "How Hypnotist and Subject Maneuver Each Other" (1963:20–40).

7. The quotation—and the idea behind it—were presents from Shelly Errington.

8. The notion of a text as a selection and ordering of motifs (or motives) is derived, ultimately, from V. Propp (1958) and Kenneth Burke (1969).

9. This point is supported and illustrated in Judith Becker (1965).

10. The text used here is Aristotle's *Politics and Poetics,* translated by Jowett and Twining (1969), especially book 2, chapters I–IX; and book 4, chapter VI.

11. The notion of iconicity is derived from Kenneth Boulding (1961), a basic text in the study of comparative epistemography. The centrality of tense in establishing textual coherence in English narrative is demonstrated in William Labov, *Transformation of Experience in Narrative Syntax* (1972).

What I call the *narrative presupposition* is the presupposition in English (and other, but not all, languages) that in two succeeding clauses with past-tense verbs, unless otherwise marked, the events referred to happened in the same order as the clauses. That is, the sentences, "The man looked at the clock. He sat down," mean, in part, that the man looked at the clock before he sat down, although this order is presupposed, not *marked* in the structure of these sentences. In many languages (e.g., Old Javanese, Burmese) this presupposition does not hold and narrative order is a *marked* strategy. This is an example of a basic linguistic difference in languages that affects text-building strategy. These basic differences usually concern iconic linguistic facts, facts assumed by native speakers to be about the nature of the world not about the nature of language. For a discussion of non-Western iconic facts, see A. Becker (1975).

12. These Javanese terms are partially described in Probohardjono (1966) currently being translated from the Javanese by Susan Walton (J. Becker, 1984). The conceptualization of a sentence as a drama, with actors, agents, scenes, actions, etc., suggests that traditional Javanese philologists shared a metaphor, at least, with modern linguists (e.g., Pike's tagmemics, Fillmore's case grammar) and literary critics (e.g., Kenneth Burke's dramatism).

13. *Pathet* in music means something slightly different, closer to our notion of mode. See Probohardjono (1966), translated by Susan Walton (J. Becker, 1984). In a wayang performance, music from the final *pathet (manjura)* is played before the play begins, creating a cyclic musical structure, since it is the first and last mode one hears. This musical redundancy is not reflected in the foregoing representation of *lakon* structure.

14. These rules are described in numerous handbooks for dalangs. Among the more complete ones are Nojowirongko (1960) and Sajid (1958). There are also numerous *pakem* (scenarios) for individual plays. See James Brandon (1970) for an English translation of one of the best of these, which combines a handbook and *pakem*, the *Serat Tuntunan Padalangan*.

15. For a description of time reckoning in Bali (and traditional Java) see Clifford Geertz, *Person, Time, and Conduct in Bali* (1973). See also Soebardi (1965). These structural principles are applied to the description of music in Judith Becker, "Time and Tune in Java."

16. For a description of the Old Javanese–Balinese semiotics of space, see C. Hooykaas (1974). I am indebted also to unpublished work on the five directions by Patricia Henry.

17. This sense of mythology is explored in Roland Barthes (1972), particularly in the final essay "Myth Today," in which Barthes writes, "Mythical speech is made of a material which has *already* been worked on so as to make it suitable for communication" (p. 110).

18. This passage was brought to my attention by Shelley Errington.

19. Ironically, most attempts to "preserve" traditional drama require deep change. This "irony" is discussed in A. Becker (1974).

20. Reported to me by Patricia Henry, personal communication from Malang, East Java.

21. These mantra are being translated by Susan Walton and will appear in J. Becker (forthcoming). Some of the mantra also appear in Hooykaas (1973).

22. The *ma'bugi* trance ritual of Sulawesi has been beautifully filmed by Eric Crystal in *Ma'bugi: Trance of the Toraja*.

23. Versions of this myth appear in Sastroamidjojo (1964:142–63); Rassers (1959); and Holt (1967). The basic source is the *Tantu Panggelaran*, written during the latter days of Majapahit. Claire Holt translates the text as follows.

> As for Lord Guru, never before was he seized by wrath, now however, he was overcome with fury; therefore, he cursed himself and became a *raksasa* [giant]. Then the Lord Guru took on the shape of a *raksasa* with three eyes and four arms; since then he has been called Kala-Rudra. All the gods were stunned, as was the whole world, when they perceived the shape of the Lord Kala-Rudra who was bent on devouring everything on earth.
>
> Directly, Icwara, Brahma, and Wisnu tried to prevent Lord Kala-Rudra from devouring the world; they descended to earth and played *wayang*; they told about the true nature of the Lord and the Lady (his consort) on earth. They had a *panggung* [an elevated place] and a *kelir* [screen]; their *wayangs* were carved out of leather and were extolled in beautiful *panjangs*. The Lord Icwara was the *udipan* [*dalang?*], Brahma and Wisnu protected him. They wandered about the earth, making music and playing *wayang*, since then there exists the *bandaginahawayang*; thus was the origin according to the old tale.
>
> Another means of defense by the Lords Icwara, Brahma, and Wisnu against the Lord Kala was they went about the earth and sought out Lord Kala who, pale-faced, agitated, moved around his *bale* [pavilion], . . . Icwara became *sori*, Brahma became *pederat*, Wisnu *tekes*; they went around singing songs (*mangidung*) and playing (*hamenamen*); since then there has been the *bandaginamen* men.

24. The term for this texture is *ruwat*, which is often translated as 'liberation', but it is "liberation" in the sense that Br'er Rabbit is "liberated" from Br'er Fox within the safety of his tangled briar patch. Wayang is a kind of conceptual briar patch. The active verbal form for *ruwat* is *ngruwat*, the term used for performing a shadow play in order to exorcise spirits. *Ruwat* is part of a series *ruwit, ruwed, ruwat* 'little, delicate tangle', 'medium-sized tangle or complication', and 'large physical or conceptual tangle, or liberation'.

The word *ruwat* is rich in folk-etymological associations, due to its phonological associations with *ruwah*, 'spirit, soul of the dead' and *(w)ruh* 'to see or know'. See the following section for discussion of the importance of this etymologizing (cf. evolution of Sanskrit *ramia* 'beautiful' > Javanese *rame* 'complicated, tangled lively').

25. My teacher tells the story of his first wayang performance in which he insisted on performing a story that was too "heavy" (*berat*) for him. All the oil lamps died mid-performance, so his grandfather pushed him aside and continued the performance, and all the lights came on again.

   On Mount Kawi, near Malang, a wayang performance goes on every day and every night, nonstop year round, performing for the essential audience and preserving the spiritual texture, the *ruwatan*.

26. This term was pointed out to me by Susan Walton, who observed that the pervasiveness of etymologizing in Javanese texts is closely related to the high value placed on coincidence. Both are considered nonarbitrary.

27. See Gregory Bateson, for further examples (chiefly Balinese) of the role of skill as a basic element in aesthetics: "Style, grace, and information in primitive art." Bateson writes, "Only the violinist who can control the quality of his notes can use variations of that quality for musical purposes" (1972:148).

28. A book dalang is insufficient for most Javanese because he fails to perform one of the important functions of a good dalang, contextualizing (the present in the past and the past in the present).

29. Thus foreign borrowings are *information* about nature. Almost all Sanskrit borrowings into Javanese (and Kawi) are nouns, the names for things. Javanese (and others) borrow from Sanskrit (or Arabic, or Dutch, or English) not primarily to appear elegant and learned—though these are secondary motivations sometimes—but to gain information. See J. Gonda (1973).

30. There are many difficult Javanese books about the mystical meaning of the language of wayang. For a sample, see Holt (1957), which is a translation of Mangkoenegoro (1973).

31. That the Javanese view wayang emblematically in this way is supported by frequent allusions in literature and by constant references in conversation. Here is a well-known and frequently quoted example from the *Serat Tjentini*, translated and explained by Zoetmulder (1971). In a discussion about wayang and its relation to Islam, a Javanese host says:

   > The illuminated screen is the visible world. The puppets, which are arranged in an orderly fashion at both edges of the screen at the beginning of the play, are the different varieties and categories created by God. The *gedebog*, the banana trunk into which the dalang sticks his puppets whenever they have no role to fulfill in the play, is the surface of the earth. The *blentjong*, the lamp over the head of the dalang behind the screen, which brings to life the shadows on the other side, is the lamp of life. The *gamelon*, the orchestra which accompanies the play with its motives and melodies fixed in accor-

dance with the various persons and events projected on the screen, represents the harmony and mutual relationship of everything that occurs in the world.

The creatures, which appear in the world in uncounted numbers and in an astounding variety of forms, may become an obstacle to true insight, impeding understanding of the deeper meaning of all that is created. He who refuses to be led by one who is wiser than he [that is: the uninitiated who is unwilling to put himself under the guidance of a guru] will never see that God is in and behind everything. He is deceived by form and shape. His sight becomes troubled and confused, and he loses himself in a void, while the true significance of the universe remains hidden to him. He goes astray on a path full of obstacles for, lacking the right knowledge, the true meaning of all that appears before his eyes continues to evade him.

32. See Hildred Geertz (1968), one of the very few explorations of the cultural context of speech pathologies.

33. Some of these attributions are listed in Sastroamidjojo (1964:265–73). Attribution is itself an interesting linguistic act. Who attributes what to whom under what circumstances? We attribute texts mostly, whereas Nukuoro attribute some words to certain individuals, as Vern Carroll pointed out to me.

34. This essay, taken together with Judith Becker's "Time and Tune," suggests the possibility of a single set of constraints running through the whole of the traditional Javanese epistemology, in music, calendars, texts, rituals, and social relations. Of course, this unity may be in part the oversimplification of an outsider, but, if true, this unity is probably a rather rare situation in a culture, as it is in a person. In both it has great power. The complex of changes we call *modernization* necessarily fragments this unity. Social change alters one by one, and in no particular order, it seems, those relations of a text to its context that constitute its meaning. Modern single time (Greenwich Mean Time, manifest in the modern necessity of life, the wristwatch) thus strongly affects plot coherence by devaluing multiple time. If multiple time is devalued, coincidence ceases to be "truth" (*kebetulan*), and is replaced, usually, by narrative/causal "truth." (In music the strategy of expanding cycles gives way to linear theme and variation.) Likewise the mythology may change and a whole new set of characters and motifs may come into currency. The unseen audience may fade, and trance communication may become just entertainment. Words may lose their naturalness and hence etymologizing its purpose. Thus conceptual worlds slowly disappear, just as new ones emerge.

REFERENCES

Anderson, Benedict R. O'G. *Mythology and the tolerance of the Javanese.* Data
Papers, no. 27. Ithaca: Cornell University Southeast Asia Program, 1965.
Aristotle. *Politics and poetics* (B. Jowett and T. Twining, trans.). New York:
Viking Press, 1969.
Barthes, Roland. *Mythologies.* New York: Hill and Wang, 1972.
Bateson, Gregory. *Steps to an ecology of mind.* New York: Ballantine, 1972.
Becker, Alton. The journey through the night: Some reflections on Burmese
traditional theatre. In Mohd. Taib Osman (ed.), *Traditional drama and mu-
sic of southeast Asia.* Kuala Lumpur: Dewan Bahasa dan Pustaka, 1974.
(Also in *The drama review,* Winter 1970.)
Becker, Alton L. A linguistic image of nature: The Burmese numerative
classifier system. *International journal of the sociology of language,* 1975, *5,*
109–21.
Becker, Alton, and I Gusti Ngurah Oka. Person in Kawi: Exploration of an
elementary semantic dimension. *Oceanic linguistics,* 1976, *13,* 229–55.
Becker, Ernest. *The birth and death of meaning.* New York: The Free Press, 1962.
Becker, Judith. *Karawitan: Source readings in Javanese gamelan and vocal music.*
Ann Arbor: Center for South and Southeast Asian Studies, University of
Michigan, 1984.
Becker, Judith. Time and tune in Java. In A. L. Becker and Aram Yengoyan
(ed.), *The imagination of reality: Essays in Southeast Asian coherence systems.*
Norwood, N.J.: Ablex, 1979.
Benveniste, Emile. Ch. 6: Categories of thought and language. Ch. 7: Re-
marks on the function of language in Freudian theory. In *Problems in
general linguistics.* Coral Gables, Fla.: University of Miami Press, 1971.
Bloch, Maurice. Symbols, song, dance, and features of articulation. *European
journal of sociology,* 1974, *XV,* 58.
Borges, J. L. *Ficciones.* New York: Grove Press, 1962.
Boulding, Kenneth. *The image.* Ann Arbor: University of Michigan Press,
1961.
Brandon, James (ed.). *On thrones of gold: Three Javanese shadow plays.* Cam-
bridge, Mass.: Harvard University Press, 1970.
Burke, Kenneth. *A grammar of motives.* Berkeley: University of California
Press, 1969.
Coomaraswamy, A. K. Hindu view of art: Theory of beauty. In *The dance of
Shiva.* New York: Noonday Press, 1957.
Croce, Benedetto. Ch. XVIII: Identity of linguistic and aesthetic. In *Aesthetic:
As science of expression and general linguistic* (D. Ainslie, trans.). New York:
Farrar, Strauss and Giroux, 1970.

Crystal, Eric. *Ma'bugi: Trance of the Toraja.* 16 mm. film, 22 min., color. Private collection.

Emerson, R. W. *Nature.* New York: Liberal Arts Press, 1948.

Emmerson, Donald. The Ramayana syndrome. Forthcoming.

Geertz, Clifford. *The interpretation of culture.* New York: Basic Books, 1973.

Geertz, Hildred. Latah in Java: A theoretical paradox. *Indonesia,* April 1968, 93–104.

Gonda, J. *Sanskrit in Indonesia* (2d ed.). Sata-Pitaka Series, vol. 92. New Delhi: International Academy of Indian Culture, 1973.

Hahn, Edward. Finite-state models of plot complexity. *Poetics: International review for the theory of literature,* 1973, 8.

Hale, Kenneth. A note on a Walbiri tradition of autonymy. In D. D. Steinberg and L. A. Jakobovits (eds.), *Semantics: An interdisciplinary reader in philosophy, linguistics, and psychology.* New York: Cambridge University Press, 1974.

Haley, Jay. *Strategies of psychotherapy.* New York: Grove and Stratton, 1963.

Hardjowirogo. *Sedjarah Wajang Purwa.* Djakarta: Balai Pustaka, 1968.

Holt, Claire. *On the wayang kulit (purwa) and its symbolic mystical elements.* Data papers, no. 27. Ithaca: Cornell University Southeast Asia Program, 1957.

Holt, Claire. *Art in Indonesia: Continuities and change.* Ithaca: Cornell University Press, 1967.

Hooykaas, C. *Kama and Kala (Materials for the study of shadow theatre in Bali).* Amsterdam: North Holland Publishing Co., 1973.

Hooykaas, C. *Cosmology and creation in the Balinese tradition.* The Hague: M. Nijhoff, 1974.

Kats, J. *Het Javaansche Jooneel I wayang poerwa.* Weltrveden, 1923.

Labov, William. *Language in the inner city.* Philadelphia: University of Pennsylvania Press, 1972.

Lacan, Jacques. *The language of self* (A. Wilden, trans.). Baltimore: Johns Hopkins University Press, 1973.

Laing, R. D. *Knots.* New York: Vintage, 1970.

Lévi-Strauss, Claude. *Structural anthropology.* New York: Basic Books, 1963.

Mangkoenegoro. Over de wajang-koelit (poerwa) in het algemeen en over de daarin voorkomende symbolishe en mysticke elementen. *Djawa,* 1973, XIII, 79–95.

Mellema, R. L. *Wayang puppets: Carving, colouring, symbolism.* Amsterdam: Koninklijk Instituut voor de Tropen, 1954.

Nojowirongko, M. Ng. *Serat tutunan padalangan.* Jogjakarta, 1960.

Pike, K. L. The hierarchical and social matrix of suprasegmentals. *Nabitka zprae filologicznych,* 1963, XVIII, 1, 95–104.

Probohardjono, R. Ngb. S. *Sulukan slendro.* Solo, 1966.

Propp, V. Morphology of the folktale. *International journal of American linguistics*, 1958, 24, 4, pt. III.

Rassers, W. H. On the origin of the Javanese theatre. In *Panji, the culture hero*. The Hague: Mouton, 1959.

Resink, G. J. From the old Mahabharta- to the new Ramayana-order. *Bijdragen tot de Taal-, Land-en Volkenkunde*, DL 131 II/III, 1975, 214–35.

Sajid, R. M. *Bauwarna Wajang*. Jogjakarta, 1958.

Sastroamidjojo, Dr. Seno. *Renungantentang pertundjukan wajangkulit*. Djakarta: Kinta, 1964.

Soebardi. Calendrical traditions in Indonesia. *Madjalah ilmu-ilmu sastra Indonesia*, 1965, 14, 1, 49–61.

Waldo, Ives. Metaknowledge and the logic of Buddhist language. In *Loka: A journal from Naropa Institute*. Garden City: N.Y.: Anchor, 1975.

Wilden, Anthony. *System and structure: Essays in communication and exchange*. London: Tavistock, 1972.

Young, R. E., and A. L. Becker. Toward a modern theory of rhetoric: A tagmemic contribution. In J. Emig, J. Fleming, and H. M. Popp (eds.). *Language and learning*. New York: Harcourt, Brace and World, 1966.

Young, R. E., A. L. Becker, and K. L. Pike. *Rhetoric, discovery and change*. New York: Harcourt, Brace and World, 1971.

Zoetmulder, P. J. The wajang as a philosophical theme. *Indonesia*, Oct. 1971, 12, 89.

Zurbuchen, Mary. Kawi discourse structure: Cycle, event, and evaluation. *Rackham literary studies*, Winter 1976, 45–60.

The Linguistics of Particularity: Interpreting Superordination in a Javanese Text

I have never translated the whole text of a wayang for reasons that now should be clear: it is an oral genre, sounded and carefully attuned to the particularities of its performance. To translate it would be to make it something it isn't, like a skinned and stuffed bird.

There are, however, books in Java called pakem, *that contain, in various degrees of detail, the plots,* suluks, *and even some of the dialogues of frequently performed plays. In this essay a scene of wayang is taken from a* pakem *for close analysis. It is a technical essay, written for an audience of linguists at the Berkeley Linguistics Society. I do not think it is too arcane for the general reader, however, and it does fill in a gap in the previous essay: a taste of the way text building happens at the level of sentences.*

Here one phenomenon in particular is explored: that which happens in Javanese discourse because in the language there is no inanimate pronoun like the English it. *How can you build a coherent sequence of sentences with no* it? *(Look at the first paragraph above, for instance, and imagine all the* its *gone and the repetitions that its absence would require.) I try to show that the absence (from the point of view of a language with* it*) of this small grammatical phenomenon opens up an esthetic possibility that in English would be awkward and much more difficult to achieve and that a good part of the coherence and esthetic power of this intriguing scene depends on it.*

❖   ❖   ❖

A definition of language is always, implicitly or explicitly, a
definition of human beings in the world
—Raymond Williams

The term that titles this essay, the linguistics of particularity, I first heard from Kenneth L. Pike many years ago. Most of my own aca-

71

demic life has been spent exploring that term, with a growing sense of its importance. At first it seems perverse, this substitution of particularity for the pursuit of generality or universality as the goal of our craft. Is it any more than an instance of the general heuristic principle (mathematical or rhetorical): always invert?

For Pike, I think, the motivation toward a linguistics of particularity is part of his strong conviction that one's understanding of another language, or another person, is a movement from an etic perspective—an outsider's perspective—to an emic understanding, a more fully contextual understanding. This change is not just an increasing awareness of regular patterns *in* the language, but a change in what Pike calls the observer. That is, the particularity involves both the observer and the text: both are in history. What we call a text—some remembered bit of language is the trace, often a very faint trace, of some event in some world in which somebody wanted to say something to someone about something, and that someone and somebody and something are particular. Likewise, that linguistic observer is a particular observer, full of biases he or she is never fully aware of—the biases of his or her own language and his or her understanding of that language. Like the horse's hoof and the prairie grass, the observer and the text co-evolve.

In the years since Pike first talked about a linguistics of particularity, I seemed to hear similar kinds of statements from several very disparate sources: from Gregory Bateson (1979:17) who wrote that "contextual shaping is only another term for grammar"; from the poststructural hermeneutic tradition in France—most clearly, perhaps, from Paul Ricoeur (1981); from the late Wittgenstein (1958) in his understanding of language as a form of life; from Raymond Williams (1977), whose penetrating Marxist critique of linguistics begins with the sentence quoted above as an epigraph; from the interpreters of Heidegger like Grassi (1980) and Ortega (1957:242) who proposed an interpretive linguistics, which the latter called "una nueva filología"; or from Clifford Geertz (1983:19) who describes a "laws and instances" approach in the social sciences being replaced by a "cases and interpretations" one.

I do not cite all those people to endorse a particular brand of linguistics. A truly interpretive linguistics, a linguistics of particularity, has yet to appear. All of them, however, if not in unison then at least in harmony, suggest alternatives to a structuralist view of language—and I mean generative as well as taxonomic structuralism. These alternatives share a resemblance in their view of language as activity in a particular context, co-evolving along with that context, in part constitutive of it.

In the unfinished job of projecting "una nueva filología," Ortega (1959) gives two axioms of this discipline.

1. Every utterance is deficient—it says less than it wishes to say.
2. Every utterance is exuberant—it says more than it plans.

The philologist helps us correct our deficiencies and exuberances in understanding those we have trouble understanding, in distant cultures or right at home. The goal is not a theory of language but something more like usefulness—usefulness in helping us make the adjustments necessary to understanding the Javanese, the Cree, our own neighbors, and ourselves. And the rigor here is not the rigor of theory (with particular bits of language as examples) but the rigor that comes from the particularity of the text-in-context.

The best method I know for doing this is what has been called "back-translation," starting from a translation and then seeking out the exuberances—those things present in the translation but not in the original—and the deficiencies—those things in the original but not in the translation. For most linguists, the translations are glosses, that is, English substitutes for words and parts of words (including labels for linguistic categories). This is an English appropriation of the text under study. And, of course, we appropriate not only the words, but also a context for them. I would argue that most of the analysis is accomplished by the glossing. In "back-translation" one reverses that process, not necessarily to improve the translation (one may be starting from what is already the best possible translation), but rather to get closer to that particular text-in-context and see it as a reasonable and sane way of being in the world.

An Episode from a Javanese Wayang

The rigor in this essay comes from a written version of a scene from a Javanese shadow play. It is taken from a *pakem*, an interesting Javanese genre of models for shadow-play performances. Sometimes they are quite abstract, other times (as here) rich with detail and very lively vocabulary. It's good data for studying Javanese discourse since it has a full Javanese past, unlike some of the new language games for which the prior texts are non-Javanese. I had been reading the whole work with a fellow Javanist, Alan Feinstein, who was working on a translation. Every week we would do back-translation—trying to find the exuberances and deficiencies of his English interpretation. The passage I've selected for close inspection here is one we worked on. Later I sent the translation to a Javanese linguist, Bambang Kaswanti Purwo, and received many corrections.

The passage is a typical episode from a wayang used to "clean" a village of a variety of real and potential evils—in people and in the air. It's the life story of the demon Kala. His name in Javanese means 'time'—as well as 'destruction'. Wayang is a means of coping with Kala; indeed, as the story recounts, wayang is used as a way not to defeat the demon but to constrain him. The demon is limited in his prey to children of various sorts—an only child, twins, a girl born between two boys, and several other categories. These constraints on the demon were imposed by his father, Siva, who conceived Kala in a moment of anger.

In this episode, Kala is chasing an orphan boy, Jaka Jatusmati. Whenever he stops to hide from Kala, the boy escapes but a traditional taboo is broken. Here a steamer of rice is upset, which saves the boy but breaks a taboo and requires a very interesting remedial act.

Let us go through the story, lightly parsing, with a bit of commentary when it gets obscure. I hope the reader will be patient and read bilingually.

Dandang Rubuh

An episode from the *Pakem Pangruwatan Murwa Kala* by Kyai Demang Reditanaja, arranged here in lines, to be read from English to Javanese. (The spelling has been brought up to date, and some clear typographic errors corrected. The punctuation is as in the original.)

1. There was a woman steaming (rice) inside of her house,
   Be person female steaming at   inside of house
   Ana wong wadon adang   ing sajroning omah,

2. the doors were all closed,
   door art. all   closed
   lawange kabeh diinebi,

3. while the one who looked after (it)—her grandfather
   while who look-after related-as grandfather
   dene kang tunggu   kaprenah kakekne

   was outside of the house,
   be   outside of house
   ana sajabaning omah,

4. concentrating on what he was doing so it happened
   while   absorbed-in thing so   happen-unnoticed
   sinambi anggegeb   barang temah katungkul

5. Jaka Jatusmati entered the house,
   Jaka Jatusmati lumebu ing omah,

6. and   watched over the steaming
   banjur unggu   dang-dangan

7. and   arranged the wood of the fire
   kalawan angutik   geni

8. Bathara Kala—something made him stop walking
   Bathara Kala   kandheg   lakune

9. And he sought the one who had put the steamer on the stove,
   then tried   person who put-on-stove steamer
   nuli ngupaya wong kang ngenteb   dandang,

10. And met her in the garden picking vegetables,
    meet   be in garden   pick   vegetables
    ketemu ana ing tegalan lagi remban janganan,

11. And urged her to order away
    and   urged   to   order go-away to
    banjur sinraban supaya akon lunga   marang

    the child who watched over the steaming,
    child who look-after steaming
    bocah kang tunggu   dangdangan,

12. But he was not paid any attention
    but   not be-reacted to
    nanging ora dipaelu

13. Bathara Kala then returned impatiently,
                    then return not patient
    Bathara Kala nuli bali   ora saranta.

14. Jaka Jatusmati was enjoying himself, sitting,
    Jaka Jatusmati still enjoy
    Jaka Jatusmati isih ngenak-enak

    embracing his knees,
    embrace   knees
    ngrangkul dhengkul

15. looking after the fire.
    and look-after fire
    karo tunggu   geni.

16. Bathara Kala opened the door
    Bathara Kala mbukak   lawang

17. and entered the house
    then enter   in house
    nuli lumebu ing omah

18. Jaka Jatsumati was spied on
    Jaka Jatsumati kadingkik

19. then seen to go hide behind the steamer,
    then evade   conceal   steamer which erect
    wis angocati ampingan dandang kang ngaded,

20. and he grabbed at him but he slithered away around the
    steamer

intend be-seized slip away circle   steamer
arep   cinandak marucut ngubengi dandang

(*Marucut* = state of being loosed, as when you catch a fish
and the fish is slippery.)

21. Bathara Kala said.
Bathara Kala ngandika.

22. Hey, slippery child!
Hey child slippery
Heh boca kesit!

23. You just give up—don't hide behind the steamer
you   follow just don't go-in-shade of steamer
kowe nuruta bae aja   ampingan   dandang

24. Don't you feel you got enough from this steamer?
ques. you   not feel   that get   full
apa   kowe ora rumasa yen nggonmu wareg

from   steamer this
saka ing dandang iki?

25. and he pounced.
banjur nubruk.

26. Jaka Jatusmati escaped and went out,
Jaka Jatusmati ngoncati   metu,

27. The steamer fell over.
dandange   rubuh.

28. Bathara Kala slipped and fell, smeared with rice, his head
moving continuously from side to side, and his legs jogging
quickly to shake off the heat.
Bathara Kala slip   fall smeared   shake-head
Bathara Kala kapleset tiba galumprut gobag-gabig,

jog
kicat-kicat.

(*Kicat-kicat* = uncomfortable feeling in feet from walking on a
hot place.)

29. The woman who owned the house came home and saw that
    the steamer was upset,
    person   who own house come see   that
    wong kang duwe   omah teka sumurup yen

    steamer   knocked-over
    dandange gumalimpang,

30. and asked her grandfather who was outside,
    ask   to   grandfather who be   outside
    takon marang kakekne   kang ana ing jaba,

31. what had happened that the steamer fell?
    what origin   steamer   get   fallen
    apa   mulane dandange nganti rubuh?

32. The one who was asked shared her remorse
    who asked   go-with regret
    kang tinakon melu   getun

33. and said almost unheard:
    and   say   very quietly
    banjur angucap lirih:

34. It was because Sang Kala (time) struck,
    that because hit   by sangkala
    Iku wong   kena ing sangkala,

35. which is fatal dressed as a woman
    get   fatal dressed-as   woman
    nganti tiwas dandananing wadon

36. so then be naked, completely, and dance
    so then   experience naked expose dance
    lha banjur nglakonana wuda byar   njoged

    (*Byar* = sudden change from darkness to light.)

37. around the house in a ring three times,
    circle   house join   bracelet times   three
    ngubengi omah tepung gelang   kaping telu,

38. and I'll beat the rhythm—dhug, dhug, brag
    I   beat   dhug, dhug, brag
    tak tabuhi dhug, dhug, brag

39. And I'll address you as a naked madwoman.
    and I   address person crazy after naked.
    sarta tak elokake wong edan bar ndhul.

40. The person who received the instructions instantly then took
    off her clothes,
    person who receive lesson   quickly   then
    wong kang tampa ujar ing sanalika banjur
    take-off clothes
    anrucat panganggone,

41. And did what her grandfather advised.
    act   advice of   grandfather.
    anindakake sawewarahing kakekne.

42. Bathara Kala felt mocked by the woman
    Bathara Kala felt   mocked
    Bathara Kala rumasa diiwi-iwi

43. then tried to shake off the mockery:
    and   shake-off:
    banjur angipat-ipati:

    (*Angipat-ipati* recalls *kicat-kicat* in line 28. It means to make a
    move to shake off something unwanted, like a cockroach on
    the arm.)

44. Hey my child of the wind!
    Heh bocahingsun   wadu barat!

    (The *wadu barat* are the child-servants of Kala.)

45. Besides taking away their wealth,
    besides deprive   wealth
    kajaba elongana kayane,

46. also take away their rice everyday,
    also deprive   rice   of every day
    uga elongana berase ing saben dina,

47. take away seven in a household,
    deprive   seven a household/family
    elongana pitung somah,

    (This line is obscure.)

48. Don't let it cease until I have captured my prey,
    don't you cease if   not yet be seized prey-my
    aja   kok uwisi yen durung kacandak beburonku,

49. Bathara Kala continued pursuing the boy, wherever he had
    gone,
    Bathara Kala continue pursue to   whichever-direction
    Bathara Kala isih   nututi ing saparan,

50. but now walking slowly.
    but   pace   slow
    nanging lakune remben.

The purpose in arranging the text this way is to emphasize the
direction of inquiry—from an English translation back toward the
Javanese. It is a difficult task to impose on a reader, to figure out how
those English words are related to the Javanese and to undo their
implicit grammatical interpretation. Here the translation is a starting
point not a goal. The task is to deconstruct the translation, to the end
of a greater authenticity or fullness in interpreting the text. It is a self-
correction in the direction of emic understanding.

As a first step it is useful to list the exuberances and deficiencies,
following Ortega's axioms for a new philology.

1. Every utterance is deficient.
2. Every utterance is exuberant.

Note that Ortega says *"every* utterance," not just some. The paradox
works even in the most intimate conversation, but the deficiencies and
exuberances are almost overwhelming when one is approaching a distant text. And so it is important to list them. Here is a partial listing. I
will focus here primarily on a few grammatical differences and set aside

the numerous lexical, pragmatic, metaphorical, phonological, and rhetorical differences, though these can only with effort be separated, for purposes of comparison.

A	B
Exuberance of Translation (only in English)	Deficiency of Translation (only in Javanese)
Number	Reduplications
Tense	Focus marked on verb
Aspect	"Zeroing" for animate anaphora
Anaphoric pronominalization	
Third-person inanimate pronoun	Repetition for inanimate anaphora

Each of these differences can be explored, with the goal of attuning oneself to the text by giving up coherences produced by things in column A—the coherence of tense, of number, of some determiners, of some pronominalization—and learning to pay attention to the coherences produced by those things in column B—reduplication, focus, "zeroing," and repetition. Each of these differences affects the kinds of textures it is possible to produce since each has to do with coherence, that is, cross-sentential constraints.

Discourse grammar has to do mostly with paradigmatic relations, with constraints on the fillers of syntagmatic slots. Continuity of topic, tense, or focus binds sentences in quite particular ways. One can follow a topic through a text and see how it changes grammatical shapes and roles and gathers significance in new contexts. Recent studies of topic continuity by Givón (1983) and others help us get these chains (or themes, or "paraphrase sets," as we called them twenty years ago) into clearer focus.

When one examines the topic chains in the Javanese text, several interesting things appear.

1. We can see that "zeroing" (i.e., not mentioning a topic after its initial mention—with "zeroing" in quotation marks lest we

forget its English bias) occurs only with animate topics and only when the topic has been mentioned one clause earlier. There are many instances of this.

2. We can see that restrictive relative clauses only reintroduce formerly identified topics after a gap (there are six instances here: 9, 11, 19, 29, 30, 40).

3. Pronouns are used in direct speech only, and only first and second person are found. There is no number. Topic chaining is not maintained by pronominalization but by "zeroing" for third-person animate topics in adjacent clauses, and by repeating elsewhere, i.e., with animate topics after a gap and with all inanimates. All inanimate chains are sustained by repeating the topic. There is no *it* in Javanese (nor in modern Indonesian, except as a very recent innovation).

I would like to examine here just this last phenomenon, repeating inanimate topics, and see how it works in building the superordinate chain in the text. Some topic chains are more important than others in two senses.

1. Superordinate chains have a larger scope within a text and hence play a more important role in creating coherence.

2. As centers of coherence, superordinate chains give relevance to subordinate chains, just as a phrasal head gives relevance to its modifiers. Here we are looking at the hypotactic relations of topic chains to each other in a paradigmatic hierarchy (see Becker 1965; and Halliday 1981).

The topic with widest scope here is marked by the term *dang* 'to steam' in all its forms. Forms of *dang* occur twelve times in the text. (The nearest rival, *Bathara Kala*, occurs only eight times.) Until near the end of the story, when the "antidote" episode occurs, this term, *dang*, appears in every sentence except two, and in these two (14–15 and 28) it is metonymically present, in the fire that produces the steam or the rice that is being steamed. Here is a minor text-building strategy, a way of topic chaining working under slightly different constraints from those we experience in English, since we have *it*. Is this a difference that makes a difference, as Gregory Bateson used to say? Does it make the sort of difference that, say, the absence of tense or number clearly makes in text building (Becker 1979)?

In answer to this question, let us first see what happens to *dang* in each of its manifestations.

1. First it appears as a verb, stative in form: *adang*. The woman is steaming something—rice is the unmarked case (line 1).
2. Then, later in the same long sentence, it is nominalized via reduplication: *dangdangan* 'the steaming'. The boy attends to the steaming (line 6).
3. Then it becomes a noun through partial reduplication: *dandang* 'steamer'. It occurs in a relative clause reidentifying the woman who put the steamer on the stove (line 9).
4. In the same sentence, it appears again, this time reidentifying the boy (line 11).
5. Next, the term in noun form (*dandang* 'steamer') appears twice in one sentence as the object of the verb. Kala sees the boy hide behind the steamer and then slither away around it (lines 19 and 20).
6. It occurs twice in the next sentence, still as object (lines 23 and 24).
7. Then, at the center of the story (line 27), the noun *dandang* takes a definite article and becomes subject. The fact that this episode is traditionally named by this line (*dandang rubuh* 'steamer falls') lends weight to this interpretation of the line as the center of the story. This interpretation is given further weight by the line that follows it, a clause with a sequence of five predicates in a row, a common way of marking a climax (line 28).
8. The noun plus definite article (*dandang* + *e*) remains a subject in two embedded clauses referring back to the incident, the falling (lines 29 and 31).
9. And then (line 35), via a near identity of form (*dandang* and *dandan* 'to dress, be adorned')—a rhyme pun of the sort very common in Javanese—the thematic term *dandang* changes to

dandan so that in a formal way the falling of the steamer gets linked to the woman's removing her clothes and hopping naked around the house three times like a crazy person—a corrective action for knocking over a rice steamer that Javanese friends assure me is not unknown in modern Java.

One might note that the topic chain that ranks second in superordination (in this episode), *Sang Kala*, is the superordinate chain for the entire shadow play—that is, it is the topic that gives coherence to the larger whole. Parallel to the pun in the *dang* chain in line 35, the *Sang Kala* chain changes, too, in the immediately preceding line, where the proper name, *Sang Kala*, becomes the common noun *sangkala* 'time'. Here, too, a sound correspondence is pivotal in linking the two parts of the story, the taboo breaking and the remedy.

By its persistence and repetition in a topic chain a certain term becomes a center around which other terms take subordinate positions—the four characters, the house, the fire, the rice—all of them get their cohesion from that steamer. It is the thing that holds the plot together. In Burkean terms, an instrument becomes thematic and shapes the plot.

The difference between Javanese and English in the management of a nonanimate topic chain involves exuberance of English, while the lack of rich possibilities of reduplication and repetition is a deficiency. In reading Javanese, we drop this form of pronominal substitution from our set of potential cohesion strategies and add reduplications of various sorts—reduplications of whole words or of parts of words. It may well be that reduplication and repetition can best be seen as variants of a single strategy at different levels—strategies of repeating. Repeating a term instead of pronominalizing or "zeroing" can be interpreted as the intersentential manifestation of a very common Austronesian strategy. Pronominal substitution, "zeroing," and repeating are, then, not alternate ways of doing the same thing since they result in very different textures. It is difficult to generalize about these different strategies, but a list of some of the differences might help us to see how they do "make a difference."

Pronominal Substitution	Repetition
1. Term is nominalized	Term freely changes categories (i.e., we follow it into predicates)
2. Processing is speeded	Processing is slowed
3. Sound of term is lost, referentiality is preserved	Sound of term is preserved, even enriched
4. Sound puns are difficult	Sound puns are easy

In chaining then, "zeroing" is, as Fred Lupke puts it, a least, repetition a most, and pronominalization is somewhere in between. Each has different effects. Note that the effects we are looking at here are not logical but might better be called esthetic—different modes of creating a satisfying texture. One homology with these differences of texture might be the general Javanese esthetic of density (corresponding to a strategy of repetition in discourse) in contrast to the general Japanese esthetic of sparsity (corresponding to the strategy of "zeroing" so common to Japanese discourse). Contrast a Noh play with a Javanese wayang, or a Japanese music ensemble with a gamelan. This kind of nonrational homology is one of the things that binds a culture (see Becker 1979).

Recapitulation

One of the basic differences between interpreting the grammar of clauses and that of discourse is, as many have noticed (e.g., Pike, Burke, and Halliday), that in discourse the patterning seems predominantly paradigmatic, while in clauses it seems predominantly syntagmatic. Chaining is not a central clausal phenomenon, although it appears, of course, in the guise of "Equi-NP" operations, in which monoclausal phenomena are usually given multiclausal interpretations (under the strange notion that a clause can have but a single predicate). Nor is discourse predominantly syntagmatic, though we can press stories into tree diagrams, with effort. Following a topic through a chain, studying its continuity and discontinuity, and then studying the relations between chains seems central to the linguistic study of texts. The likeness between many modifiers sharing a single headword and many subordinate topic chains sharing a single superordinate topic chain may be a bit forced; likewise, the likeness between word-level reduplication and the repeating of a term in a topic chain may be no more than that—a likeness. On the other hand, language, like culture, may be bound by just such homologies.

A final word, then, about particularity. The topic chain we followed here is a particular thread in the texture of a particular tale. All discourse—unlike the study of syntax—is of necessity the study of particularity, as Ricoeur has pointed out (1981:198). Ortega, too, saw this many years ago, when he wrote:

> the splendid intellectual achievement represented by linguistics as it is constituted today obliges it (*noblesse oblige*) to attain a second and more precise and forceful approximation in its knowledge of the reality, "language." And this it can do only if it studies language not as an accomplished fact, as a thing made and finished, but as in the process of being made, hence *in statu nascendi,* in the very roots that engender it. (1957:242)

The actual a priori of any language event—the real deep structure—is an accumulation of remembered prior texts just like the one studied here: particular prior texts, acquired from particular sources. From the perspective of particularity, generality is a kind of epiphenomenon produced by the reshaping of a particular prior text to a new context. And our real language competence is access, via memory, to this accumulation of prior text.

ACKNOWLEDGMENTS

Several people have helped in this essay: Alan Feinstein and Bambang Kaswanti Purwo in reading the Javanese; Eric Rabkin in expanding the interpretation to include the *Sang Kala* topic chain; Deborah Tannen for very insightful discussions about repetition in text building, particularly her paper presented at the Linguistic Society of America meeting held in Minneapolis in December 1983, entitled "Repetition and Variation as Formulaicity in Conversation"; Fred Lupke for insisting on the relevance of leasts and mosts; and Judith Becker for many useful suggestions.

REFERENCES

Bateson, Gregory (1979) *Mind and Nature*. New York: Dutton.
Becker, A. L. (1965) "Tagmemic Approach to Paragraph Analysis," *College Composition and Communication*, XVI.
—— (1979) "Text-Building, Epistemology, and Aesthetics in Javanese Shadow Theatre," in A. L. Becker and Aram Yengoyan (eds.), *The Imagination of Reality: Essays on Southeast Asian Coherence Systems*. Norwood, N.J.: Ablex.
Geertz, Clifford (1983) *Local Knowledge: Further Essays in Interpretive Anthropology*. New York: Basic Books.
Givon, Talmy (1983) *Topic Continuity in Discourse: A Quantitative Cross-Language Study*. Amsterdam: J. Benjamins.
Grassi, Ernesto (1980) *Rhetoric as Philosophy: The Humanist Tradition*. University Park: Pennsylvania State University Press.
Halliday, M. A. K. (1981) "Text Semantics and Clause Grammar: Some Patterns of Realization," *The Seventh LACUS Forum, 1980*.
Ortega y Gasset, José (1959) "The Difficulty of Reading," *Diogenes* 28.
—— (1957) *Man and People*. New York: Norton.
Pike, Kenneth L. (1972) "Toward a Theory of the Structure of Human Behavior," in Ruth Brend (ed.), *Kenneth L. Pike: Selected Writings*. The Hague: Mouton.
Reditanaja, Kjai Demang (1964) *Pakem Pangruwatan Murwa Kala*. Surakarta: Tri-Jasa.
Ricoeur, Paul (1981) *Hermeneutics and the Human Sciences*. London: Cambridge University Press.
Williams, Raymond (1977) *Marxism and Literature*. Oxford: Oxford University Press.
Wittgenstein, Ludwig (1958) *Philosophical Investigations*. New York: Macmillan.

Binding Wild Words:
Cohesion in Old Javanese Prose

with Thomas Hunter

The following essay is very similar in plot to the last one—taking a relatively small text like a proverb and attempting to sketch the framework of prior texts within which it has meaning. In order to do the close and multicontextful kind of study I was developing, a very small text is necessary since the amount of detail that piles up in the process is overwhelming. These essays report on a process that is prolonged but very engaging nonetheless: the detailed study of a single, particular sentence over a period of months, even years.

That's not everyone's cup of tea, but philologists know how interesting, even esthetically powerful, it can be. The problem is, finally, how to write up the results of this prolonged "meditation" in summary fashion; how to take a reader through an experience without reproducing that experience. One friendly critic referred to my kind of study as being akin to S. J. Perelman's mock stage direction: "the curtain goes down for seven days to mark the passage of a week."

The only solution for this that I know of is to work on small texts, either freestanding ones, like proverbs, or key sentences (e.g., initial sentences) from larger works.

In "Binding Wild Words" I report on some of the things I discovered in meditating on a sentence of Old Javanese from a much larger text, one I was using at the time to teach the language, a collection of tales retold, not necessarily translated, from Sanskrit. I worked very closely on this sentence with Thomas Hunter who knows Sanskrit far better than I.

The sentence is a translation into Old Javanese from Sanskrit, and so a comparison with the original Sanskrit revealed a little of what happened in that process. The essay is an account in English of how an Old Javanese "proverb" was translated from Sanskrit. Not only is there a single curtain that goes down for seven days, but now two curtains of crosslingual obscurity.

If the task is utopian, so are many other important tasks (marriage, writing, friendship, lexicography). Besides, in reading distant texts it is proba-

bly not necessary to meditate on every sentence this way, though, I would argue, it is important to do one or two—to remind us that much of great importance is lost and added in translation. An obligatory act of retribution for philologists.

This essay was written for a festschrift (published in Indonesia) for Fr. John W. M. Verhaar, a continual source for me of new insight and deep support. Rama John is the grammarian referred to in the first sentence.

❖   ❖   ❖

Introduction

The Old Javanese *Tantri Kāmandaka* (Hooykaas 1931) begins with a very interesting sentence—and one whose meanings seem appropriate in an essay honoring a grammarian. The passage reads as follows:

> Ikang wwang tan wruh ring warga nikang çāstra mwang çabda-paçabda, umara madhya ning sabhā, mahyun mangucap-ucapa kalawan sang mahāpurusa, ikang wwang mangkana niyantanya n paḍa lawan ikang wwang mareng alas, mahyun sumikĕpeng gajah alas ri sĕdĕngnya matta mamawa bĕsan ing tunjung sahĕle, kangkĕna pangikatannya.

Hooykaas puts it into Dutch as follows.

> Een persoon die geen kennis bezit van de hoofdstukken der grammatica, van woord-en-stem, en dan in een gezelschap zich begeeft, met het voornemen om gesprekken to houden met geleerden, die is als een man die zich in een bosch begeeft met het voornemen om een wilden olifant te vangen als deze juist bronstig is, met één lotosstengel als middel om hem te binden. (Hooykaas 1931:12)

The following display provides glosses and some idea of the constituent structure, with parallel clauses arranged at equal indentations.

Separate clauses, dependent and independent, are numbered; the whole is a complex sentence, an elaborate simile.

1. Ikang wwang tan wruh ring   warga nikang çāstra   mwang
   that person not know about form of   sastra-s and
   çabda-paçabda
   words (?)

2.   umara madhya ning sabhā
        go   center of   hall

3.   mahyun mangucap-ucapa kalawan sang mahāpurusa
            want   to speak   with   great man

4. (Ikang wwang mangkana niyantanya n   pada lawan
   that   person do   clearly-it that same with
   ikang wwang)
   that person

5.   mareng alas
        go   forest

6.   mahyun sumikĕpeng gajah   alas ri sĕdĕngnya matta
            want   to bind   elephant forest while in   rut

7.   mamawa bĕsan   ing tunjung sahele
              carry   stamen (?) of   lotus   one blade

8.   kangkĕna pangikatannya
                          which hit binding-place-it

In this display, clause 1 is parallel to two later clauses, clause 4 via subject, clause 7 via predicate. Clause 2 is parallel to clause 5, and clause 3 to clause 6. The fourth clause is at a higher structural level than the others since it describes the relationship of clauses 1–3 to clauses 5–8. That is to say, clause 4 is of a different logical type from the other clauses: it serves to define the rhetorical function of the sentence as a whole.

There are several lexical problems in the passage, particularly the word *bĕsan*, perhaps a translation for the Sanskrit word *tantu* 'stamen' (also 'thread'), but I have not found the word in any dictionary available to me, nor do Javanese friends recognize it; another lexical problem is the Javanese shaping of the Sanskrit word *çabda* into *çabda-paçabda* ('woord-en-stem'). These problems, like those of establishing the text itself, are problems of primary philology.

But there are further levels of philology, resting on the essential foundation of the primary philology—the dictionary making, editing, and translation that makes the further study possible but does not exhaust the problems of philology. At these later levels of philology, one looks long and hard at the text and tries to understand it using all the tools of modern linguistics, modern rhetoric, and modern theories of culture and literature: who is speaking to whom in this text, about what? What here is the invention of the author—or multiple authors and emenders—and what is stereotypic? Why did he or she weave the text as it is woven? What constraints was he or she operating under, grammatical and epistemological? None of these questions have obvious answers.

After a few answers to these questions begin to shape themselves, the modern philologist begins to fear he may be gazing at the mirror of his own imagination. Surely what is modern in modern philology[1] is a certain self-consciousness about the observer along with the observed. One feels that in the older philology such a concern with the observer was indeed rare and would seem self-indulgent and even disloyal if one exposed too fully the deepest biases of one's own culture.

However, as a point of departure, the quotation from the *Tantri Kāmandaka* given above offers in the simile it develops a model for its own analysis. What one must not lack in entering a hall to discourse with a great man are *warga nikang çāstra mwang çabda-paçabda*, which translate—and elaborate—the Sanskrit compound *çabdaçāstram* 'grammar'—but grammar in its broadest sense, closer to Kenneth Burke's notion of logology or Walter Ong's noetics: the shaping, storage, retrieval, and communication of knowledge (Burke 1961; Ong 1977).

With Sanskrit writing and Sanskrit texts came Sanskrit attitudes about language. At the center of these attitudes was an epistemology of language quite different from that of most of us today, Eastern or Western. Madhav Deshpande (1979:65) describes this epistemology as follows.

> The status of Sanskrit in classical and medieval times resembles that of the world of Platonic Ideas. This is clearly reflected in the linguistic speculations of the Sanskrit grammarians, ritualists, and logicians. Therefore, the process of Sanskritization of non-Sanskrit languages continued to dominate the Indian linguistic scene and remained a very significant way of increasing the prestige of those languages. . . . In later times, the Persian and English compete with Sanskrit in this regard.

Within such a view, knowing about words—knowing grammar—is as basic to understanding the phenomenal world as biochemistry, neurobiology, or electronics seems to many today. In grammatical awareness was to be found the key to things.

Here clearly lies one of the powerful Sanskrit cultural challenges to the ancient Javanese. With the technology of writing came texts, terms, concepts, and new beliefs about language itself. If Sanskrit is in a deep, divine sense "true," what of the local languages? To put it briefly, only by becoming more like Sanskrit, or even, through imaginative etymologizing, by finding Sanskrit roots in Javanese words, could other languages approach the divine and true of Sanskrit. A written language, enough like Sanskrit to translate çāstras, became a *bahasa*, which, like its many cognates in Southeast Asia, is from the Sanskrit root *bhāṣ*. Old Javanese is one of the oldest and best preserved of the Southeast Asian *bahasa*-s.

The other part of the simile about grammar fills in the rest of the elaborate paradigm: trying to speak well without "grammar" (note that here writing underlies speech) was like trying to bind an elephant in rut ("boiling in his rut" in the Sanskrit original) with a single stalk ("stamen" in the original) of lotus. Besides the outrageous impossibility of the task, the elaborate simile says more. The paradigm might be broken down like this.

	A	B
Instrument	'grammar'	'stalk of lotus'
Location	'hall'	'forest'
Agent	'a man'	'a man'
Patient	('words')	'a wild elephant'
Intent	'to speak'	'to bind'

Within the simile, both grammar and the lotus stalk are modes of binding something powerful/holding words together. This metaphor of grammar as binding is a familiar one to many modern linguists for whom the notion of cohesion or binding is as intriguing a problem as segmentation was a generation earlier.[2]

The elaborate simile and a dozen of the words in the Old Javanese text are from Sanskrit, but the grammatical cohesion—the binding—is not. In Old Javanese the Sanskrit words are bound and made to cohere in a different way—a new way, each affecting the other to shape the literary language we call Old Javanese or Kawi. Old Javanese grammar bound—and so altered the meaning of—Sanskrit words and figures. What this alteration or difference might have meant will be the subject of the rest of this essay.

The Problem of Translation

The Old Javanese *Tantri Kāmandaka*, from which the passage we are looking at was taken, was in some ways a translation and in some ways not. That is, there is no Sanskrit original of the whole work. *Tantri* is both the name of the heroine of the frame story and the name of the genre of gnomic or philosophical literature of which this work is an example. *Kāmandaka* seems to refer to the name of a famous Indian author/compiler of this kind of literature, Kāmandakī, whose work, usually referred to as the *Kamandakīya Nīti-Sāra*, was translated into Old Javanese several times (Hooykaas 1956). Kāmandakī's more illustrious predecessor was Cāṇakya, whose practical philosophical works were translated into all South and Southeast

Asian *bahasa*-s. Cāṇakya is mentioned in the seventh section of the *Tantri Kāmandaka*:

Iti çāstra Cāṇakya, kanggěha Hyang Aditya tunggal; sādhanaa(?) ning katon ing buddhing atīta, ring anāgata, ring wartamāna de sang prajña, saha dharmōpaḍeça, katingalan ing kārya ala ayu; ikang yogya gawayakěna, aywa kang tan yogya.

Hooykaas (1931:18–19) renders it into Dutch as:

Zoo is het çāstra van Tjāṇakya, dat als de eenige zon moet worden beschouwd, als middel van den geleerde om te kunnen doorgronden den geest van het verleden, de toekomst en het heden, tegelijk met de leeringen van den dharma; om te kunnen onderscheiden het goede en het slechte; wat goed is moet men toepassen, maar niet wat niet goed is.

What both Cāṇakya and Kāmandakī compiled were collections of *subhāṣita*-s, bits of wisdom of all sorts, neatly and concisely stated in verse. Collections or anthologies of *subhāṣita*-s were very highly valued throughout South and Southeast Asia, particularly the political ones, which promised to reveal the secrets for the success of the powerful Indian kingdoms. Though at times Cāṇakya and Kāmandakī sound cynically Machiavellian in their political advice, political stratagems make up only a small part of the total *subhāṣita* literature. Wisdom about duty in marriage, sex, even agriculture and cooking, is of equal importance. Recent works by Ludwik Sternbach (1963, 1969, 1974) have opened up this genre and its history to the reader of English, as Otto Böhtlingk did for German (1870). The late Professor C. Hooykaas (1956) along with Professor Poerbatjaraka (1933) have traced their history in Indonesia.

The *Tantri Kāmandaka* is not a collection of *subhāṣita*-s, however. It is an unbelievably intricate structure of tales embedded in tales, throughout which the *subhāṣita*-s are used to evaluate the action. We use the term *evaluate* here as a technical term: as William Labov first showed (1967), a narrative (in English) has to have at least two features—at least one temporal sequence and an evaluation. Livia Polanyi (1978:33) calls evaluations "devices . . . to explain why the narrator thought these texts were worth telling, or to highlight which aspects of the dense cluster of events should be considered the *peak* of the story."

Throughout the text of the *Tantri Kāmandaka*, events are evaluated with *subhāṣita*-s first stated in Sanskrit and then translated and explained in Old Javanese. *Pantun*-s have a similar function in Classical Malay literature. As evaluations the *subhāṣita*-s give meaning to—and thus "bind"—the events of the story. As such they can be seen as *paradigms of action*, a term borrowed from Paul Fussell whose recent book, *The Great War and Modern Memory*, discusses evaluatory figures in language about the First World War. In the following passage he is discussing the rhetorical figure of irony as a device for framing the events of the war.

> By applying to the past a paradigm of ironic action, a rememberer is enabled to locate, draw forth, and finally shape into significance an event or a moment which otherwise would merge without meaning into the general undifferentiated stream. (Fussell 1975:30)

Subhāṣita-s provided paradigms in which events could be shaped and evaluated.

The *Tantri Kāmandaka* is clearly a translation from and recombination of three different genres: *subhāṣita*-s, animal tales (from the *Pancatantra* and the *Hitopadesa*), and a frame story, which sets up the moral dilemma that the animal tales explore from different sides, one inside the other. The frame story has a number of archetypal features: a king wants to know what makes a successful king. After some discussion his minister tells him that a ruler is successful because of the effectiveness of his orders. After seeing from his window a village wedding, the king wants a wife, and then a new wife every day, until the ministers can find no more girls in the kingdom. The minister is in a bind, for if the king's orders are not obeyed, they are not effective, and his only source of authority disappears. In despair the minister enters a beautiful temple garden, explicitly Javanese, which is described in great detail. His wife sends to him his daughter, Tantri, who has been well educated in the *çāstras*. She, in turn, volunteers to face the king and, through tales, to instruct him.

The tales she tells center on the problem of the source of evil— the proper paradigm for evaluating evil actions. There are two proposals: (1) that all living creatures are fundamentally different and friendship between them is, by nature, impossible, whether they be lion and bull, hunter and monkey, or tick and self-satisfying bedbug; and (2) that individuals are evil, and lying is the main source of that evil. This opposition is stated over and over again, tale in contrast to tale, all evaluated by *subhāṣita*-s, until in the end, in the triumph of the lying jackal, the second view is ironically confirmed.

That is how the larger tale is bound, in a combination of three sources, probably uniquely combined through recombination and expansion of prior texts. This way of translation and invention still remains common in the inventions of the Javanese shadow puppeteer (Becker 1979) who embeds story in story and evaluates each with quotations from Old Javanese.

The first *subhāṣita* in the *Tantri Kāmandaka* is the one quoted above, which begins the work. In the original Sanskrit, it reads as follows.

çabdaçāstram anadhītya yaḥ   pumān
grammar   not know which man

vaktum icchati vacaḥ sabhāntare
speak   want to words in hall

bandhum icchati   vane madotkaṭam
bind   want to in forest rut-boiling-over

kuñjaram kamalatantunā   hi saḥ
elephant lotus-stamen-with emphasis he

                        —*Indische Sprüche*, number 6401

If we compare the Sanskrit original with the Old Javanese "translation," we notice several important differences.

Conciseness and Elaboration

While the Sanskrit version contains only sixteen words, the Old Javanese version contains forty-four words. There are four basic reasons
for this.

(*a*) Compounding. While there are four compounds in the Sanskrit, there is none in the Old Javanese, except perhaps *mahāpurusa*. In
translating each of the compounds, the Old Javanese uses phrases:

çabdaçāstram becomes *warga nikang çāstra mwang çabda-paçabda*

sabhāntare becomes *madhya ning sabhă*

madotkaṭam becomes *ri sĕdĕngnya matta*

kamalantunā becomes *bĕsan ing tunjung sahĕle*

While Old Javanese authors can imitate Sanskrit compounding, particularly in verse translation, it is not what one might call a regular
grammatical option (Gonda 1973:456–70).

(*b*) Reduplication and repetition. Although compounding in Old
Javanese is awkward, density increases in words by reduplication
(e. g., *çabda-paçabda* and *mangucap-ucapa*) or by repetition. The repetition
of *ikang wwang* seems necessary to the Old Javanese in order to keep
clear the grammatical relations within clauses and across clauses.

In comparing the Sanskrit version with the Old Javanese, we find
two different kinds of cohesion or binding: case inflexion and compounding in Sanskrit on one hand, and deictic prepositions and repetition (including reduplication) in Old Javanese on the other.

The deictic prepositions in Old Javanese make a neat paradigm.

	direct	oblique	directional
indefinite, nonspecific	i	ni	ri
definite	ing	ning	ring
definite and specific	ikang	nikang	rikang

Within this system lies much of the clause-level binding power of
Old Javanese. For a speaker of English this system is somewhat like

the intersection of contrasts between functions like subject, object, and adjunct with demonstratives or articles. When combined with role (or case) marking affixes in the predicate, the clause-level cohesion system of Old Javanese becomes even clearer.

Let us look only at the system described so far, as it appears in the passage from the *Tantri Kāmandaka:*

Clause 1: *ikang wwang* = subject, definite and specific (specific probably because of the comparison to follow)
wruh = unmarked predicate
ring warga nikang çastra, etc. = directional adjunct, definite (*nikang* is at phrase level)

Clause 2: subject carried from clause 1
*um*para (*um* + para) = subject is agentive

Clause 3: subject carried from clause 1
*ma*hyun (*ma* + hyun) = subject is "stative"
*mang*ucap-ucapa (*manN* + ucap(redup) + a) = subject is agentive
*ka*lawan (*ka* + lawan) = subject is dative

Clause 4: *ikang* wwang = repeated subject, direct, definite, specific
*mang*kana = subject is agentive

Clause 5: subject carried from 4/1
*ma*reng (*um* + para + ing) = subject is agentive

Clause 6: subject carried from 4/1
*ma*hyun (*ma* + hyun) = subject is "stative"
*sumi*kĕpeng (*um* + sikĕp + a + ing) = subject is agentive
ing gajah alas, etc. = object is direct, definite

Clause 7: subject carried from 4/1
*ma*mawa (*maN* + wawa) = subject is agentive

At clause level, then, a combination of prepositions, marking definiteness, specificity and grammatical function, and predicate affixation, marking role (plus something like aspect, to be discussed below), serves to bind together the nuclear constituents of the clause. (Nonnuclear clausal constituents are marked by a large set of nonnuclear prepositions.) Word order is SVO or VSO.

These same prepositions mark at phrase level the relations of modifier to head.

Phrase binding in clause 1:	*nikang* = oblique, definite, specific, binds noun head and noun modifier
Phrase binding in clause 2:	*ning* = oblique, definite, binds noun head and noun modifier
Phrase binding in clause 3:	none
Phrase binding in clause 4:	*n* = makes following clause a nominal, binds nominalized clause and pronominal head (-nya), with the sense of 'such that' in English. *ikang* (the second one) = marks object of preposition *lawan*, direct, definite, specific
Phrase binding in clause 5:	none
Phrase binding in clause 6:	*ri* = directional, indefinite, nonspecific, binds noun head and clause
Phrase binding in clause 7:	*ing* = from *ning* with initial *n* fused with the final -*n* of *bĕsan*, therefore oblique, definite, binds noun to noun
Phrase binding in clause 8:	*(i)kang* = direct, definite, and specific, with initial vowel fused with final vowel of *sahĕle*, binds noun head and dependent clause

One important difference, then, between the Sanskrit and Old Javanese versions is in the mode of binding or cohesion at word level (compounding versus reduplication); at phrase level (compounding versus deictic prepositions); at clause level (inflexion versus deictic prepositions); and across clause, that is, the sentence level, which will be discussed below. The contrast between the two systems of binding becomes even more clear when one notes that Sanskrit compounding overlaps two distinct levels in Old Javanese, word and phrase, whereas the Old Javanese system of deictic prepositions overlaps two distinct levels in Sanskrit, phrase and clause. It seems distinctively Austronesian that the cohesion markers at phrase and clause levels should be nearly identical, while in Indo-European languages they are so often different, for example, a gender system at phrase level and a case system at clause level.

(c) Elaboration of detail. Another difference between the two texts that can help explain the conciseness of the Sanskrit and the elaboration of the Old Javanese is the way terms and events are provided with more detail in the latter. That is, *çabdaçāstram* is deconstructed and elaborated into *warga nikang* çāstra *mwang çabda-paçabda*. We might call this the elaboration of a term. An event is elaborated in the details of the hall (*sabhā*), which in Old Javanese contains a *mahāpurusa*, and the purpose of the lotus stalk/stamen, which in Old Javanese is "als middel om hem te binden" (*kangkena pangikatanya*). Such elaboration seems necessary to fill in background or knowledge presupposed in the source language, about, for instance, what the term *çabdaçāstram* includes, or about what one might meet in a *sabhā*, or about what to do with the lotus stalk/stamen.

(d) Explicit linkage. Looking now at interclausal, or sentence level, cohesion, see that, while the relationship of the two parts of the simile is left quite implicit in the Sanskrit, it is heavily marked in the Old Javanese. In the Sanskrit version there is only the parallelism of

> vaktum icchati vacaḥ
> bandhum icchati vane

to link the two parts structurally. (There are, of course, paradigmatic links.) In the Old Javanese version, on the other hand, there is a whole clause.

> *ikan wwang mangkana niyantanya n   pada   lawan ikang wwang*
> that person do   clearly-it that same with that person

That probably would have seemed awkward and verbose to Cāṇakya or Kāmandakī, but its verbosity may well reflect what Walter Ong calls its "copiousness," that is, a characteristic abundance (Latin *copia*) or flow of words more common in oral modes of discourse than in written ones (Ong 1977:114). Old Javanese may well be written in a more oral style than Sanskrit, and hence the two modes of cohesion across clauses may reflect the differences between basically oral noetics and visual noetics, or some stage in between (Ong 1977:92 ff.).

The conciseness of the Sanskrit figure and the elaboration of the Old Javanese seem to be describable, then, under those four headings: compounding as a strategy, reduplication as a strategy, elaboration of detail (terms or events), and explicit linkage interclausally. All have to do with binding or cohesion. The differences seem to go deep. To the extent that both passages illustrate what they are talking about—that is, binding words, they mean different things. There are, however, some other differences, not related to copiousness, which must be discussed before the differences in the meaning of the two versions can be more fully uncovered.

Basic Word Order

We also notice in comparing the Sanskrit and Old Javanese versions of the *subhāṣita* that the grammatical order is different.[3] In the Sanskrit the order shows the characteristic O(bject)-V(erb) strategies:

object before predicate

modifier before head

main verb before auxiliary

postposition

In Old Javanese, objects never occur before predicates, although subjects can have any of four roles: actor, undergoer, scope, or item, to use tagmemic terminology; they might also be called agentive, objective (as distinct from the function "object"), dative-directive, and stative (the subject of a stative or equative predicate). In Old Javanese, modifiers follow headwords (with the exception of quantifiers and deictics), auxiliaries precede main verbs (e.g., *mahyun sumikĕpeng*), and there are prepositions, as we have just seen above. The passage under exploration here illustrates all these points. In this sense the two versions are what Verhaar calls mirror images of each other (1980:35).

This mirror imagery can be observed in the way the constituents are "inverted" in the two versions of the first two lines.

1. Sanskrit:

çabdaçāstram anādhītya yah   pumān
grammar   not know which man

Old Javanese:

Ikang wwang tan wruh ring   warga etc.
that person not know about form etc.

2. Sanskrit:

vaktum icchati   vacaḥ sabhāntare
speak want to words in hall

Old Javanese:

umara madhya ning sabhā mahyun
go   center of   hall want to

mangucap-ucapa   etc.
speak   etc.

This basic word-order difference seems to be the grammatical foundation on which all the higher-level differences rest. Here are the constraints most "within" the language and least constrained by the situation "outside" language. To use Verhaar's terms, word order is more "articulatory" or "mental" than "iconic" or "situational" (1980).

Verse and Prose

The major interclausal binding force of the Sanskrit *subhāṣita* is its sound, in this case a meter called Rathodahata: -v- / vvv / -v- / v-. Sound binding might be called prelogical, but nonetheless it is deeply true in a language in which sound-meaning relations are anything but arbitrary. That is, if the word for the name of a thing is more real than the thing, then one gains some important kinds of understanding by examining the sounds of that word, at least as important kinds of understanding as one might get to by measuring the thing. (If it is the thing one is after, sounds get in the way.)

Thus the Old Javanese translator preserves the original Sanskrit text for its sounds, doing the best he can, and explains it in his own language. There is no need to translate the meter. He is glossing the Sanskrit, just as in Kawi reading groups of modern Bali the learners read the sounds of the language (Old Javanese) and the teachers interpret them in Balinese—an old, slow, and very effective method of language learning for those who have patience.

The Binding Force of the Old Javanese Predicate

The Old Javanese predicate is the center of several systems of cohesion: it may mark the roles of the subject and object, the distance of the observer, the relation of the clause to other clauses, and the relation of the event it describes to other events. Notice that all of these binding functions are quite different: marking roles binds the constituents of the nucleus of the clause, marking observer distance binds the clause to the speech act, marking interclausal prominence binds the clauses in a sentence, and marking the relationship of events binds the clause to the referential world.

Only the two latter binding functions will be discussed here, since in the single sentence we are interpreting the predicates mark mainly agentive subjects and no object roles, and there is no change of observer distance (see Becker and Oka 1974). What changes is the prominence of the clauses in relation to each other and the "reality" or "unreality" of the events referred to.

Clausal prominence is marked by the infix -um- (which is prefixed to a word beginning with a vowel or, sometimes, a bilabial). The subject of a verb so marked is always agentive, and the clause in which it appears will always be a background for another clause, almost always a following clause. There are three examples of this infix in the passage we are studying in clause 2, 'going' (umara) is marked as background to the following 'wanting' (mahyun) in clause 3; in clause 5, 'going' (mareng < um + para + ing) is background to the following 'wanting' (*mahyun*) in clause 6; and, in one of the more subtle grammatical turns of the sentence, in clause 6 'binding' (*sumikĕpa*) is background to 'carrying' (*mamawa*) in clause 7. (This latter is interestingly subtle because it would be more common, probably, that carrying the tool be background to the act of using it [here 'binding']: but the point of the *subhāṣita* is the absurdity of carrying that tool, and so it is foregrounded.)

The "reality" of the events is marked by the irrealis suffix *-a*, which appears twice, first in line 3 on *mangucap-ucapa*, and second on *sumikĕpa* (*-a* + *ing* = *eng*) in line 6. Both mark intended actions. Thus *-um-* and *-a* bind clauses in two different ways: prominence (i.e., ground and figure) and "reality" (i.e., realis and irrealis).

Conclusion

Thus we have seen the different ways that a sentence in Old Javanese shapes a context and makes it cohere. Looking only at the *subhāṣita* that begins the *Tantri Kāmandaka* we note several kinds of cohesion,

1. the plot-binding cohesion of an evaluation
2. the word-binding cohesion of compounding
3. the multilevel cohesion of repetition
4. the clause- and-phrase-binding cohesion of deictic prepositions
5. the clause-binding cohesion of explicit linkage
6. the sentence-binding cohesion of meter
7. the multilevel cohesion of the predicate
8. and the paradigm-binding cohesion of the metaphor,

which provided a starting point for the *Tantri Kāmandaka* and for this essay. In the unfolding of the metaphor lies a view of language as a cohesive, binding force. To the extent that this cohesion is different in Sanskrit and Old Javanese, the "same" text must mean different things, as it must also in Dutch or in English.

ACKNOWLEDGMENTS

We are grateful to Madhav Deshpande for his aid with the Sanskrit text of the *subhāṣita*, and to Suzanne Sutro, Winnifred Anthonio, and Nangsari Ahmad for discussion of the Old Javanese. Many of the ideas developed here grew from reading and talking with John Verhaar.

NOTES

1. Modern philology has its roots in the later work of the great Spanish philosopher José Ortega y Gasset, particularly his essay "The Difficulty of Reading" (1959) in which he states the two central axioms that define the double problem of modern philology.

   1. Every utterance is deficient—it says less than it wishes to say.
   2. Every utterance is exuberant—it conveys more than it plans.

   The modern philologist seeks meaningful interpretations between the inherent deficiencies and exuberances of the texts he studies. The work of Kenneth Burke (especially Burke 1961) has been central, too, in our attempt to reexamine the aims and methods of the text-centered study of language. See also Ong 1977; Bateson 1979; Pike and Pike 1977; Ricoeur 1978; and Geertz 1980. In this last work, Geertz contrasts two kinds of explanation: laws-and-instances versus cases-and-interpretation. Philology, old or new, contrasts with linguistics in its methodology in just this way: the case (or particular text) comes first, not the law (or rule).

2. Problems of cohesion are discussed in Pike and Pike (1977) and applied in Zurbuchen (1976). See also Halliday and Hasan (1973). The notion of *binding* is developed in Foley (1976), particularly in chapter 2. This notion of binding seems to underlie a metaphor for language that was widespread in Old Javanese Sanskritic literature, in the terms *tantra, tantri,* and *tantu,* all of which involve notions of thread and weaving. The reference to *tantu* in the passage we are examining could well be a subtle pun.

3. Pudjosudarmo (1976) has described the development of word order in Javanese from Old Javanese Verb-Subject-Object to modern Javanese Subject-Verb-Object, noting in this development several changes: the loss of the Old Javanese deictic prepositions, a change from information focus on the initial constituent in Old Javanese to information focus marked by intonation in modern Javanese, and a change from role-marking "passive" in Old Javanese to person-marking "passive" in modern Javanese.

In this process, it is the subject that changes position, while the typologically more crucial verb-object order remains stable.

REFERENCES

Bateson, Gregory. 1979. *Mind and Nature: A Necessary Unity.* New York: E. P. Dutton.

Becker, A. L. 1979. "Text-Building, Epistemology, and Aesthetics in Javanese Shadow Theatre." In Becker and Yengoyan (eds.), 211–43.

Becker, Alton L., and I Gusti Ngurah Oka. 1974. "Person in Kawi: Exploration of an Elementary Semantic Dimension," *Oceanic Linguistics* 13:229–25.

Becker, A. L., and Aram A. Yengoyan (eds.). 1979. *The Imagination of Reality: Essays in Southeast Asian Coherence Systems.* Norwood, N.J.: Ablex.

Böhtlingk, Otto. 1870. *Indische Sprüche.* St. Petersburg: Commissionare der Kaiserlichen Akademie der Wissenschaften.

Burke, Kenneth. 1961. *The Rhetoric of Religion: Studies in Logology.* Boston: Beacon Press.

Deshpande, Madhav. 1979. *Sociolinguistic Attitudes in India: An Historical Reconstruction.* Ann Arbor: Karoma.

Foley, William. 1976. *Comparative Syntax in Austronesian.* Ann Arbor: University Microfilms.

Fussell, Paul. 1975. *The Great War and Modern Memory.* New York: Oxford University Press.

Geertz, Clifford. 1980. "Blurred Genres: The Refiguration of Social Thought," *The American Scholar* 49:165–79.

Gonda, J. 1973. *Sanskrit in Indonesia.* New Delhi: International Academy of Indian Culture.

Halliday, M. A. K., and Ruqaiya Hasan. 1973. *Cohesion in Spoken and Written English.* London: Longmans.

Helm, June (ed.). 1967. *Essays on the Verbal and Visual Arts.* Seattle: University of Washington Press.

Hooykaas, C. 1931. *Tantri Kāmandaka: Een Oudjavaansche Pantjatantra-Bewerking in Tekst en Vertaling Uitgegeven.* Bandoeng: Bibliotheca Javanica 2.

Hooykaas, C. 1956. "Kāmandakīya Nītisāra, etc., in Old-Javanese," *Journal of the Greater India Society* XV:18–50.

Labov, William, and Joshua Waletzky. 1967. "Narrative Analysis: Oral Versions of Personal Experience." In Helm (ed.).

Natanson, Maurice (ed.). 1973. *Phenomenology and the Social Sciences.* Evanston, Ill.: Northwestern University Press.

Naylor, Paz Buenaventura (ed.). 1980. *Austronesian Studies*. Ann Arbor: Center for South and Southeast Asian Studies, University of Michigan.

Ong, Walter J. 1977. *Interfaces of the Word: Studies in the Evolution of Consciousness and Culture*. Ithaca: Cornell University Press.

Ortega y Gasset, José. 1959. "The Difficulty of Reading," *Diogenes* 28:1–17.

Pike, Kenneth L., and Evelyn G. Pike. 1977. *Grammatical Analysis*. Dallas, Tex.: Summer Institute of Linguistics.

Poerbatjaraka, R. Ng. 1933. *Nītiśāstra Oud-Javaansche Tekst met Vertaling Uitgegeven*. Bandoeng: Bibliotheca Javanica 4.

Polanyi, Livia. 1978. *The American Story: Cultural Constraints on the Meaning and Structure of Stories in Conversation*. Ann Arbor: University Microfilms.

Pudjosudarmo, Gloria. 1976. "Hipotese Perkembangan Sintaksis Bahasa Jawa," *Bahasa dan Sastra* II/4:2–22.

Reagan, Charles E., and David Stewart (eds.). 1978. *The Philosophy of Paul Ricoeur*. Boston: Beacon Press.

Ricoeur, Paul. 1978. "Explanation and Understanding." In Reagan and Stewart (eds.), 149–66. English translation of "Expliquer et comprendre."

Sternbach, Ludwik (ed.). 1963. *Cānakya-Rāja-Nīti*. Adyar, Madras: Adyar Library and Research Centre.

Sternbach, Ludwik. 1969. *The Spreading of Cānakya's Aphorisms over "Greater India."* Calcutta: Calcutta Oriental Book Agency.

Sternbach, Ludwik. 1974. *Subhāṣita, Gnomic, and Didactic Literature*. Wiesbaden: Otto Harrassowitz.

Verhaar, John W. M. 1973. "Phenomenology and Present-day Linguistics." In Natanson (ed.), 361–464.

Verhaar, John W. M. 1980. "Tipologi Struktural dan Bahasa Indonesia" dalam buku *Teori Lingguistik dan Bahasa Indonesia*. Yogyakarta: Penerbitan Kanisius.

Zurbuchen, Mary. 1976. "Kawi Discourse Structure: Cycle, Event, and Evaluation." *Rackham Literary Studies*, Winter, 45–60.

Person in Kawi:
Exploration of an Elementary
Semantic Dimension

with I Gusti Ngurah Oka

The cline of person in languages seems to me basic in the process of text building. A cline of person is a grammatical continuum from oneself to the most distant "other" upon which all the people, things, and events of experience are arrayed. Languages seem to differ profoundly in the ways they order this cline of person.

In Old Javanese (Kawi) the paradigm of person seems to have a centrality and complexity like that of tense in English. Furthermore, person can be very subtle in Old Javanese literature, allowing figures and tropes that would be very hard, if not impossible, to duplicate in English.

Although this essay, too, was written primarily for linguists (an international gathering of Austronesionists in Hawaii), I do not think it is difficult to read. The importance of person in any poetics of Javanese makes it appropriate to include this rather technical essay here, since it is in just such sensitive areas that retribution is demanded of a translator.

It was written along with a Balinese linguist, I Gusti Ngurah Oka, who teaches Kawi in Indonesia and understands it far more profoundly than I do.

❖   ❖   ❖

1. The Cline of Person

A central thread—perhaps *the* central thread in the semantic structure of all languages[1]—is the cline of person, an ordering of linguistic forms according to their distance from the speaker. Between the subjective, pointed, specific pronominal "I" and the objective, generic common noun, between these poles, the words of all languages—words for people, animals, food, time space, indeed, words for everything—are ordered and categorized according to their distance—spatial, temporal, social, biological, and metaphorical—from the first person, the speaker. The cline of person also underlies most linguistic systems, as well as words, systems of deixis, number, definiteness, tense, and nominal classification, among others.[2]

As only one example of the indirect grammatical manifestation of the cline of person, notice that the modifiers in an English noun phrase are ordered between the poles of speaker-related meaning over against detached, nonsubjective nominal meaning.

  1. The two lovely big (square) yellow brick houses . . .

The order is from subjective judgments of the speaker-observer (particular reference, number, evaluation, relative size) to those qualities that seem to be inherent in a class of objects and hence to be least affected by *personal* differences in the observer (shape, color, material).[3] Metaphors, too, are anchored in the cline of person, as Edmund Leach and others have demonstrated. The fact that the names of body parts, pets and domestic animals, and sexual intimates can substitute for each other metaphorically means that they are related in a single paradigm, the basic recurring dimension of which is person.[4]

While person appears to be a universal semantic dimension of language, structures of person and linguistic manifestations of person—particularly personal pronouns—differ from language to language. Language students and linguists have to learn that "I" is not "I," "you" is not "you," and "we" is not "we" from one language to the next. Within a language family, however, these differences may not be so great as across genetic boundaries, and many Indo-European scholars have demonstrated the formal and semantic similarities of Indo-European pronoun systems.[5] In Austronesian languages, too, one comes to expect certain paradigmatic regularities. This experience gives rise to a conception of Common Austronesian, a set of constraints that appears to operate throughout the family.

One way to approach the problem of describing person in Austronesian is to compare personal pronoun systems in many languages and extract common features. If one is primarily interested in the phonological shapes of personal pronouns, this approach is fruitful. The forms *aku, ka(N)u, (s)ia, kami,* and perhaps *kita* have more or less transparent reflexes in other Austronesian languages, often with articles and numbers affixed to them. Brandstetter (1916) has argued convincingly that these forms (except *kita*) are common for Western Austronesian, while Grace (1959) has posited related forms (*au, koe, ia, ta,* and *ma*) as proto-Polynesian.[6] If one's goal is to discover and describe the semantics of person, however, comparing paradigms is not illuminating, partly because analysts more often than not force Austronesian pronouns into an Indo-European paradigm, but mainly because they do not give us enough information about the semantics and pragmatics of the personal pronouns. Unfortunately, new questions usually demand new data.

The first step, then, must be a thorough exploration of the cline of person in *full context* in a single Austronesian language, from which one can then look out at other languages in the family.

Old Javanese, or Kawi,[7] is an appropriate beginning point. As Brandstetter observes, exaggerating only slightly, it is the only Austronesian language that has a history. We have available to us vast amounts of linguistic data in Kawi from ancient times: the texts used in this paper originate between the ninth and the fourteenth centuries. The data include full contextual information; that is, we know from the stories in the texts who was speaking to whom, about what, and in what situation. Furthermore, there is sufficient variation for us to observe changes in the systems of person.

This latter is an important point, though one that extends a bit beyond the scope of this paper: grammatical systems, like phonological systems, have family-wide weak points—points of apparent genetic instability that are as much a common feature of the family as particular forms. At these points we *expect* change from language to language, just as we do with the various "r" reflexes in Austronesian phonology. Hence, particular points of variation can be extremely useful in reconstructing linguistic history. Part of the goal of this paper, in addition to showing the complex role of person in Kawi grammar, will be to isolate points of predictable variation in paradigms.

2. Personal Pronouns in Kawi

As we have observed, we need more than isolated sentences to study person. We must know who the speech act participants are, what they are talking about, and what the setting is. In this study, therefore, our data are sentences in context. Where relevant we shall provide contextual information. It is interesting to note, too, that once we see how personal systems operate we can use them to reconstruct Kawi speech acts and thereby gain solid information about the society in which these speech acts were used.

The basic pronoun paradigm in Kawi (at all periods) is relatively simple, as is shown in figure 2. In examining this paradigm in detail, one familiar with other Austronesian languages is struck by the fact that there are no plural pronouns. (There are also no grammatically plural nouns.) Plurality in Kawi is marked by conjoining pronouns (e.g., *you* and *I*) or by quantifiers (e.g., *many, all,* etc.) or it is simply assumed from context. There is, hence, no first-person plural *we*, either exclusive or inclusive. The difference between the A column and the B column is, rather, personal, a distinction between close or intimate (A) and more distant or formal interpersonal relations. If the speaker feels on intimate terms with the hearer (or the other)—and has a social right to intimacy—he will use pronouns from column A of the paradigm. If, on the other hand, he feels a proper social distance should be maintained or he wants to detach himself in some way from the hearer (or the other), he will use pronouns from column B. In Kawi, to treat someone as intimate or close who is not properly in that relationship is to insult him—unless one were a ruler, all of whose subjects are ipso facto servants and may be treated as intimates. It is interesting that both power and intimacy are expressed in the same way in Kawi, and many other languages. This may well be because both give one essentially the same rights over another—his person, his services, his productivity, etc. When these rights are reciprocal, then the relationship is truly intimate. When the rights are not reciprocal, then the relationship is based on power.

Only one Kawi text, the *Wirataparwa*, which is rather atypical,[8]

| | A | B |
	Close	Distant
Speaker	aku	kami
Hearer	ka(N)u	kita
Other	ia	sira

Fig. 2.   Pronouns of Kawi

has pronominal usages that might be taken as plural, though even many of these are ambiguous. In all other texts, *kami, kita,* and *sira* are unambiguously singular distant, as in the following example from the *Uttarakanda,* which describes the birth of Waisrawana. The god Brahma is speaking to Waisrawana with clear singular intent.

    2. T aminta kitānugraha ri kami sakahyunta.
        You ask you receive of me   all wish you.
        'You ask that you receive from me all that you wish'.[9]

As we shall see, the semantics of column B forms is complex, and it is unstable in many Austronesian languages.

All of the forms in column A, and perhaps all those in B, too, are complex morphemes. That is, each is further analyzable into formatives, which, while not clear and distinct morphemes, mark some regular meaning such as, for instance, that marked by the final consonants in the English pronominal forms *they, their,* and *them.* The meanings marked by one or another *part* of a Kawi pronoun often have to do with differences of focus within a sentence. Some of these meanings of pronominal formatives will be discussed below. Let us note now, however, that *aku* has focus variants *a* (~*k*~*dak*) and *ku. Ka(N)u* breaks into *ka* and *mu* (~*nyu*);[10] *ia* into *i* (~*si*) and *a.* The form *kami,* on the other hand, is not broken in Kawi, although short forms are found in many other Austronesian languages.[11] The second-person distant form *kita* has variants *t* and *ta*. *Sira*, like column A forms, includes two morphemes, *si* and *ra*.

The formative *ka* (or *k* alone) is the basic deictic formative in Kawi and many other languages, a "pointer." Note that it occurs in all first- and second-person forms, separating these "shifters," to use Jespersen's term, which point to participants in the speech act, from third-person forms, all of which include the basic and widespread locative formative *i*.

By analyzing the pronouns into formatives, one isolates distinctive vowels and consonants associated with each person. These are not arbitrary analyses, as we will demonstrate when we examine the dimension of person outside the pronoun system. Notice, now, that first person is marked by the high vowels *u* (< *aku*) or *i* (< *kami*); second person by high, mid, and low vowels, *u* (< *kamu*), *o* (< *ko*), and *a* (< *kita*); third person by the low vowel *a* (< *ia/sira*). First person is opposed to third person as high vowel against low, while second person is mixed, though it can be marked uniquely by a mid vowel.

In addition to these vowel oppositions, there are consonants associated with person. These can be observed in the genitive forms *-ku*, *-mu* or *nyu*, and *-ya:* first person is marked by a back consonant *k*, second by the labial nasal *m* or the palatal nasal *ny*, third person by Ø, although in many languages the genitive particle *n* becomes associated with third person.[12] These person-marking vowels and consonants appear in Kawi and related languages on forms other than personal pronouns, thus extending in interesting ways the cline of person far beyond its pronominal function. The vowels, for example, appear on Kawi demonstratives, which are personal.

iki	here (by me)
iku	there (by you)
ika	yonder (by neither you nor me)

The person-marking consonants appear in Kawi as reduced, non-focused forms of subject pronouns, as in

3. Yan *k* mātya . . .
   If   I die

4. *T* aminta kitānugraha ri kami sakahyunta.
   You ask you receive of me   all ask you.
   'You ask that you receive from me all that you wish'.

5. Ngka ta   ya *n* mangso   bhagawān Bhisma.
   then (topic) he he advanced Lord Bhisma.
   'Then he who advanced was Lord Bhisma'.

These same consonants appear in a language closely related to
Kawi, the archaic Praja dialect of Sasak (Lombok) where personal
inflections appear on active verbs.

mekgita'an   'I see him'
memgita'an   'You see him'
mengita'an   'He sees him' (*-an* 'him')

Though person is marked in these and many more Kawi grammatical systems, number is not. The morpheme often posited for
plural in other Austronesian languages, *ra* (R_1a), indicates only distance and respect in Kawi. The *-ra* that appears in *sira* (third person
distant) also appears as an honorific prefix (or personal article) on
words like *rama* 'father' (< *ra* + ama), *rena* 'mother' (< *ra* + *ina*), and
rabi 'wife' (< *ra* + *bi*). It also appears independently.

6. Pirengön ra   putu   mpungku.
   Be heard hon. grandson you.
   'Let it be heard by you, grandson'.

7. Masö   ta   sang Pandawa saha   lawan ra
   Advance topic the Pandawa   together with honored
   Pancala . . .
   Pancala . . .
   'The Pandawas advanced together with (their allies) the
   Pancalas'.

There is, of course, a frequently observed link between distancing (respect) and plurality. Intimacy is basically dyadic, as Goffman (1956) observes.

> Where an actor need show no concern about penetrating the recipient's usual personal reserve, and need have no fear of contaminating him by any penetration into his privacy, we say that the actor is on terms of familiarity with the recipient.

On the other hand, to respect the hearer is to avoid any suggestion that the relationship is dyadic but rather to assume an objective, impersonal structure in which there are one or more intermediaries always potentially present, an inherently triadic—and hence plural—situation.

It is clear that in Kawi distance and respect are the primary meaning of the column B pronouns. This fact is reflected in many other Austronesian languages where the so-called plural forms are used in singular situations to indicate social distance. We can identify column B in the pronoun paradigm as a point of paradigmatic instability in Common Austronesian: all these forms (*kami*, *kita*, and *sira*) are unstable semantically. The second-person intimate form *kamu*, on the other hand, is unstable in form, though not in meaning. Perhaps if we knew more about the medial nasal, however, this apparent variation in form might be resolved.

Examples of Kawi personal pronouns in context may be found in appendix I.

3. Articles and Deixis in Kawi

Probably the most frequent kind of pronominal variation within Austronesian (aside from that caused by regular phonological differences) results from the affixation of deictic particles and definite articles to personal pronouns. Earlier in our analysis of Kawi pronouns we identified three forms as deictics or articles in Kawi: *k(a)*, *i*, and *si*. *K(a)* is basically a "pointer," indicating motion or attention *to* someone or something. *I* appears to be locative and static, while *si* is the personal definite article (which also functions as a relative clause marker; see appendix I, example 10).

In contrast to the personal article *si*, there is the impersonal definite article *ang* or *ng*, which is used primarily with inanimate nouns and nonhuman creatures.

8. *Ang* kata . . .
   The story . . .

9. Mangrengö ta   *ng* danawa.
   listen   topic the ogre.
   'the ogre listened'.

The article (*a*)*ng* precedes the headword. It often blends with the genitive form *ni* to form the compound *ning* ('of the') and the locative *i* or *ri* to form *ing* or *ring* ('at the' or 'to the'). (See appendix I for examples.)

There are other human articles besides *si*. *Si* marks the lowest status and is used sometimes for personified animals. Marking higher status than *si* is the form *sang*, used for heroes and rulers. Notice once again the vowel progression: close or familiar is *i*, distant or respectful is *a*. The speaker uses *si* in referring to himself, even though others may use *sang*, as in the following example.

10. Tadanantara dateng ta   sang Kānana . . . mājar ta   sira . . .
    Then   come   topic Sir Kanana . . .   say   topic he
    "Pinakanghulun si   Kānana, kinon ārya Widura."
    I   the Kanana, sent   Hon. Widura.
    'Then Sir Kanana came. . . . He said, "I am Kanana, sent by Arya Widura." ' (Like *si*, *sang* also functions as a relative clause marker; see appendix I, example 12.)

Beyond *sang* there are higher-status personal articles: *dang* and *dang hyang*, used for saints, teachers, and holy people (see appendix I, example 15), and *sang hyang*, the personal article for gods, mountains, heavenly bodies, and holy things (see appendix I, examples 13–15).

Sira, the third-person distant pronoun, also functions as a personal article in Kawi, marking human status between *si* (low) and *sang* (high), as in the following example.

11. Mangkana ling sang Jaratkaru ring sira strī.
    Thus   say Sir   Jaratkaru to   the wife.

In English we would probably translate that sentence as

'Thus said Sir Jaratkaru to his wife'.

although the Kawi *sira* here is not genitive but refers to the wife. We know this from the position and the form of *sira*. 'To *his* wife' would be *ring strī nira*. Genitives follow headwords and are marked by initial *n*.

It is when articles and deictic particles combine with person that forms of great semantic complexity—and also great importance in textual cohesion—appear. There is no convenient label for this Kawi paradigm—as we apparently have no single paradigm for these forms in modern Indo-European languages. The closely related set of forms we wish to discuss includes demonstratives, temporal and logical adverbials, and clausal nominalizers. Because all the forms are built around the deictic formative *k*, we will call them deictics.

Kawi deictic forms are complexes of at least three formatives, but they may include as many as six formatives. The simplest deictics, given above, include:

iki (*i* locative + *k* deictic formative + *i* first person)
    'this, here, near speaker'

iku (*i* + *k* + *u* second person)
    'that, there, near hearer'

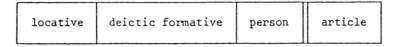

locative	deictic formative	person	article

Fig. 3.   Basic structure of the deictic

ika (*i* + *k* + *a* third person)
'That yonder, over there, near neither
first nor second person'

Following a convention of the Kawi writing system, when the
deictic form is followed by a noun the article for the following noun
is added to the deictic form, producing the common variants *iking*
(*iki* 'this' + *ng* 'the'), *ikung*, and *ikang* (see appendix I, examples 16,
22). The structure of the deictic can thus be represented as shown in
figure 3.

Deictic forms not only resemble pronouns in marking person but
also function as *anaphoric* pronouns, as in the following.

12. Ri telas mahārāja Yudhisthira masalin sarira, pada ik
     After   king   Y.   change body, same he
     halep nira lawan hyang Dharma.
     beauty his with   the God Dharma.
     'After King Yudhisthira changed his form, his beauty equaled
     that of the God Dharma'.

4. Time in Deixis: The Inflection of Deictic Forms

A close relation between spatial deixis (*this, that*) and temporal deixis
(*now, then*) has been observed in many languages. In Kawi, deictic
forms are inflected in several ways to show temporal relations. These
inflections lead to derived deictic forms (some essentially untranslatable), which are complicated and very subtle. Here, in deictic inflection, some of the special beauty of Kawi grammar appears.

First, the basic third-person deictic *ika* ('that over there, near neither speaker nor the hearer') may be further inflected for person. That is, person-marking vowels (*i*, *u*, or *a*) are added to the base *ika*, and the form now refers to something in the past related to speaker, hearer, or other.

> *ike* (< *ika* + *i*) 'that relating to speaker that happened in the past'
>
> *iko* (< *ika* + *u*) 'that relating to hearer that happened in the past'
>
> *ikana* ~ *ikā* (< *ika* + *a*) 'that relating to neither speaker nor hearer that happened in the past'[13]

The following sentence from the Kawi *Ramayana* illustrates the use of these forms in building textual cohesion; in the gloss of this sentence, deictics with first-person reference will be marked with (*i*) and deictics with second-person reference with (*u*).

> 13. Ndan *ike*   tasen anak ras*ike iko*   bhujangga kalih
>   Thus that(i) take child her(i) that(u) priest   two
>
>   siki kemar pada-pada, prasiddhanak mahārāja
>   ones twin   same   true child   king
>
>   *iko*   tan waneh.
>   that(u) not other.

Here Valmiki is speaking to Rama about his (Rama's) twin sons, who with their mother (Sita) have been staying with a priest. Valmiki is telling Rama that they are his (Rama's) true children. And so he says:

> 'Those (with me in the past, the twins) take her (with me in the past, Sita) children from that (you met before) priest two identical twins, true children of the king (you), that (related to you) not other'.

More freely,

i		i u	∅	
	k			ng
ng		a	i u a	
Definite-loc.	Deictic	Person	Person	Definite

Fig. 4.   Paradigm of deictic forms

'Those children I spoke of, take them, her children, from that priest you saw. They are identical twins, none other than your true children, King Rama'.[14]

(See also appendix I, examples 17–19.)

The other way of introducing a time reference into the deictic forms is to prefix the form with the definite article *ng* rather than the locative *i*. *Ngka* generally has a temporal or anaphoric meaning, in contrast to the more locative *ika*. Only *ngka* can be used as a temporal adverbial, as in the following.

14. *Ngka* ta   ya n mangsö bhagawan Bhisma.
    *Ika
    Then (topic) he he advanced Lord Bhisma.
    'Then he who advanced was Lord Bhisma'.

It does not appear possible (i.e., no forms were found) to mark simple first- or second-person deictics with the definite article. Thus, we have not found *ngki* or *ngku*—and it is difficult to imagine what they might mean. Personal past reference is possible, however, and we do find *ngke, ngko,* and *ngkana* (see appendix I, example 20), which always have temporal meanings.

The deictic has, so far, the structure shown in figure 4.

Like the English temporal adverbs *now* and *then*, which in some contexts have sequential as well as temporal meanings (*now* 'this time' or 'after this'; *then* 'that time' or 'after that'), deictics with *ng-* (i.e., *ngka, ngke, ngko,* and *ngkana*) can show sequential relationships in a text. In this case the stative verb prefix *ma-* (see section 5, below) is added to the deictic form, yielding a kind of sentential predicate *mangkā, mangke, mangko,* and *mangkana. Mangkā* means roughly 'with that before, having that before' or 'thus'. The other forms add the personal dimension: 'with that related to speaker, hearer, or other'. For example:

> 15. Matang yan geleng ni nghulun mangke ri kita,
>   Because if   anger of me   thus(i) to you
>
>   ya ya galakta   ri nghulun.
>   same anger you to me.
>   'That's why my anger thus toward you is like your anger toward me!'

Finally, on the expanded deictic forms *mangkā* and *mangkana* the prefix *sa-* appears. The prefix *sa-* means roughly 'at that same time' or 'altogether' from the basic meaning *sa* 'one'. For example:

> 16. Nis ksatriya ikang bhūmi samangkā.
>   Not warriors that   world at that time.
>   'There will be no warriors in the world at that time'.

> 17. Muwah hanā   ta   dwipa samangkā lwirnya.
>   And   will be (topic) island all like   that appearance of it.
>   'And there will be an island just like that'.

Further examples of these forms may be found in appendix I, examples 20–21.

The shape of the deictic forms can now be described in general, as shown in figure 5.

We have seen, then, how complex deictic forms can be understood as repeated applications of a rather small number of inflections, all of them marked in some way for person. That is, person is an obligatory inflection in deictic usage. Indeed, as we have begun to demonstrate, it is primarily person—the marked shifts in point of view—that gives

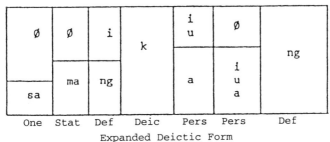

Fig. 5. Expanded paradigm of deictic forms

formal coherence to Kawi texts, somewhat as tense—and the sequence of tenses—gives cohesion to English texts. One could talk with real sense of the "sequence of persons" in Kawi. Furthermore, notions like plurality, temporality, sequence, and tense are, in a sense, secondary, metaphorical developments of the interplay of person, location, and definiteness.

Within this same paradigm of person many nouns and verbs in Kawi are also arrayed. Indeed, here are the roots of what later became distinct speech levels in Javanese and related languages. On the scale of close versus distant (which could be labeled in various other ways: personal versus impersonal, intimate versus formal, subjective versus objective) actions, people, animals, body parts, plants, and many other things are symbolically ordered.[15]

To illustrate this symbolic extension of person, we will consider only body parts. The most intimate and personal part of the body (linguistically, at any rate) is the head, particularly the eyes. Mentioning the hearer's eyes (but not the speaker's) is still taboo in Java. To make oneself humble before another is to linguistically offer him one's head in Kawi—and many other languages. The most respectful, and hence most self-effacing, word for the speaker ("I") in Kawi is the word for head, *hulun*, which has many variant forms (see sentences 10 and 15 above, and examples in appendix I). It may be preceded by an article (*nghulun, anghulun, sanghulun*), a topic marker and article (*pwangkulun*), an object-focus verb *pinaka* (*paka* 'use' plus object-focus infix -*in*-) 'used as, considered as': *pinakanghulun* 'considered as the head = "I," and several other related forms'.

Opposed to the head is either the body (*sarira*), or the blood (*rah*), or even the shoe (*paduka*) of the hearer. From the word for blood come several complex forms, particularly the 'royal you', *rahadyan* (< *rah* 'blood' + *adi* 'honored' + -*an* passive suffix). From 'blood' and 'head' comes the elegant form for 'you', *rahadyan sang hulun*. (In modern Javanese *rahadyan* becomes *raden* 'prince'.) From the interpretation of the body on the personal dimension of language the symbolism extends quite literally in all directions. Head versus blood is associated with colors (white versus red), directions (north versus south—never sleep with your head south!), gods (Shiva versus Brahma), geography (mountain versus sea)—the extensions are vast until on one linguistic dimension the rules and categories of a culture are built. It is from this perspective that we might justify the suggestion in the first sentence of this essay that the cline of person is perhaps the central thread in the semantic structure of language.

5. Person, Predicate Inflection, and Point of View in Kawi.

In this section we would like to demonstrate that the same structure, using many of the same forms, that underlies pronouns and deictics is also found in the basic Kawi verb inflections. Let us begin with the Kawi verb (or noun) *hwan* 'care for or tend animals', which is selected because its range of inflection is more extensive than many other verbs, and hence it is more useful as an illustration. *Hwan* is a two-place predicate, which takes an agent and a patient. There are several ways to express in Kawi the proposition TEND(x,y).

(a) Mahwan ta   sira lembu.
    Tend   (topic) he cow.

(b) Ahwan ta   sira (lembu).
    Tend   (topic) he (cow).

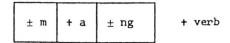

Fig. 6.   Structure of a Kawi verb prefix

(c) Manghwan ta   sira lembu.
     Tend   (topic) he cow.

(d) Anghwan ta   sira (lembu).
     Tend   (topic) he (cow).

Note that there is a two-way contrast in the predicates of sentences
(a–d). The initial and final nasals of the verb prefix vary. That prefix
can be described as shown in figure 6. The initial *m-*, paralleling the
distinction that separated columns A and B in the Kawi pronoun
paradigm, marks the distance of the speaker (or writer) of the sentence from what is being predicated, that is, the "action" of the verb.
The absence of the initial *m-* (examples b and d) indicates distance or
detachment from the "action" of the verb. Presence of the *m-* marks
closeness or involvement of the speaker (or writer).

The final *-ng* of the verb prefix is clearly—in both form and
meaning—the definite article discussed above, as Brandstetter observed briefly in his essay on the Indonesian verb ([1912] 1916:163).
As we saw in discussing the deictic complex, definiteness is semantically linked with past time. Here, too, it marks a specified, definite
act. If the act of the verb, on the other hand, is potential, future,
generic, habitual, stative, or otherwise indefinite (all here labeled
"stative"), then the final *ng* is not present. These choices of verb prefix
can be displayed paradigmatically as in figure 7. The four sentences
can then be glossed as follows.

(a) Mahwan ta sira lembu. 'He tends cows,' though he may not
    be doing so at the time of the utterance and the speaker has
    no definite instance in mind. The speaker is involved in some
    way.

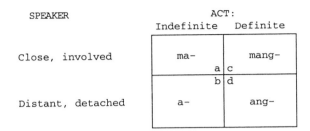

Fig. 7.   Paradigm of Kawi verb prefixes

(*b*) Ahwan ta sira (lembu). Same as (a), except the speaker is detached and the patient is optional.

(*c*) Manghwan ta sira lembu. 'He is tending cows' or 'He tended cows'. The speaker has a definite instance in mind and is involved in some way.

(*d*) Anghwan ta sira (lembu). Same as (c), except the speaker is detached or distant.

Notice that when the speaker is detached or distant (sentences b and d), the object (*lembu*) is optional, which is not the case when the speaker is involved or close. It is not clear how this fact can be explained, except by the general—and circular—comment that a diffuse, detached perspective renders otherwise obligatory information optional. There is probably a "conversational postulate" of some sort behind this fact (Gordon and Lakoff 1971).

A few examples in context can illustrate these choices. In the first, Bima is speaking to the giantess Hidimbī (whom he marries) about his mother, Kunti, who is sleeping. The verb for sleep (*turu*) is inherently stative, so the definite formative *ng* is impossible. The contrast here is between *m* and not *m*.

18. Ling sang Bhima: "Ndā tan wenang   mungwāturu
    Say   Bima   "That not desirable wake-sleep

    (+ mungu + a + aturu) mwang ibu   ni nghulun,
                          with   mother of me

tuwi sedeng   nirenak   maturu."
true specially she-enjoy sleeping."
Bima said, "It is not good to wake my sleeping mother, especially as she (appears to be) enjoying her sleep."

The purely descriptive, detached reference to sleep is *aturu*, but
when Bima shifts to an involved perspective and uses *maturu*, the
implication is that he has glanced at her or shifted his perspective in
some way. This is a common, rather subtle feature of Kawi style,
which we found to be common also in the descriptive and narrative
passages of the modern Javanese shadow play: a shifting of the author's or speaker's perspective. It also serves to distinguish direct
quotations from narration and description (which are not marked by
punctuation in Kawi text), though this is not its main function. In the
following interesting example, the author begins narrating with a
detached perspective. When the god Siva speaks to Uttangka, the
perspective is involved, in keeping with direct quotation. The final
words are the author's close-up, involved summary.

19. Ri lampah nira *am*anggih ta   sira wwang *an*unggang
    On way   his meet   (topic) he man   ride

    ri wrsabha; ya tojar   i sira: "Bhoh Uttangka!
    on bull;   he (topic) say to him: "Hey Uttangka!

    mahyun kita datengery Ayodhya mene gelek
    wish   you to come to Ayuthia now fast

    mūtrapurisam bhaksayaswa: pangan tahi ni lembungku
    (Sanskrit for what follows): eat   shit of bull of me

    inum uyuhnya. Saksana kita dateng ry Ayodhya denya."
    drink urine of it. Fast   you come to Ayuthia by it."

    Mangkana ling   ning wwang manunggangi lembu ri sira.
    Thus   word of   the man riding   bull to him.
    'On his way he met (definite detached: *ang*) a man riding
    (definite detached: *ang*) on a bull; he (as yet unknown as Siva,
    hence nonrespectful *ya*) said to him, "Hey Uttangka! You

wish (stative involved: *ma*) to go to Ayodhya right away. Eat the dung of my bull, drink its urine. In that way you will go quickly to Ayodhya." Those were the words of the man who rode (now definite, involved: *mang*) on the bull to him.'

(See also appendix I, examples 23–27.)

In addition to the distinction discussed here, the Kawi verb is also marked for aspect (*-um-*), focus (*ka-*, *-in-*), arealis (*-a*, *-an*), and causative (*-akna*). However, the basic dimensions of the paradigm, the basic thread running through the verb system, is the interplay of person (close versus distant) and definiteness. Mastering Kawi, and appreciating the subtlety of Kawi literature, requires first of all understanding the ways that this thread is woven into text.

6. Conclusion

Brandstetter has already demonstrated the widespread occurrence of most of the forms described here. Their formal status as Common Western Austronesian is probably established. What Brandstetter did not comment on directly—though one suspects he must have noticed—is the close relation of person, definiteness, and deixis, the recurring structural contrast between close and distant, involved and detached, now and then, head and blood, mountain and sea—all of which seem basic to much of Kawi grammar, probably much of Western Austronesian grammar as well, and perhaps also that set of general constraints we may one day call Common Austronesian grammar.

NOTES

1. There are two wide-ranging and careful studies of person in language, Forchheimer (1953) and Majtinskaja (1969). Forchheimer notes that he had not been able to find even one language or dialect that did not have a category of person. He goes on, "Next to person we find number, but there are languages that have not developed number into a category" (p. 1).
2. For discussion of person and deixis, see Forchheimer (1953) and Fillmore

(n.d.). The relation of person and number is discussed in Forchheimer (pp. 11–20) and in Bean (1970). The relation between person and definiteness is explored in this paper. Person in relation to tense is discussed in Lakoff (1970).

3. See Vendler (1968).

4. One version of this paradigm is displayed in Hall (1969, 126–27). It is now richly and provocatively explicated in a structuralist framework in Leach (1964).

5. See, for instance, Jespersen (1924, 212 ff.). See also Bopp (1856).

6. See Brandstetter (1916, 110–13). Brandstetter writes, "The following forms can be shown to be Common IN: *aku*, 'I', *kaw*, 'thou', *ia*, 'he', *kami*, 'we', *kamu*, 'you'; in the pronoun of the third person plural only the nucleus *ra* is Common IN, the attendant articles vary, they are chiefly *i* or *si*, thus forming *ira* or *sira*" (pp. 110–11). We will see later that Brandstetter's glosses are probably wrong, particularly in regard to plural forms. See also Grace (1959). Grace also posits *la* (Brandstetter's *ra*) as a pronoun.

7. Both names are used interchangeably by some, or they may refer to different things. Without tracing the history of these terms, we would prefer to use the term Kawi here, because (1) our data will be the literature called Kawi in Java, Bali, and Lombok plus the ritual language drawn from that literature still in use in Bali and Lombok; (2) the term Old Javanese implies that the language under discussion is a direct ancestor of Middle and modern Javanese, which may well not be the case; and (3) the living Balinese ritual language (called Kawi) is not properly called Old Javanese.

8. The *Wirataparwa* is the fourth book of the *Mahabharaba*, a pure work of about A.D. 996. For a description, see Poerbatjaraka (1952, 9). See also Zoetmulder and Poedjwijatna (1954, 35).

9. From the *Ramayana Uttarakanda Dasamukkacarita*, line 24, excerpted in Zoetmulder (1958, 1:10). See appendix II for texts used in this study.

10. The basic second-person form has many variants, all explainable by the presence or absence of the nasal *m* or *ny* (represented morphophonemically as *N* here). Thus there is *kau*, and by Kawi sandhi rules $(a + u > o)$ *ko*, as well as *kamu* (*mu*) and *kanyu* (*nyu*). In some languages of Eastern Indonesia (e.g., Rotinese) the independent pronoun is *o* alone. There is another second-person form in Kawi, *tva*, which is borrowed from Sanskrit.

11. Shortened variants of *kami* in other languages include *ai* (Rotinese), *mia* (Tsou), *mi* (Cebuano), *nay* (Malagasy), and *m* (Marshallese).

12. Grace (1959) posits for proto-Polynesian the independent personal-pronouns speaker: *au*; Hearer: *koe*; Other: *ia*; and the corresponding possessive forms -*ku*, -(*m*)*u*, and -*na*. Note that the *n* is a nominalizing suffix, which gives it further third-person associations.

13. These vowel combinations follow regular sandhi rules in Kawi: a + a = ā;
    i + i = ī; u + u = ū; a + ĕ = a; u + ĕ = u; i + ĕ = i; a + u = o; a + i = e;
    i = y before a; u and ö = w before a.
14. The form *rasika* 'she' and *sarika* 'he' are the only sex-marked pronominal
    or deictic forms in Kawi. They appear related but their analysis is unclear.
    The final *-ika* is probably the demonstrative; like the demonstratives,
    these forms take personal vowels.
15. For an exposition of this symbolic ordering of words (and by implication
    also things in the world) in a related language, Rotinese, see Fox (1971).
    For a more general discussion of the personal element in language, see
    also Thass-Thienemann (1973).

APPENDIX I

FURTHER EXAMPLES OF PERSONAL FORMS IN KAWI

I. *Pronouns*

1. *Aku* dinalihta   swāmin*yu*
   I   considered you husband your
   'You consider me your husband'.

   (spoken in irritation by King Ducwanta to Cakuntaka)

2. Yan ana wwang mara ngke maturu mene, warah *aku*,
   If be man come here sleep now, tell me,

   dak mangsane
   I   eat will
   'If the man who came here is asleep now, tell me and I'll eat
   him'.

   (serpent to a crow)

3. Ya ta   pajarakna ri *kami*
   It (topic) tell   to me
   'Tell it to me'.

   (teacher to student)

4. Matang yan dateng *kami* mangke ri *kita* . . .

Result if   come I   thus   to you . . .
'The reason I came to you now . . .'

5. Mrtyuwyasana muhāran*ya* teke   kan*yu*
   Demon-mischief mad-name it come you
   'Mad acts of demons possess you'.

   (Krishna to Duryodana)

6. *T*   ahuwusan tāna*ku*   mangayat laras
   You stop   (topic) son my draw   bow
   (Tānaku = ta + anak + ku)
   'My son, stop drawing your bow'.

   (Drona, the Brahman teacher, to young Yudhisthira)

7. Lumaku ta   *ya* ring   lwah
   Go   (topic) he to the valley
   'He went to the valley'.

8. Haywa tan masih i   *sira*
   Don't not love   to him
   'Don't not love him'.

   (father to son, referring to the king)

II. *Articles*

9. Warna ni kuda ni*ng*   ripu
   Color of horse of the enemy
   'The color of the horse of the enemy'.

10. Ikang kadi sanghulun ksatriya *si*
    That like me   warrior he who

    pejah ring   rana   ya pangan inum ngarannya
    die   in the battle it food   drink name his
    'For warriors like me, to die in battle is our food and drink'.

11. Mangkana ling   *sang* Brahmana kanyā.
    Thus   speak the Brahman daughter
    'Thus spoke the daughter of the Brahman'.

12. Sukhenak aturu *sang* Santa ngaran ira
    Like   sleep the Santa name   his

    sang   tan ahyun ring jayaparājaya
    he-who not wish   for   victory
    'The one who likes to sleep is named Santa—the one who
    doesn't want to win'.

13. Nguniweh   *sang hyang* Mahāmeru tan hana ring nusa Jawa
    Furthermore the holy Meru   not be on the island Jawa
    'Furthermore the holy Mt. Meru was not (yet) on the island
    of Jawa'.

14. Wanan ta   *sang* hyang sastra Mahābhārata wacanen   ira
    Take   (topic) the holy   book Mahābhārata to be read it
    'Take the holy Mahabharata and read it'.

15. Kinon   ta   *dang hyang* purohita magawaya
    Ordered (topic) the   priest   make

    wiwāhamanggala
    wedding ceremony
    'The royal priest was ordered to make preparations for the
    wedding'.

III. *Deictics*

16. *Ikang*   wre   mungguh ing   pang
    That the monkey sat   on the branch.

17. Sajna haji   mahārāja Dharmaputra wruth *ike* nghulun
    Your majesty king   Dharmaputra know that I

    yan rahadyan sanghulun nimitta ning   mentasa sangkeng
    if   you   cause of the free   from

    Yamaniloka
    hell
    'Your majesty King Dharmaputra (Yudhisthira) I (with past
    reference) know that you are the cause of my freedom from hell'.

18. Tan yukti ulahta *iko*
    Not right act you this
    'Your previous act was not right'.

19. Tan yogya *ika*nang rāh yan   tarpanakna ri sira
    Not proper that   the blood if offered   to him
    'It is not proper to offer to him that blood (referred to by
    another)'.

20. *Ngkana* ta   siran panemu rare rwang siki   jalu-stri
    Then   (topic) he   met   child two   people boy-girl
    'Then he met two children, a boy and a girl'.

21. Kunang panglawan sang Arjuna ring   sanjata *samangkana*
    Be   attack   the Arjuna against weapon like that
    'There was the attack by Arjuna against all weapons of that
    kind'.

22. Mangrengö ta   rahadyan sanghulun kabeh, *iking*   carita
    Hear   (topic) you   all   this the story
    'Listen, all of you, to my story'.

IV. *Predicates*

23. *Aputih* hulu nira, *ahireng* warna nira
    White head her   black   color her
    'Her hair is white, her color black'.

    (description of Kali, wife of Shiva, by narrator of the story—
    detached perspective, stative/indefinite)

24. *Mahireng* ekĕl rambutnya
    Black   curl hair his
    'His hair was curly and black'.

    (description of Dhrstadyumna—involved perspective,
    stative/indefinite)

25. Ing   ūni ri kāla ning *aprang* lawan sang Korawacata
    In the past at time of   fight with the Korawas
    'In the past, when (he) used to fight with the Korawas'.

(Dharmawangsa to Bima, on the path to paradise—detached perspective, indefinite)

26. *Anangis* ta   sira mwang sira stri mwang anak nira sajalwistr
Weep   (topic) he   with   wife   with child   his boy-girl
'He wept along with his wife and all his children, sons and daughters'.

(narrator describing a Brahman family—detached perspective, definite)

27. Bapa. Ibu.   Haywa kita prihati. Pahuwusan *manangis* . . .
Father. Mother. Don't you sad.   Stop   crying . . .
'Father, mother. Don't be sad. Stop crying . . .'

(Same situation as example 26. Now Bima is speaking— involved perspective, definite.)

APPENDIX II

The authors have collected data from many texts and from the ritual Kawi language of modern Bali. We are grateful to Drs. Imam Hanafi, Professor Drs. Soewojo Wojowasito, Professor Robbins Burling, Patricia Henry, and Will Vroman for numerous suggestions and examples. The following are the major sources used in this essay.

J. Gonda, *Sanskrit in Indonesia* (Nagpus, 1952).

R. D. S. Hadiwidjana, *Sarwacastra* (Djakarta, 1963).

H. Kern, *Rāmayāna kakawin* ('s-Gravenhage, 1900).

Prof. Dr. R. M. Ng. Poerbatjaraka, *Kapustakan Djawi* (Djakarta, 1952).

Siman Widyatmanta, ed., *Adiparwa* (*djilid* 1) (Jogjakarta, 1958).

C. F. Winter, *Kawi-Javaansch Woordenboek* (Djakarta, 1920).

Dr. Soewojo Wojowasito, *Kamus Kawi-Indonesia* (Malang, 1970).

Dr. S. Wojowasito, *Kawicastra* (Djakarta, 1963).

Drs. P. J. Zoetmulder and I. R. Poedjawijatna, *Bahasa Parwa* (Djakarta, 1954).

Dr. P. J. Zoetmulder, *De Taal van het Adiparwa* (Bandung, 1950).

Dr. P. J. Zoetmulder, *Sekar Sumarwur,* vols. I and II (Djakarta, 1958).

REFERENCES

Bean, Susan. 1970. Two's company, three's a crowd. American Anthropologist 72:562–64.
Bopp, Franz. 1856. A comparative grammar of the Sanskrit, Zend, Greek, Latin, Lithuanian, Gothic, German, and Slavonic languages, trans. E. B. Eastwick. London, Williams & Norgate.
Brandstetter, Renward. 1916. Common Indonesian and original Indonesian. In: An introduction to Indonesian linguistics, trans. C. O. Blagden, 67–133. Royal Asiatic Society Monographs, vol. 15.
Fillmore, Charles. N.d. Six lectures on deixis. Unpublished.
Forchheimer, Paul. 1953. The category of person in language. Berlin, Walter de Gruyter & Co.
Fox, James. 1971. Sister's child as plant. In: Rethinking kinship and marriage, ed. Rodney Needham. London, Tavistock.
Goffman, Erving. 1956. The nature of deference and demeanor. American Anthropologist 58:473–502.
Gordon, David, and George Lakoff. 1971. Conversational postulates. Papers from the Seventh Regional Meeting of the Chicago Linguistic Society, Chicago.
Grace, George W. 1959. The position of the Polynesian languages within the Austronesian (Malayo-Polynesian) language family. Supplement to International Journal of American Linguistics 25(3).
Hall, Edward T. 1969. The hidden dimension. New York, Doubleday.
Jespersen, Otto. 1924. The philosophy of grammar. London.
Lakoff, Robin. 1970. Tense and its relation to participants. Language 46:838–49.
Leach, Edmund. 1964. Animal categories and verbal abuse. In: New directions in the study of language, ed. Eric Lenneberg, 23–63. Cambridge, Mass., MIT Press.
Majtinskaja, K. 1969. Mestoimenija v jazkax raznyz sistem [Pronouns in languages of different systems]. Moscow.

Poerbatjaraka. 1952. Kapustakan Djawi. Djakarta, Djambatan.

Thass-Thienemann, Theodore. 1973. The interpretation of language, vols. I, II. New York, Aronson.

Vendler, Zeno. 1968. Adjectives and nominalizations. Papers on Formal Linguistics, no. 5. The Hague, Mouton.

Zoetmulder, P. J. 1958. Sekar Sumawar. Vol. I. Djakarta, Ober.

Zoetmulder, P. J., and I. R. Poedjwijatna. 1954. Bahasa Parma I. Djakarta, Ober.

Aridharma:
Framing an Old Javanese Tale

This is a much later work than the previous essay and as such it is much more philological than linguistic. Indeed, it begins with an attempt to contrast modern philology—the philology of a time that postdates modern linguistics—with the traditional sort of philology.

The text is the same one from which the sentence in "Binding Wild Words" is taken, the Old Javanese Tantri Kamandaka, *a collection of tales translated from Sanskrit. While that sentence is the initial sentence in the text, the story translated and discussed here is the final section of the work. Like a scene from a shadow play, it is a story inside a story inside a story. Unlike a shadow play, this is a written text, ancient yet frequently revived and performed in modern Java and Bali.*

❖   ❖   ❖

All of these sounds, the crowing of cocks, the baying of dogs,
and the hum of insects at noon, are the evidence of nature's
health or sound state. Such is the never failing beauty and
accuracy of language, the most perfect art in the world; the chisel
of a thousand years retouches it.
                                        —H. D. Thoreau

The Philological Frame

A philologist faces two tasks, so different that they often bear different names. Textual criticism, which must for both historical and procedural reasons be called primary philology, is concerned with "the art of judging rightly the genuineness of written works and passages."[1] Secondary philology is what Schleiermacher (1838) called hermeneutics, "the art of understanding rightly another man's language, particularly his written language." Martin Heidegger quotes these two definitions from Schleiermacher in "A Dialogue Between a Japanese and an Inquirer," a work in which the philosopher as inquirer confronts the abyss that the philologist knows well, the abyss between the ways two languages mean, so that, in his dialogue with the Japanese, Heidegger (1971:5) writes, "the language of dialogue constantly destroyed the possibility of saying what the dialogue was about." The final step in primary philology is often translation, so that one text becomes two. Translation is the bridge—the only bridge—across the abyss. For the secondary philologist, the interpreter, translation is the point of departure, something to be *deconstructed* (to use the current philological term for it) in a movement back toward an understanding of the original text, the source of the translation, in order to correct the exuberances and deficiencies of the translation.[2] The goal in this case is not a better translation but some understanding of things beyond translation.

To those laboring in the intricacies of textual criticism, hermeneutics can appear arrogantly subjective, while to the modern interpreter textual criticism itself seems blind to the possibility that even such basic acts as transliteration involve interpretation—to the extent that there is meaning in the medium itself. For instance, the shaping of the Old Javanese syllable, with its consonantal center and modifications above, below, before, and after it, is deeply metaphoric in a different way than is the more linear, Roman alphabet.[3] In transliteration itself there is exuberance (that is, meaning is added) and deficiency (meaning is lost). Self-correction of this sort, the self-consciousness of one facing a text in a distant language, should not be confused with subjectivism, as some have suggested, for it is just the opposite—a respect for another voice not an obsession with one's own.

The Old Javanese (or Kawi) story that gives occasion to these philological meditations[4] is from a collection of framed tales called the *Tantri Kamandaka,* composed by an unknown author. The language suggests "the late Hindu-Javanese period as the time of origin."[5] The primary philology has been done by one of the great philologists of our time, the late Christiaan Hooykaas. Pigeaud lists three versions of the work in the Leiden collection, the more complete of which was studied, transliterated, and translated into Dutch by Hooykaas in 1931.[6] The *Tantri Kamandaka* is usually classified as moralistic, didactic, or sometimes gnomic literature, and therefore it lies outside the scope of *kalangwan*, the Javanese term Zoetmulder uses to distinguish belles lettres from other preserved texts, although we must remember that these classifications are European not Javanese. Later, more "literary" versions are found in Middle Javanese and Balinese *kidung* poetry, though in Zoetmulder's opinion these newer versions have "a certain artificiality which goes less well with the subject matter than did the more simple approach of the Old Javanese original."[7]

Versions of the *Tantri Kamandaka* continue to be shaped in the present. There is a new Indonesian version (Kawi and Indonesian in parallel columns) by L. Mardiwarsito[8] and a grammar of Old Javanese (*Struktur Bahasa Jawa Kuno*) by L. Mardiwarsito and Harimurti Kridalaksana, which is based on the *Tantri Kamandaka*.[9] In Bali, the well-known *dalang*, Wayan Wija, has created a new genre of shadow theater, with new puppets, based on the *Tantri Kamandaka*. And in his last book Gregory Bateson retells the story in English in order to develop a notion of silence or basic discontinuity across species and genders.[10]

The story of Aridharma (later Anglingdarma and Ajidarma), which is the final full story of the *Tantri Kamandaka*, has a life of its own apart from that work. The author first saw it carved in stone on Candi Jago in East Java, and then as a *ketoprak* performance by the Siswa Budaya Company in Malang in 1970 (a videotape was made of that performance for later study). Later I found a comic book about King Anglingdarma, by Jachja, printed in Bandung. It is well known in the *wayang* repertoire and appears in the *Serat Kanda ning Ringgit* ('Book of tales of the *wayang purwa* theater'). In the *Sangkala ning Bumi*, Angling Darma is listed as the sixth incarnation of Wisnu in Java, and the story is recounted in Ranggawarsita's encyclopedic, universal history, *Pustaka Raja*, written in the late nineteenth century. This latter work, along with the *Serat Kanda* and several other versions, is summarized in G. W. J. Drewes's recent book, *The Romance of King Angling Darma in Javanese Literature*, which also contains a translation (with the original text) of a Javanese poetic version.[11] Similar stories with different names are found in Malay (the *Hikayat Shah Mardan*), in Thai (*Lin Ton*), in the Buddhist Jatakas (the *Kharaputta-Jataka*, number 386), and in the *Arabian Nights*, where it is the second tale, called "The Ox, the Ass, and the Farmer."[12] In each of these settings, the tale takes on different meanings depending upon the frame: who is saying what to whom, about what, and in what language. In this sense, the tale provides a ground upon which to compare the different contexts it evokes.

A good deal, then, of the primary philology for the *Tantri Kamandaka* has been done, although we may not yet have achieved an entirely "genuine" text, dictionary, and grammar. Indeed, to identify one stage in the life of a lingual artifact as genuine is itself open to very serious question. However, the primary philology gives us access to this story and makes possible more attention to understanding it and the context it shapes. Both of the tasks of philology—textual criticism and hermeneutics—are clearly utopian, in the sense that Ortega uses the term in order to designate a task "whose initial intention cannot be fulfilled in the development of its activity and which has to be satisfied with approximations essentially contradictory to the purpose which had started it."[13] Finding the "genuine" text is utopian, translation is utopian, just as finding any final understanding is always necessarily utopian, too.

The Sounding of Voices

Before entering the translated text of the Aridharma story, one should consider for a moment the performance of the text. Visual scanning is not the same as sounding. One might take exception to Pigeaud when he writes of works like the *Tantri Kamandaka*, "probably moralistic and didactic texts were read by all cultured men and women, both ecclesiastics and laymen. . . ."[14] On the evidence of the present—the way the texts are performed today—and on the evidence of the story itself—the way stories are experienced by the characters in the story, one would suspect that more people heard than read them. In the *Tantri Kamandaka*, Tantri, the daughter of the king's minister, teaches by telling stories, and her skill is a skill in telling. Since the stories are mostly dialogues and monologues, not reported but presented as direct discourse, it is not unreasonable to assume that skill in telling those stories meant skill with voices: the voices of Tantri, her mother, the king, the lion, the wolf, the turtles, the swans, the louse, and the bedbug—all the creatures of its vast world.

To the modern hearer—and in my own case I listened repeatedly to a taped performance of the text made by a traditional Javanese actor (R. M. Soedarsono)—the language of the characters seems varied and distinctive. One character does not sound like another. As a clear instance, let us examine the language of a female lizard on the wall who is overheard by King Aridharma. It is markedly alliterative and comical, and the king begins to chuckle, until he bursts out laughing.

> Duh antyanta kapengin mami rumenge
> pañumbana sang nātha ri patnīnira
>
> Tan kadi tuwuhku tinambang tan kinasihan tuwi
> tan tinunggal. [Note all the t's!]
>
> Ah ah sang ratu aridharma saphala sihta
>
> Oh, I feel it so sharply, listening to the
> love words of the king to his wife.
>
> She's not like me—abandoned, unloved,
> uncoupled.
>
> Oh, oh, King Aridharma, your love ripens.

Likewise, it is distinctive of King Aridharma's mode of speaking that he lectures others and pontificates like a scholar, always giving the proper Sanskrit terms for things.

> Yeku warna-sanghāra ngaranya. . . .
>
> It is called *warna-sanghāra*, the destruction of differences—

The performance of a tale—the skill that is being taught in this kind of literature—seems to require, like a good shadow play, the shaping of voices. Therein lies the liveliness of the text, which, with rhythm, and pitch, and voice dynamics, the reader must supply by sounding it, not just scanning it with the eyes like a printed book. One might imagine the text being presented to a class of young nobles in pre-Islamic Java. I have imagined the story that way, on the model of lessons from an old teacher, Lalu Mesir, who taught me in a traditional way in eastern Lombok in 1970. Each day Lalu Mesir dressed up formally, with *batik sarong*, black jacket, turban, and an old *kris* tucked into his waistband. At first there were just the two of us, but after about a week young men from the village began to join us and ask questions. The teacher sat on one side of a low round table. I sat on the other side with the young men around me, a bit behind. He would open a palm-leaf book and begin to perform it, with great variety in his voicings. He often stopped to explain things. Since it was in that setting that I experienced this kind of literature, I have taken it as a context for the following translation, to replace, if I may be allowed to, the desk, lamp, and typewriter of my study in Ann Arbor. I hope the reader can imagine it sounded in such a setting, in the late afternoon air on the wide porch of Lalu Mesir's house.

The Tale of Aridharma from the Old Javanese
Tantri Kamandaka

There was a king who was given the name Aridharma, which means 'attuned to the laws of nature'. Once, while he was hunting in the forest, he came upon a *nagini*, a daughter of the *naga* king, doing wrong, having sex there with a common snake. Seeing that, Aridharma said: "Ha! How wrong it is for a *nagini* like you to take the maleness of a common snake. It is called *warṇa-sanghāra*, the destruction of differences—and that is why it is not right. You may think that this is an overly harsh judgment, but for a king it is not. The name for it is *wiparita*, perversion."

So said the king, and he killed the common snake and slapped the *nagini*. She went home very upset and spoke to her father, the *naga* king.

"Why are you sobbing, my child?"

And his daughter answered: "There is a king called Aridharma. He was hunting in the forest and he saw how beautiful I was. I refused to be one body with him, but he tried to force me, out of his passion, and he chased me and hurt me. And he slapped me. That's why your daughter is sobbing."

"Now, now, be calm my child. I will kill King Aridharma and soothe your heart."

Without hesitation, the *naga* king went to the city of Sri Aridharma, and, taking the form of a *brahmin*, he entered the palace. Inside he became a *naga* again, and making his body small he hid under the king's bed.

Just then the king was arm-in-arm with his wife, called Mayawati, which means 'mistress of appearances'. He was daydreaming and he moaned out loud, and Mayawati spoke these words to him: "Ha! Maharaja! You are acting strangely. You are not like yourself."

King Aridharma answered his wife: "There was a *nagini* I came upon when I was hunting in the forest. She was doing wrong. She was taking the maleness of a common snake. That is not right. It is like a well-born woman, a *brahmin*, taking the maleness of a low-born man, a *sudra*. It turns the world upside down. The word for it is *warna-sanghāra*, the destruction of differences. Better she take the maleness of another *brahmin*. It's the same with the *nagini*. It would not be wrong conduct if she were not the daughter of the *naga* king, but she had sex with a common snake, and that is not right, so I killed the snake and I slapped the *nagini*."

That is what Aridharma said, and when the *naga* king heard it he thought in his heart: "My child . . . you went too far. The *nagini* is deceitful. King Aridharma really did act unselfishly. It is proper that he should hold the world together. He has a right to wipe away the filth of the world . . . and whoever it is that acts wrongly."

That is what the *naga* king said in his heart. He left the bed, returning to the form of a *brahmin*, and he was greeted graciously by Maharaja Aridharma. The sage responded with wise words: "I am the father of the *nagini* you struck. She acted out of bad motives. You were correct to punish her as you did for her bad actions. I give you a boon, king. Ask as you wish."

The king answered with these words: "I wish to know the speech of all animals and to understand it."

"Your request is quite proper, have no fear, but there is one condition: you may not tell anyone else. If you do, may you die."

The *naga* king carried out his promise and then returned to the *naga* world.

King Aridharma remained.

He was lying in the daytime, arm-in-arm with his beloved Mayawati. From above the place where the king was, a lizard said: "Oh, I feel it so sharply, listening to the love words of the king to his wife. She's not like me, abandoned, unloved, uncoupled. Oh, oh, King Aridharma, your love ripens."

This was the meaning of the language of the lizard.

The king was watching and he suddenly burst out laughing.

His wife said: "Oh my lord, what is it now? I don't understand why you are laughing."

"Nothing, dear one. I just felt good and I laughed."

That is what the king said, then he added: "I cannot tell you more than that."

Queen Mayawati said: "I still want to know what it is."

"Don't ask, dear one, just believe me. I will die if I tell you."

The queen answered: "If that is all you can say, then I must die, too . . . if you do not tell me what you mean."

"If that is what you say, dear one, let the funeral pyre be built. Go order those who do these things to make the pyre, with a platform, and coffins, and an arch, a pavilion, and gifts. Let all these things be beautiful."

After this was done, King Aridharma gave gifts of merit to the *brahmins*, the *rishiis*, the followers of Shiva, and the followers of Buddha. Everything precious in the palace was given: royal gifts of gold, jewels, silver, clothing, and money. He gave them these things.

When the flames of the holy fire were blazing, he walked up the steps, leading Mayawati. When they were on the platform, the two of them together, there emerged from the bushes goats, a pair of goats, the female named Wiwita and the male Banggali. They came to the edge of the blazing pyre. Wiwita said to her husband: "Father of my children, get me some leaves from the fire. I feel a craving to eat them. That's what I want! Don't just do nothing."

These were the words of her husband: "Ha! You don't know how dangerous that is. Don't you see those guards circling the fire holding weapons? Swords! Spears! *Krises!* What do you think would happen?"

Wiwita said: "Ha! Maybe you don't love me then. Ha! I'll die on the spot if I don't get what I want!"

The male goat answered: "Ha! Go ahead then, and die. Why am I to suffer for you? I will not do as King Aridharma does—carried away by his wife's words. If that's what it is, I don't want it. That's not the way of someone called a *mahapurusha*, a noble being—such a one may love or not love. Even though I am a beast, I do not want to be like that and do only as you wish me to."

Those were the words of Banggali, berating his wife.

Meanwhile, the words of both the goats were overheard by Maharaja Aridharma. He remembered them and thought about them: "How wise the goat's words are and how wretched he is. What makes it so bad is that his wife's words are entirely improper."

He reflected a moment.

"Even though he is in fact an animal, he is not easily led by his wife. And I, after all, am a king, and if I enjoy being subordinate to a wife, who then can call me lord? The one called Wiwita is not following *dharma*. Banggali must not accept her pressure."

So Maharaja Aridharma thought in his heart, and he suddenly descended from the pyre and went into the palace. He took to heart the words of the goat Banggali and put aside the idea of throwing himself into the fire.

As for all the things he had given away—regalia, clothes, and treasures—they were now offered in ritual as expiation and redemption of Maharaja Aridharma by the priests of Shiva and Buddha and by all the *rishiis* and scholars. This ritual act restored the well-being of Sri Maharaja Aridharma and the stability of his *negara*, the realm he ruled.

But Queen Mayawati persisted and fell into the fire by herself, and the goat wife also threw herself into the fire.

And, reflecting on this, Vasubaga, the great scholar, made a *sloka*.

uttama-madhya-kaniṣṭham kottamam wacano bhawet /
tasya mahatagrastawa wākyam samadya wijayet //

That means: "Whether something is said by someone of highest
status, or middle status, or lowest status, whatsoever is fitting and
proper should be done and whatsoever is not should be set aside.
That is what happened when the great King Aridharma took to heart
the words of the goat."

In this way, what I am saying is also true.

❖   ❖   ❖

With these last words we move out of the story and into its frame, the
first of the many frames that shape the *Tantri Kamandaka*, the larger
text from which this story comes. The story of Aridharma and the
sloka that evaluates the story (attributed here to Vasubaga) are told by
a wild dog, or wolf, named Sambada. He tells it to Candapinggala,
the lion king.

The story of Aridharma is the last in the Candapinggala frame,
and so we must go back a bit to pick up the frame story, so that we can
see how the story of Aridharma was used within it.

The frame story of Candapinggala begins with a poor *brahmin*
named Dharmaswami, master of *dharma*, who begs Shiva for a way out
of poverty. Shiva sends him a young bull called Nandaka, the offspring
of Shiva's own vehicle, Nandini. Dharmaswami uses Nandaka to carry
wood and slowly builds up a caravan of a thousand carts. On a long
journey to Udyani the *brahmin* so overloads the aging Nandaka that he
collapses. The *brahmin* tells two of his men to stay behind with
Nandaka until the bull either recovers or dies. If he dies, they are to
make a fire and burn him.

But Dharmaswami's men get bored and frightened in the wild
forest of Udyani, so they abandon Nandaka and make a big bonfire,
knowing that Dharmaswami will see the smoke and think it is
Nandaka's pyre.

Left alone, Nandaka the bull wanders in the Udyani forest. He meets a pack of wild dogs, hunters for the lion king, Candapinggala. The dogs attack the bull, but he runs amuck, killing many dogs with his horns. The survivors run to king Candapinggala and tell him about the bull.

The next day Candapinggala goes out himself, with the pack of wild dogs, and he is impressed at the bull's great size and strength, even though, as the king notices, he eats only grass and leaves. In admiration, Candapinggala befriends Nandaka and vows to eat only grass and leaves, too. The lion and the bull live in peace and equality.

The leader of the hunting pack, however, the wild dog Sambada, is deeply threatened. In his view, like should stay with like. The source of evil is the mixing of categories, including unnatural relations across kinds such as friendships between carnivores and herbivores. He righteously vows to the pack that he will undo the unnatural friendship, and he does it by telling tale after tale, separately, to Nandaka the bull and Candapinggala the lion. All of them concern betrayal and deceit and each story is evaluated with one or more *slokas*. A few times the bull Nandaka answers with his own stories—which demonstrate that evil results from lying and bearing false witness not from friendships across categories as Sambada would have it.

Most of the stories have stories within them, and stories within those stories, each framing the other, so that the texture is thick and full of nice resonances, like gamelan music. By the device of these stories, the friendship is shattered and Candapinggala and Nandaka die, bound together in combat, a final feast for the wild dogs.

And the strange tale that Sambada tells to Candapinggala, the one that finally turns friendship to hatred, is the story of Aridharma. Sambada tells Candapinggala that the story of Aridharma shows that the lion king should not let Sambada's low status influence his credibility. Now we can continue with the text to the end, from the point at which Sambada has just said "In this way, what I am saying is also true." The translation continues:

❖   ❖   ❖

These were the words of Sambada, the wild dog, and he added a *sloka:*

nakhinām ca nadīnām çṛngginām ca çastrapāninām /
viçvāso naiva kartavyaḥ strīṣu rājakuleṣu ca //

That is to say: "This is the teaching of the scholars. There are those one ought not befriend: evil people, animals with horns, those with sharp claws, wives of kings, those who accost one in the street, the family of a king. Do not make friends with these, say the scholars. My lord, you yourself must confront Nandaka the bull. His horns are broad and sharp, like swords. Life takers! Agony makers!"

And those were the words of Sambada, the wild dog, provoking the lion king, and he believed them.

And so he went to Nandaka, along with Sambada and his pack of dogs. All of them gathered around the terrible one, all of them roaring. They approached with mouths wide open.

But, lulled by the stories Sambada had been telling him, Nandaka the bull was not frightened. He snorted playfully and stabbed at the earth with his horns, full of friendship, as he watched Candapinggala, thinking: "Ha! He's coming to warn me of something."

They attacked Nandaka. Their teeth went straight to his neck. Nandaka was confused. He thrust his horns and tore out the stomach of the lion king, so that his entrails were wrapped around him like garlands.

They both died, the lion and Nandaka.

They returned again, the lion to the realm of Vishnu, Nandaka to the realm of Shiva.

It was all interpreted by Bhagawan Vasubaga in a *sloka:*

niccotyesapateduhkam niccohutpāpatemrĕtyu /
paramwatāwikasyanti tasmat nicca wisarjayet //

This means: "Ignorance is the cause of misfortune. Ignorance is the condition under which danger and death thrive. That is why the goal of all those with understanding, those who seek happiness in the world, is to avoid friendship with the ignorant. Such friendships are not good because the evil character of the ignorant poisons the hearts of those who are good. If they play, they scratch and bite. How can anyone with insight want such a one for a friend? That is what happened in the mutual destruction of Nandaka and the lion Candapinggala. They both died, deceived by the provocations of the wild dog Sambada."

❖   ❖   ❖

With this *sloka* we again shift frames. The person telling the story of Candapinggala and Nandaka is a wise and clever woman, the daughter of a court official in the palace of King Ecwaryapala. The king is young and tyrannical, a smart but sexually aggressive ruler who has forced his ministers to bring him women, a new one every night. The ministers, who finally can find no more unwed women, do not know what to do. Tantri, the teller of these tales, is sent by her mother to relieve the despair of her father, the chief minister, as he lies moaning in the darkness by the pool in their temple garden. (The garden is described in distinctly Javanese terms.) She confidently volunteers to go to the king and teach him morality, using all of her skill in the arts of *tantric* instruction. And so she tells the king the long tale of Candapinggala, and the *sloka* above is her evaluation of the story. Following the *sloka*, she continues:

❖   ❖   ❖

"The dead bodies of Nandaka and the lion were eaten by Patih Sambada, the wild dog, and he ate his fill. In the end Sambada the wild dog died from gorging himself, and his followers, too, died of stuffing themselves, in greed. The soul of Sambada returned to the crater of the copper-headed caldron on the crust of hell to experience the five kinds of rebirth. As many as the hairs of his body, that was the time he spent in suffering, ten years for every hair. So he suffered in misery, along with his pack of killers, and that is what happens to those not attuned to *dharma*, rejected in the world because they are thoughtlessly excessive, scheming grievous schemes, endlessly."

And so ends Candapinggala,
Tantri's tale, tantric words.

Framing a Fable

The story ends there, abruptly, with no fulfillment of the frame story about Tantri and King Ecwaryapala. The story Tantri tells, however, the tale of Nandaka and Candapinggala, does have an end. Sambada's telling of it to the lion king frames the story of Aridharma, just as Aridharma's telling frames the story of the *nagini* and the common snake. Who is telling what to whom? And why?

Each frame frames a question about what lies beyond the frame.[15] Beyond the story of Aridharma is Sambada's scheme, beyond Sambada's is Tantri's, and beyond Tantri's is some particular place, time, and motivation in which the text is performed. For my translation I have imagined the setting to be an informal class in Lombok with Lalu Mesir, but beyond that class, as an outer frame, we find ourselves— modern readers of an old literature, reading Hooykaas's text and trying to look beyond it. At each level, meaning is determined by use—the use to which we put the tale.

Each of these tales contains within it a statement of the use to which it is put, inserted there by the teller as a commentary— sometimes by a prior teller like Vasubaga, and sometimes by the present teller, Sambada or Tantri in the section translated here. These statements are called *subhasitas*, quotations from Sanskrit, which form the core of the *Niti-sastras*, the lore and science of government. The power of the *subhasitas* lies in their existence apart from the stories, in a different language, a form of Sanskrit, taken from a realm of accepted truths. They are active proverbs. As Kenneth Burke wrote,

Proverbs are strategies for dealing with situations. Insofar as situations are typical and recurrent in a given social structure, people develop names for them and strategies for handling them. Another name for strategies might be attitudes.[16]

The story of Aridharma is a strategy or attitude, too, a guide to dealing with a particular situation, and as a story it is separable from the Sanskrit *subhasitas* that frame it. There are many tellings of the story, in different frames. In its Buddhist version (Jataka 386; see appendix 2) it is used by the Buddha as a lesson for one of his followers about the dangers of being caught in an unwise commitment to a wife.

The master told this tale in Jetvana, concerning temptation of a brother by his former wife. When the brother confessed that he was longing for the world, the master said, "Brother, this woman does you harm: formerly also you came into the fire through her and were saved from death by sages," so he told an old tale.

The old tale is a version of the Aridharma tale, in which the king is called Senaka, and the Buddha is Sakka in the form of the goat. In the *Tantri Kamandaka*, however, the story has a different point: to persuade the lion king to listen to advice from an inferior (Sambada himself in this case), and this point is carried by the *subhasita* within the tale.

The words of the low, the middle status, and the great,
Whoever is wise should heed them:
What is not right should be put aside.[17]

Subhasitas like this were collected in books, the most famous of which were compiled by Canakya and Kamandaki,[18] the latter being the probable source of the "Kamandaka" of the title, where the word seems to name a genre of texts.[19] These collections were translated into many of the languages of Southeast Asia, as effective strategies for dealing with difficult situations. They are generalized to extend beyond the particular combination of events of any one instance and they impose on events a transcendental generality.

Literature of this sort clearly is, as Burke puts it, "equipment for living." With it one learns to identify allies and enemies and to size up situations wisely. There seems to be no other way to read the *Tantri Kamandaka*.

And yet the story seems to overpower any one point. If the tale of Aridharma is performed, and it has been performed over and over again, it is not just to say, indirectly, that one should listen to good advice from humble sources. Even within the *Tantri Kamandaka*, this tale seems to say more than that. Tantri is a woman teaching a powerful man, and, although Sambada is using the story to destroy a peaceable kingdom, Tantri is using it to restore one. And there are other resonances across the frames: the sexual tension of Tantri's situation with Ecwaryapala, who expects to sleep with her when the long tale is over; or the resonances of Aridharma's ability to understand animal languages, which legitimizes as more than fiction the animal tales Tantri has been telling. These and other resonances make it seem that more than the motivation of Sambada in undermining the friendship of Candapinggala and Nandaka makes this story appropriate as the final tale of the *Tantri Kamandaka*, since its themes extend to the outer frame and beyond. It is also the only tale Tantri tells in which the hero is a human being, a king, and therefore quite directly relevant to the king of the outer frame, Ecwaryapala, whom Tantri is seeking to influence.

Thus, multiple-framed stories create an excess of meaning. The sorts of resonances that emerge across the frames tie the story to its context in ways that, even if they do remain in the background (to be seen properly from the corner of one's eye), create a very thick texture. The artistry of telling stories this way—one within the other, piling perspective on perspective—is in some ways almost too simple, like the depth achieved in the multiple, self-reflexive framings of an Escher drawing. Of course, this very involution is part of what makes the story interesting to us today.

The tale of Aridharma, then, is contextualized within a hierarchy of frames, each of which gives rise to questions about what lies beyond the frame. To many of these questions the reader or hearer responds with acts of imagination. For instance, where in relation to the couch on which the king and queen were lying was the small lizard? What does a *nagini* look like? When they ascended the steps to the flaming pyre, where were Aridharma and Mayawati in relation to the goats? Even the least imaginative reading necessarily evokes details of this sort, none of which are in the text. For me, seeing the staged *ketoprak* version provided a source for some of these details. Others will fill them in from their own memories and imaginations. There is no way that one can read only the words of the story and not provide a great many details oneself.

In just this sense, the story is itself a frame for an active experience, which goes beyond the frame. It asks questions and evokes answers about what is beyond it. There remains, however, an "it"—a frame within which these details are evoked. This frame is made of words—nouns, verbs, adjectives, connectives, affixes, pronouns, and so on—all bound into clauses, sentences, and clusters of sentences, which serve a particular function of plot. The difficult question is just how to think about this tremendously complex, verbal texture.

Consider, first, plot. We tend to think of plot as a sequence of actions or episodes, in an Aristotelian way. A particular sequence of actions characterizes a particular plot, so that we recognize Jataka 386 as a variant of the Aridharma tale. As a sequence of actions, we might describe the plot of the Aridharma tale as follows.

1. King Aridharma finds the *nagini* lying with the snake.
2. King Aridharma punishes the *nagini* and the snake.
3. The *nagini* reports to her father.
4. The father promises vengeance.
5. The father enters the king's palace and hides.
6. The father hears the true story.
   And so on.

One can easily and quite naturally abstract the story still further by a strategy of explaining via the substitution of more abstract terms.

1. The hero confronts evil.
2. The hero punishes the evildoer(s).
3. The evildoer seeks vengeance.
4. The evildoer finds an agent of vengeance.
5. The agent takes on a disguise.
6. The agent hears the true story of the evildoer.
   And so on.

In this way one can build a general etics of stories, interpreting all stories as instances (or tokens) of abstract archetypes. One may even want to suggest that these archetypes are universal. Plot of this sort can be called fable.[20]

There is another way to think of plot, not as a sequence of episodes but as a sequence of language acts, which might also be called rhetorical functions. There are ways, particular ways, of presenting the fable. For instance, a character in the story may relate some of the actions, while other actions are told by the storyteller or writer directly. Plot at this level is a mode of framing action in some coherent way. If we look at the Aridharma tale in this way, an interesting pattern emerges, one that reveals the artistry of the Old Javanese author in shaping a Sanskrit tale. As told here, the plot of the Aridharma story is a series of monologues and dialogues connected by movements—goings and comings. It is much more dramatic than narrative. The episode of the *nagini* and the common snake is told four times. First, the narrator, Sambada, tells it in the third person. Then it is immediately retold by Aridharma in a monologue directed partly to the *nagini* and partly to himself, in which he interprets (using a Sanskrit term) this act of sex as a mixing of categories, and for that reason wrong. The story is retold again by the *nagini* to her father, in which telling she reinterprets Aridharma's acts as sexual aggression. In the next scene, Aridharma tells the story to his wife, overheard this time by the *naga* king from his hiding place under the bed. The plot, in this second sense, progresses by repetition of the same story.

1. Report, third-person account by the storyteller
2. Monologue by Aridharma, overheard by the *nagini*

3. Dialogue, the *nagini* to her father
4. Triadic dialogue, Aridharma to Mayawati, overheard by the *naga* king

One can fill in the rest of the plot in this way, describing language acts rather than the events of the fable.

5. Inner monologue by the *naga* king
6. Dialogue, the *naga* king and Aridharma (symmetrical center of the plot)
7. Overheard monologue, lizard overheard by Aridharma (parallel to number 2, above)
8. Dialogue, Aridharma and Mayawati (parallel to number 3)
9. Triadic dialogue, the goats are overheard by Aridharma (parallel to number 4)
10. Inner monologue, Aridharma (parallel to number 5)
11. Report, third-person account by the storyteller of the return to the palace and the deaths of Mayawati and the female goat (parallel to number 1)

Structural parallels of this sort evoke thematic symmetry between what happens before the center of the story (the dialogue between the *naga* king and Aridharma) and what happens after it: for instance, the observing of a couple engaged in sex, an account of the prior event in which the whole truth is withheld, learning the truth by overhearing it, changing understanding of the initial event in an interior monologue, and so forth.

As a plot, then, the fulfillment of the story is the building of its symmetry, the balancing of one episode with another, so that unexpected resonances emerge. Overlaid upon this are the multiple frames of the containing stories and their *subhasitas*. In these frames, perspectives shift and hence new interpretations of the contained event emerge. The Indian fable gives rise to the Old Javanese plot, which, in its repetitions, its speech-act symmetry, and its multiple embeddings, suggests a kinship with the structures of Javanese shadow plays and gamelan music.[21]

One might see more clearly the difference between plot and fable by comparing the Aridharma story from the *Tantri Kamandaka* with the *Kharaputta Jataka* (number 386) mentioned above (the complete text is to be found in appendix 2). There are many more episodes in the Jataka version of the story, and found among them, in the same order, are the episodes of the Aridharma fable. The symmetry of plot is not there, however, nor are the developed speeches and voices. It is a more completely narrative version. The frame of the Jataka version—the Buddha speaking to his followers—is completely different. By comparing different versions (including the very different version in the *Arabian Nights*, given in appendix 3), one might come up with a general scheme of the fable, perhaps in the form of a formula with optional and obligatory narremes, filled by variant sets of events and personae. One would again be on the path away from understanding.

Using the Tale

There is so much more to learn about the tale: one can pile note upon note until it is all but impossible to look through the dense philological texture. But the value of gnomic literature has to be its usefulness, for this kind of literature is not an end in itself; it is rather "equipment for living."[22] Every translator dreams of becoming what Emerson called a "transparent eyeball"—to see and let others see through the text, to make it not opaque but transparent, in the way that, when I say to my son, "Look at the moose standing there in the weeds," I want him to look through my words at the moose standing there in the weeds. The text, the tale of Aridharma, finally has to become subsidiary to a focus beyond the text.[23]

In the *Tantri Kamandaka*, the tale of Aridharma is used by the wolf to undermine the friendship of the lion and the bull, in the Buddhist Jataka a related tale is used to admonish a disciple about sexual distractions, and in the *Arabian Nights* the father of Scheherazade uses the same fable in another plot to persuade her to give up her suicidal scheme to confront the Sultan of Bagdad. There is no family resemblance in the uses of the fable in the way that there is a family resemblance in the motifs of the three versions considered here. Trusting the wolf's words, even if he is an inferior creature, being distracted by sex, or being foolishly obstinate are only three evaluations of the story.[24] None of them may be very useful to us today, and without a use the tale is only mildly amusing, not "equipment for living."

And then, to make it even less useful, there is the sexism of the tale. Aridharma does not shed a tear for the queen he liked to lie with in the daytime. He does not try to save her from the fire. Obstinacy does not seem a sufficient motivation for death, although we try to remember the lessons of Kenneth Burke: that motives are also part of the grammars of our languages. It is interesting to note that in later elaborations of the fable in Java and Bali this sexism was confronted. One might even speculate that the sexism—this uneasiness about Mayawati's role in the scheme of things—may have contributed to further elaboration of the tale. In these later versions, Mayawati complains about her mistreatment after her death. A goddess (usually Uma) curses Aridharma to madness in some versions, and in most later versions he wanders for seven years in the body of one or more animals, including the pet duck or parrot of a beautiful princess. More male fantasy, perhaps, but the curse is interesting as a motivation for continuing the fable, one that we can fully share, since seeking justice for Mayawati helps us appropriate the tale more easily to our late-twentieth-century uses. According to Ricoeur, appropriation is the only way to correct the distanciation of the analysis we have been conducting. Without it, meaning is incomplete. One must be able to see another possible world through it.[25]

Besides the fact that sexism makes the tale less useful to us, there is the issue of talking with animals. In spite of all the lore about whales, dolphins, and chimps, few people I know believe that one can communicate with animals via language. Most believe that language is what chiefly distinguishes humans from other animals—the modern equivalent of the soul. But communication with animals via language was not implausible in the traditional Javanese and Balinese episteme, and this is still true for many Javanese and Balinese today:

the tradition is alive. Among the stories about the great nineteenth-century Javanese poet and scholar Ranggawarsita is one stating that he claimed to know the languages of animals.[26] If we are to make this claim plausible, we have to change our understanding of language—appropriation seems to require it. More than any other of its themes, including sex, the tale of Aridharma is about language.

Figure 8 is a Balinese drawing of the *naga* king inscribing a written syllable on Aridharma's tongue. There is a great deal of resonance in this image. In many stories from around the world the tongue is metonymic of language and serpents are guides into the animal realm. Perhaps this is due to the relationship between snakes and birds, either through snakes eating birds' eggs or through a common descent. And birds are the preeminent nonhuman candidates for talkers.[27]

In the Aridharma tale the mode of transmission for the language of animals is not specified. The narrator says only, "The *naga* king carried out his promise and then returned to the *naga* world." What is striking in both the drawing and the tale is that this transmission occurs in such a brief time, that the essence of language can somehow be condensed. What is most tantric about the tale is this view of language. The root metaphor in this tantric view of language may well be sexual—that knowledge is like an implanted seed. This association of the formation of the body and the formation of language shapes a metaphoric language well known in tantric writing and picturing in both Java and Bali and also throughout South and Southeast Asia. In the best-known tantric work in Java and Bali, the *Sang Hyang Kamahāyānikan,* the doctrine of *sabda-prapañca* describes the evolution of the world of sound in man, a microcosm of the universe.

> I will teach you again concerning the following: the body inside and outside is a stûpa-prâsâda. The letters are namaḥ siddhaṃ, a, â; i, î; u, û; rĕ, rö; lĕ, lö; e, ai; o, au; ang, ah; ka, kha; ga, gha; nga; ca, cha; ja, jha; ña; ṭa, ṭha; ḍa, ḍha; ṇa; ta, tha; da, dha; na; pa, pha; ba, bha; ma; ya, ra, la, wa; ça, ṣa, sa, ha. Such are the letters, which form the inwardness of the reality of the çarîra-prâsâda.[28]

Fig. 8. *Naga* king inscribing tongue of Aridharma. (By I Boengklik and Dewa Ketoet Pasek, from the Bateson-Mead Collection of Balinese Art.)

Hadiwijono, in *Man in the Present Javanese Mysticism* (1967), comments on this passage.

It must be acknowledged that much of this passage is obscure. But so much is obvious, that the body of man is considered as being composed of the verbal manifestation of the absolute.

A more detailed explanation of the manifestation of the absolute is given in Sang Hyang Kamahāyānikan 48, which says that *na* is bone, *maḥ* is blood, *si* is flesh, *ddhaṃ* is skin, *a* is knowledge, *i* is color, *u* is form, *rě* is eye, *lě* is ear, *e* is nose, *o* is anus and genital, *ang* is the sun, *aḥ* is the rest of the moon.

Further it is explained that *ka, kha, ga, gha, nga* and *ca, cha, ja, jha, ña* is the eye and the object of seeing, and that *ṭa, ṭha, ḍa, ḍha, ṇa* is the ear and the object of hearing, and *ta, tha, da, dha, na* is the nose and the object of smelling, that *pa, pha, ba, bha, ma* is the anus and the genital, that *ya, ra, la, wa* is the earth, that *ça, ṣa* are the two feet, that *sa, ha* are the two hands.

In this way the absolute pervades the whole universe and man. The whole verbal-speculation is therefore closed with the statement that the 37 letters contain the nature of non-duality (*adwayamaka*) and that they, mixed with the passions, have the form of a circle, which is a stūpa that is equal to the body (carīra-stūpa), and that inside and outside it is a stūpa-prāsāda (a building that is equal to a stūpa). On the top of the stūpa-prāsāda-body (the body which is equal to a stūpa-prāsāda) is the abode of Lord Divine Buddha, with a meditating form of revelation.[29]

Sounds and their corresponding letters are eternal, the foundation of the universe, and are themselves thought of as *mantra*, religious or magical formulae. There is a clear description of this doctrine in Dasgupta's *An Introduction to Tantric Buddhism*.

In this matter the Buddhist Tantras agree fully with the Hindu Tantras. It is a general custom with the Tantras to place these Mantras in the form of the letters in different parts of the body for the purification of the body, and there are often elaborate systems for the arrangement of the letters on the different plexus (cakras) situated within the body along the spinal cord. . . . In this transformation of the letters into the Mantras . . . the Tantras seem to have adopted the Mimamsa theory of sabda or sound. The Mimamsakas hold that sound is eternal, and is always in the form of the letters of the alphabet, and a word is also nothing more than the letters that compose it. The meaning of a word is absolutely independent of any human agency and belongs to the word by virtue of its very nature and some peculiar power is required for the realization of this inherent meaning. The words themselves are also eternal, but they require the auxiliary agency of pronunciation to be recognisable to our consciousness. The Tantras accept this view of the eternal nature of the sabdas and further hold that "the movement that produced the world shows itself, or is represented to us in miniature, in the production of the sound." The process of the production of the sound is the epitome of the notion, as it were, of the cosmic process of creation.[30]

Lest one think this doctrine too arcane for the simple tale we are studying here, let us turn to the first *subhasita* at the beginning of the *Tantri Kamandaka*, whose concluding pages we have been considering. This is the outermost frame of the whole work.

A person who does not know the forms of writing and sound and goes to the center of a hall to speak with a great man, that person is like one who goes to the forest to capture a wild elephant in rut carrying only the stamen of a lotus to bind him with.[31]

The term used here for *sound* is rather strange, *çabda-paçabda*, probably a distortion of the term found above, in the passage from the

Sang Hyang Kamahāyānikan, so that it ought to read *çabda-prāsāda* 'sound-*stūpa*'.

The stated purpose of the collection of tales in the *Tantri Kamandaka* is to teach skill in language to those who would advise kings—"go to the center of a hall to speak with a great man."[32] What makes Tantri's tale also a set of tantric words, in the last line of the text, is the adoption of this tantric image of language. It is very different from the widely accepted, modern, academic image of language as an arbitrary set of signs, which represent reality. In the tantric view, the *sabdas* (*çabdas*) shape reality, and they are not arbitrary.

The power and authority of Aridharma, like the power and authority of Tantri herself in her instruction of the young king, lie in knowing the right names for things, apart from any human agency. A great deal makes sense in the tale when we take this view. Aridharma correctly names the act of the *nagini,* just as the goat correctly describes the act of the king in following his wife into the flames. And, if knowing the *sabdas* alienates Aridharma from his own people, it also marks him as a rightful and righteous king. It all holds together.

A cohesive image emerges, within which the tale of Aridharma can make sense to us—eternal Sanskrit aside—for the notion that by languaging we constitute our worlds (our sound-*stūpas*) is also a very modern notion. One might think of Wittgenstein, who wrote:

> One thinks that one is tracing the outline of the thing's nature over and over again, and one is merely tracing round the frame through which we look at it.[33]

The best use of the tale of Aridharma may be to teach us to know these frames we look through and how completely they bind us.

NOTES

1. This and the following quotation from Schleiermacher appeared in Heidegger (1971:10–11). The essay confronts the problem of the two kinds of philology in a discussion between Heidegger and a Japanese philosopher, a student of Nishida, one of Japan's most prominent language philoso-

phers. The subject of the discussion is esthetics. Heidegger comments, "The danger of our dialogue was hidden in the language itself, not in what we discussed, nor in the way in which we tried to do so" (1971:4).

2. *Exuberancy* and *deficiency* are Ortega's terms for the differences with which secondary philology is primarily concerned. He stated the two axioms of modern philology as:

> 1. Every utterance is deficient—it says less than it wishes to say.
> 2. Every utterance is exuberant—it conveys more than it plans.

See Ortega (1959:2; 1957, chaps. 11, 12) for further elaboration of these axioms.

3. The many important differences between roman and pallava writing are described in A. Becker (1983, 1984) based on Zurbuchen (1987).

4. The term *meditation* used as a name for one of the forms in which modern philologists write was first used in a secular mode by Ortega, in his *Meditations on Quixote*, to mean sustained thought about a text from several different perspectives. Of course, it has an origin in religious rhetoric and practice, like the term *hermeneutics.*

5. The periodization and classification of Javanese literature, like the term *literature* itself, are an outsider's framing of certain Javanese-Balinese-Sasak philologies (using the term *philology* here in Kroeber's sense of an accumulation of prior texts plus the apparatus necessary to get at them). Late Old Javanese has been characterized on the basis of the forms of the deictic, personal, and topicalizing particles, by the verb morphology, and by the forms of negation. See Zoetmulder (1974) for details.

6. Catalogued in Pigeaud (1967–70) in I.13.120. I have used here a photocopy of codex 4533. The *Tantri Kamandaka* was edited and translated into Dutch by Hooykaas (1931). In the margin of Codex Or 4533 are notes and corrections ascribed to van der Tuuk.

7. Zoetmulder (1974:438). Zoetmulder does not classify gnomic prose works like the *Tantri Kamandaka* as literature (*kalangwan*). In our philological tradition didactic works are often anomalous.

8. Mardiwarsito (1983) is based on Hooykaas (1931) but it contains only the second part of the Hooykaas text (i.e., it includes the animal tales but not the frame story).

9. Mardiwarsito and Kridalaksana (1984) is a description of the grammar of the section of the *Tantri Kamandaka* translated here. This work was used in seminars on the *Tantri Kamandaka* at the University of Michigan, in 1984–85, led by L. Mardiwarsito.

10. Bateson (1987) raises the question of why the hero, Aridharma, will lose his knowledge of the language of animals if he tells anybody that he understands it.

11. Drewes discusses the *Tantri Kamandaka* version of the Aridharma tale only

briefly and in passing, since it relates only the initial episodes of the longer fable he is concerned with. He does not discuss the framing of the tale, the topic of the present study. Nevertheless, it must be emphasized that the careful primary philology of van der Tuuk, Hooykaas, Mardiwarsito, and Drewes is what makes secondary interpretive philology possible. The present essay is only a long footnote on their work.

12. The Jataka and *Arabian Nights* versions of the fable are given in appendixes 2 and 3. Note that the framing and evaluation of the fable are completely different in these versions.

13. Ortega (1959:1). It is worth including the entire passage from which this quotation is taken, since it frames his axioms for a new philology, given in note 2, above, and is the theoretical basis for this essay.

> To read, to read a book, is, like all other really human occupations, a utopian task. I call "utopian" every action whose initial intention cannot be fulfilled in the development of its activity and which has to be satisfied with approximations essentially contradictory to the purpose which had started it. Thus "to read" begins by signifying the project of understanding a text fully. Now this is impossible. It is only possible with a great effort to extract a more or less important portion of what the text has tried to say, communicate, make known; but there will always remain an "illegible" residue. It is, on the other hand, probable that, while we are making this effort, we may read, at the same time, into the text; that is, we may understand things which the author has not "meant" to say, and, nevertheless, he has "said" them; he has presented them to us involuntarily—even more, against his professed purpose. This twofold condition of speech, so strange and antithetical, appears in two principles of my "Axioms for a New Philology," which are as follows: "(1) Every utterance is deficient—it says less than it wishes to say; (2) Every utterance is exuberant—it conveys more than it plans."

14. Pigeaud (1967–70, 1:69). One might dwell on Pigeaud's statement as a rich example of cross-cultural appropriation, since it isn't only the word *read* that is exuberant here.

15. I am indebted to Alan Trachtenberg and his studies of photography for stimulating discussions of frames. I am paraphrasing here some of his observations in a conversation we had about the acts of framing and "reading" frames.

16. The brief essay from which this passage is taken, "Literature as Equipment for Living," gives us the term *strategy* as it is used below. Ortega's term for *strategy* in *Man and People* is *usage*.

17. Much of the Sanskrit in the *Tantri Kamandaka* is deviant from the standardized versions found in Sternbach (1963, 1969, 1974). I am grateful to

Thomas Hunter and Madhav Deshpande for guidance in the study of the
Sanskrit sources of the *subhasitas*.

18. These are discussed in Hooykaas (1956) and Sternbach (1963, 1969, 1974).

19. In Zoetmulder and Robson's *Old Javanese–English Dictionary* (1982), on
    page 783, the word *kamandaka* is glossed as 'work on the science of govern-
    ment and politics, named after Kamandaki, the Indian author of a
    Nitisastra'. Hooykaas (1959) gives further uses of the word *kamandaka* in
    modern Javanese, where it comes to mean 'fabricated' and, as a verb, 'to
    disguise, fabricate, or mislead'.

20. See Thompson (1946:83) and Thompson and Roberts (1960:93) for a fuller
    list of cognate tales. These references were provided by A. K. Ramanujan.

21. For a comparison of the plot of *wayang* with musical and calendric plots,
    see A. Becker (1979:211–43) and J. Becker (1979:197–210).

22. For insightful work on the study of literature in context, see Burke (1964)
    and Ortega (1957, chaps. 9, 10).

23. On this notion of transparency, see M. Polanyi and Prosch (1975), particu-
    larly chapter 4, "From Perception to Metaphor." A similar idea appears in
    the chapter "Appropriation" in Ricoeur (1981).

24. *Evaluation* in this sense first appears in Labov (1967). The term is devel-
    oped and qualified in L. Polanyi (1985). As Polanyi points out, evaluation
    is often negotiated: a single evaluation is not inherent in a story.

25. Again, the reference is to the work of M. Polanyi and Prosch (1975) and
    Ricoeur (1981).

26. See Errington's translation of one of his greatest works (1989).

27. I am paraphrasing here from James G. Frazer (1888). See also Guss (1985)
    for insights by Frazer and many others on this intriguing topic.

28. Quoted from the *Sang Hyang Kamahāyānikan*. See Kats (1910, sec. 47, 48).
    The translation is by Hadiwijono (1967:42–43). The last sentence of the
    passage quoted here reads in Old Javanese *Nihan lwir ning aksara pina-
    kantara nikang carira-prasadatattwa.*

29. Hadiwijono (1967:42–43). I am not sure what he finds obscure in this
    rather widespread tantric abduction.

30. Dasgupta (1974:60–61). I am grateful to Judith Becker for instruction in
    tantric Buddhism and for these sources, and to Alan Feinstein for his
    unpublished translation of and commentary on the *Serat Kridhaksara,*
    "which tells of the unfolding of the Javanese letters, when they were still
    part of the human body, of their creation by Bathara Panyarikan and their
    recreation by Prabu Widdhayaka, and so forth."

31. In Old Javanese this passage reads:

    > Ikang wwang tan wruh ring warga nikang çāstra mwang çabda-
    > paçabda, umara madya ning sabhā mahyun mangucap-ucap kalawan
    > sang mahāpuruṣa ikang wang mangkana niyatanya n pada lawan

ikang wwang mareng alas mahyun sumikepeng gajah alas ri se-
dengnya matta mamawa besan ing tunjung sahele kangkena pangikatanya. (Hooykaas 1931:12)

The standard Sanskrit version is:

çabdaçāstram anādhītya yah pumān
vaktum icchati vacaḥ sabhāntare
bandhum icchati vane madotkaṭam
kunjaram kamalatantunā hi saḥ.
(Böhtlingk 1870, no. 6401)

For a detailed comparison of the Sanskrit and the Old Javanese translation, see A. Becker and Hunter (1982). See pages 89–108 in this volume.

32. As Rao (1916:6) states, "some of these saivacharyas became rajagurus or
the preceptors of kings, and appear to have wielded such great influence
and power that they have sometimes set aside even the royal command-
ments and acted on their own authority." The *Tantri Kamandaka* might
well have been a basic text for Saivacharyas who would advise rulers.
Tantri, the ideal preceptor of kings, had studied "sarwa castra mwang
ring sarwa tantra tattwagama, tattwa-jnana. Nguni n pamutus ning sarwa
tattwa tasak sira ring sarwopadeca mwang hasta-kocala. Matangnya n
dyah Tantri kaprakacitanira nama nira ring rat." That is, Tantri had studied in "all written texts and in all tantras of true knowledge. In addition to
completing the study of all philosophy, she had thoroughly mastered the
arts of teaching and music. And so the name of the young maiden Tantri
was widely known in the world." See Hooykaas (1931:26) for the Old
Javanese text.

33. Wittgenstein (1958, para. 114).

APPENDIX 1

KAWI TEXT OF THE ARIDHARMA STORY AND FOLLOWING
EPISODES
(FROM HOOYKAAS'S *TANTRI KAMANDAKA* [1931:192–
204])

Ana sira ratu mahārājâridharmâbhiṣekanira prabhu, ri tadanantāra
mara sireng alas mabuburu sira. Amanggih ta sira nāginī-kanyā
duryaça, malaki ring ula dĕlĕs. Umulat pwa ya sira: "Uḍuh salah çīla

arah, nāginī-kanyā kapwa kita, malaki pwa yeng ula dĕlĕs. Yeku
warṇa-sanghāra ngaranya, tan yogya ika çīlanya, mangkanaa. Tan
kawaçâku niṣṭhuraa, apan aku ratwa ning prajā; mapa kalinganya?
Wiparīta ika!" Ling Mahārāja; pinatyan ikang ula dĕlĕs; ikang nāginī-
kanyā pinupuh de sang nātha.

Mulih ikang nāginī-kanyā saçoka, mawarah ring bapanya sang
Nāga-Rāja, saha tangis denya mojar. Matakwan sang Nāga-Rāja:
"Mapa ikang pinangisakĕn, anaku?"—Awuwus ikang nāginī-kanyā:
"Ana sira ratu Mahārājâridharma ngaranya, wanacara maburu-buru.
Tinonira juga pwa ngulun rahayu, sinomahira ta ngulun tan angga.
Mamakṣakĕn juga sira, sawet ning hyunira. Binuru ngulun sinakitan,
pinupuh juga. Mangkana panangis ning tanyanta."—"Ndah jugâ-
naku pangĕr kita sakarĕng, aku mĕjahana sang ratu Aridharma
pahenakĕn jugâmbĕktânaku." Tan masowe lunga sang Nāga-Rāja.

Umareng kaḍatwan Çri Aridharma, mĕnggĕp arūpa brāhmaṇa
tumameng dalĕm pura. Mulaya nāga-rāja muwah pinahalitnya awak-
nira, masĕnĕtan ring sor ing palangka. Kunang sang Ratu sĕḍĕng-
nira pagugulingan lawan kasihnira dewī Māyāwatī ngaranira. Uman-
gĕn-angĕn umĕnĕng ta sira; mojar dewī Māyāwatī, lingnira: "E
Mahārāja, dingaryan pwa Aji tan kadi sosowen."—Sumahur sang
Nāthâridharma ri swāmīnira: "Ana nāginī-kanyā, katemw ing alas
de mami, nguni mamy aburu-buru. Salah ulah pwa ya: malaki ring
ula dĕlĕs; tan yogya ika çīlanya. Kadyangga nikang brāhmaṇī malaki
açūdra-janma, apan ika gawe wiparīta ring bhūmi, warṇa-sanghāra
ngaranya. Muwah kenakanya malakya sang brāhmaṇa juga. Mangkana ta sang nāginī, tan salah kramaa, yan tan nāga-rāja-putra. Ika
ta malaki ula dĕlĕs, tan yogya ika. Matangnya n ngwang mĕjahi ula
dĕlĕs; kunang ikang nāginī-kanyā, pinupuh ni ngulun." Mangkana
ling sang Nāthâridharma.

Marĕngĕ ta sang Nāga-rāja, mangĕn-angĕn pwa yeng atinya:
"Anaku kita karih lukan denya salah çīlanya, juti dahat ikang nāginī;
mahādibya paramârtha kapwa sang Nāthâridharma. Tuhu-tuhu yan
mamawa rat; wĕnang sira umilangakĕna kalĕngka ning jagat, ikang
ala çīlanya." Mangkana ling nikang nāga-rāja ri atinya. Mijil pwa ya
sakeng sor ning palangka, waluy arūpa brāhmaṇa muwah.

Sinwāgata de Mahārājâridharma, sumahur sādhu wāk: "Sangu-

lun bapa ning nāginī, ikang pinalu nguni de Sang Nātha denya
duṣtanyâmběknya. Wěnang Sang Nātha mamīḍanaha, yan ana dur-
wyasananya. Malampah anugraha ta Sang Nātha sakahyun Çrī Mahārāja."—Sumahur Sang Nātha, lingnira: "Mahyun wruha mami çabda
ning satwa kabeh, pangartyan ika."—"Rahayu ling Sang Nātha, lah
aywa sangçaya, Çri Mahārāja, kunang samaya ni ngulun. Tar wěnang
yan weraha ing lyan, Aji; joh tasmāt matya kita, lan mawaraheng
lyan."—Mamastwani sang Nāga-Rāja; lunga ta ya mulih ing pātāla.
       Kari Mahārājâridharma, magugulingan sira ring dina-kāla, lawan
kasih-nira Dewī Māyāwatī. Umulat iking cěcěk ri ruhur Sang Nāthâ-
guling, kunang lingnya: "Duh antyanta kapengin mami ruměngě
pañumbara Sang Nātha ri patnīnira; tan kadi tuwuhku, tinambang tan
kinasihan tuwi tan tinunggal. Ah ah Sang Ratu Aridharma saphala
sihta." Mangkanârtinya çabda ning cěcěk.
       Umulat Sang Nātha, těhěr gumuyu sira, miděm sirâpacěh. Mo-
jar dewīnira: "Sang Nātha, uḍuh tan anggěh amběk ni ngulun
mulat. Taha mapa tikang ginuyu de Sang Nātha?"—"Taha dewī, ya
ta sukha guywan juga ngulun," mangkana ling sang Prabhu, "ana
ndatan warahakěna ika."—Mojar Dewī Māyāwatī: "Ngulun juga
mahyun wruha."—"Aywa dewī, matya rakwa ngwang yan umaraha
iri kita."—Sumahur dewīnira: "Sâjñā Aji, ngulun juga misan pějaha,
yan tanpawarah Sang Prabhu ri kalinganya."—"Taha, Dewī, kita yan
warahěnkwa, pagawayakěn tunwan tumangan, rumuhun, lah koněn
taṇḍa rakryan, makāryaa kang tumangan, panggungan, mwang la-
rung, gopura, witāna biddhanāga, pakarmanya, cara-cara pahayun."
       Tělas ika kinārya; mapuṇya-dāna Sang Prabhu Aridharma, ring
sang brāhmaṇa, sang rěsi, mwang çiwa-boddha, asing mūlya ring
kaḍaton, rājayogya, mas, maṇi, rajata, wastrâdi mwang artha—ya ta
sinungakěnira.
       Sěḍěng dumilah ujjwala urubnya Hyang Agni, munggah ta sirâ-
tuntunan lawan Dewī Māyāwatī; sěḍěngnira aneng ruhur lantaran
kapwa sira kalih—ana ta wěḍus lakîstrī, mětu sakeng sukět. Si
Wiwitā ngaran kang wadon, Si Banggali kang lanang. Ya ta mareng
tunga ning tunwan; mojar si Wiwitā ri lakinya: "E bapanyânaku, pan-
galapakěna ngulun wawar ing tunwan; mahyun panganěn mami,
manginakanya pangiḍam mami. Ndan ika kahyun mami, aywân-

ginak-inak!"—Mojar lakinya, lingnya: "Uḍuh, tan wruh ing wiṣṭi
kapwa kita, tan tonĕn ta kang rumakṣa, kumuliling ring tunwan, saha
sañjatanya lwirnya, tuhuk kaṇḍaga mwang tumbak. Paranta tĕma-
hanta?"—Mojar si Wiwitā: "Lah tan sihta gane kiteng aku; lah pĕjaha
pisan aku, yan tan katĕkana kahyun mami."—Sumahur ikang lanang: "Lah mara ngke pwa kita pĕjaha; mapa ta kalaran aku iri kita?
Bwat tan kadi sang Ratu Aridharma ngulun, koluyan dening wuwus
ning strīnira. Wis tan ahyun pwâku yan mangkanaa, apan tan
mangkana sang mahāpuruṣa ngaranira, wĕnang masih wĕnang tan
masih. Nistanyâku satwa, tan mahyun yan mangkanaa, kunang
kahyunta, milwa angkwa ri kita." Nahan wuwusnya si Banggali,
manguman-uman i rabinya.

Kunang wuwusnya kalih ikang wĕḍus, ya ta rinĕngwakĕn de
Mahārājâridharma; udhāni sira wĕkasan. Lingnireng ati: "Antyanta
sādhu wuwusnya ikang wĕḍus. Ya ta kari pāpa, yukti dahat ika;
mapan tuhu dudu, wuwus ning strīnya," rumaseng twasira. "Satwa
jātinya, ndatan gya kapitut eng strīnya. Ngulun iky apan Ratu; yan
ahyuna kasorana dening strīnya, syapa ya sumirangery aku? Ikang
Wiwitā satwâdhamā, tan anggga kawiçwāsa ning strī." Mangkanân-
gĕn-angĕn Mahārājâridharma.

Moga ta sira tumurun sakeng tumangan, mantuk mareng kaḍat-
wanira. Mamintuhu ta sira ri wuwus ning meṣa si Banggali, wande
sirâlabĕh agni. Kunang sakweh nikang drĕwya pinuṇyakĕnira nguni,
lwirnya sadhana, bhūṣaṇa mwang upakāra, ya ta prasiddha pinaka-
prayaçcitta pinariçuddha Mahārājâridharma dening sang mahādwija
çiwa boddha mwang rĕsi paṇḍita samudaya. Ya ta mangun swasthā
Çri Mahārājâridharma, nguniweh pagĕh ning swanagara. Kunang
Dewī Māyāwatī lastari tumĕḍun ing agni, prihawak sira; kunang
ikang wĕḍus wadwan tumut yâlabuh agni.

Tinon de bhagawān Basubhāga, magawe çloka:

uttama-madhya-kaniṣṭham kottamam wacano bhawet
tasya mahatagrastawa wākyam samadya wijayet.

kalinganya: Ujar ing kaniṣṭha-madhya-uttama, asing yogya yukti ika
iḍĕpĕn; ikang tan yukti tilarakĕna, kadyangga ning wuwus ning

mesa—kathamapi iniḍĕp de Mahārājâridharma. Matangnya n yukti wuwus ni ngulun.

Mangkana wuwus nikang Sambaddha çrĕgala saha çloka:

"nakhinām ca nadīnām ca çṛngginām çastrapāninām
viçvāso naiva kartavyaḥ strīṣu rājakuleṣu ca

kalinganya: Rakwa warah-warah sang paṇḍita, ikang tan wĕnang rowangan ing sangsara, wwang duṣṭa, satwâlaṇḍĕp sungunya, malaṇḍĕp kukunya matwas, strīnira sang ratu, anambĕbĕng ing awan, warga sang Ratu, tan yogya ika makasangsargaa."

"Mangkana ling sang Paṇḍita.—Pāduka Ra Sangulun kapwa wiçeṣa ri sang Nandaka; sungunya magĕng alungid kadi khadgatulya, sākṣāt pangalap urip, pati umĕntak kita."

Nahan ling nikang Sambaddha çrĕgala, mangadu-adu; mamintuhu ta sang Singa-rāja. Wĕkasan lumakwa pwa ya mareng sang Nandaka, dinulur denikang patih Sambaddha çrĕgala saha wadwanya. Kabeh masĕ ta mareng sang Bherawa, sadā masinga-nāda, mangakakĕn tiking wulatnya. Kunang sang Nandaka tan matakut dening wuwus nikang Sambaddheng uni. Wijawijah ta ya sang Nandaka mangambusan maningat lĕmah, angra tuṣṭâmbĕknya, umulat pwa ya sang singa Çrī Caṇḍapinggala; walingnya: "Ih ya makira-kira urip tumandang ta sang singa Caṇḍapinggala." Mangdĕmak ring sang Nandaka, tan salah sahutnya, puṇḍak sang Nandaka. Kagyat ta sang Nandaka, siningatakĕn ta sungunya, makoleran usus sang Singa-rajā, pinakasampĕt de sang Nandaka, kadi sawitnya. Pĕjah pwa ya kalih sang singa lawan sang Nandaka, mapulang pwa ya, ikang singa mulih in Wiṣṇubhawana, ikang Nandaka mulih ing Çiwa-pada.

Tinon de bhagawān Basubhāga, magawe çloka:

niccotyesapateduhkam niccohutpāpatemrĕtyu
paramwatāwikasyanti tasmat nicca wisarjayet

kalinganya: Nīca buddhi pinakamārganyâmanggih pāpa; nīca sangka ning mamanggih bhaya mwang pati. Matangya n deya sang sādhu-jana kabeh, sang mahyun ing sukhawāhya, aywa juga masangsara lawan ikang nīcabuddhi. Tan yogya mitranya, apan caṇḍa-bherawa buddhinya. Ikang duṣṭa wiṣâmběknya, sopadi kang ayu; yan siniwo-siwo bwat manggarut, nguniweh panahutnya. Matangnya n sang sādhu-jana, ayo tanpamilih ika mitra. Darçana ika pějah sang Nan-daka kalawan sang Caṇḍapinggala. Pějah pwa sira kalih, piniçunā dening Sambaddha çrěgala mapuhara.

Mināngsa wangkenya sang Nandaka, mwang sang singa, dening patih Sambaddha çrěgala, denyâmāngsa mawarěg-warěgan. Mawa-sana pějah kawěkarěn si Sambaddha çrěgala, těkeng wadwanya sama pějah kawěkarěn dening lobhanya. Kunang ātmanya Sambaddha, mulih maring Wālukârṇawa Tāmbragohmukha, pinakaitip ing kawah ring Yamanīloka, denyâmukti pañcagati-sangsāra. Amilang wulunyâ-waknya lawasnya, mangěmasi pāpa, sapuluh tahun ing wulunya tunggal-tunggal. Samangkana denyâmukti pātaka, sama kalawan sang Pāpaka. Mangkana kapangguh ing tan yukti ring jagat pinakaelik ning bhūmi, apan dalurung denyâweh larâmběk, nityâkire duḥkha satata.

ITI CAṆḌAPINGGALA SAMĀPTA,
TANTRI-CARITA, TANTRA-WĀKYA.

NOTE

As noted above, the text is taken from Hooykaas (1931:192–204). Footnotes and variant readings have been omitted, and only the corrected versions of the *subhasita* have been given. It is important to note that the punctuation is almost entirely exuberant (that is, it has no counterpart in the original texts), including the capitalization and paragraphing. Two original punctuation marks give way in this roman transliteration to twelve marks: capitalization, period, comma, semicolon, colon, question mark, exclamation mark, quota-tion marks, dash, hyphen, paragraph indentation, and word separation. The original marks correspond to none of these twelve in function. This is an example of exuberancy and deficiency in the medium itself. I am grateful to Stuart Robson for providing me with one of the original Kawi versions from which Hooykaas worked, codex 4533 in the Leiden collection.

APPENDIX 2

KHARAPUTTA-JATAKA (NO. 386)
(QUOTED FROM COWELL [1973:174–77])

"Goats are stupid," etc.—The Master told this tale in Jetavana, concerning temptation of a Brother by his former wife. When the Brother confessed that he was longing for the world, the Master said, "Brother, this woman does you harm: formerly also you came into the fire through her and were saved from death by sages," so he told an old tale.

Once upon a time when a king named Senaka was reigning in Benares, the Bodhisatta was Sakka. The king Senaka was friendly with a certain naga-king. This naga-king, they say, left the naga-world and ranged the earth seeking food. The village boys seeing him said, "This is a snake," and struck him with clods and other things. The king, going to amuse himself in his garden, saw them, and being told they were beating a snake, said, "Don't let them beat him, drive them away"; and this was done. So the naga-king got his life, and when he went back to the naga-world, he took many jewels, and coming at midnight to the king's bedchamber he gave them to him, saying, "I got my life through you": so he made friendship with the king and came again and again to see him. He appointed one of his naga girls, insatiate in pleasures, to be near the king and protect him: and he gave the king a charm, saying, "If ever you do not see her, repeat this charm." One day the king went to the garden with the naga girl and was amusing himself in the lotus-tank. The naga girl seeing a water-snake quitted her human shape and made love with him. The king not seeing the girl said, "Where is she gone?" and repeated the spell: Then he saw her in her misconduct and struck her with a piece of bamboo. She went in anger to the naga-world and when she was asked, "Why are you come?" she said, "Your friend struck me on the back because I did not do his bidding," shewing the mark of the blow. The naga-king, not knowing the truth, called four naga youths and sent them with orders to enter Senaka's bed cham-

ber and destroy him like chaff by the breath of their nostrils. They
entered the chamber at the royal bed-time. As they came in, the king
was saying to the queen: "Lady, do you know where the naga girl has
gone?" "King, I do not." "Today when we were bathing in the tank,
she quitted her shape and misconducted herself with a water-snake: I
said, 'Don't do that,' and struck her with a piece of bamboo to give
her a lesson: and now I fear she may have gone to the naga-world and
told some lie to my friend, destroying his good-will to me." The
young nagas hearing this turned back at once to the naga-world and
told their king. He being moved went instantly to the king's chamber,
told him all and was forgiven: then he said, "In this way I make
amends," and gave the king a charm giving knowledge of all sounds:
"This, O king, is a priceless spell: if you give anyone this spell you will
at once enter the fire and die." The king said, "It is well," and accepted it. From that time he understood the voice even of ants. One
day he was sitting on the dais eating solid food with honey and
molasses: a drop of honey, a drop of molasses, and a morsel of cake
fell on the ground. An ant seeing this comes crying, "The king's
honey-jar is broken on the dais, his molasses-cart and cake-cart are
upset; come and eat honey and molasses and cake." The king hearing
the cry laughed. The queen being near him thought, "What has the
king seen that he laughs?" When the king had eaten his solid food
and bathed and sat down cross-legged, a fly said to his wife, "Come,
lady, let us enjoy love." She said, "Excuse me for a little, husband:
they will soon be bringing perfumes to the king; as he perfumes
himself some powder will fall at his feet: I will stay there and become
fragrant, then we will enjoy ourselves lying on the king's back." The
king hearing the voice laughed again. The queen thought again,
"What has he seen that he laughs?" Again when the king was eating
his supper, a lump of rice fell on the ground. The ants cried, "A
wagon of rice has broken in the king's palace, and there is none to eat
it." The king hearing this laughed again. The queen took a golden
spoon and helping him reflected, "Is it at the sight of me that the king
laughs?" She went to the bed chamber with the king and at bed-time
she asked, "Why do you laugh, O king?" He said, "What have you to

do with why I laugh?" but being asked again and again he told her. Then she said, "Give me your spell of knowledge." He said, "It cannot be given": but though repulsed she pressed him again.

The king said, "If I give you this spell, I shall die." "Even though you die, give it me." The king, being in the power of womankind, saying, "It is well," consented and went to the park in a chariot, saying, "I shall enter the fire after giving away this spell." At that moment, Sakka, king of gods, looked down on the earth and seeing this case said, "This foolish king, knowing that he will enter the fire through womankind, is on his way; I will give him his life": so he took Suja, daughter of the Asuras, and went to Benares. He became a he-goat and made her a she-goat, and resolving that the people should not see them, he stood before the king's chariot. The king and the Sindh asses yoked in the chariot saw him, but nobody else saw him. For the sake of starting talk he was as if making love with the she-goat. One of the Sindh asses yoked in the chariot seeing him said, "Friend goat, we have heard before, but not seen, that goats are stupid and shameless: but you are doing, with all of us looking on, this thing that should be done in secret and in a private place, and are not ashamed: what we have heard before agrees with this that we see": and so he spoke the first stanza:

> 'Goats are stupid,' says the wise man,
>   and the words are surely true:
> This one knows not he's parading
>   what in secret he should do.

The goat hearing him spoke two stanzas:

> O, sir donkey, think and realize
>   your own stupidity,
> You're tied with ropes, your jaw is wrenched,
>   and very downcast is your eye.

> When you're loosed, you don't escape, Sir,
>   that's a stupid habit too:

And that Senaka you carry,
    he's more stupid still than you.

The king understood the talk of both animals, and hearing it he quickly sent away the chariot. The ass, hearing the goat's talk, spoke the fourth stanza:

Well, Sir king of goats,
    you fully know my great stupidity:
But how Senaka is stupid,
    prithee do explain to me.

The goat explaining this spoke the fifth stanza:

He who his own special treasure
    on his wife will throw away,
Cannot keep her faithful ever
    and his life he must betray.

The king hearing his words said, "King of goats, *you* will surely act for my advantage: tell me now what is right for to do." Then the goat said, "King to all animals no one is dearer than self: it is not good to destroy oneself and abandon the honour one has gained for the sake of anything that is dear": so he spake the sixth stanza:

A king, like thee, may have conceived desire
    And yet renounced it if his life's the cost:
Life is the chief thing: what can man seek higher?
    If life's secured, desires need ne'er be crossed.

So the Bodhisatta exhorted the king. The king, delighted, asked, "King of goats, whence come you?" "I am Sakka, O king, come to save you from death out of pity for you." "King of gods, I promised to give her the charm: what am I to do now?" "There is no need for the ruin of both of you: you say, 'It is the way of the craft,' and have her beaten with some blows: by this means she will not get it." The king

said, "It is well," and agreed. The Bodhisatta after exhortation to the
king went to Sakka's heaven. The king went to the garden, had the
queen summoned and then said, "Lady, will you have the charm?"
"Yes, lord." "Then go through the usual custom." "What custom?" "A
hundred stripes on the back, but you must not make a sound." She
consented through greed for the charm. The king made his slaves
take whips and beat her on both sides. She endured two or three
stripes and then cried, "I don't want the charm." The king said, "You
would have killed me to get the charm," and so flogging the skin off
her back he sent her away. After that she could not bear to talk of it
again.

❖   ❖   ❖

*At the end of the lesson the Master declared the Truths, and identified the
Birth:—at the end of the Truths, the Brother was established in the First
Path:—"At that time the king was the discontented brother, the queen his
former wife, the steed Sariputta, and Sakka was myself."*

APPENDIX 3

A TALE FROM THE *ARABIAN NIGHTS*

This tale includes a bit of the frame story, which is in many ways
parallel to the *Tantri Kamandaka*. It is reprinted from the *Arabian Nights'
Entertainments*, edited by George F. Townesend (New York: Frederick
A. Stokes, 1891), pages 9–13.

❖   ❖   ❖

The implicit obedience which good Mussulmen owe to the com-
mander of the Faithful, had as yet restrained the inhabitants of
Bagdad from rebellion, nor had they taken any measure to preserve
their children from so new a calamity [the sultan's taking a new bride
each night and having her killed in the morning]; when the beauteous

and accomplished Scheherazade, daughter of the grand vizier, undertook to deliver them from it, by becoming the destined bride. Her father was astonished when she declared her design. He used every argument and entreaty to persuade her from it; and agreeably to the custom of the East, he endeavored to enforce his reasoning by the following apologue.

The Ox, the Ass, and the Farmer

There lived in a certain country a very wealthy farmer whose lands were cultivated with the greatest care, and abounded with all sorts of cattle and poultry. It so happened that he had an opportunity to render essential service to a very powerful genie; who, in return, at the farmer's request, endowed him with the faculty of understanding the language of all animals; but on this express condition, that he should never interpret it to any one, on pain of death.

Some time after this event, the farmer was walking leisurely in his yard, when he heard the following conversation between an ox and an ass: "Sprightly," said the ox, "how much do I envy your condition! you have no labor, except now and then to carry our master little journies; in return for which you are well fed with the best corn, carefully cleaned, and lodged in fresh straw every night; while I, who work from daylight till dark, and am urged by the blows of the plowman to toil almost beyond my strength, when my hard task is performed, am scantily supplied with coarse food, and pass the night on the common."

"Those," replied the ass, "who call you a foolish beast, are not much mistaken. Why do you not with all that strength, exert a little courage, and resist such ill treatment? If they give you bad corn, smell at it and leave it! and when they are about to fasten you to the plough, bellow aloud, stamp with your foot, and even strike them with your horns. Be assured a little resolution will soon procure you better treatment."

The farmer having heard this conversation, was not long in coming to a resolution. The next morning the laborer found the ox restive, when he attempted to yoke him; on which, by his master's orders, he left him, and putting the collar on the ass, he fixed him to the plough, and with many blows compelled him to perform the work the ox should have done. Nor was this all; for when he returned at night, more dead than alive, he found no straw to lie on; and instead of a plentiful supply of the best oats, there was nothing in his manger but a handful of coarse beans, ill-cleansed, which even his extreme hunger could scarcely prevail with him to eat.

The ox, who had rested the whole day, and been fed with the provender usually given to his companion, received him on his return with many compliments, and avowals of obligation. To these ceremonies the ass had no relish; without answering a word he threw himself on the ground, and, in thought, began to upbraid his own folly: "Was ever such imprudence as mine?" said he within himself; "how has a silly officiousness undone me? what had I to wish for that I did not enjoy? when did sorrow ever approach me? All this happiness I have deservedly lost, by meddling with that which did not concern me."

The grand vizier applied the obvious moral to Scheherazade. But finding she persisted, he became angry. "If you will continue thus obstinate," said he, "you will oblige me to treat you in the same manner the farmer did his wife in the sequel of the story."

The farmer hearing that the ass was in bad plight, was curious to know what would pass between him and the ox. Accordingly, after supper, he took a walk with his wife into the yard, when he heard the sufferer say to his companion: "Comrade, what do you intend to do tomorrow, when the laborer brings your meat?" "Do! my best friend," replied the ox, "why, I will carefully attend to your instructions; if my corn is not of the very best quality, I will not deign to touch it; and if he presumes to lay a halter on me, I will not fail to knock him down."

"I fancy," replied the ass, "you will think it prudent to alter that resolution, when I relate to you what I heard our master say to the laborer just now." The ass having thus excited the attention and fear of the ox, told him very gravely, that the farmer had ordered his servant, if the ox continued restive, to knock him on the head the day following, and distribute his flesh among the poor.

The ox, alarmed at this story, bellowed aloud for fear, and vowed submission to the laborer, which resolution the ass was forward to commend.

The farmer was so pleased with the cunning of the ass, and the terrors of the ox, that he burst into an immoderate fit of laughter. His wife, who saw no reason for this extraordinary mirth, was curious to know the cause of it. He tried to evade her question; but the more he sought to divert her attention, the more earnest she became in her inquiry; at length, tired with her importunity, he told her that the cause of his laughing must continue a secret: "You will not, I suppose," added he, "urge me any further, when I acquaint you that my revealing it would certainly cost me my life."

The assertion, which she affected not to believe, made the wife redouble her importunities; the farmer, however, continued resolute, and suffered her to pass the night in tears without much concern. But when he found next day that the same obstinate desire of the fatal information continued, he was exceedingly distressed. He called in the assistance of his neighbors and relations, who in vain represented to her the unreasonableness of her request. She persisted, and the unhappy farmer was on the point of gratifying her, at the expense of his life, when an incident determined him to alter his intention.

Going out of his door, he heard his faithful dog relating with concern the story of his embarrassment to a cock, who heard it with much contempt: "A pretty fellow, truly," replied the cock, "is this master of ours, who cannot manage one wife, when I govern fifty! Let him take a good crabstick, and use it properly, I will engage she will soon dismiss her impertinent curiosity." The honest farmer took the hint; his wife returned to her duty; and you, my daughter, if treated in the same manner, would no doubt be as conformable to my desires, and forego so desperate an experiment.

Notwithstanding this and every other method taken to shake her determination, Scheherazade continued unmoved; and the grand vizier was obliged to announce to his sovereign the ambition of his daughter. . . .

REFERENCES

Bateson, Gregory, and Mary Catherine Bateson. *Angels Fear: Towards an Episte-mology of the Sacred.* New York: Macmillan, 1987.

Becker, A. L. "Text-Building, Epistemology, and Aesthetics in Javanese Shadow Theatre." In *The Imagination of Reality,* ed. A. L. Becker and A. Yengoyan. Norwood, N.J.: Ablex, 1979.

Becker, A. L. "Literacy and Cultural Change: Some Experiences." In *Literacy for Life,* ed. Richard W. Bailey and Robin Melanie Fosheim. New York: Modern Language Association, 1983.

Becker, A. L. "Biography of a Sentence: A Burmese Proverb." In *Text, Play, and Story: The Construction and Reconstruction of Self and Society,* ed. Edward Bruner. Washington, D.C.: American Ethnological Society, 1984.

Becker, A. L., and Thomas Hunter. "Binding Wild Words: Cohesion in Old Javanese Prose." In *Pelangi Bahasa,* ed. Harimurti Kridalaksana and Anton M. Moeliono. Jakarta: Penerbit Bhratara Karya Aksara, 1982.

Becker, Judith. "Time and Tune in Java." In *The Imagination of Reality,* ed. A. L. Becker and A. Yengoyan. Norwood, N.J.: Ablex, 1979.

Böhtlingk, Otto. *Indische Sprüche.* St. Petersburg: Commissionaire der Kaiserlichen Akademie der Wissenschaten, 1870.

Burke, Kenneth. "Literature as Equipment for Living." In *Perspectives by Incongruity.* Bloomington: Indiana University Press, 1964.

Cowell, E. B., ed. *The Jatakas (or Stories of the Buddha's Former Births),* vol. 3. London: Pali Text Society, 1973.

Dasgupta, Shashi Bhushan. *An Introduction to Tantric Buddhism.* Calcutta: University of Calcutta, 1974.

Drewes, Gerardus W. J. *The Romance of King Angling Darma in Javanese Literature.* Bibliotheca Indonisica, no. 11. The Hague: Martinus Nijhoff, 1975.

Errington, J. Joseph. "To Know Oneself the Troubled Times: Ronggawarsita's *Serat Kala Tidha,*" in *Writing on the Tongue,* ed. A. L. Becker, 95–138. Ann Arbor: Center for South and Southeast Asian Studies, University of Michigan, 1989.

Frazer, James G. "The Language of Animals." *Archaeological Review* 1, no. 2 (1888).

Guss, David M. *The Language of the Birds.* San Francisco: North Point Press, 1985.

Hadiwijono, Harun. *Man in the Present Javanese Mysticism.* Bern: Bosch and Keuning, 1967.

Heidegger, Martin. *Holzwege.* Frankfurt: Klostermann, 1950.

Heidegger, Martin. *On the Way to Language,* trans. Peter D. Hertz. San Francisco: Harper and Row, 1971.

Hooykaas, C. *Tantri Kamandaka*. Bibliotheca Javanica, no. 2. Bandung: A. C. Nix, 1931.

Hooykaas, C. "Kamandakiya Nitisara etc. in Old-Javanese." *Journal of the Greater India Society* 15, no. 1 (1956).

Kats, J. *Sang Hyang Kamahāyānikan*. The Hague: 1910.

Labov, William, and Joshua Waletzky. "Narrative Analysis: Oral Versions of Personal Experience." In *Essays on the Verbal and Visual Arts*, ed. June Helm. Seattle: The University of Washington Press, 1967.

Mardiwarsito, L. *Tantri Kamandaka*. Ende-Flores: Nusa Indah, 1983.

Mardiwarsito, L., and Harimurti Kridalaksana. *Struktur Bahasa Jawa Kuno*. Ende-Flores: Nusa Indah, 1984.

Ortega y Gasset, José. *Man and People*, trans. Willard R. Trask. New York: W. W. Norton, 1957.

Ortega y Gasset, José. "The Difficulty of Reading." *Diogenes* 28 (Winter 1959).

Ortega y Gasset, José. *Meditations on Quixote*, trans. Evelyn Rugg and Diego Marin. New York: W. W. Norton, 1961.

Pigeaud, Theodore G. T. *Literature of Java*. 3 vols. The Hague: Martinus Nijhoff, 1967–70.

Polanyi, Livia. *Telling the American Story: A Structural and Cultural Analysis of Conversational Story Telling*. Norwood, N.J.: Ablex, 1985.

Polanyi, Michael, and Harry Prosch. *Meaning*. Chicago: University of Chicago Press, 1975.

Rao, Gopinatha T. A. *Elements of Hindu Iconography*. Madras: Law Printing House, 1916.

Ricoeur, Paul. "Appropriation." In *Hermeneutics and the Human Sciences*. New York: Cambridge University Press, 1981.

Sternbach, Ludwik. *Canakya-Raja-Niti*. Adyar-Madras: Adyar Library and Research Centre, 1963.

Sternbach, Ludwik. *The Spreading of Canakya's Aphorisms Over "Greater India."* Calcutta: Calcutta Oriental Book Agency, 1969.

Sternbach, Ludwik. *Subhasita, Gnomic, and Didactic Literature*. Weisbaden: Otto Harrassowitz, 1974.

Thompson, Stith. *The Folktale*. New York: Holt, Rinehart and Winston, 1946.

Thompson, Stith, and Warren E. Roberts. *The Types of Indic Oral Tales*. Helsinki: Academia Scientiarum Fennica, 1960.

Wittgenstein, Ludwig. *Philosophical Investigations*. New York: Macmillan, 1958.

Zoetmulder, P. J. *Kalangwan: A Survey of Old Javanese Literature*. The Hague: Martinus Nijhoff, 1974.

Zoetmulder, P. J., and S. O. Robson. *Old Javanese–English Dictionary*. The Hague: Martinus Nijhoff, 1982.

Zurbuchen, Mary Sabina. *The Language of Balinese Shadow Theater*. Princeton: Princeton University Press, 1987.

PART 2
SOME BURMESE FIGURES

Biography of a Sentence:
A Burmese Proverb

When I left Burma in 1961, after three years of daily study with Saya U San Htwe, I mentioned to him that I would be lost without him as a teacher. A few days later he presented me with a small, handwritten notebook full of what I took to be proverbs, arranged by number—in sets of two's, three's, four's, etc. He told me that I would find them useful.

This essay explores one of them, until in the end it does prove itself useful in describing its own analysis.

Here the notion of prior text is in the foreground—the way we take old pieces of languaging from memory and reshape them into new contexts. Everything we say has a past, and its meaning depends on that past. Equally, everything we say has a future into which we push it. All languaging is what in Java is called jarwa dhosok, *taking old language (*jarwa*) and pushing (*dhosok*) it into new contexts. This seems to me to be one of the most important things I learned in Southeast Asia.*

❖   ❖   ❖

Three Kinds of Mistakes

There are three kinds of mistakes: those resulting from lack of
memory, from lack of planning ahead, or from misguided beliefs.
> —Burmese proverb

I call this essay "Biography of a Sentence" in order to evoke Wittgenstein's way of thinking about language as a form of life, a mode of being in the world, and so to depart from an atomistic picture of language and meaning and to move toward a contextual one. In using language one shapes old words into new contexts—*jarwa dhosok*, the Javanese call it, pushing old language into the present. All language use is, in this sense, translation to some degree; and translation from one language to another is only the extreme case. I argue here that translation for the philologist—one who would guide us across the terra incognita between distant languages—is not the final goal but only a first step, a necessary first step, in understanding a distant text; necessary because it opens up for us the exuberances and deficiencies of our own interpretations and so helps us see what kinds of self-correction must be made. And so the goal of this essay is to begin with a Burmese proverb, a simple sentence, a minimal text, and to move step by step from a translation (provided by a bilingual Burmese) closer to the original. Each step is a correction of an exuberance or a deficiency of meaning as presented to us in the English translation.

In moving from an atomistic mode of interpretation to a more contextual one, new kinds of questions appear just as old ones lose their force. One asks not how some phenomenon is built up in a rule-governed way out of minimal bits but rather in what ways context constrains particular language—real text (i.e., remembered or preserved language). There are many ways to answer that question, depending on how one defines context. One way to see context is as sources of constraints on text. Linguists and language philosophers could agree on five or six sources of constraints, although they would group and name them differently, I suspect. Let me for present purposes identify these six kinds of contextual relations, none of which seems to me to be reducible to another.

1. *Structural relations*, relations of parts to wholes
2. *Generic relations*, relations of text to prior text
3. *Medial relations*, relations of text to medium
4. *Interpersonal relations*, relations of text to participants in a text-act
5. *Referential relations*, relations of a text to nature, the world one believes to lie beyond language
6. *Silential relations*, relations of a text to the unsaid and the unsayable

There is nothing particularly original about these six, and there has been a great deal of work on each, except perhaps the last one. Together they define context. A text is the interaction of the constraints they provide.

The terms have one great weakness: they are all too categorial—too "nouny," too liberally neutral. As Kenneth Burke might say, their "improvisational" quality is weak. The life of a text is in the weighting and balancing and counterbalancing of the terms and figures and in the conceptual dramas they evoke. To transcend these neutral terms, one can make them active—as a text strategy—and say that a text has meaning because it is structuring and remembering and sounding and interacting and referring and not doing something else . . . all at once. The interaction of these *acts* is the basic drama of every sentence.

The sentence—simple or complex—is, in any language, the minimal unit in which all these actions are happening, in which the drama is fully staged. Only with sentences—and larger units—are there speakers and hearers and times and worlds; that is, particular speakers, particular hearers, particular times, and particular worlds. Paul Ricoeur (1981) calls sentences the "minimal units of discourse," the "minimal units of exchange." Jan Mukarovsky (1977:15) wrote of the sentence as "the component mediating between the language and the theme, the lowest dynamic (realized in time) semantic unit, a miniature model of the entire semantic structuring of the discourse."

Words and phrases are *staged* only as sentences. Much of our language about sentences overlaps with our language about drama, an iconicity we share with many other languages. That is, in both there are actors or agents, goals, undergoers, instruments, accompaniments, times, and settings—all bound into an act or state, or just plain *being*, and all shaped to a context in subtle ways. To see the drama of a sentence requires only a bit of contemplation: stepping back (as a friend puts it) to take a closer look. To hide that drama with neutral terms—what Burke (1964) calls "bureaucratizing" knowledge—is to lose the essential liveliness and excitement of that contemplation. And it is to miss the considerable aesthetic pleasure one gets in contemplating a text and seeing the drama of terms and figures unfold, a good deal of it at the level of sentences.

Not all sentences are whole texts in themselves. Most are parts of larger texts. Yet there are sentences free enough of lingual context to be treated as texts. Proverbs, perhaps, which are not really self-sufficient texts but rather small texts used to evaluate (give value to) new situations. They are recurrent evaluatory statements, part of whose job is to sound like proverbs, language in the public domain. Proverbs are a mode of sounding, referring, interacting, remembering, and shaping small enough to be discussable in an essay (a ratio of 1 sentence of text to 320 sentences of commentary, in this case). In larger texts, one is forced to sample.

Contemplating single sentences or very small texts brings one into the world of the grammarian, the world of delicate parsing. It thus brings one up against a very large, wildly ill-defined, grammatical terminology: all the names for the categories, processes, and relations that grammarians talk about, often very intimidatingly. One can get the feeling that from grammar school to graduate school the prime use of grammar has been some variety of intimidation.

However, the *pleasures of the text* (one of the phrases Roland Barthes left us) are too important not to encourage people to enter as amateurs and to experience the whole of the journey to a distant text. There is a skill in parsing that a good linguist can be led to display on small persuasion, but it should be only inspiring to the amateur not intimidating—like Billie Holiday's singing.

There are two basic ways to think about grammar (as a prelude to the contemplation of a small text). One view leads us to think of the field of study as a system of rules that somehow maps abstract and a priori semantic categories and relations onto phonic substance—or in different terms, map a logical deep structure onto a surface structure. Language in this structural sense is "rule governed," and the task of the grammarian is to find the most economical, least "subjective" formulation of the rules. Theory is exclusively formal. In this view the computer is a natural metaphor for the language-processing mind. Grammars—or tiny fragments of unfinished grammars—tend to be written as rules accompanied by examples, illustrating problems of theory shaping (Geertz 1983:19).

There is another kind of grammar, based on a different perspective on language, one involving time and memory; or, in terms of contextual relations, a set of prior texts that one accumulates throughout one's lifetime, from simple social exchanges to long, semimemorized recitations. One learns these texts in action, by repetitions and corrections, starting with the simplest utterances of a baby. One learns to reshape these texts to new context, by imitation and by trial and error. One learns to interact with more and more people, in a greater and greater variety of environments. The different ways one shapes a prior text to a new environment make up the grammar of a language. Grammar is context-shaping (Bateson 1979:17) and context shaping is a skill we acquire over a lifetime. We learn it essentially by continual internal and external corrections, in response to change and lack of change in the environment. From the first point of view, constraints common to all languages tend to be structural (or logical); from the second, pragmatic (or rhetorical). What I call philology might also be called a rhetorically based linguistics.

The ways one shapes a text to new contexts include such operations as substitution of words or other larger or smaller lingual units, rearrangements, repetition, expansion, inflexion, and embedding. These are all things one can do with a word or a sentence or a larger text, all general strategies, which one learns to do more and more skillfully and which become (potentially) more and more complex. The problem with stating them all as rules is that the constraints on shaping are not entirely structural; and they are not a closed system but open to context. We are not so much compositors of sentences from bits as reshapers of prior texts (the self-evident a prioris of language). The modes of reshaping are in large part conventional but also in some unpredictable part innovative and unpredictable— except for the most formulaic of utterances. Language interaction is not a closed system (i.e., rule-governed).

Even very formulaic utterances have interesting histories. The strange imperative greeting that has blossomed (along with the three-piece smiling face) in the currency of noetic exchange over the past few years in American English has been, "Have a nice day." The reader is invited to notice how many different shapings of that formula he or she encounters over the next few days. This morning, in a good New Jersey accent, I got, "Have one, y'hear," from an exuberant gas station attendant. "I will," I answered, not knowing what I was saying. In all language, there are prior norms and present deviations going on constantly.

Proverbs tend to be slower changing than nonproverbs, since they are public language and not private language and depend on recognition as proverbs in order to work. But there are a whole range of things we recognize as proverbs—not just wise, comfortable ones but also banal clichés and even original evaluations not yet fully in the public domain. Here are a few.

> He who hesitates is lost.
>
> Well, it takes all kinds. . . .
>
> Sometimes a man just has to stand up for his rights.
>
> We're all in it for the money.
>
> He leaped before he looked.

Here are some not yet in the public domain, perhaps never to be.

> Progress: that long steep path which leads to me. (Jean-Paul Sartre)
>
> Contextual shaping is only another term for grammar. (Gregory Bateson)
>
> Art and the equipment to grasp it are made in the same shop. (Clifford Geertz)
>
> Do not be overwhelmed by all that there is to know. It is a myth of the oppressor. (Kenneth Koch)

Public evaluatory sentences are of many sorts. One need only look through the *Oxford Dictionary of Proverbs* to see the great variety in even so small a sample. But the goal here is not to provide a classification scheme for proverbs (as Burke [1964:108] writes in his short essay on proverbs, "The range of possible academic classifications is endless"—a good and useful candidate for the public domain). They are sometimes "generic" sentences, in two senses: they are often marked by indefinite subjects and indefinite tense and thus meant to refer to a large class of phenomena; but they are also generic in the sense that they are quite overtly drawn from the past and help to identify a present text as belonging to a *genre*, a set of prior texts. They are meant to stand apart. Their power comes from one's recognition of them as shared public opinion, and one is not supposed to argue with them in situations that call for politeness. They are part of the credit of society on which one lives.

As prevailing opinions, public opinions are uttered differently than private opinions are. They need no support, since they do not depend on the adherence of individuals and are not presented as hypotheses to be proved. They are there, to be reckoned with, as authoritative as law. We sometimes think of public opinion as a collection of private opinions (polls operate on this fallacy) rather than as a collection of evaluatory statements, there in the language— like proverbs—on which we are free to draw (Ortega 1957:266). This collection is not identical for each of us and like much of language is broader in recognition than in use. The closer we are to people, in a communal sense, the more we share evaluations—and the less we seem willing to tolerate evaluatory differences.

There is a continuum of evaluatory utterances from those, like proverbs, that we share exactly (i.e., with identical wording) to those that we recognize as having some family resemblance with our own evaluatory stock sufficient to be accepted as equivalent or nearly so. For example, "He who hesitates is lost" is always said in just those words—even when referring to women. Here, context shaping is minimal, a matter only of one's voice, its qualities, pitches, and rhythms. By contrast, the cynical observation "We're all in it for the money" is less frozen and more likely to be reshaped—softened or strengthened—each time it is used.

These small texts—proverbs, semiproverbs, and clichés—are a form of speaking the past. But uttering them—even with all the controls over rhythm, pitch, and voice quality that music can provide—is also to some extent speaking the present. They evoke a norm and to some degree, however small, deviate from it.

Utterances with a family resemblance to, for instance, the cliché "We're all in it for the money" include those utterances that can be seen to have a connection with it via substitution, rearrangement, repetition, expansion, inflexion, and/or embedding. As a figure, the cliché sets up points of substitution.

> We are all in it for the money.
>
> They were partly in it for the money.
>
> He was in it because of his interest.

The sentence is a frame for the substitution of words, affixes, phrases, and whole clauses—all the levels of lingual units.

Besides substitution, context shaping can involve rearrangement and the consequent readjustments, which contribute much of the complexity to syntax (Givón 1979:235 ff.):

> It's the money that we're all in it for.
>
> Money is what we're all in it for.

Or expansion:

> We're all—you, me, and everyone—in it right now for the money we can get out of it.

Or repetition:

> We're all in it for the money . . . for the money.

Or inflexion:

> He's in it for the money.

Or the whole can be embedded:

> I don't believe that we're all in it for the money.
>
> Our all being in it for the money disturbs me.

(One can reduce these modes of context shaping by considering inflexion a structural type of substitution and by considering repetition and some embedding as types of expansion.) Mostly one uses combinations of these strategies to shape prior text into new contexts—and to recognize someone else's shaping.

The important thing here is not whether one can describe all the shapings that are possible, singly and in combination, and all the remedial strategies that they entail, in some formalism, but rather where family resemblance fades in the reshaping that keeps lingual strategies alive. Most people—our cousins and aunts—are not often aware of the extent to which one constantly reshapes old language into new contexts. The process is rapid, and only if there is a breakdown do we normally become conscious of it—when something doesn't *sound* right (under analysis, as Wittgenstein [1958] put it, language is on holiday).

The difference between looking at grammar as rules that map logical categories and relations onto a medium and looking at it as ways of reshaping old language to new contexts is, primarily, that in the first case one begins with a priori or "universal" categories as being common to all languages, while in the second case what is common are pragmatic or rhetorical situations—common features of the context—and what is a priori is prior text. To assume a universal logic seems to be to take very abstract representations of the categories and relations of Indo-European languages as inherent in all languages (see Benveniste 1971). One learns, of course, to confront all new experience in one's own language, including experience of another language. It is not difficult to assume that these categories and relations are "there" *in* the phenomena, a priori to language. However, it seems more conducive to cross-cultural understanding that one not assume an abstract realm of absolute categories and relations—some kind of extralingual logic—as a ground for all languages, but rather start in language, with actual remembered texts (however they are preserved). Recall Wittgenstein's (1958:114) caution: "One thinks that one is tracing the outline of the thing's nature over and over again, and one is merely tracing round the frame through which we look at it."

The meaning of a word, then, is not a combination of atomic

categories and relations or underlying features or properties but the past and present contexts it evokes. Then how do grammars and dictionaries of distant languages work? They work as abductions: one language in terms of another. A grammar of Burmese in English is an English version of certain aspects of Burmese—that is, those having English analogs. A Burmese grammar of English does not yet exist, except as a translation into Burmese of an English grammar of English; but if it did, it would be a Burmese interpretation of English in which, for instance, the simplicity of our numeral classifiers and verb particles might be noted. Grammars and dictionaries are as much cultural artifacts as newspapers or shadow plays.

In understanding a distant text, even for the writer of the most formal of grammars, there is an essential first step—a gloss or rough word-for-word translation. It is always present and is always meant to be invisible, like the invisible man, dressed in black, in the Japanese Noh drama, who moves props, adjusts costumes, and generally keeps things tidy on stage. The gloss, rather than the abstract representations of categories, features, and relations, is the underlying vehicle for understanding. The only mode that we have of understanding a distant text is first to jump to an interpretation, to guess (or have someone guess for us), and then to sort out the exuberances and deficiencies of one's guess. One's own language is the initial model for another language, a metaphor of it (Pike and Pike 1977:69).

A philologist does well to be always self-conscious that his understanding of another language is initially metaphoric and not "pure" meaning. To do otherwise is to add to the exuberancy of thinking of logical categories as reified "things," the further exuberancy of assuming that they are the categories of one's own language. It is at this point that grammatical explanation becomes political: when we assume that there is one grammar for the Greek and the Barbarian—and it is Greek. To ask, for instance, what the passive is in Burmese is to assume (1) that "the passive" exists a priori to any language, and (2) that "it" has an English name or an English function in shaping context, whatever one calls it. To translate some Burmese clause as an English passive, however, is both necessary and reasonable.

A methodology for parsing should be a lightly held thing, as one

confronts the distant text with it. When methodology and text conflict, it is the methodology that should give way first. In this sense,
one's discipline is the text. Methodologies come and go, but the discipline of the text and its language remain. Perhaps a particular experience can illuminate this point.

On arriving in Burma in 1958, I began to learn Burmese from a
very kind and patient old teacher, U San Htwe. As I had been taught
to do, I would ask him words for things and then write them down.
He watched me writing for a while and then said, "That's not how
you write it," and he wrote the word in Burmese script. For the word
evoked by English "speak," I wrote /PYɔ/ and he wrote ေြၣ. I
insisted it made no difference. He insisted it did and told me I was
hurting his language. And so I began, somewhat reluctantly, to learn
to write Burmese: /p——/ was a central ဎ, and /-y-/ wrapped around
the ဎ to make ၣ and the vowel /ɛ——ɔ/ fit before and after it:
ေြၣ.

This difference in medial representation made a great difference
on at least two levels. For one thing, I could not segment the Burmese
syllable into a linear sequence, as I could /PYɔ/, as one can see clearly
by studying the two representations. But segmentation into linear
sequence is a prerequisite for doing linguistics as most of us have
been taught it: normally, sounds string together to make morphemes
and words, and words string together to make phrases, and so on. We
analyze strings, with analog phenomena relegated to super- or sub-
segmental status. To write my kind of grammar I had to violate his
writing.

At first it seemed to me a small price to pay, to phonemicize his
language. But over the years—particularly twenty years later, in Java
and Bali—I learned how that kind of written figure (a center and
marks above, below, before, and after it; the figure of the Burmese
and Javanese and Balinese syllable) was for many Southeast Asians a
mnemonic frame: everything in the encyclopedic repertoire of terms
was ordered that way: directions (the compass rose), diseases, gods,
colors, social roles, foods—everything (see Zurbuchen 1981:75 ff.). It
was the natural shape of remembered knowledge, a basic icon.

As Zurbuchen (1981) has shown us, this notion of the syllable is

the ground even of the gods: it is evoked at the beginning of every
Balinese shadow play. Even though the shadow play is taught and
performed orally, it begins with an invocation of the written symbol as
a source of power.

> Just as the boundaries of awareness become perceptible,
> There is perfect tranquility, undisturbed by any threat,
> And even the utterances of the gods subside.
> It is none other which forms the beginning of my obeisance to
>   the Divine.
> Greatly may I be forgiven for my intention to call forth a story.
> And where dwells the story?
> There is a god unsupported by the divine mother earth,
> Unsheltered by the sky,
> Unilluminated by the sun, moon, stars, or constellations.
> Yes, Lord, you dwell in the void, and are situated thus:
> You reside in a golden jewel,
> Regaled on a golden palanquin,
> Umbrellaed by a floating lotus.
> There approached in audience by all the gods of the cardinal
>   directions. . . .
>
> [1981:vi]

These last lines, after locating the written symbol outside of time and
space, describe metaphorically the shaping of the written symbol as a
focal point for natural order. Zurbuchen's (1981:vi–vii) translation continues, describing the implements of writing.

> There, there are the young palm leaves, the one *lontar*,
> Which, when taken and split apart, carefully measured are the
>   lengths and widths.
> It is this which is brought to life with *hasta, gangga, uwira, tanu*.
> And what are the things so named?
> *Hasta* means "hand"
> *Gangga* means "water"
> *Uwira* means "writing instrument"

Taru means "ink."
What is that which is called "ink"?
That is the name for
And none other than
The smoke of the oil lamp,
Collected on the bark of the kepuh-tree,
On a base of copper leaf.
It is these things which are gathered together
And given shape on leaf.
"Written symbol" is its name,
Of one substance and different soundings. . . .

The translation, which I have taken the liberty of arranging in lines (mainly to slow down the reader), goes on slowly to evolve the story from the written symbol.

My point, however, is not to explore this image further, or to retell Mary Zurbuchen's fascinating stories, but to try to understand why U San Htwe had insisted on my learning Burmese this way. I think it was that the traditional learning was organized around that shape, that it was a root metaphor (see Lakoff and Johnson 1980), the stuff that holds learning together—just as our sequential writing lines up so well with our sequential tense system or our notions of causality and history. That is a great deal to ask anyone to give up—the metaphoric power of his writing system. And I had tried to argue with that wise old man that it did not matter.

One of the most subtle forces of colonialism, ancient or modern, is the undermining of not just the substance but the framework of someone's learning. As Gregory Bateson put it, in his oft-quoted letter to the other regents of the University of California, "Break the pattern which connects the items of learning and you necessarily destroy all quality." I see now that what I had been suggesting to my teacher, though neither of us could articulate it, was that we break the pattern that connects the items of his learning. When methodology and language conflict, it is the methodology that should give way first.

The proverb that serves as an epigraph to this essay comes from a small book my teacher gave to me just before I left Burma in 1961, after studying with him for three years and mostly reading Burmese classics, after I had grasped a bit of the language. I read with a great deal of what Keats called "negative capability": Keats spoke of Shakespeare as one who was "capable of being in uncertainties, mysteries, doubts, without any irritable reaching after fact and reason" (quoted in Dewey 1934:33). I read with half-understanding the children's histories, poems, plays, chronicles, and *jataka* tales he brought me, and heard with half-understanding his commentaries and corrections of me. I taught English to children in the morning—funny, uninhibited Burmese children—and studied Burmese in the late afternoon, at twilight, at U San Htwe's house. Just before I left, he gave me a small notebook, a child's copybook with a picture of a mountain on the front, in which he had copied lists of sets: the two thises, five thats, and fifteen whatevers. I had asked him how I might continue studying Burmese without him and this book was his solution and gift. I stared at it for years, and with the help of a Burmese friend, U Thein Swe, began to understand some of it, much later.

In the book, written in U San Htwe's fine hand, are all classes of things, abstract as well as concrete, in this world and out of it—a syllabus for study. It begins with sets of twos and grows, as if paralleling the growing complexity of one's experience, to larger and larger sets. The initial sets are sometimes obvious, like the two parents and the two strengths (strength of arm and strength of heart), but are sometimes more exotic pairs like the two worlds (the zero world—in which Buddhas, monks, supernatural beings, and so on do not appear, exist, or flourish—and the nonzero world—in which the above appear, exist, and flourish). The sets in my book continue to sets of eighteen. (I learned later that other lists go on to bigger sets and that my teacher may have censored a bit.) To understand the sets, he said, is to understand the world, both inner and outer, seen and unseen. They represent, taken together, a taxonomy of the phenomenal and noumenal universe of at least some traditional Burmese.

Each set is itself a kind of plot from a universal plot book, around which to build a discourse. For example, a sermon can be built around, say, the four cardinal virtues (love, attention, happiness, detachment), or a political speech around those three kinds of mistakes mentioned in the epigraph (resulting from lack of memory, from lack of planning ahead, or from misguided beliefs). Or a play might be constructed around some other appropriate set, perhaps the four false hopes (hoping to get rich by reading treasure maps, hoping to get healthy by reading medical literature, hoping for wisdom by following a learned man, and hoping for a girlfriend by dressing up). These sets are assumed a priori to any discourse as impersonal frames to which nature, both human and nonhuman, properly and appropriately corresponds. A true sermon, a wise foreign policy, or a well-constructed drama can be rooted in one or more of them. One can contemplate these sets with continual fascination and increasing insight as one learns to see things in new ways. Like a good poem, a new set can defamiliarize one's world.

The proverb used as the epigraph to this paper appears in my copybook as in figure 9. U San Htwe copied this from a manuscript book that one of his teachers had given to him. Similar books were common in traditional Buddhist monastic education. They were learned first then gradually understood over the years, like most things in traditional Southeast Asian education. Memory preceded understanding, an order practiced by few in our culture other than classical pianists. The closer one gets to nonliteracy (and a chirographic culture is, in this sense, less literate than a print culture), the more a student seems to be expected to *perform* the past like a classical pianist. Language classes in traditional schools were not so much the acquiring of a neutral tool as a set of prior texts, serious cultural wisdom.

Neither had writing come to Burma, as it never does anywhere, as a neutral tool. It had come with content: a religion, a calendar, and a new set of cultural prior texts in Pali, the language of Buddhism. The new writing was, first of all, access to those Pali texts, the real sources of knowledge. Only gradually did the local language begin to be written in the new writing, at first only for translation. Later, this translation language—far from the language acts and strategies of everyday discourse (the vernacular)—began to be used for creating local texts and replacing individual memory. Very much later, some

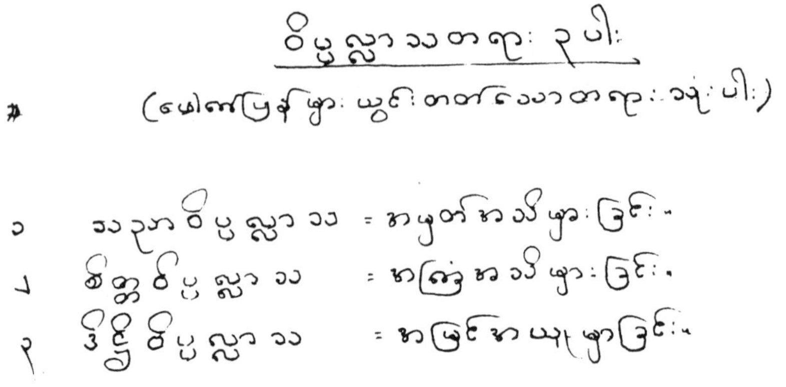

Fig. 9.   Proverb as it appears in U San Htwe's copybook

bold innovator began to write the vernacular. In a very general way, that is what happened throughout Southeast Asia under the noetic impact of Sanskritic languages.

And so this set about mistakes is not a proverb in our sense but rather Buddhist categories indicating natural laws of human nature, stated first in Pali and then in Burmese. Phrase-by-phrase translation of this sort is also common in Southeast Asia, and no doubt elsewhere, as a way of *performing* a translation. It has had profound effect on literary styles and performance techniques, where translating is a very common speech act (Okell 1965). These traditional styles make most foreigners feel that about half the words should be crossed out: we get impatient with that extra step of glossing so many words.

In order to parse the Burmese passage, we must first transliterate it, or else learn Burmese writing. Taking the former, faster course means both addition and loss of meaning: what is lost is the powerful iconicity of the image of the Burmese syllable, the visual gesture and pace of reading it and sounding it, and the aesthetic possibilities of the shaping and combining of syllables. Using a Burmese typewriter, even, is like decorating a Christmas tree: the central symbol is struck and the carriage does not automatically jump ahead but just sits there, while one adds things above, below, before, and after the central syllable. One focuses on syllables, not phonemes.

Figure 10 gives an interpretation (meant to be read slowly) of the

wippallāthą	ta ya:	thoñ:	pa:
error	law	3	classifier

(hpau'	pyañ	hma:	ywiñ:	ta'	thaw	ta yą	thoñ: pa:)
(perforate	return	error	misplace	do	connective law	3 classifier)

1. thą nya	wippallāthą	=	ą hma'	ą thi	hma:	hkyiñ:
perceive-mark	error		sign-mark	know-witness	error	doing

2. sitta	wippallāthą	=	ą kyañ	ą thi	hma:	hkyiñ:
mind-thought	error		plan	know-witness	error	doing

3. ḍiti	wippallāthą	=	ą myiñ	ą yu	hma:	hkyiñ:
opinion-doctrine	error		appearance	belief	error	doing

Fig. 10.   Transliteration and glossing of the proverb

Burmese text in Roman letters, a transliteration, with rough glosses in English, taken from dictionaries and bilingual Burmese friends. With this, let us go back to the original English translation (the epigraph of this paper) and remove from it all the exuberance we can by taking out everything that has no counterpart in the Burmese (in this passage):

three kind mistake

error memory   error plan   error belief

Everything else in the English is there because of the demands of English: existential frame ("There are. . . ."), tense, number, of, deictics, prepositions, connective. Nearly none of the things that give the English passage its cohesion by relating the parts to each other is left. What remains is that thin, sparse wordscape that characterizes "literal" translation. It might be argued further that only one of the English words comes reasonably close to the range of meaning of its Burmese counterpart: three (၃).

The cohesion of the Burmese passage comes from grammatical phenomena that we do not have in English or that we have but do not exploit in the way Burmese does. One deficiency, one of the things missing from the English, is *classification*. It occurs twice, once in the top line (*pa:*) and again in the parenthetical explanation in the second line. It is used in counting, but it also has several other grammatical-rhetorical functions in Burmese. It evokes a universe of discourse, that is, a particular perspective on the word classified (Becker 1975). It marks, by its special prominence, a discourse topic, and therefore shares some of the function of the English existential sentence ("There be . . ."). The classifier *pa:* is one of a paradigm of classifiers that mark the status of beings and some things associated with them. There are five categories, which might be conceptualized as a center and four concentric rings radiating from that center. In the center are Buddhas, relics, images, and the Buddhist Law. In the next ring, closest to the center, are the things classified as *pa::* deities, saints, monks, royalty, scriptures, and Pali terms. The word *pa:* itself is felt to be related to the term for 'close' by some Burmese friends, while others are skeptical about that etymology. In the next orbit are things associated with the head, metaphorically: people of status, teachers, and scholars. And next are ordinary humans, followed by an outer realm of animals, ghosts, dead bodies, depraved people, and children. A classifier is a locus on a conceptual map, not the name of a genus all members of which have some attribute. Animate beings are ordered according to their distance from Buddhahood: spiritual progression is a movement from animality to Buddhahood. The three mistakes as a set are Buddhist wisdom and so are closest to the center in this conceptual map.

Classifiers almost seem to add another level of reality to the world as seen through Burmese. We are accustomed to quantifiers, like two pounds of something or three yards of something else, but we do not regularly and obligatorily classify everyone and everything with the same unconscious thoroughness that, by contrast, we mark relative times in our tense-aspect system. Classifiers give special salience to terms as they are introduced, marking out the topics of a discourse. What linguists call *zero anaphora* (marking a discourse role as unchanged by *not* mentioning it) indicates the domain of a term in a Burmese discourse. My own Burmese was always very confusing because I kept overmentioning things, a particular form of exuberance to which English conditions us.

Most other terms a foreigner usually undermentions. These are the so-called elaborate expressions (Haas 1964:xvii–xviii; Matisoff 1973:81 ff.). Although words are almost all monosyllabic in Burmese (with the exception of foreign terms like *wippallātha* and the other Pali terms in the text), they are used in pairs. There are examples in lines 2 through 5.

1. *hpau' pyañ*   'perforate-return' meaning to 'fall-away' (as from a religion)
2. *hma: ywiñ:*   'error-misplace' meaning 'mistake'
3. *a hma' a thi*   'mark-know' meaning 'perceiving and remembering' (no English term of this scope)
4. *a kyañ a thi*   'intent-know' meaning 'planning ahead', 'intending'
5. *a myiñ a yu*   'appearance-belief' meaning 'belief' in a broad sense

There are no precise English equivalents for any of these pairs of terms, but via their Burkean dialectic they help us to imagine what they might mean. Like the classifiers, they tend to make phrases double-headed. Few foreigners manage this very well and so speak very *thin* Burmese, while we find them, as our name for this phenomenon suggests, elaborate.

The rhythm of good Burmese seems to demand these expressions, and rhythm is probably the most basic and powerful cohesive force in language. When two people speak comfortably to each other, they both join in the creation of a rhythm, marked by stresses, nods, grunts, gestures, and sentence rhythms. On the basis of this created rhythm they exchange words. If the conversation is not going well, the discomfort will be manifested in arhythmic responses and repairs, until they get rolling again. Speaking a language requires skill in those background rhythms, which are not the same in all languages. Our basic, elusive unease in speaking to foreigners is in large part inexplicable because it is often in large part rhythmic (Erickson and Shultz 1982; Scollon 1981). Here, the rhythmic elaborate expressions mark the parallelism of the three pairs of terms, perhaps also bringing the Burmese terms into balance with the heavier Pali terms.

Slowly, by a process of self-correction after a ventured glossing, the Burmese passage is emerging: the drama of the classifiers and the elaborate expressions. This slow emergence is the aesthetic of philology. It emerges in all the dimensions of meaning: as a structure, as a genre, as an exchange, as a sounding, and as a potential reference to (or evaluation of) an appropriate event.

If we look at the overall syntax of the text, we can clearly identify two strategies. One is the strategy of the title and its paraphrase, which might be interpreted as:

X	law	three	"close" things
X	taya:	*thoñ:*	*pa:*

Here the X represents the variable term, the difference between the first and second lines. This is a particular classifier strategy, to give it a name based on its final constituent. By comparing other sets in the little book, we might make a more general formula for classifier strategies, but that would be to move away from understanding how this strategy is shaped in this context. A strategy is not an abstract pattern but an actual bit of text, used as a point of departure, either across texts or in a single text. Here, the first line is a frame for the second, in which the Pali term is paraphrased in Burmese. To give the most generalized formulation of the strategy is to move too far from the text in separating formal meaning from the four other kinds of meaning. It is possible to do so, as a long period of structural analysis has proved, yet it is also a movement away from understanding.

The second strategy is what we might call (after the distinctive sign =) an equative strategy, and it might be interpreted as: NUMBER Y *wippallāthạ* = Z error-ing. This is the strategy of the final three lines. In this small text, a system has been established in which certain slots in a frame are varied, others kept unchanged (other entries in the little book almost all use variants of these strategies). These repeated strategies give *structural* coherence to the text and provide a ground for thematic coherence.

By looking at the relation of the three slots (X, Y, and Z), we find a further pattern. The fillers of X are modifiers of *taya* (law). In the first line the filler is the Pali term (Burmanized) *wippallātha*, and this term becomes part of the *frame* of the second strategy (i.e., the term that Y modifies). In the second line, the paraphrase, the filler of X is *"hpau' pyañ hma: ywiñ: tat thaw"* (a modifying clause: 'perforate-return error-misplace doing + connective term and clause particle'—a Burmese paraphrase of *wippallātha*, the Pali origins of which are discussed later in the paper). Part of this Burmese paraphrase (the word *hma:* 'error') is the key framing term in the second part of the equative strategy (i.e., the term that Z modifies). The two fillers of X are Pali and Burmese, respectively, while the fillers of Y and Z are also, respectively, Pali and Burmese. Furthermore, each filler of Y is structurally parallel, as is each filler of Z. And, one might add, the number *three* of the first two lines constrains the number of equative figures in the list. The structural figure might be represented as in figure 11.

As a structure, the text is very elegant. Each part is tightly bound into a very symmetrical overall pattern. At the lower levels of structure in this text are the varieties of relations of modifier terms to modified terms and the internal structure of the elaborate expressions:

a hma'	*a thį*	'mark know'
a kyañ	*a thį*	'plan know'
a myiñ	*a yu*	'appearance belief'

Here, the particle *a* marks a noun derived from a verb (Okell 1969:243). However, what phonological and semantic constraints there are on the order of these constituents is still unclear.

Probably, it takes a close parsing to make us aware how tightly structured this figure is. It is a structure used throughout the book U San Htwe gave me and hence quite appropriately called a frame for a certain kind of language—a coherence system, a language-game, an episteme.

The kind of knowledge that these frames "contain"—to use our English metaphor for the relation of knowledge to language (Lakoff and Johnson 1980:92)—or better, that these "frames" are the formal

X law three revered things
(X-law three revered things)
1 Y *wippallāthą* = Z error-ing
2 Y *wippallāthą* = Z error-ing
3 Y *wippallāthą* = Z error-ing

Fig. 11.   Structure of the rhetorical figure

meaning of—is for the most part originally in Pali and is being shaped into Burmese in these figures. There are two lingual interfaces here: from English back to Burmese, and from Burmese back to Pali. These can be seen as two sets of prior texts, although the relations are not that simple, if we consider, for instance, the curious use of the equal sign—the source of which in Burma may well have been English—or the intrusion of Burmese into the Pali words—where a Burmese writer's possible confusion over long and short vowels in Pali led to the "misspelling" of *wippallāthą* (only one *p* in Pali). Or, both these things may be U San Htwe's own deviations. One of the hardest things to know in reading a distant text is what is stereotypic and what is innovative.

The term *wippallāthą* is a Burmese interpretation of Pali *vipallasa* from Sanskrit *viparyasa*. Edward Conze (1957, 1962a, 1962b) translates it as 'perverted views'. The noun *viparyasa* is from a root *as*, which means, roughly, 'to throw'. The whole term is used for the 'overthrowing' of a wagon, or even, as a Sanskrit pundit told me, 'turning a pancake'. It has been translated as 'inversion', 'perverseness', 'wrong notion', 'error', 'what can be upset', or 'missearches'—that is, looking for permanence in the wrong places. I think it quite appropriate to call them 'mistakes of interpretation' and so underscore their special relevance for philologists. "The Scriptures," writes Conze (1957:314; 1962a:40), "identify the *viparyasas* with 'unwise attention' (*ayoniso manasikaro*)—the root of all unwholesome dharmas—and with ignorance, delusion, and false appearance." In another place, he writes, "The *viparyasa* are sometimes treated as psychological attitudes, sometimes as logical propositions, and sometimes even as an ontological condition" (1962b:39). When considered as features of the world they distort, the *viparyasas* are four in number; but when considered as *locations* in the mind, they are three.

samjna	(Pali-Burmese *thanya*)	= 'perception'
citta	(Pali-Burmese *sitta*)	= 'thought'
dṛṣṭi	(Pali-Burmese *diṭi*)	= 'theoretical opinions'

All of these mistakes of interpretation lead us to habitually act as if things were different from what they are. Perception (blending in Burmese with what we might call memory) is perverted when we forget that what we perceive is impermanent, ultimately unpleasant, and not us (not to be seen ego-fully). And so we meditate on the rise and fall of the thing, breaking it down into dharmas. Thought (blending in Burmese with planning) is perverted by our wishes and fears. Both fear and hope make us overstress the permanence of things, make us close our eyes to suffering and exaggerate the importance of our own existence. Belief is perverted when we formulate a theory that the world contains permanent objects, with permanent properties, or that good outweighs suffering, or that there is a self.

These are all empirical mistakes, summarized in the formula that these views lead one to seek "the Permanent in the impermanent, Ease in suffering, the Self in what is not the self." As Conze (1962a:41) writes,

> All this we can see quite clearly in our more lucid moments—though they be rather rare and infrequent. The techniques of Buddhist meditation aims at increasing their frequency, and innumerable devices have been designed with the one purpose of impressing the actual state of affairs on our all too reluctant minds.

Even yet there remains what Ricoeur has called a "surplus of meaning"—an open-endedness about what I first saw as a proverb (translated for me by a non-Buddhist Burmese) but later came to see as a translated bit of Buddhist philosophy. We have sampled each of the contextual sources of meaning—the interpersonal uses of public language, the metaphoric power of the medium, the kinds of references the proverb might be appropriate with, the tight symmetry of its structure, and the prior (and posterior) Buddhist texts it evokes. We have moved back from translation toward the original text, and beyond. The text was our discipline and the unfinished process has been one of self-correction: removing exuberances of interpretation, filling in deficiencies. The Burmese text eventually overtakes us, as a Buddhist injunction to philologists.

There are three kinds of perversions of interpretation, three kinds of mistakes of philology:

1. Perversions of perception, including memory = perversions of the past, of prior texts
2. Perversions of thought . . . forethought, planning, hopes and fears = perversions of the future
3. Perversions of appearances and beliefs = perversions of theory

ACKNOWLEDGMENTS

The author is grateful to Madhav Deshpande and Luis Gómez for help with the Pali terms; to Michael Aung Thwin and U Thein Swe for help with the Burmese; and to Clifford Geertz and others at the Institute for Advanced Study, Princeton, for many valuable suggestions when a version of this essay was presented there in March 1982. This paper is dedicated to Saya U San Htwe, my teacher in Taunggyi, Burma, 1958–61.

REFERENCES

Bateson, Gregory
   1979   Mind and Nature. New York: E. P. Dutton.
Becker, A. L.
   1975   A Linguistic Image of Nature: The Burmese Numerative Classifier System. International Journal of the Sociology of Language 5:109–21.

Benveniste, Emile
1971   Categories of Thought and Language. *In* Problems in General Linguistics. pp. 55–64. Coral Gables: University of Miami Press.
Burke, Kenneth
1964   Literature as Equipment for Living. *In* Perspectives by Incongruity. pp. 100–109. Bloomington: Indiana University Press.
Conze, Edward
1957   On "Perverted Views." East and West 7(4):313–18.
1962a   The Three Marks and the Perverted Views. *In* Buddhist Thought in India. pp. 34–46. London: George Allen & Unwin.
1962b   The Maháyána Treatment of the Viparyāsas. Orientemus Jk. 1:34–46.
Dewey, John
1934   Art as Experience. New York: G. P. Putnam's Sons.
Erickson, Frederick, and Jeffrey Shultz
1982   The Counselor as Gatekeeper: Social Action in Interviews. New York: Academic Press.
Geertz, Clifford
1983   Blurred Genres: The Refiguration of Social Thought. *In* Local Knowledge: Further Essays in Interpretive Anthropology. pp. 19–35. New York: Basic Books.
Givón, Talmy
1979   On Understanding Grammar. New York: Academic Press.
Haas, Mary R.
1964   Thai-English Student's Dictionary. Palo Alto: Stanford University Press.
Lakoff, George, and Mark Johnson
1980   Metaphors We Live By. Chicago: University of Chicago Press.
Matisoff, James A.
1973   The Grammar of Lahu. Berkeley: University of California Press.
Mukarovsky, Jan
1977   The Word and Verbal Art. New Haven: Yale University Press.
Okell, John
1965   Nissaya Burmese. *In* Indo-Pacific Linguistic Studies, G. B. Milner and Eugenie J. A. Henderson, eds. pp. 186–227. Amsterdam: North-Holland Publishing Company.
1969   A Reference Grammar of Colloquial Burmese. London: Oxford University Press.
Ortega y Gasset, José
1957   Man and People. New York: W. W. Norton & Company.
Pike, Kenneth L., and Evelyn G. Pike
1977   Grammatical Analysis. Arlington: Summer Institute of Linguistics and University of Texas.

Ricoeur, Paul
    1981   The Model of the Text: Meaningful Action Considered as a Text. *In* Hermeneutics and the Human Sciences, John B. Thompson, ed. and transl. pp. 197–221. Cambridge: Cambridge University Press.
Scollon, Ronald
    1981   The Rhythmic Integration of Ordinary Talk. *In* Georgetown University Round Table on Language and Linguistics, 1981. pp. 335–49. Washington, D.C.: Georgetown University Press.
Wittgenstein, Ludwig
    1958   Philosophical Investigations. New York: Macmillan.
Zurbuchen, Mary S.
    1981   The Shadow Theater of Bali: Explorations in Language and Text. Ph.D. dissertation. University of Michigan, Ann Arbor.

The Figure a Classifier Makes: Describing a Particular Burmese Classifier

There are two kinds of moves a linguist makes in studying a distant language, glossing and parsing. The latter has reached in modern linguistics a very high degree of sophistication, but the former, glossing, is still done in a way that suggests it is a simple preliminary to the more complex act of parsing. Word-by-word glossings are given to passages, and then, for all readers who do not already know the language under study, the rest of the discussion is carried out on the basis of the glossings. My argument is that a particular glossing, a deceptively simple form of translation, determines the parsing to a large degree. To gloss, say, a Burmese sentence into English is to anticipate an analysis using English categories. And then to go on to say, on the basis of that analysis, that "universals of language" had been demonstrated seemed to me highly suspect. I began to see the "universals" lurking in our procedures themselves. Wittgenstein put this succinctly in paragraph 114 of his Philosophical Investigations, *which he begins, as he frequently does, by quoting his former work and then arguing against it.*

> *114. (Tractatus Logico-Philosophicus, 4.5): "The general form of propositions is: This is how things are."—That is the kind of proposition that one repeats to oneself countless times. One thinks that one is tracing the outline of the thing's nature over and over again, and one is merely tracing round the frame through which we look at it.*

This kind of error is particularly evident, I think, in the description of distant languages. To counter it, not entirely but at least in part, requires putting translation in the foreground and using it, rather than parsing, as the key tool of philological study.

❖   ❖   ❖

> Incidentally, a classifier or repeater, because of its peculiar nature,
> can never be directly rendered into a language that has no such
> linguistic features.
>
> —U Hla Pe (1967:179)

This essay is about that "peculiar nature" Professor Hla Pe writes
about, and the problems of interpreting classifiers in English, "a language that has no such linguistic features." I would like to focus on
one particular classifier in a Burmese poem, on the assumption that
seeing a classifier in full context—seeing the ways it shapes and is
shaped by that context—can help the philologist correct the exuberances and deficiencies of his or her own understanding.

On Translation

One method for doing this is to begin with a translation and then
deconstruct the translation in such a way as to get closer to the Burmese original. A necessary first step in understanding a distant text
and the context it shapes is *glossing*, a kind of minimal translation in
which English words (and sometimes abbreviated category names,
like *art*[icle], *pa*[st], *def*[inite], or *f*[irst] *p*[erson]) are substituted for
Burmese forms. As necessary as this glossing may be, most of the
interpretive act of parsing is done in that first step. Given glossing, a
Burmese sentence can be parsed as a deviation from English and give
rise to a strong sense of universality.

   Any linguistic work on typology depends on other people's examples, approachable only via these minimal translations, often called
"literal" or "word-for-word" translations. There is a misplaced confidence here, a belief that these glossings and labelings are more objective, less interpretive, than a more complete translation. It is clear to
me that when we read a text in a foreign language via glosses and
labels we quite necessarily and unselfconsciously appropriate (i.e., fill
in by habit) much of the coherence and context that allows a "reading" of that text, be it only a single sentence. A simple example would
be assuming that tense is "understood" in a tenseless language, and

so avoid the fact that it just isn't there and that one must learn what it means to do without it.

A further kind of glossing is involved in the assumption that there is some sort of propositional counterpart of any sentence, a logical or "deep" representation of that sentence that is fully express-ible in some version of English. In a very subtle and politically power-ful way we thus appropriate distant language into English—taking from translations a sense of universality.

One thing a philologist can do is try to defamiliarize those texts, retracing glossing and labeling in order to discover what has been added in the translation and what has been left behind. In order to do this, one can only work with a particular text and sort out contextual relations one by one, searching for exuberances and deficiencies of interpretation. By contextual relations I mean the relations of any given text (oral or written, larger or smaller) to the intentionality of the people who shape and receive it, to the prior texts it evokes in their memories, to the natural world outside of language that it consti-tutes and presupposes, to the larger text it may be a part of, to the medium that forms it, and even to the kind of silence that frames it. All of these together shape the particularity of any bit of language one may study.

I would like in this essay not to generalize about classifiers—even classifiers in Burmese—but rather to particularize about them, start-ing with a translation and then trying to defamiliarize it, in the direc-tion of what K. L. Pike would call *emic* understanding.

A Burmese Poem

One of the best-known Burmese poems is a *linka* (from Pali *alamkara* 'ornamentation') thought to have been written in 1173 by a courtier named Anatathuriya shortly before he was executed by order of the new king. It is felt to exemplify a Buddhist attitude toward death, an "anger-allaying" *kabya* ('poem'), as my teacher, U San Htwe, explained to me. The anger to be allayed is not the poet's but the king's—a complex rhetorical situation (and a neat double bind for the king).

Here, in a passage translated from the *Glass Palace Chronicle*, by U Pe Maung Tin and Gordon Luce, with some changes by U Hla Pe, Anna Allott, and John Okell (1963:560–61), is the poem.

When one attains prosperity,
Another is sure to perish.
It is the law of nature.

Happiness of life as a king—
Having a golden palace to dwell in,
Court-life, with a host of ministers about one,
Enjoyment—shade—peace,
No break to felicity—
Last but a lifetime, is but a bubble mounting
    for a moment to the surface of the ocean.

Though he kill me not,
But in mercy and pity release me,
I shall not escape my karma.
Man's stark-seeming body
Lasteth not ever:
All living creatures are subject to
    inexorable decay.

Thy slave, I beg
But to bow down in homage and adore thee!
If in the wheel of samsara
My past deeds offer me vantage,
I seek not for vengeance.
Nay, master, mine awe of thee is too strong!

If I might, yet I would not touch thee;
I would let thee pass without scathe;
For the law of Impermanence lures the elements
    of my body.

Now when these four stanzas were read before
the king and he heard them, he commanded, stating
"Set him free." But the executioners spake
into his ear and said "The deed is done."

The English style here in many ways appropriates the poem by making it seem Victorian and hence, to us, cliché-ridden—so familiar that it evokes minimal wonder and delight, evokes no "defamiliarization" (Schlovsky's *ostranenie*). Without entering the dispute about the possibilities of translation, let's just say that there are two extremes, reflecting the demands of the two languages—totally familiar language and totally unfamiliar—and that this translation approaches the former in familiarizing Burmese.

Exuberances and Deficiencies of a Translation

I would like to look now only at the first few lines (where the classifier is), sorting out some of the exuberances and deficiencies of an English understanding, and seeing, too, something of the figure a classifier makes, a particular classifier.

The first rhetorical figure of the poem includes these lines.

When one attains prosperity
Another is sure to perish.
It is the law of nature.

An earlier translator rendered the passage this way.

Yes, he is one who, wealth attained,
Shall pass away and disappear:
    'Tis Nature's law.

This second translation is much more distant from the Burmese original than the one we are studying. It overlooks entirely the strategy of the classifier, evidenced by the translator's assumption that there was only one "he." We can compare each translation with the Burmese original, transliterated here into Roman letters (an exuberance that changes the meaning in basic ways that I have described elsewhere, in Becker 1983) and given here word-for-word glosses based on Judson's dictionary (1953 [1852]) and on explanations given me by U San Htwe, my teacher, in 1959. Here are the first lines of the poem.

thu ti: tə   yau'
3° only one human (classifier)

kaung: bǫ yau'   mu
good   to arrive perform

thu tə   yau' hma
3° one (clf) at/concerning

pye'   ling   ka   tha
destroyed imperative continuative   only
                prior   (balances mu)

dhammata ti:
dharma   only

There are many un-English phenomena here that are lost if we move too quickly to an English understanding, an appropriation (Ricoeur 1981:182). In the glosses above, the Burmese and English terms do not match very closely. Using Derrida's punctuation "under erasure," let us eliminate the English words in the first translation that are there only because of the demands of English and have no counterpart in the Burmese.

~~When~~ one attains prosperity,
Another ~~is sure~~ to perish.
~~It is the~~ law of nature.

These are some of the exuberances of English. The word translated as 'attain' (which is homophonous with the classifier translated so far as 'human') should probably be under erasure, too, since the Burmese word, *yau'*, means only to arrive or to reach something or some place, and does not carry the notion of 'a step up' or 'a desired goal' that seems a part of *attain*. Now let us reverse the process and put under erasure the Burmese words that do not appear in the English. These are *some* of the deficiencies of the translation.

~~*thu ti:*~~   *tə*   ~~*yau'*~~
3° only one (clf)

kaung: ~~bə~~ *yau'   mu*
good   to arrive perform/adversative/continuative

~~thu~~ *tə   ~~yau'~~ ~~hma~~*
3°   one (clf) at/concerning

pye'   ~~ling~~   ~~ka~~   ~~tha~~
destroyed imperative continuative   only
            prior   (balances *mu*)

dhammata ~~ti:~~
dharma   only

There is nothing very precise about this comparison nor is it really any test of the quality of a translation. It does, however, focus attention on some of the differences. Note that these differences involve mostly nonreferential terms that mark the relations of the words to each other, the attitude of the first person to the second and third persons in the language act, and the cohesion of the whole. Each difference is worth exploring: the compound predicates are especially interesting. Here, however, we will look only at the classifier (*yau'*), to see how it works.

A Classifier Figure

The classifier *yau'* appears first in the phrase,

thu ti: tə   yau'
3°   only one (clf)

and again in the third line,

thu tə   yau' hma
3°   one (clf) at/concerning

If one asks what rhetorical or pragmatic function this classifier figure fills, one would be hard pressed to answer, since apparently we do get on well without them, and hence there does not seem to be any

English necessity that is being met by them. They seem, rather, to add a dimension to the lingual landscape, evoked in the act of counting (and elsewhere)—as if to say that counting one kind of thing must be distinguished from counting another, perhaps at about the same grammatical depth at which we distinguish mass and count nouns, only far more elaborately articulated.

A classifier figure is prototypically tripartite, with three kinds of nouns in three slots.

| 1 | 2 | 3 |
| the classified | the numeral | the classifier |

Although the numeral (or, more generally, a quantifier) may be an important part of these figures, it may not be the most important part— as evidenced by the fact that normally unstressed variants of *one* and *two* occur there, and in many of the uses of these figures the numeral *one* alone may normally occur there, having lost most if not all of its quantifier force and functioning only to identify and bind the figure. I am thinking of phrases like the following, given in Hla Pe (1967).

> *sąni'   tə   kya*
> system one fit   (i.e., 'be systematic')
>
> *hma'   tə   mę*
> notice one lack (i.e., 'be unthinkable')

There are many others like these, in which the form is that of a classifier figure, but the function is not numerative.

In my judgment, the English figures most like Burmese classifier figures are some of those with *of*:

> a tale of destruction
>
> a book of stories
>
> two cans of peaches
>
> a gaggle of geese

a whale of a story

a peach of a girl

In these figures at least one of the nouns is usually referential—in "a tale of destruction" it seems to be the first noun, while in "a peach of a girl" it seems to be the second, as Verhaar points out (1979). In "two cans of peaches" both nouns seem equally referential, and so perhaps the list can be shaped into a cline. In all cases, however, the noun phrases are double headed: one term frames another, referentially or metaphorically. This process seems quite distinct from quantification.

Linguists have classified classifier figures primarily in terms of paradigmatics rather than syntax. That is, we more often look at the kinds of nouns that go into the slots rather than the types of relations between them. Classification as a mode of metaphor, for instance, is rarely described. An exception is Hla Pe, who writes (in an interesting, Burmese-flavored English):

> because of their natural tendency to bestow a certain imagery on a conceptual object, something sacred or having a shape or characteristics usually associated with concrete objects, the poets begin to bring in the classifier to fit their imagery. In one of these poems, the five causes of a woman's insolent behavior to her husband are given as maŋ—'ŋa—'gwiŋ 'insolence-five-ring'. (Hla Pe 1967:185)

If poets did it, one can bet the people did, too. There is a metaphoric open-endedness to the system. Hla Pe continues,

> Up to the downfall of the Burmese monarchy in 1886, as already stated, poetry which played no small part in the dissemination of Buddhism played a major part in the lives of Burmese scholars, and they in turn perpetuated in their various works many of these expressions, that have been adhered to by the mass from generation to generation, until these expressions became conventionalized by the end of the 19th century!

These conventionalized classifications Professor Hla Pe refers to are the books of "established sets of forms" (*thu-te-thana thayouk-pya abhiddan*) of which there are many versions. I have described some of these elsewhere (Becker 1975, 1984). The point here is that the grammatical figure of classification can be seen, as Hla Pe sees it, as corresponding to a rhetorical strategy—a strategy in which one builds plots and policies around the "three this's, eight that's, and fifteen whatever's," as one rather disrespectful foreigner always referred to them. As but one sample, from a collection my teacher, U San Htwe, gave me in 1961, let me give (in English) the four disappointments.

> hoping to get rich by reading treasure maps
>
> hoping to get healthy by reading medical literature
>
> hoping for wisdom by following a learned man
>
> hoping for a girlfriend by dressing up

The Semantic Field of the Classifier

But let us return to the more prosaic figure from the poem, having seen some of the more elaborate uses of this grammatico-rhetorical figure.

> *thu ti: tə   yau'*
> 3°   only one (clf)

Setting aside *ti:* for a moment (and the syntactic pressure it creates), let us look at the prototypical fillers of the three slots: (1) classified, (2) numeral, and (3) classifier. James Matisoff (1973), in one of the finest and most detailed descriptions of classifiers in a single language (Lahu, the classifier system of which closely resembles Burmese), writes about several important kinds of classifiers—the fillers of slot 3. He lists seven kinds.

> 1. autoclassifiers (what Hla Pe and others call repeaters, i.e., slots 1 and 3 are filled by identical forms)

2. special classifiers (i.e., nouns that function only as classifiers)
3. measures
4. times (with which slot 1 is often missing)
5. groups (with which slot 2 is always filled by *one*)
6. all-purpose (never used in place of 3, 4, and 5 above)
7. round-number classifiers (units of ten)

Only a few fillers of slot 1 are normally used with all these different kinds of fillers of slot 3. Hla Pe gives the Burmese word *myi'* 'river' with examples of most of these types.

> To cite just one example *myi'*, 'a river', Burmese scholars may claim, has at least eight 'classifiers'—*myi'* itself, *tan* 'a line', *hmwa* 'a section', *sin* 'a straight thing', *θwε* 'a connection', *pa* (for sacred beings or objects) and *khu'* 'a unit'. Other words besides may be made to serve as numeratives for *myi'*. (Hla Pe 1967:181)

Here, *myi'* used for itself is an example of 1, autoclassification, while *sin*, *pa:*, and *θwε* are 2, special classifiers. *Khu* is an all-purpose classifier, and the rest are measures (what Hla Pe calls quantifiers). *River* has not to my knowledge been used as a temporal unit, but it could be one of a unit of tens or be used with one of the group classifiers.

Rather strangely, I feel, Hla Pe and Okell (and others) do not consider this last kind, Matisoff's 5 groups, to be a classifier strategy at all, mainly on account of the constraint limiting slot 2 only to the numeral *one*. As Hla Pe writes:

> There are phrases particularly in Burmese songs which fall into these numerative patterns, but these have only *tə* 'a' or 'the', never other numbers. These are therefore not numeratives. E.g. *yin—tə* + *me* 'graceful—a + maiden, a (or the) graceful maiden', *au'—tə* + *nε* 'lower—the + country, The Lower Burma'. Cf. also *lu—tə* + *cho* 'some people', and *ye—tə* + *shei* 'a small amount of water'.

Types like "some people" and "a small amount of water" are what Matisoff calls group classifiers. Note that "graceful a maiden" is somewhat like "peach of a girl," where syntax and referentiality seem reversed, and the referential or "manipulable" noun (in Hopper and Thompson's term) is the maiden/girl. For me, these types all have a strong enough family resemblance in form and function to other classifiers that I would want to include them in one category, just as I would want to include temporal expressions, even though they often have nothing in slot 1.

The classifier in the first line of the anger-allaying poem, *yau'*, is what Matisoff calls a special classifier; that is, it can only appear in slot 3 (except in a few compounds like *yau'kya:* 'male, man' or *yau'hpạ* 'brother-in-law'). Hla Pe divides the set of special classifiers into three subsets, animate, inanimate, and conceptual. Let's look at the last subset first, since it is the smallest. His conceptual subset overlaps with Matisoff's all-purpose classifiers. It is a subset of three terms, in his words.

1. *pa:* n [proximity] (1) concepts which have a sacred or precious connotation—the attributes of Buddha, the law and the like; (2) composite-terms, having as their second member the word tə'ya (law, nature, condition, duties, etc.) e.g. 'lɔgadan tə'ya the law or nature of the world i.e. the vicissitudes of life, min jin tə'ya royal duties; (3) established sets of religious as well as secular concepts.
2. *ya'* n [a place] chiefly with intellectual concepts—knowledge, arts, and science: statements.
3. *khụ* n [a unit] with any concept, except those which have sacred, precious or intellectual connotation (Hla Pe 1967:183)

Here the order seems to be a continuum from sacred, to scientific, to everyday kinds of concepts. The order is clearly hierarchical, as it is for animate beings and inanimate objects as well (see Becker 1975). There are five classes of animate beings, among them the *yau'* of the poem under study. Hla Pe describes the hierarchy as follows.

The Burmese people have been Buddhist since before the language was reduced to writing sometime in the 12th century. They have apparently classed all beings by grades according to their intellectual and spiritual attainments. The hierarchy thus emerged reflected the attitude of the people toward the classified. (Note: each classifier is followed in square brackets by its meaning, or by a query where the meaning is uncertain, and then by the objects arranged as far as possible in the chronological order in which it seems likely that each has come to be included in that class. Wherever necessary, comments are given in round brackets: n noun, vn verbal noun.)

> 1. *shu* n [?] supernormal entities—Buddhas, Minor Buddhas; (anthropomorphic) Buddhas' relics, pagodas, images; recorded words of Buddha i.e. the Law, treatises and folded paper; (in olden days) teachers and scholars. (exceptions: mosquito-nets, fishing-nets, gardens and staircases.)

This is clearly a most interesting class. The term is usually written *hsu*. It has a Jinghpaw cognate *tsu* with a range of meanings like 'stale', 'dry', 'congested', 'disembodied spirit', and, as a verb, 'to propitiate' (James Matisoff, personal communication). This suggests a pre-Buddhist history for the term. Hla Pe continues:

> 2. *pa:* n [proximity] supernormal persons—Buddhas, Minor Buddhas, saints, monks; (anthropomorphic) the Law; precious things e.g. gems; deities, members of royalty! (in olden days) Court officials.
> 3. *u:* n [?the head] individual beings; (modern tendency) persons with status—officials, teachers, scholars and wealthy people.
> 4. *yau'* n [?person] ordinary human beings.
> 5. kauŋ n [the body] subhuman beings—animals; dead people's spirits, ghosts, etc.; morally or intellectually depraved persons; (facetiously or in anger) any person.

None of these classifiers, with the exception of *kaung*, can ever be a determinatum of the designatory word. (Hla Pe 1967:183)

The important thing here is to see that the classifier is selected from a kind of conceptual space that has been historically shaped. Emerson put it nicely when he wrote "The whole of nature is a metaphor of the human mind." Part of what the classifier in the poem says is that the two people in contrast in the figure are of the same category, *yau'*, under the same reality or *dharma*. And this, really, is the main point of what Anantathuriya is telling the king: your good fortune and my misfortune are within the same reality. The classifier is crucial in this statement.

With some understanding, then, of the semantic field being evoked by the classifier, let us turn back to the first lines of the poem and say something about the syntax—both the internal structure of the figure and its part in a larger figure.

A Rhetorical Figure

A figure is a unit of language considered from more than just structural perspectives: a unit of language in which interpersonal and generic (prior-text) constraints are also in view. A figure is a unit of language considered thus from a rhetorical rather than a logical point of view, a move in what Wittgenstein called a language game. (In the sense that I am using the terms here, Wittgenstein's *Tractatus* is a logical view of language, *Philosophical Investigations* a rhetorical view. See also Grassi [1980], and Ducrot and Todorov [1972] for further discussion of these senses of the terms *figure* and *rhetoric*.) To understand the figure that the classifier makes, in the first few lines of the anger-allaying poem, would require some broader sense of the repertoire of Burmese rhetorical figures—for example, Burmese language games, epistemes, or coherence systems—whatever we call them. We cannot assume an a priori set of rhetorical categories any more than we can assume an a priori set of grammatical or logical categories, or an a priori set of poetic categories. And, while we in the West know something of Burmese grammar and poetics, we know next to nothing about Burmese—indeed, any Southeast Asian—rhetoric. Hence, to call this Burmese figure, for instance, an antithesis and synthesis is to evoke a Western rhetorical tradition that is surely inappropriate here, though to what degree inappropriate cannot yet be said. Yet this is the only way that we have, using our terms, to describe their language, knowing from the start that our language is, at best, a metaphor for theirs, hoping quite sincerely for correction.

Interpreting, then, the figure as antithesis and synthesis, we might display it as follows.

A. — *thu ti: tə yau'   kaung: bǫ yau'*
   3°   only one (clf) good   to arrive

   mu
   perform/continuative

Antithesis: B.   —   *thu tə   yau' hma   pye'   ling*
   3°   one (clf) at/concerning destroy imperative,
                                                   prior

   ka   tha
   continuative   only

Synthesis: C.   —   *dhammata ti:*
   dharma   only

Line A is opposed to line B, which is at many points parallel with it. The contrast is marked by the terms *mu* and *ka*. While one person is enjoying success, another is *of necessity* (marked by *ling*) suffering destruction: the relation is not causal but simultaneous. Line C is the synthesis: the very antithesis itself is called *dharma*. Line C is thus at a different level from A and B, is of a different logical type, a meta-statement on A and B.

The repeated classifier phrase also marks the antithesis. A full classifier figure is used in Burmese, with very high frequency, to introduce a topic rather than to sustain one. Under Givón's iconicity principle (Givón 1984) that a heavier noun phrase will be more likely to introduce a topic in discourse than a light one, it is appropriate to describe full classifier phrases as heavy noun phrases. Classification is typically an initial strategy in Burmese language games: a way of identifying a topic. Here, in the lines we are studying, the full classifier phrase is repeated, suggesting different topics rather than the sustaining of a single topic. This is what makes that nineteenth-century translation of these lines (quoted earlier) so completely wrong.

> Yes, he is one who, wealth attained,
> Shall pass away and disappear:
>   'Tis Nature's Law.

To translate *dharma* as 'Nature's Law' (or, as in the more modern translation, 'the law of nature') seems to introduce a notion of temporal causality to this figure, so strong, perhaps, that the nineteenth-century translator overlooked the evidence of the repeated classifier phrases. A common Western exuberance in translating Southeast Asian texts is to add temporal causality, the basic coherence system in tense-marking languages.

Although in lines A and B the classifier phrases are parallel, they are not identical. In line A, the second word, *ti:*, does not appear in line B. Interpreting that *ti:* gives rise to a most interesting syntactic problem. That this is not just a problem for overanalytic philologists but for Burmese readers as well is evidenced by the variant readings of line A in various versions of the poem. That word, *ti:*, seems to have been the least stable word in the whole poem in the historical transmission of the poem. Here are the variant readings (see Hla Pe et al. 1963) of the classifier phrase in A.

1. *thu ti: tə   yau'*
    3° only one (clf)

2. *thu tə   yau' ti:*
    3°   one (clf) only

3. *thu tə   yau' thi*
    3°   one (clf) topic marker

This variation seems interpretable as the result of conflicting constraints. On the one hand, Burmese rhyming is usually backward-moving, often in couplets of four syllables, as here.

x x x a (*thu ti: tə yau'*)
x x a x (*kaung: bọ yau' mu*)

The second and third variants of the classifier phrase in A destroy this rhyme pattern, found throughout the poem. For this reason, I suspect, the first variant is usually accepted as the norm. However, the first variant is odd syntactically. The pressure in modern Burmese would be to have the *ti:* (pronounced tɛ) in final position, forming what Matisoff (1973:94) calls a coda to the classifier phrase, an additional slot in the figure. In modern Burmese, a common phrase resembling English *alone* is a headless classifier phrase, written

təyau'   *ti:*
one (clf) only

It seems quite possible, on the evidence of the variation, that the order of the first variant of line A is a *marked* or deviant order, or at least has become so over time. And so the problem is: is the deviant order significant, and if so, how?

There are further problems, however, with the lexical interpretation of this word, *ti:*. Some will argue, on the basis of the universality or convenience of our grammatical categories, that there are several homophonous forms of *ti:*. Judson in his dictionary (1953 [1852]:458–59) defines them this way.

—as a verb *ti:* means "to remain for a little while; to lodge in another person's house; to detain for a little while; to tack or tie together slightly; to collate, compare."

—as an adjective, *ti:* means "only, no more; used with numerals."

—as an "adverbial emphatic distinctive," *ti:* is "used to designate an object with some particularity."

—as a "verbal affix, closing a sentence; equivalent to the substantive verb *ši thi*, 'to be', etc." [An example of this use is the final word in line C.]

With reluctance I pass over the problems of categorization Judson's terms give rise to, and that mystifying final "etc." above. He was an excellent nineteenth-century American describer of languages whose interpretation of Burmese remains among the best. The question is whether this interpretation of *ti:* is not a bit exuberant and a more emic view might be to see one form in several different functions not four homophonous words. If the use of the term as an adjective ("only, no more") and its use as a verbal affix ("closing a sentence") can be associated, then *ti:* has a structural prominence in the poem as a whole. It occurs (and this is not marked but quite normal) as the final word in every "stanza"—every main rhetorical figure, thus marking the rhythm of the poem at the highest structural level, like falling intonation in English. In the soundscape of the poem, then, *ti:* has a major function. Its use as the second word of the poem may well serve to topicalize emphatically the first word, *thu,* and establish the recurring rhetorical figure of the whole poem, antithesis, via a kind of lexical contrastive stress.

This is the kind of grammatical puzzle a philologist can get into, in the attempt to correct exuberances and deficiencies of understanding. I would argue that questioning things that seem most obvious to us, not settling for too rapid a glossing, too rapid an appropriation of the meaning, serves to make the poem less familiar and thus to correct the translation. This defamiliarization is part of the aesthetic of "back-translation," and it runs to the deepest levels of grammatical understanding. One of the uses of grammatical analysis is to help us cross the terra incognita between English and Burmese, moving further from English, closer to Burmese.

A Summary

A classifier figure can be seen as an overlay of constraints—structural, generic, pragmatic, and referential—a few of which have been described here: the three-slot pattern plus coda, its rhetorical uses in metaphor and contrast, the way it shapes a relationship between writer and reader (poet and king or poet and us) far away in time and language, and the way it shapes a conceptual world. Said differently, a classifier figure is a system of systems, multiply constrained by the demands of structure, of genre (prior texts), of interpersonal relations, and of a construed natural world.

This interplay of systems is quite particular and cannot be seen or described apart from particular contexts. The interaction of these constraints happens only at the level of the particular. Only particular utterances have speakers, hearers, times, places, worlds—the irreducible conditions of their existence. Particularity, finally, is the source of a philologist's rigor.

ACKNOWLEDGMENTS

The author is grateful to John Musgrave and James Matisoff for help in preparing this essay. It draws heavily on the work of Professor Hla Pe (1967) and on lessons and discussions on Burmese literature with Saya U San Htwe in Taunggyi, Burma, 1958–61. Primary philology on Anantathuriya's poem is from Hla Pe, Allott, and Okell (1963). The earlier translation is by R. F. Andrew St. John, published in Harvey (1965:54–55). The notion of modern philology draws on Ortega (1957, 1959), Wittgenstein (1958), Grassi (1980), and Ricoeur (1981). For an overview on modern philology, see Becker (1984).

REFERENCES

Becker, Alton L. 1975. "A Linguistic Image of Nature: The Burmese Numerative Classifier System." *International Journal of the Sociology of Language* 5.109–21.

———. 1983. "Literacy and Cultural Change: Some Experiences." In *Literacy for Life: The Demand for Reading and Writing*, ed. Richard W. Bailey and Robin Melanie Fosheim. New York: Modern Language Association of America.

———. 1984. "Biography of a Sentence: A Burmese Proverb." In *Text, Play, and Story*, ed. Edward M. Bruner (1983 Proceedings of the American Ethnological Society). Washington, D.C.: The American Ethnological Society.

Ducrot, Oswald, and Tzvetan Todorov. 1979. *Encyclopedic Dictionary of the Sciences of Language*. Baltimore and London: Johns Hopkins University Press.

Emerson, Ralph Waldo. 1891. "Nature." In *Nature: Addresses and Lectures.* Boston: Houghton, Mifflin and Company.

Givón, Talmy (ed.). 1984. "Topic Continuity in Discourse: An Introduction." In *Topic Continuity in Discourse: A Quantitative Cross-Language Study.* Amsterdam: John Benjamins.

Grassi, Ernesto. 1980. *Rhetoric as Philosophy: The Humanist Tradition.* University Park and London: Pennsylvania State University Press.

Harvey, G. E. 1925, 1967. *History of Burma.* London: Frank Cass and Company, Ltd.

Hla Pe. 1967. "A Re-examination of Burmese Classifiers." *Journal of the Burma Research Society* 50.

Hla Pe, Anna J. Allott, and John Okell. 1963. "Three 'Immortal' Burmese Songs." *Bulletin of the School of Oriental and African Studies* XXVI: part 3.

Judson, Adoniram. 1852, 1953. *Burmese-English Dictionary.* Rangoon: Baptist Board of Publications.

Matisoff, James. 1973. *The Grammar of Lahu.* (University of California Publications in Linguistics 75). Berkeley: University of California Press.

Ortega y Gasset, José. 1957. *Man and People.* New York: W. W. Norton and Company.

———. 1959. "The Difficulty of Reading." *Diogenes,* no. 28, Winter.

Pe Maung Tin and G. H. Luce. 1923. *The Glass Palace Chronicle of the Kings of Burma.* Oxford: Oxford University Press.

Ricoeur, Paul. 1981. "Appropriation." In *Hermeneutics and the Human Sciences,* ed. and transl. John B. Thompson. Cambridge: Cambridge University Press.

Stacy, R. H. 1977. *Defamiliarization in Language and Literature.* Syracuse: Syracuse University Press.

Verhaar, John W. M. 1979. "Neutralization and Hierarchy." Sophia Linguistica Working Papers in Linguistics 5.

Wittgenstein, Ludwig. 1958. *Philosophical Investigations.* New York: Macmillan.

The Elusive Figures of Burmese Grammar

Most of these essays were written because someone asked that they be. This one answers a request from William Foley for "an emic, Burmese-eye view of the Burmese verb phrase" to be presented at what turned out to be a real treat, a week-long Wenner-Gren conference in Jamaica. The topic of the conference was "The Role of Theory in Language Description." It was the only conference I ever attended where all of the papers were very good. It was also the last gathering arranged by Lita Osmundsen, the arranger of so many now mythic Wenner-Gren conferences of the past.

The essay is probably the most difficult in this collection—unavoidably so, I think. An emic view (the term, like so much in these pages, comes from Kenneth L. Pike) is not an insider's view of his/her own language but an outsider's attempt to move toward one, in this case a Burmese-eye view. The distinction is crucial. To a Burmese, my labored, awkward attempt to describe a Burmese verb phrase will seem an obfuscation of the obvious. From the outside, however, that obviousness is anything but.

Translation, particularly of grammatical figures, is usually a familiarization of a distant text, but here I try to resist that move and attempt to describe in English what seems to me to be a grammatical wordscape very different from English or Indo-European wordscapes. A distant language very often defamiliarizes one's own view of things grammatical, and that makes for a certain degree of difficulty.

❖   ❖   ❖

Exuberance and Deficiency

The unavoidable problem we face in understanding a distant language is that our understanding begins within the bounds of our own language, and, although we can try very hard to overcome this problem and with new experiences go beyond these bounds, we remain to the very end outsiders engaged in a utopian task—one of those many human tasks in which we must always settle for approximations.[1]

This is not an exotic condition, faced only by explorers of distant wordscapes, but—as every linguist knows—the ordinary condition of using language, of *languaging*. Our understanding of another person's words is always approximate, always on the one hand exuberant, for we *add* much to what we hear or read, and, on the other hand, deficient, for there is much the sayer (or the writer) intended that we *miss*. In my experience, any translation of any sentence from Burmese, Malay, or Javanese (the Southeast Asian languages I have studied) is always at least 50 percent exuberant and 50 percent deficient—that is, at least 50 percent of the lingual material of the translation has no counterpart in the original and at least 50 percent of the original has no counterpart in the translation. I would like to bring this disparity into the foreground.

For linguists there are two steps in analysis that put into the background most differences between unrelated languages. The first of these is glossing, a kind of "literal," word-by-word, morpheme-by-morpheme translation, which, though it might be done with care, almost never is. Most of the analysis is done in the glossing, for the reader's understanding and, hence, the analyst's argument depend on the familiarity of those glosses.

Glossing is clearly a political process. How often do two languages meet as equals, with equal and reciprocal authority? How often, for instance, are the root metaphors[2] of the "exotic" language considered equal in analytic power to those of the language of analysis? Many find the deepest metaphors of another language poetic and defamiliarizing, but few find them to be as useful in analysis as one's own, that is, as pictures of the world "as it is." It takes considerable effort even to see one's own root metaphors as metaphors.

The second step in analysis by which dissimilarities are put into the background is abstraction, or, as linguists call it, parsing—putting the glossed language into a grammatical framework, the terms of which are terms in the language of the glossing. This language about language, or metalanguage, is also rarely if ever seen as equal in power in the two languages, and so there is an interesting politics here, too, which is only beginning to be unfolded: the politics of claiming universal explanations from within a particular language.

One alternative is to look to local (versus universal) explanations. In Southeast Asia there is plenty of local language about language, much of it involving new metaphors for the shapes and uses of the many things people can do with words. And there are also plenty of local grammars, but in these grammars, with rare exceptions, the parsing is done with an imported metalanguage, Sanskritic or European. (The major exception I know of is Zainal Abidin bin Ahmad's introduction to Malay for schoolchildren, called *Pelita Bahasa Melayu*, which was written in the forties and fifties largely in reaction to colonial grammars of Malay.) And so, although local language about language is rich and interesting in almost all societies, there are few independent analyses based on local traditions. The language game called parsing is not universally played.[3]

An emic understanding, then, is not an insider's understanding, for the insider may have no counterpart to the language game being played in the analysis, or the game itself may be a kind of calque of a borrowed game. Rather, emic understanding is a kind of self-conscious understanding, a process that the *outsider* undergoes: a deliberate process of foregrounding dissimilarity and self-consciously, methodically correcting the exuberances and deficiencies of one's outside understanding.

Defamiliarizing Burmese

I would like to describe some of this dissimilarity in modern Burmese by studying a narrative, the author of which I know and will send a copy of this essay to in hope of correction. It is a passage of about 134 sentences, a tentative number since Burmese punctuation does not consistently mark units we would call sentences. Let me illustrate this punctuation (and some of the dissimilarity it evokes) with the first sentencelike unit of the story in figure 12; in it, a narrator persona of the author is speaking.

As I have written elsewhere,[4] transliteration of this passage into Roman writing is not a "meaning-preserving" act, for the writing

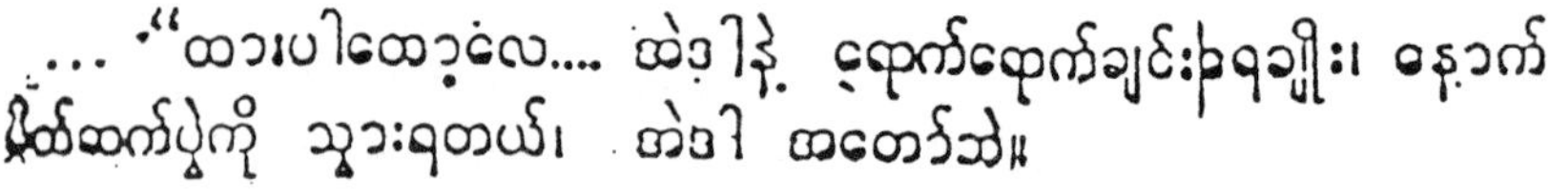

... "ထၢးပါ၊ထေၣ၆လ.... ထဲၣ]ၣ့ ၄ဧၢက်�၄ဧၢက်ချင်းၣ့ရ၍ျ်း၊ ၀န္ၣၢက် �`ိၲထ်ထက်ပ့ံၤက့ံ သှၣးရတယ်၊ ထဲ၅] ၊ ဘေတၣ်ဘ](

Fig. 12.   Passage from a Burmese story. ("A Burmese in England and
America" by Dr. Maung Maung Nyo.)

system one uses shapes the way one imagines one's language and
thinks about it. Our linear representation of sound units underlies
both our phonetic and our phonemic practice and becomes a root
metaphor for the sequencing of language itself, as scholars like
Jacques Derrida and Walter Ong have taught us to see more clearly.
Without going into that here, where the distant goal is to describe
"the Burmese verb phrase," suffice it to say that writing systems (and
other systems of representation) are among the deepest metaphors in
a language, that they resonate richly throughout a culture, and so for
us to substitute one technology of writing for another is not a neutral
act, a mere notational variation. It means to reimagine language itself.

One way to begin to do that is to look at a Burmese typewriter. A
Burmese typewriter does not automatically move along to the next
space when a letter is struck. It sits still. One strikes a central symbol,
the syllable "initial" consonant in most cases, and then one may mod-
ify it by adding marks above, below, behind, and in front of it. (I must
add that for many Southeast Asians in my classes in Burma, Java, and
Malaysia, the "front" of a word is the side facing the direction of
writing, that is, the right side; for most of us the "front" of a word is
the side facing away from the direction of writing, that is, the left
side.) The central cultural metaphor, the figure of Burmese writing
itself, at the level of morphemes and monosyllabic words, is much
more one of center and periphery than linear sequence. I will return
to this root metaphor later. The point here is that putting Burmese
words into linear, phonemic writing (romanizing it) obliterates a very
deep metaphor (center and periphery), which resonates widely in
Burmese culture. Much traditional philology and modern linguistics
depends upon this romanization as a first step (even before glossing)
in analysis. The illusion is that nothing important is lost.

One clear indication of emic Burmese parsing is Burmese punctuation. It is influenced, in part, by Roman conventions: there are quotation marks and an ellipsis in figure 12, probably borrowed from English punctuation. There is also in the text of this story an interesting new convention of putting commas between serial verbs, marking open rather than close phonological juncture. The traditional Burmese marks (which have Indic origins) include spacing between phrases (not words) and single or double vertical lines marking what might in translation be called clauses and sentences, respectively. Let me now just go ahead and Romanize and gloss this passage (retaining the original punctuation), and then discuss some more of the exuberances and deficiencies of the translation.

> 'hta:bato.le . . . e:dane.   yau'   yau'hcin: yeihco: |
> put   this with arrive arrive   bathe
>
> nau' mei'hse'pweko thwa: yate |
> after reception to go   must
>
> e: da   atobe: ||
> this just right
>
> 'Let that be . . . as soon as we arrived we bathed |
> After that we had a reception |
> That's just what I wanted || . . .'

The point here is not to argue that, for instance, *hta:* has a different range of meaning from English *put*, although that is certainly true. It is rather that many of the English words in the translation have no counterpart in the Burmese text at all, words like *be, as, we, a, is, I*, and past tense. I don't think it is possible to say that these words are somehow "understood" from the context in the Burmese text. They just aren't there, necessary as they may be to the coherence of English, for it is the English gloss that implies them, not the Burmese original. Concerning things like copula, articles, and tense, Burmese is silent.[5] These are some of the exuberances of the English translation, and it is important, I think, that they represent the core of the English system of discourse coherence: tense, copula, pronouns, and articles.

The deficiencies of the translation—those things in the Burmese that have no counterpart in the translation—include things at the core of the Burmese system of discourse coherence. These are primarily nonreferential terms in the sector of clauses that might be parsed as the predicate or the verb phrase. In typological terms, Burmese is O(bject), V(erb), and S(ubject) anywhere before V when it's there at all. (S seems more nearly a sentential rather than a clausal constituent in Burmese.) The Burmese words I am narrowing in on are in the sector labeled V, the predicate.

Many parts of the predicate have relevance to functions well outside that sector, at many different levels of context. For instance, one might parse the first clause in the example above as:

(hta:)ba)to.)lei) . . .
(put)polite)change of state)persistive) . . .
'Let that be . . .'

Imagine concentric circles: the openness of the last three parentheses is meant to suggest that the last three terms have relevance to context outside the clause and, in part, outside the text. The second word, *ba*, takes us to the level of the speech situation of the narrator since it marks politeness of the utterance vis-à-vis the recipient, that is, the one the narrator is talking to within the story. The third word, *to.*, is described in Judson's (1852) dictionary as "verb affix, denoting a slight necessity," but more recent descriptions[6] agree that it marks an imminent (as here) or recent change of state, which perhaps gives, in Judson's terms, "slight necessity" to the request to "put something aside, please." The final term, *lei*, is tough to gloss: it has been called "euphonic," "slightly emphatic or persistive." It makes the clause a little longer and the imperative perhaps a little more gentle, more friendly.

Although their dynamics can be suggested in English, these terms have no clear English counterparts. Like English tense, they follow the verb but have reference to the speech act: the speaker is being persistent, not saying what the subject of the sentence should be; the speaker is being polite and is marking a change of state in the telling of the story. In Foley and Van Valin's (1984) terms, their position is near the nucleus of the clause, but they are functionally part of the periphery and beyond.[7] Their use is to put the clause into context.

On Defining "Context"

I would like to explore for a moment what "putting a clause into context" might mean, before going further into the parsing and analysis of "the Burmese verb phrase."

Linguists and philologists would recognize, I think, at least six different kinds of context for any chunk of language from sentences on up to whole texts: (1) the context of other language before this chunk or after it within the text (thinking of text as any recorded instance of languaging); (2) the context of the language act itself, in which someone is languaging to someone, somewhere, sometime; (3) the context of memory—the prior texts and remembered contexts this bit has the power to evoke; (4) the context of a world beyond languaging, a world we observe through words, whatever we may believe about the ontology of that world—so that if I say "Look at Bill over there" I don't normally mean for you to look at my words but through them; I mean them to be transparent; (5) the context of the medium—sound, inscription, gesture, and the neural medium of inner languaging we call thought. None of these five kinds of context can be reduced to one of the others, and all are within a context we might call (6) the context of silence—the unsaid (in any particular utterance) and the unsayable (in any particular language).

"Putting a clause into context," to return to the question of what that can mean, can mean relating that clause to (1) other parts of the text, including other clauses; (2) the language act; (3) the memories it evokes; (4) a world beyond language; (5) a medium; and (6) silence. Languages may differ in all six kinds of relation to context, I believe, and so describing "the verb phrase in Burmese" means describing dissimilarities in all six. Various parts of "the verb phrase" relate to various kinds of context.

One more word, an aside, about the six kinds of context, before I start to use them. I hope that they are clear. They are meant to be noncontroversial, though I realize that they are merely one "take" on languaging. It is a Deweyan take[8] in which one focuses on languaging as one means by which a live being attunes itself to context. Animals and plants also can be seen as relating to context in these six ways: they build structures; form communities; have memories; construe worlds; manipulate media; and live against a background of emptiness. For humans, of course, all six are more complex than for algae, although that belief, too, may rest on too much exuberant universalizing. Each of us is thrown at birth into a particular tradition of attunement, a philology (or language considered over time). English and Burmese are two different traditions of attunement, two different philologies, which only recently in human history have come to interact.

Framing Burmese in English

The picture of Burmese that has developed in English, in spite of important differences of detail, has been rather consistent from the beginning of the historic interaction of the two, from the time Carey and Judson first began to familiarize Burmese to speakers and readers of English in the early nineteenth century to, in our own day, the recent, very thoughtful descriptions by Okell (1969), Allott (1965), and Wheatley (1982). I do not mean to be negative about that tradition, for it is my own; however, by taking our tradition itself to be within the scope of study, it may seem negative at first. One major goal of many modern philologists and anthropological linguists, however, is to be as self-conscious about our own traditions as we can be, in a move toward emic understanding. A powerful quotation from Wittgenstein says it well and memorably: "One thinks one is tracing the outline of the thing's nature over and over again, and one is merely tracing round the frame through which we look at it" (*Philosophical Investigations*, para. 114).

The discipline in this self-conscious endeavor is not to be taken from theory, that is, from the metalanguage, since that metalanguage is part of what is being examined. Rather, the discipline for the philologist is of another kind: the discipline of particular texts, in particular places and particular times, so that as much of the context as possible is made accessible for study. Here I will describe "the verb phrase in Burmese" in the context of a five-page excerpt from an account of a trip that a group of students from Burma took to the Edinburgh Festival. It was written by Dr. Maung Maung Nyo (a well-known Burmese author and professor of medicine) who is narrating the story. He is frequently interrupted by friends who are joking with him about his relationship with one of the group, a young Chinese woman. Burmese friends assure me that Dr. Maung Maung Nyo's prose is good modern colloquial writing.[9]

For about four months I read over this little text nearly every day, until its dissimilarities began to emerge. Using the six different kinds of context as a heuristic, I will try to describe some of the exuberances and deficiencies I have noticed.

A String of Metaphors

Let me return to that first clause, an imperative that might be translated 'Let that be. . . .' The whole thing can be seen as a string of metaphors.

hta: ('put') is a metaphoric "putting down" of a topic of discourse prior to picking up a new one. The context it relates to is prior discourse, although the object is unsaid.

ba (polite) is a metaphoric use of a verb that we might translate as 'include', 'be with', 'accompany'. It is a very old metaphor for politeness, with no originality at all, except to the foreign learner for whom it is fresh and exotic. The context it relates to is the social situation, the language act.

to. (change of state) is a metaphoric use of a verb that describes the act of hitting something into the air with hand, foot, or stick—as in the widespread Southeast Asian game (Burmese *hcin:loun:*) in which the players, either singly or in a group, keep a rattan ball in the air with their feet. The context it relates to is, again, the discourse itself, as an "object."

lei (euphonic) is a metaphoric use of a verb that Judson (1852) translates as 'to be scattered, lost, evaporated, as camphor, quicksilver, etc.'. The verb seems close, too, to a noun meaning 'air, wind'. It seems appropriate at the very end of a clause, and it seems to relate to the texture of the discourse itself.

To think of "the verb phrase in Burmese" as a string of metaphors foregrounds dissimilarity. For many linguists it may seem to exoticize Burmese in a way that is perhaps historically accurate (and perhaps not), but it is certainly not the way native speakers would imagine their own language. Over time, as one learns the language, the recurring metaphors become bleached and ordinary, but for the comparative philologist (interested in how that ordinariness came about), it seems emic and right to try to see the elasticity of the metaphors first and then to see their present use as extensions (or deviations) into new contexts. I realize I am skating on thin ice in ascribing particular metaphors in English to these Burmese terms, and I am far surer that it is warranted to see them as a string of metaphors than I am of my own glossing of them.

The study of the rhetoric of metaphor traditionally focuses on single words and has usually been classed, since Aristotle, as a single-word figure in which there is a displacement and extension of a word from one context into another. (One notices that our English metalanguage here, like that of most European languages, is built around metaphors of spatial movement: meta-*phor*, dis-*place*, rhetorical *moves*.) A verb phrase, however, is a more complex figure than a single word, often even an overlay of figures. Paul Ricoeur (1975) makes much of the distinction between metaphors as words and metaphors in sentences (thinking of sentences as the minimal units of discourse, i.e., the minimal units with full context, as context is defined above). This distinction parallels Benveniste's between semiotics (the study of signs in a code) and semantics (the study of sentences in context).[10]

Let's look at these words at first semiotically (i.e., as individual words and as sets of words) not semantically as parts of a particular verb phrase. There is much that can be said about them as metaphors. As many have noted, almost all the "auxiliary verbs" and "particles" have or once had status as main verbs. There are probably about a hundred of these and the sets may be open.[11] Here are some that seem transparent.

Main Verb (with gloss)	Used as Auxiliary or Particle
thwa: 'go'	'arrive in a state'
la 'come'	'becoming'
mi. 'catch'	'inadvertent'
pi: 'finish'	'and'
pyan 'return'	'repeat, [go] back'
pei: 'give'	'[do] for'
ci. 'look at'	'try to'
san: 'try, test'	'polite urgency'

In these cases we either have English counterparts that resemble these Burmese root metaphors, or we know languages that do, or we can easily imagine how they might make sense. The following are less transparent.

to. 'to hit in air with foot, hand, or stick'	'change of state'
lei 'to be scattered, lost, evaporated'	'persistive'
hpu: 'to behold'	'already achieved'
thei: 'small, insignificant'	'still, yet'
hke. 'do bit by bit'	'different time, place'
oun: 'surround, cover'	'further action'

One might classify these and the other metaphors of the Burmese verb phrase in various ways, perhaps sketching out semiotic fields, for example, the metaphoric extensions of movement or of vision. It certainly is possible to create semiotic paradigms of these verbs and imagine a kind of map of Burmese "thought" in terms of root metaphors.[12] However, the focus here is their use in a particular Burmese verb phrase.

Metaphors in Context: The Verb Phrase

At its simplest, a Burmese sentence is a verb phrase, and the simplest verb phrase has two parts, like many Burmese grammatical phenomena: a VERB and a FINAL. Around these two the structure is built.

The two, VERB and FINAL, do not stand in any dependency relationship to each other but rather might be described as making a polarity, between more referential and less referential, or least grammatical and most. The problem with these terms *referential* and *grammatical* is that both poles of the Burmese verb phrase "refer," and both have grammatical roles. In terms of the six kinds of context presented above, it might be better to say (putting aside cases of self-reflexivity) that the VERB refers primarily to the context of the world outside the language act and the FINAL refers primarily to the context of the language act itself. What constrains the VERB (again, putting aside self-reflexivity) is what I'll call (after Emerson) Nature, and what constrains the FINAL is the particular social event of languaging.

Around the VERB, before and after it, cluster the words (many used figuratively) that particularize the natural event by identifying and specifying it.

Around the FINAL, before and after it, cluster the words (also usually figurative) that particularize the language event by identifying and specifying it.

Between the VERB and the FINAL, things are not all that tidy. A lot of the elusiveness happens there.

If the poles of the verb phrase have their feet in two different contexts, the one in the natural event, the other in the language event, where do the other four kinds of context come in: intertextual relations (memory), intratext relations (structure), medium, and silence? Some, as we will see, work on the very edges, and some at the center, of this polarity between VERB and FINAL.

The Right Pole: The FINAL

The set of VERBS is open-ended, and that of FINALS rather small, though there are many variant forms of the latter. Julian Wheatley (1982) lays out the final particles this way.

INDICATIVE

	positive	negative
actual	-*te*	
hypothetical	-*me*	-*hpu:*
change of state	-*pi*	

IMPERATIVE

	-Ø	-*ne·*

In consideration of the self-consciousness that an emic ideal re-quires of us, we must not give too much power to those latinate English terms in the chart above, as familiarizing as they are, but see them, too, as metaphors brought over into an alien wordscape. Among these final particles, the oddest and least familiar is probably *pi*. Among realis-irrealis, mood, and negative-positive polarity, we find "change of state," which seems like a displaced aspect. Allott calls that same *pi* "punctative." As Professor Allott writes (1965:289), "*pi* has caused much trouble to grammarians and students alike. It is difficult to describe in terms of English grammatical categories the type of sentence marked by the final particle *pi* in Burmese."

There is not time now to go through the history of that trouble, except to note that *pi* was enough like "tense" for Judson (1853) to call it "past" in the last century, and Stewart (1936) to call it "perfect" in this, and for traditional Burmese translators to use it to represent a Pali past participle.[13] A modern Burmese grammarian, U Pe Maung Tin, has said (quoted and translated by Allott [1965:290]) "*pi* shows that a different situation, indicated by the verb, has really been reached." It is clear that the final particle *pi* is like a tense particle in at least two ways: it has reference to the moment of speaking; and it marks an act as specific. The important thing seems to be that, with *pi*, some specific thing either has happened or is happening. Here, again, we meet tenselessness; we already met it in discussing the "change of state" particle (i.e., tossing the rattan ball) *to.*, which (from our per-spective) does not distinguish an accomplished change of state from an imminent one. Another way to say this (to extend the metaphor of the writing system) is that the event of speech is not a moving point but a center.[14]

Let me now put aside details about individual particles in order to fill in some of the grammatical space around and between the two obligatory poles of the verb phrase, the VERB and the FINAL. As we will see, elements of the verb phrase (now better called the two-headed verb + final phrase) cluster around the two poles.

Categories Close to the FINAL

Close to the FINAL cluster "optional" words that have been called evidentials, references to the speech event, politeness markers, vague words called euphonic or "intonation carriers," and an interesting small set of mutually exclusive (nearly) words that according to Allott (1965) mark "aspect," although this term may clash somewhat with more recent definitions of *aspect*. There are three words in this category: *to.* (which we have seen several times already), *oun:*, and *thei:*. They occur just before or after the FINAL in the verb phrase.

The first of these (*to.*) marks something we have called a change of state, either already accomplished or imminent. It is very like *pi* and never (or very rarely) co-occurs with *pi*. Like *pi*, it seems to say that something happening is stopping or something new is beginning. Unlike *pi*, it can occur with negatives and other final particles. Allott (1965) calls it "culminative."

The other two (*oun:* and *thei:*) she calls "cumulative." They both mark continuation of an occurrence, and, as Okell (1973) has shown, continuation of a nonoccurrence, essentially the opposite of a change of state. One of them, *oun:*, marks imperatives and hypotheticals, the other, *thei:*, marks indicatives.

With imperatives, *to.* and *oun:* occur after the final particle. With indicatives, *to.* and *thei:* occur before the final particle. We can only speculate why this should be.[15] What it does, however, is complicate the act of describing the Burmese verb + final phrase since there are now two positions for this category, which Allott (1965) calls "aspect." As we will see, this is not unusual in Burmese and it reinforces, I think, the image of the verb + final phrase not as a linear sequence but as two polarities with elements clustering around each, in orbits.

As with *pi*, the point of reference for these "aspect" particles is the speech event. There is another category that has reference to the speech event. There are only two particles in the category. Allot calls them "location" and distinguishes them as "junctive" and "nonjunctive." They occur with all finals (but not after stative verbs), and they are mutually exclusive. They occur before optional "aspect" particles, near the FINAL. Allott (p. 299) writes, "Without one of these two particles a verbal sentence does not refer to one specific action. (There are other ways, however, of specifying a definite action)."

The one that she calls "junctive" (*hke.*) says that there are two locations involved in the specific event, one of them associated with the speaker. The other, which she calls "nonjunctive" (*lai'*), says that the specific event is carried through and finished with.

One might represent the Burmese verb + final phrase described so far as:

(VERB) . . . (junctive (change of state (FINAL)))

Let us continue to look at the things that cluster around the FINAL a bit longer before turning to the VERB end of the phrase. We have seen some things that occur just before the FINAL (junctive, change of state). After the FINAL there are (1) question markers; (2) tags (e.g., *hsou* 'It is said'); (3) evidentials, like *hpe:* ('really'), *po* ('for sure'); (4) a quotative (*te.*); and (5) an array of "euphonic," "emphatic," or "intonation-bearing" particles whose meanings remain elusive and which may have more to do with the medium than the other contexts. One always feels defeated by these last things, as if there were more to them than there appears. Perhaps not.

At the very end of the phrase, there can be a formal pronoun for the second person, so that men use a masculine for 'you' (*hkinbya*) and women a feminine (*shin*). A proper name for the addressee, too, might go into that final slot.

One might argue that all of these are outside the verb + final phrase, even outside the clause, and that they mark the closure of the sentence. Functionally they are certainly peripheral operators, but so are many of the final particles. It is impossible, I think, in a verb-final language, ultimately, to define the end of the verb phrase and the beginning of the sentence operators. They may be in double function. And it may well be that this diffuse boundary makes no trouble for anyone except philologists.

All of these things cluster on the right polarity of the phrase and are related to the speech event—identifying it and expressing attitudes toward it—except tags like 'it is said' (*hsou*) and the quotative particle (*te.*). These two explicitly relate the sentence to prior text, the context of memory.

It was mentioned earlier that there are variant forms of the final particles. These different forms serve two major purposes: (1) the variant forms serve to mark the phrase or clause as a part of a larger structure: coordinate, subordinate, or cosubordinate (Foley and Van Valin 1984); (2) the variant forms serve to distinguish spoken and written language. The story under examination here uses this latter phenomenon to good purpose. Most of the story is written in spoken Burmese, but when the author wants to make a comment outside the story he shifts to written Burmese, marked only by the written variant of final particles (i.e., the spoken final particle *te* becomes the written form *thi*).

There is one word that seems to wander about in this right-hand polarity of the double-headed verb + final phrase. It is *pa*, the "polite" particle, although the term *polite* in English fails to convey the importance of this word. It might be better to think of it as "inclusive," on the basis of the meaning of the corresponding independent verb, as discussed above. Allott (1965:302) states bluntly that it "occupies a position third from the end." By "the end" she means the final particle, which she takes as the end of the verb phrase (the verbal syntagma). She goes on, "*pa* precedes the category of aspect with all final verb particles except *hpu:*, when it follows it." (*hpu:*, you may recall, marks a negative assertive. It probably attracts *pa* for reasons of sound—a constraint of the medium itself.) Allott (p. 302) also says, "Starting from *pa* to the end of the sentence, we have particles whose function is to establish the nature and purpose of the sentence in relation to the situational context." We might then think of *pa* (except with *hpu:*) as marking a boundary between the two polarities of the verb + final phrase, a kind of transition from the context of Nature to the context of the speech event.

The Left Pole: The VERB

I would like to make that transition myself now and begin to describe the other end of the phrase, the VERB and the things that cluster around it.

Distinctions like transitive and intransitive seem to play as little part in Burmese as tense. In describing the particles, it does seem useful to distinguish active and stative verbs: the junctive/nonjunctive category, for instance, never occurs with stative verbs. This seems, however, more a matter of the unlikeliness of a junctive/nonjunctive "state" than an important grammatical constraint.

What is interesting—and dissimilar—about the Burmese verb is how seldom it is single and simple, one verb with one final particle. In the story under consideration here, only 12 out of 134 sentences have a single, simple verb, and 8 of those are verbs that take sentence complements (i.e., *pyo:* 'say'; *me:* 'ask'; and *thi.* 'know'). Usually the verb is part of a compound verb or is modified by an auxiliary (i.e., cosubordinate) verb, or both. Like the verb phrase as a whole, the verb itself is almost always made of two parts.

Word building itself, in Burmese, seems to happen by compounding, so that there are not just transparent serial compounds like *thwa:we* ('go' + 'buy') but also many nonserial pairs like *ceina'* ('be ground down' + 'be cooked') meaning 'to be satisfied, contented', or *hma:ywin:* ('error' + 'misplace') meaning 'mistake', or *neihtain:* ('stay' + 'sit') meaning 'reside'. In the serial compounds, there is an optional particle *pi:* ('and' < *pi:* 'finish'), which can be put between the two verbs without altering the meaning: *thwa:pi:we* ('go and buy'). This particle cannot be inserted between nonserial pairs.

There are many interesting things to say about these compounds. For instance, some are formed artificially, in which case the second member of the compound is a rhyme syllable or a reduplication, not an independent word at all: for example, *ne'ne:* (from *ne'* 'deep' + *ne:* rhyme syllable) = 'profound'. In some, the two words are of nearly identical meaning: for example, *pyo:hsou* ('speak' + 'speak') = 'speak'. Okell (1969) has described these compounds in detail, and most of the examples here have been taken from his study. The point is not that Burmese has compound verbs and English doesn't, for we clearly do, but rather that Burmese does it so much and so freely, almost as if there were, in a monosyllabic language, pressure from the medium itself to make words weightier and a little slower in passing. Whatever the reason, there seems to be a pressure toward double-headedness throughout the language. For us to speak Burmese is to learn to use two or more words where, in our own noetic economy, one would do.[16]

This pervasive compounding gives rise to a major problem in describing the verb + final phrase: how does one distinguish a compound of verb + verb from verb + auxiliary, given the fact that most auxiliaries are also regular verbs and many can occur both after and before the main verb? Some combinations are clearly compounds, for neither the first nor the second member occurs frequently with other verbs. Some combinations are clearly verb + auxiliary, for the auxiliary in these cases either does not occur independently as a regular verb or else it occurs with almost any verb. Most combinations, however, fall somewhere in between. Again the picture is not very tidy.

There are a few interesting tests, none of them conclusive. One of them is the placement of the negative marker *ma*. We have already seen that one of the final particles is another negative marker (*hpu:*), which, as discussed above, attracts the polite word *pa*. Negation, it should come as no surprise to notice, is also a double-headed structure: one foot (*ma*) marks the verb and the other (*hpu:*) is a final particle. The placement of *ma*, then, should tell us where the main verb is. There are some interesting complications, however.

With an ordinary, lexical compound (as with a single verb) the negative *ma* precedes it, or in some cases is prefixed to both members, as in:

> *ma-hsaun-ywe'* ('not-bear-carry on head') 'not execute, carry out'
>
> *ma-htein:-ma-thein:* ('not-restrain-not put away') 'not put under detention'

When there is a verb followed by an auxiliary, the negative *ma* either precedes the verb or the auxiliary. John Okell (1969), whose explanations and examples I am using at this point, considers the order neg-verb-aux to be the general rule and verb-neg-aux to be the exception, but then he goes on to list twenty-two exceptional auxiliaries that seem to attract the negative. As far as I know, no one has yet described the significance of this variation. It seems to make no difference if you say *ma-yu-thwa:* (not-take-go) 'not take away' or *yu-ma-thwa:* (take-not-go) 'not take away'. That is to say, the scope of the negative does not change with its position.

One solution, essentially the one suggested by Allott (1965), is to consider that any erstwhile auxiliary becomes a main verb if it attracts the negative, and this makes perfect sense when you consider that almost all auxiliaries also occur as main verbs (certainly all those that attract negatives occur as main verbs). Wheatley's (1982) argument against this, that even under negation these auxiliaries retain their auxiliary meaning, makes sense, too.

Perhaps the problem, once again, is trying to think of a single headword in the basic grammatical configuration. Perhaps there is something like a grammatical pressure (or a deeply resonant metaphor) in Burmese toward building double-headed figures, so that where English tends toward modifier-head relations, Burmese tends toward double-headed ones.

This negation of the second verb, then, becomes like several other processes that are possible at this position in the verb + final phrase in Burmese. Like negation of the auxiliary verb, all these other optional alternatives also seem to give prominence to the erstwhile auxiliary without any apparent change of meaning. So that, according to Okell (1969:33), one can say either *pou.hkain:* ('send' + 'tell') (verb + AUX) or *pou.hpou.hkain:* (('send' + 'to') + 'tell') (COMPL + verb) and both would be rendered in English 'tell (him) to send (it)'. Note that in the first form 'send' is the main verb, while in the second 'tell' is—suggesting, among other things, that either position in the figure could be prominent. What is not at all clear is what this area of apparent optionality really does in Burmese, that is, what kind of context it relates to.

And, if *pou.hkain:* is an instance of verb + auxiliary, then one of the other things this figure suggests is that verb and auxiliary need not have the same agent. And, if the verb and auxiliary need not have the same agent, then we are pushing the notion of auxiliary too far. This is clausal nexus. And yet . . .

And yet at this point Burmese remains elusive, as if we had not yet asked of it the right questions. Or asked softly enough.

There can be more than one "auxiliary," and it is difficult finding any other general constraint on their order than scope: each new verb seems to include all to the left of it, so that a reversal of order produces a reversal of scope. For example, from Wheatley (1982:230):

> *-hcin   hpu:*   = 'have wanted to-'
> 'want' 'already'

while

> *-hpu: hcin* = 'wanted to have-'

But consider such phrases as the following, quoted (from literary Burmese) in Okell (1969:39).

> *ca.yau'kwe:hmanhti.hkai'hya.na.cou:kan:sou'pya'theiceipye'si*
>
> drop-explode-strike-splinter-break-tear-die-perish
>
> (describing an armed attack on a garrison)

or

> *su.hsaun:siyinhnyi.hnain:thou'thinye:ku:mutinti:hpya'pyinhsi*
>
> collect-arrange-compare-purify-write-set down-edit-amend
>
> (describing the compilation of a learned book)[17]

These are extreme cases. There are ordering constraints on the auxiliaries in spoken Burmese, but since there are over fifty auxiliaries (fifty-nine in Okell) let me only say in this essay that within the continuum between the verb (or verb cluster) and the final (or final cluster) those things closer to the verb have more to do with the event beyond language (Nature) and those closer to the final have more to do with the language event.

Many more things of note in the Burmese verb + final phrase have been described in English by Okell (1969); Allott (1965); and Wheatley (1982); and in French by Denise Bernot (1980).[18] There are several types of "pre-verbs," which occur before the main verb (both intensifiers and "pre-auxiliaries"), incorporated objects, and the frozen relic of a prefix (*h-*) on the verb that once marked an active-stative distinction. And there are all the ways verb + final phrases can be subordinated and embedded. None of these things have been discussed here. I invite the reader to learn of them from the four fine scholars I have mentioned above and whose work I have drawn upon throughout. What has been discussed here has been enough, I hope, to begin to shape a picture of the area between the verb and the final particle in a Burmese sentence. It is a grammatical landscape altogether different from anything we have in English. It has two centers, like many of the elusive figures of Burmese, and because of that there are different possibilities—different things you can do—with a Burmese verb + final phrase than with an English verb phrase.

Some Examples

But rather than describe further complexities it may be more useful here to present a few more examples, drawn from the story that I have used as my discipline in this study, about Dr. Maung Maung Nyo in England pursuing a Chinese girl. I would like to describe in context, by way of summary and illustration, a couple of the more interesting verb + final phrases.

We have already looked at the first clause of the story and described it as a string of metaphors.

hta:bato.le

PUT INCLUDE TOSS EVAPORATE

'Let that be . . .'

I have argued that auxiliary verbs work, in part, as metaphors. They retain echoes of their nonmetaphoric uses now displaced into new contexts. That is, words that have nonmetaphoric uses in identifying and specifying acts and events in Nature (PUT INCLUDE TOSS EVAPORATE) have been displaced in order to identify and specify acts and events in the management of the text and the speech event itself. What are PUT, TOSSed, and EVAPORATEd are other words. We all wince, of course, when the everyday metaphors that language uses to manage itself are uncovered: they are things to be seen only, as Gregory Bateson used to say, from the corner of the eye.

And so, to translate the passage above as PUT INCLUDE TOSS EVAPORATE is not an acceptable English translation of the Burmese. I would only argue that an acceptable translation may well have to pass by that blatant string of metaphors and note them and hear their echo, "under erasure."

A more grammatical view of the passage might describe the Burmese as:

PUT polite change-of-state persistive

or as:

VERB aux (FINAL-Ø) aspect euphonic

But 'let that be'.

Let me turn to another interesting example, later in the episode. The narrator is interrupted here for a bit of teasing about his skill in interacting with women, and someone says what might be translated as 'After all, he's doing a Ph.D'. What the Burmese says (retaining *Ph.D.* in English) is:

Ph.D. *lou'netapo*
DO STAY FINAL LIGHT (i.e., not heavy)

or:

VERB aux FINAL evidential

or:

Do-ing-assert-obvious

In this verb + final phrase there is a focus-shifting variant of the final particle (*te* > *ta*) and a strong evidential. The two parts are clear: verb + aux (DO STAY) and FINAL + evidential (ASSERT + OBVIOUS). Here we see how the FINAL part of the phrase can have two parts, with emphasis shifted away from the final to the evidential. This is another example of shifting focus or emphasis in the phrase. We have seen shift of focus from VERB to aux and now, from FINAL to evidential.

One more. The narrator has a difficult time with a rival, a young Chinese who speaks with the girl in Chinese so that he can't understand. Then she says she's thirsty and he says he bought her some orangeade, ending the sentence with the phrase:

welai'thei:te

BUY FOLLOW SMALL ASSERT

VERB AUX ASPECT FINAL

BUY do-to-completion[19] no-change-of-state ASSERT

'(I) just went ahead and bought (it)'.

Here is an example of an "unsaid," a silence that is possible with this verbal technology. What was the change of state that did *not* happen? I think it is that he did not give in to the provoking situation, that is, his not understanding the Chinese conversation.

In Conclusion

And still there are many things that remain elusive—persistently dissimilar. Particularly now, having brought in the notion of "unsaids," I am well over my head in Burmese and it is time to bring things together and to a close.

The study of another language is always comparative, one language in terms of another. Between the two languages there are always two kinds of dissimilarities: exuberances and deficiencies. An important role of theory in language description is to bring to the foreground both exuberances and deficiencies.

The theory sketched here is a theory of contexts, based on the notion that the meaning of anything is its relation to context, and that context is multiple, and that dissimilarities between languages are to be expected in all of them: dissimilarities in intratextual relations (structure); in interpersonal relations (the speech event); in intertextual relations (memory of prior text); in constituting a world of Nature believed to exist beyond language; in shaping media; and in what is said or unsaid, sayable or unsayable. All of these dissimilarities may lead one to a relativistic, nonuniversalist attitude toward languages that Kenneth Pike called "emic."

An English interpretation of Burmese has evolved over the past century and a half and throughout that time the verb and verb phrase have remained elusive due to basic dissimilarities of all these sorts. I have tried to describe a few of them, particularly the two-poled, or double-headed, structure of the verb phrase, with one pole, the verb, related to the world outside language, and the other, the final, related to the language event and the shaping of coherent text. This double figure can be found throughout Burmese: in compounds, in negation, in classifier constructions, and elsewhere. Identifying and specifying both poles are several categories of verbs used metaphorically: words referring to natural events that are used to define language events. Finally, I gave a few examples of this two-poled figure from a particular text, in order to demonstrate some of the things that can be done with it.

I cannot resist adding one more.

Coda

The final sentence of the story ends:

yeneiya.leithi

It is a comment by the author on the story, since the phrase ends with the literary final particle *thi* rather than the spoken final particle *te*, which is used elsewhere. As metaphor it is:

LAUGH STAY GET EVAPORATE ASSERT

VERB AUX AUX euphonic FINAL

or:

> Laugh-ing-had to-really
>
> Really had to keep on laughing . . .
>
> (at himself, in pursuit of . . .

An emic view demands no less.

ACKNOWLEDGMENTS

Besides the participants in the Wenner-Gren seminar, and in particular William Foley, I received generous help from John Okell and Fred Lupke, neither of whom would be comfortable with all that is written here.

NOTES

1. Several terms in this section, including *exuberance, deficiency,* and *utopian task,* are taken from the work of the Spanish philologist José Ortega y Gasset. See particularly Ortega (1959); (1957, chap. 11).
2. For further elaboration of this term, *root metaphors,* see Pepper (1952). One's own root metaphors are not normally seen as metaphors. See also Lakoff and Johnson (1980).
3. Kroeber (1944) discusses philology as a cultural system. For Kroeber a philology of a culture is its accumulation of prior texts plus the means of sustaining access to them. Across cultures, we may notice, philology (grammar writing, lexicography, translation, etc.) is also a means of sustaining access. Within an indigenous philology, built to sustain access to its own past, it doesn't usually matter that the access is one way

(now to then), while across cultures (here to there) it almost always does matter. For a study of English philology at the time when Burmese was first being analyzed in English, see Aarsleff (1983), and Becker (1986).

4. See Becker (1983, 1984, 1986).

5. As Ortega (1957:246) writes, "The stupendous reality that is language cannot be understood unless we begin by observing that speech consists above all in silences. . . . And each language represents a different equation between manifestations and silences. Each people leaves some things unsaid *in order to* be able to say others. . . . Hence the immense difficulty of translation: translation is a matter of saying in a language precisely what that language tends to pass over in silence."

6. Four works that describe Burmese in English, cited throughout this essay, are Judson (1852); Allott (1965); Okell (1969); and Wheatley (1982).

7. Grammatical terms used here (e.g., *periphery* and *nucleus*) are defined in Foley and Van Valin (1984). Closely parallel terms in tagmemics are *clause margin, clause root,* and *clause nucleus.*

8. See also Rorty (1989). Dewey's observations about language are scattered throughout his work, but see, in particular, references to language in his correspondence with Arthur Bentley, in Ratner et al. 1964.

9. The passage is from Dr. Maung Maung Nyo, *ingalan ameiyikanhnin. myanmapyitha:* (1977:155 ff.). It was excerpted, copied, translated, and used pedagogically by John Okell who passed it on to me.

10. Benveniste is quoted in Ricoeur (1975).

11. These lists, including the glosses, are based on Wheatley (1982:234–48).

12. I have attempted this in Becker (1975).

13. Burmese evolved a literary language especially for translating Pali texts, and this is described in Okell (1965). The title for the present essay is taken from that most excellent work (p. 191).

14. For a detailed discussion of *pi*, see Allott (1965:289–92); Okell (1969:382–86); and Wheatley (1982:219–22).

15. See Allott (1965:295–96) for a historical interpretation.

16. This point is the basis for very different literary esthetics in Burmese and English. When I was teaching in Burma (1958–61) I noticed that my students wrote very "wordy" English, and they noticed that I spoke very "thin" Burmese. I think now that these different tendencies are "in" the languages.

17. It is worth noting that in these long strings all of the verbs fall into pairs (e.g., drop-explode; strike-splinter; break-tear; die-perish) and that each member of a pair is itself a compound, so that the pair 'drop-explode' is made up of what one might more literally translate as 'fall-arrive' (= 'drop') and 'divide-hit mark' (= 'explode'). This is further instance of embedded double-headedness as a grammatical figure.

18. I have not discussed this excellent study since I am focused here on familiarization between English and Burmese.
19. Okell (private communication) questions the glossing of *lai'* as 'to completion'. He writes, "I think there's a temptation to overdo the 'completion' idea. *V lai'* often seems to me to have the effect of minimalizing the fuss and effort involved in the verb. . . . I agree that 'completion' is often (perhaps always) there, but perhaps it isn't the only message."

REFERENCES

Aarsleff, Hans
  1983   *The study of language in England, 1780–1860.* London: Athlone Press.
Allott, Anna
  1965   'The verbal syntagma in Burmese," *Lingua* 15:283–309.
Bailey, Richard, and Robin Fosheim (eds.)
  1983   *Literacy for life: The demand for reading and writing.* New York: Modern Language Association of America.
Becker, Alton L.
  1975   "A linguistic image of nature: The Burmese numerative classifier system," *International Journal of the Sociology of Language* 5:109–21.
  1983   "Literacy and cultural life," in: Bailey and Fosheim (eds.), 45–51.
  1984   "Biography of a sentence: A Burmese proverb," in: Bruner (ed.), 135–55.
  1986   "The figure a classifier makes: Describing a particular Burmese classifier," in: Craig (ed.), 327–43.
Bernot, Denise
  1980   *Le predicat en Birman parlé.* Langues et civilizations de l'Asie du Sud-Est et du monde Insulinde, 8. Paris: SELAF.
Bruner, Edward (ed.)
  1984   *Text, play and story: The construction and reconstruction of self and society.* Washington, D.C.: American Ethnological Society.
Craig, Colette (ed.)
  1986   *Noun classes and categorization.* Amsterdam: Benjamins.
Foley, William, and Robert Van Valin
  1984   *Functional syntax and universal grammar.* Cambridge: Cambridge University Press.
Judson, Adoniram
  1852   [Reprinted 1953] *Burmese-English dictionary.* Rangoon: Baptist Board of Publications.
Kroeber, Alfred
  1944   *Configurations of cultural growth.* Berkeley: University of California Press.

Lakoff, George
  1987   *Women, fire, and dangerous things.* Chicago: University of Chicago Press.
Lakoff, George, and Mark Johnson
  1980   *Metaphors we live by.* Chicago: University of Chicago Press.
Maung Maung Nyo
  1977   *ingalam ameiyikanhnin. myanmapyitha* [A Burmese in England and America]. Rangoon.
Okell, John
  1965   'Nissaya Burmese: A case of systematic adaptation to a foreign grammar and syntax," *Lingua* 15:186–227.
  1969   *A reference grammar of colloquial Burmese.* London: Oxford University Press.
  1973   "Still" and "anymore" in Burmese: Another look at /*thei, loun*/ and *to.* [Paper presented at the Sixth Conference on Sino-Tibetan Languages and Linguistics, San Diego.]
Ortega y Gasset, José
  1957   *Man and people.* New York: Norton.
  1959   "The difficulty of reading," *Diogenes* 28:1–17.
Pepper, Stephen
  1952   *World hypotheses: A study in evidence.* Berkeley: University of California Press.
Ratner, Sidney, Jules Altman, and James Wheeler (eds.)
  1964   *John Dewey and Arthur F. Bentley: A philosophical correspondence, 1932–1951.* New Brunswick, N.J.: Rutgers University Press.
Ricoeur, Paul
  1975   *The rule of metaphor: Multi-disciplinary studies of the creation of meaning in language.* Toronto: University of Toronto Press.
Rorty, Richard
  1989   *Contingency, irony and solidarity.* Cambridge: Cambridge University Press.
Stewart, J. A.
  1936   *Manual of colloquial Burmese.* London: Luzac and Company.
Wheatley, Julian
  1982   Burmese: A grammatical sketch. [Unpublished Ph.D. dissertation, University of California, Berkeley.]

PART 3
LEARNING MALAY

The Figure a Sentence Makes:
An Interpretation of a Classical
Malay Sentence

The word figure *here is meant to recall both the well-known essay "The Figure a Poem Makes" ("The figure is the same as for love"), by Robert Frost, and the very old notion of a rhetorical or poetic figure: a lingual form, a minimal prior text—both words and grammar—which is reshaped to new contexts. The sentence at the center of this meditation is of a type one meets frequently in a Classical Malay text. To look at it carefully as a cultural artifact (just as one might a calendar, a song, or a painting, for instance) seemed to reveal deep and important differences between Malay lingual esthetics and American English.*

❖   ❖   ❖

To understand a sentence means to understand a language. To understand a language means to be master of a technique.
—Ludwig Wittgenstein, 1958

This essay is an examination of a single sentence in Classical Malay, a sentence that I puzzled over and discussed with my friends for many months, until it began to yield its meaning and allow us, readers of Classical Malay far away in space and time, to join imaginatively in its shaping. Understanding sentences[1]—a level in the hierarchy of discourse structures—is a necessary level of competence in modern philology. Sentences have been defined by Paul Ricoeur (1971) and others (see Mukarovsky 1977)[2] as the basic units of discourse, the minimal unit of the text. Ricoeur makes an insightful distinction between *language* and *discourse* in terms of the different kinds of relations that must be taken account of to describe each. That is, discourse-internal relations [structural information] and discourse-external relations, particular relations with speaking and hearing people or reading and writing people (which are very different, since the mode of interpreta-

261

tion is so different for dialogue or for reading) in particular times and places. Unlike *language* (which many linguists see as their field of study), discourse (the field of modern philology) is studied in relation to a complex set of external constraints, grouped by Ricoeur into these kinds of relations: (*a*) temporality, relation to a particular time of utterance or writing; (*b*) subjectivity, relation to a particular speaker or writer; (*c*) referentiality, relations to nature, the referential world; and (*d*) intersubjectivity, relations to hearer or reader (as a potential speaker or writer) who depends upon his experience in the other role—that is, as speaker or writer—to help him interpret the text.[3] Just as the sign can be seen as the minimal unit of *language* ("worldless" systems and structures), so sentences—described differently for different languages—can be seen as the basic, nonreducible units of discourse—that is, the least complex units that are constrained for temporality, subjectivity, referentiality, *and* intersubjectivity, the discourse constraints. Structuralist linguistics (generative or nongenerative)—the description of language-internal relations—is far too reductive to describe discourse, the experiential context of language, as linguists have been learning in many different ways.[4]

The meaning of a sentence in discourse can be described as its relations to its discourse contexts (roughly, temporality, subjectivity, referentiality, and intersubjectivity) as well as its relations to its more specifically linguistic contexts (prior text, or scripts, and present text, the immediate linguistic context). A sentence in a written discourse can be an attempt to decontextualize the meaning of an oral discourse, at least partially, like tape-recording a conversation. Written discourse, in this sense, is more like *language* than dialogue is—that is, freer of constraints of temporality, subjectivity, referentiality, and intersubjectivity than dialogue is. The moment of reading supplies these via interpretation, and here discourse study becomes hermeneutic.[5]

Taking the perspective from sentence to context (or, in somewhat archaic terms, studying the "distribution" of sentences), one can see that the density of contextual constraints on sentences (i.e., possible distributions) varies greatly. In terms of Givón (1977), some sentences are more marked than others, and, the more marked the sentence, the more constrained the discourse context. Sentences that evoke more detailed context also may have a kind of power[6] as metonymic representations of that context: Miltonic periodic sentences, Kennedian balanced antitheses ("ask not . . ."), or the figure (unnamed, as far as I know) of Shakespeare's "A horse, a horse, my kingdom for a horse." Can that figure ever be free of its context (even to someone who doesn't know it is Shakespeare's), so that we might say A ———, A ———, my ——— for a ——— ("A theory, a theory, my tenure for a theory"!) without evoking a battlefield, near the end of the battle, on the loser's side?

Gertrude Stein (1975) made much of this power of context evocation in her dense little book, *How to Write*. She called context evocation "emotion" and observed (p. 23): "A sentence is not emotional a paragraph is." Stein did not use the same terms Ricoeur does, but she was also struck by the distinction between language and discourse. In Stein's own words (cited by Meyerowitz [1975:XX, XXI] in her introduction to *How to Write*):

> I once said in How to Write a book I wrote about Sentences and Paragraphs, that paragraphs were emotional and sentences were not. Paragraphs are emotional not because they express an emotion but because they register or limit an emotion. Compare paragraphs with sentences any paragraph or any sentence and you will see what I mean.

> In a book I wrote called How to Write I made a discovery which I considered fundamental, that sentences are not emotional and that paragraphs are. I found out about language that paragraphs are emotional and sentences are not and I found out something else about it. I found out that this difference was not a contradiction but a combination and that this combination causes one to think endlessly about sentences and paragraphs because the emotional paragraphs are made up of unemotional sentences.

> In a book called How to Write I worked a lot at this thing trying to find out just exactly what the balance the unemotional balance of a sentence is and what the emotional balance of a paragraph is

and if it were possible to make even in a short sentence the two things come to be one. I think I did a few times succeed.

The following sentences (from Gass 1973) are ones in which she thinks she succeeded in making a sentence with the qualities of a paragraph—the context evoking qualities.

It looks like a garden but he had hurt himself by accident.

A dog which you have never had before has sighed.

A bay and hills hills are surrounded by their having their distance very near.

Gass puts these sentences next to Laurence Sterne's sentence:

A cow broke in tomorrow to my Uncle Toby's fortifications.

Everyone can best describe for himself the nonstereotypic figures these sentences make when you read them and thus study that hermeneutic act of reading in her own consciousness, the growing awareness of a context for the sentence. Like poems, and like love, as Robert Frost (1979) wrote in his brief essay on poetics, they begin in delight and end in wisdom.[7]

In Classical Malay, the sentence is more like a paragraph, in Gertrude Stein's sense, and in the sense of most rhetoric books: It *establishes* a topic and *develops* it, *contextualizes* it. In seeking to understand more about establishing and developing a topic in Classical Malay— as potential readers—we must step back from some of our presuppositions about the figure a sentence makes. The experience of a Classical Malay sentence is different from the experiences of the sentences of Milton, Kennedy, Shakespeare, Stein, and Sterne. These are all more similar to each other than they are to Classical Malay figures, since they are all in English—which is why a foreigner has to start further back in the process of reading-interpretation. Reading Classical Malay is harder than reading Gertrude Stein: One must first clean his mental

palate, like a wine taster, and stop treating Malay as deviant—usually
rather bland and incomplete—English, and then try to discover the
dimensions of its own world, as a reader—which is one of the two
ways (there are only two, dialogue and reading) we can enter that
world.

A Classical Malay Figure

Sa-telah demikian maka Sang Bimanyu pun berjalan-lah sambil
                                    Bimanyu   walk   while

menchium bau   bunga2an menghiborkan hati-nya itu, naik   bukit
sniff   smell flowers   entertain   heart (liver) ascend hill

turun   bukit berapa gunong   dan jurang dilalui.[8]
descend hill   many mountain and valley pass-over

I hope the reader who doesn't know Malay will be patient without a
translation. A "good" English translation at this point would give an
illusion of understanding before we know what a "good" English
translation would have to include if it were to be at all close to the
original Malay. Let me begin describing the untranslatable parts first.

This Classical Malay figure, which will later be called a Classical
Malay sentence, is from Hussain (1964). This text is a "translation,"
whatever that meant to a Moslem Malay translating a Hindu work
from a Middle Javanese "translation" (the *Mahabharata Kawedar*)[9] of a
Sanskrit text. I have been trying to trace this process backward
through time to see how the text was recontextualized from Sanskrit
to Javanese to Classical Malay. What did it mean to "Javanese" Sanskrit and to "Malay" Javanese? It would be premature to generalize
about this larger process—the task has just begun. Suffice it to say
that the kind of sentence to be discussed here has no very close
Javanese or Sanskrit counterparts that I am aware of, though perhaps
they will emerge under closer rhetorical examination. It seems a distinctly Malay figure—very common in classical texts but clearly archaic. That is, it does not seem to be found at all in what urban native
speakers of Malay or Indonesian would call modern Malay or Indone-

sian (Bahasa Melayu or Bahasa Indonesia). It might be argued that it is
a more Austronesian figure than many found in these modern languages and that its counterparts can be more clearly seen in Old
Javanese (Kawi) or written Tagalog. In any case, the figure was chosen
because it is common in Classical Malay (sentences resembling this
one syntactically occur at a density of about one or two per page in
Classical Malay texts I have studied), because it is archaic, and because it seems distinctly Malay.[10]

The sentence has three sections—to begin from a structuralist
perspective (i.e., focusing on part-to-part relations within the text).

> Section I. The Pre-Core: *Sa-telah demikian maka*
> Section II. The Core: *Sang Bimanyu pun berjalan-lah*
> Section III. The Elaboration: *sambil menchium*, etc.

These three sections are formally marked. At the core of the figure is a
structure that may be called a *pun, -lah* structure.

> Section II. The Core
>
> . . . *Sang Bimanyu pun*   *berjalan-lah* . . .
> topic   general event
> 'Bimanyu'   'walk (travel on road)'

It has been a major error, I think, to describe this structure (A + *pun*, B
+ *lah*) as if A were necessarily a noun phrase and B a verb phrase, or
as if A were a subject and B a predicate. There are several kinds of
problems with these Western grammatical labels.

1. The distinction between "nouns" and "verbs" is not yet established for Classical Malay and is best not presupposed, particularly now that many feel Austronesian languages did/do not
   always distinguish grammatically between endocentric and
   exocentric clause relations.[11]
2. The subject-predicate relation in English is not identical with
   the *pun, -lah* relation.[12] (Some of these differences will emerge

later.) These two objections are objections to the use of a priori universal categories (noun, verb, subject, predicate) to describe Classical Malay.

However, leaving aside the difficulty of describing Classical Malay parts of speech in some "universal grammar," there is a clear need in Classical Malay to distinguish between sentence structure and clause structure—and between sentence function and clause function; the categories subject and predicate (or the relation subject-predicate) come from a tradition (Western, Greek-based grammar) in which sentences and clauses are seldom clearly and categorically distinguished (to say nothing of their further association with logical propositions).[13] Malay and other Austronesian languages clearly distinguished clauses and sentences, though this distinction is fading as Malay and Indonesian become more and more "Western" in system and structure.[14] Some features of sentences, as distinct from clauses, in Classical Malay are:

Sentences	Clauses
Topic-event structure	Subject-predicate structure
Topic initial is unmarked	Predicate initial is unmarked
Postpositional particles	Prefixes on predicates
(*pun, -lah*) mark topic-event	(*meng-, di-*) mark agentive
relations	relations (focus-nonfocus)
Referentially constrained topic	Role-focus constrained subject[15]

In Classical Malay, case relations are not relevant at sentence level, which helps to explain some of the special features of *pun, -lah* structures, particularly the observation that case-marked predicates do not in Classical Malay precede *-lah*. (This means only "verbs" with *ber-* [marking, roughly, external states and intentional motions] or *ter-* [marking nonintentional, "dative-like" involvement] or no prefixes [marking internal states and locationals] appear before *-lah* in Classical Malay, at least until quite late. The loss of this constraint appears to me central in the history of Malay.)[16]

The *pun, -lah* structure has several variant forms, explainable, perhaps, as the result of the other sections of the sentence, which precede and follow the central *pun, -lah* structure, overlapping or merging with the *pun, -lah* structure. This overlapping will be described after the other constituents of this figure are described.

The referential relations of a *pun, -lah* structure are to prior text, either an earlier part of the text in which the sentence containing the *pun, -lah* structure occurs, or a source text. A source text can be a particular work from which a translation comes (as in the example under investigation here) or it can be a stereotypic script (i.e., a conventional or prototypical event).[17] In terms used by Longacre (1976), the sequence of *pun, -lah* structures forms the "backbone" or the "skeleton" of the text.[18] It indexes an event (*-lah*) and the participant (——— *pun*) who or which will be in a single case role—in the sentence under investigation, this role is actor or agent—in the clauses that follow the *pun, -lah* core, clauses (section III of the sentence) that fill in the details and particularize the event, *in relation to this participant.* Temporal order is neither regularly marked nor presupposed, either between sentences or between clauses, though it may be inherent in some scripts (i.e., stereotypic events) or in a prior text being translated. Temporal sequence in Classical Malay is usually marked by a combination of the two terms *sa-telah* (roughly, 'end of one observation') and *sudah* ('finished', 'over').

Following the *pun, -lah* structure are one or more clauses (section III) involving the topic (marked in section II by *pun*) and within the event (marked in section II by *-lah*). In this sentence, *Sang Bimanyu* (the *-pun* topic) is the agent (though not always in focus) throughout the section of the sentence following the *pun, -lah* core. He sniffs the smell of the flowers, entertains his heart, ascends hill(s), descends hill(s), and passes mountain(s) and valley(s)—except that this last act is put so that mountain(s) and valley(s) are in focus as a location.

> *beberapa gunong dan jurang dilalui.*
> many   mount and valley pass-over

Up to that point the predicates focused on the agent (the *pun* topic) or were unmarked for focus, as in the case of *naik* ('ascend') and *turun* ('descend'). The progression of the clauses is: agent focus to no marked focus to nonagent focus (*meng-* 'agent-focus' to *di-* 'nonagent focus', morphologically).

Section III. The Elaboration

sambil **men***chium bau* *bunga2an*
      agent-focus verb object
'while' 'sniff'   'smell of flowers'

men*ghiborkan* *hati-nya itu*
agent-focus verb object + article-deixis
'entertain'   'heart'   'it-that'

naik   *bukit turun*   *bukit*
no marked-focus verbs plus locations
'ascend' 'hill' 'descend' 'hill'

berapa   *gunong*   *dan*   *jurang*
di-lalu-i
quantifier location   conj. location
nonagent focus = verb + locative suffix
'many'   'mountain' 'and' 'valley'
'he pass-over'

This part of the sentence is like a flowering (to use a Javanese musical metaphor that seems appropriate, a *sekaran*, referring to a musical elaboration) of the script-indexing *pun, -lah* core. Because Classical Malay (and Javanese)[19] aesthetics are so closely tied to nature, this elaboration very frequently includes details of landscape—the physical setting, including, often, lists of names of local plants and animals found in Malaya or Java. The stereotypic act (or the translated act) is contextualized in a Malay landscape. At the end of the sentence the landscape is in focus—background becomes foreground—and in this way the limits of the domain of the *pun, -lah* core, the scope of the topic and event, are marked—a kind of syntactic fade-out. In the next sentence they may be reestablished or changed. The "passive" turn (the *di-* verb) at the end of the sentence gives it closure. The kinds of elaboration possible here in the final section of the sentence are constrained by the syntactic possibilities of the Classical Malay clause in playing role against focus. As readers we experience topics moving in and out of roles and roles moving in and out of focus, the former at the sentence level, the latter at the clause level.

The order of the verbs in the elaboration is significant here, but it is not clear to me just where to find the sources of the constraints on this order. The progression in the elaboration section from individual, agent-focused events to location-focused events (marked by the *di-* prefix and the *-i* suffix on the final verb) appears to reflect what has been called variously the *cline of person* (Becker and Oka 1977 [presented 1974]), the *referentiality hierarchy* (Foley 1976), the *natural topic hierarchy* (Hawkinson and Hyman 1975), or the *inherent lexical content hierarchy* (Silverstein 1977), all of which seem to be quite similar, a continuum from self to other, marked off in strikingly similar ways from language to language. In most general terms, this cline or hierarchy can be represented as:

speaker > hearer > human proper > human common >
animate > inanimate (> location)[20]

It manifests itself, both syntagmatically and paradigmatically, in such varying linguistic processes as modifier order in the English noun phrase, the structure of the Burmese classifier system, inherent topic-worthiness in Navaho, pronominal systems everywhere (which is why the label "cline of person" seems appropriate), and in the deictic inflexions of Kawi (Old Javanese), Malagasy, and many other languages.[21] If the role-referent (or role-topic, in this paper) distinction is at the heart of language, conceptually prior to metaphor and person, even, then a second order of categories grows out of the role-referent split, categories of role (cases and pronouns, for instance) and categories of referent (nominal subclassifications of various sorts, for instance, *classifiers*), with the principle of classification remaining the same throughout both categories of role and categories of referent: I-other, and all its relatives, here-there, now-then, source-goal, observer-observed, and by extension even such linguistic metaphysics as mind-matter, slot-filler, and so forth.[22] Metaphor seems to work around the same distinction, the separability of role and referent.[23]

Whereas the elaboration section of the Classical Malay figure contextualizes the *pun, -lah* core in the Malay landscape (as represented in the Malay language), the first section of the sentence contextualizes that same core in the hierarchy of the prior text. We can distinguish two kinds of coherence, referential coherence (relations to a single event of a series of events in a stereotypic script) and textual coherence (marked relations between sentences, with sentences defined as discourse units). In those terms, we could say that the first section marks the textual coherence of the core, the final section the referential coherence of the core. The *referential* coherence is provided by the event (or script) of a man moving through a landscape, with perspective shifting from man to landscape. The *textual* coherence is established by the first part of the figure, with the words:

Section I. The Pre-Core

Sa-telah demikian maka . . .

It has taken me a long time to begin to understand these words. The first step in this gradual understanding was to experience the elaborate inflexion of deixis in Kawi, as I Gusti Ngurah Oka revealed it to me (and the very similar system in Malagassy, as described by S. Rajaona [1971, 1972]). The widespread Austronesian deictic formative *-k-* (varying with *-t-* and *-n-* or $\emptyset$ at the center of the simplest deictic word, which has the form vowel + consonant + vowel, with inflexion appearing sometimes in all three positions) was elaborated in Kawi by prefixing, suffixing, and compounding in more than one grammatical system. That same *-k-* (meaning very generally 'to' or 'toward' or even 'shifter', to use Jespersen's term for this changing deixis as it appears in first- and second-person pronouns) appears in the center of Classical Malay connectives like:

maka

demikian

arakian

maki(a)n

kalakian

These connective terms break easily into parts, though the English equivalents for the meanings of these parts remain a problem. *Maka* can be analyzed into *ma-* + (*k* + *a*), in which *ma-* is a stative prefix,[24] *-k-* is a deictic formative, and *-a* is a third person/there/then. *Demikian* can be analyzed into *demi-* + (*k* + *i* + *an*). *Demi-* is a word that can be translated by English 'in the name of' (as in a prayer or an oath), by English 'by' (as in 'one by one' *seorang demi seorang*), or by English 'for' (as in 'for the good of the people' *demi kepentigan rakyat*). *Demi-* followed by *-k-* is a deictic formative, *-i-* is a first person/here/now, and *-an* is a nominalizing suffix. The other forms have similar etymologies.

The other word in the first section of the sentence is *sa-telah*, which dictionaries usually translate as 'after' or 'finished'. But this word, like those above, has no clear English equivalent. It frequently combines with *sudah* in Classical Malay, a word that is given an identical gloss in English, to mark temporal junctures. The *sa-* in *sa-telah* is clearly a prefix (meaning, roughly, 'one' or 'the same'), and *telah* may be derivative of *te(r)-* + *laah* (meaning, roughly, 'investigated', 'goneover', 'studied').[25]

The combined form

Sa-telah demikian maka . . .

may then "mean" something like 'having gone over, thus, then . . .' or, in some contexts, 'after this, then', if one remembers that the meaning is not necessarily temporal or sequential, though it may be. Clear temporal sequencing in the text from which this sentence comes is nearly always marked by *sa-telah sudah*.

Etymological explanations, fascinating though they are as a conceptual strategy, do not clearly reveal the text-building functions of these words. Part of the meaning of English connective words like *however, nevertheless, furthermore*, etc., is the sum of their semantic parts, but I don't think that when we use them we are building them out of parts: it is hard to make a joke with *hownever, *everaless, or *furtherless. The main point, it seems to me, has to do with the sheer heaviness of these terms, a density in both sound and meaning that is very reminiscent of the basic principle of heaviness and lightness in Southeast Asian calendars, music, dramatic plots, and elsewhere: the coincidence of gongs at structural boundaries (the more gongs sounding together, the higher level the boundary) or—in calendric terms— the coincidence between marked (highly valued) days in simultaneously occurring "weeks" of different lengths.[26] At the level of sentences, the Classical Malay text uses just *maka* (or another single-word connective like *shahadan* or *hatta*, both borrowed from Indo-Persian languages) to mark separate units. At the boundary of a larger (i.e., larger in scope) unit, a cluster of sentences of some sort, heavier or denser connectives are used, two-word connectives (e.g., *arakian maka, demikian maka, hatta sa-telah, arakian sa-telah, sa-telah demikian*, and a few other combinations of these few connective words), and for larger units, three-word connectives (e.g., *maka sa-telah sudah, hatta sa-telah sudah, sa-telah itu maka*, and the form we are looking at here, *sa-telah demikian maka*). Aside from the rich meanings and significant variant orders of these words,[27] it is the "heaviness" itself that marks the figure we are observing—that Classical Malay sentence—as a *major* boundary in the hierarchical structure of the text, somewhat like a paragraph in English. More coinciding deictics or connectives mean a higher-level plot boundary: new place, new time, new state, new major character, etc. To put it another way, this sentence is (or, for the reader, will be) the context or background for a potentially large number of lower-level sentences. Or we might say that the scope of influence of a heavier sentence is wider than that of a lighter sentence— with heaviness defined purely in terms of the number of words in the first section of the sentence.

Thus, the first part of the figure links the *pun, -lah* core to the prior text at the proper level of generalization. The figure the sentence makes is emerging. We are, I think, learning to read more and more like a reader or hearer of Classical Malay. From the ways that the sentence evokes context, we can begin to interpret—as a reader must—and reconstruct the missing context. Whether read or heard, the text is not a dialogue; it is displaced from the full discourse context and must be interpreted.

So far we have looked at the three parts of the figure, this kind of Classical Malay sentence, and something of their relations to each other:

I	II	III
deictic connectives	*pun, -lah* core	elaboration
plot-level relations	topic-event relations	role-focus relations
textual coherence	script indexing	referential coherence
Sa-telah demikian maka	*Sang Bimanyu pun berjalan-lah*	*sambil menchium . . .*

Notice further that the movement of the sentence is from generality to particularity in several senses.

1. The sentence moves from nonrole and case-marking "verbs" to role and case-marking "verbs" (e.g., from *ber-* prefixed verbs to *meng-/di-* prefixed "verbs").
2. The sentence moves from least referential terms to most, in the sense that *maka* is less referential than *menchium* 'sniff'.
3. It moves from metacomment (about the telling) to comment (the telling), that is, from information about *the text* to information about *the story*.
4. The sentence moves from language to nature.

This last is perhaps the most interesting feature of all in this particular Classical Malay sentence strategy. From language to nature. In translating the Sanskrit-Javanese text, the writer is contextualizing in the Malay world an old, old event. It is in the third section of the sentence that the distinctly Malay setting is expressed. The writer is making the text Malay, thus enriching the Malay landscape itself by association, making it historically dense.[28]

The aesthetic possibilities of the sentence seem, too, to be far richer in the third section of the sentence, the first two sections being far more constrained by prior text. In Gertrude Stein's sense, the third section is more "emotional"—more reflective of the imagination and skill of the author, into whose "subjectivity" we as readers enter in this third section.

This Malay sentence is what might be called a *prototypical* sentence, related not by derivation but by partial resemblances in several dimensions to a great many other Classical Malay sentences with which it shares some or nearly all its meanings. In this essay I have tried to describe some of those kinds of properties, some of the nonspecific meanings the figure has. Some will be more widespread than others; that is, not all related sentences will have three sections, *and* have "heavy" deictic connectives, *and* have an agent-to-location focus progression. This figure we have been studying is the overlay of these strategies. There are less complex sentences, related to this one, with only a *pun* structure in the core and no general event marked by *lah* but, rather, an immediate movement into the clauses of the elaboration. There are less complex sentences in which a deictic connective (usually *demikian*) "enters" the core and is marked by *-lah* (e.g., *demikianlah*), indicating that the whole figure is a comment on the prior section of the text. The figure or sentence we have been examining is prototypic in the sense that it shows nearly maximal complexity at the level of the sentence: it displays the possibilities of the sentence.

These steps into the landscape of Classical Malay discourse[29] are steps into a cultural past. This Malay figure is no longer alive, in the sense that a great many of the constraints that characterize it are no longer in force.

1. The boundary between sections II and III (core and elaboration) is no longer clear, and the functions of the two systems (referential-topic and role-focus) no longer distinguish clauses and sentences in modern urban Malay or Indonesian. *-pun* still can be used to topicalize (that is, it retains its referential function), whereas *-lah* appears now to mark imperative predicates (*Pergilah!* 'Go!'), and the terms used to translate the Indo-European copula (*ialah* and *adalah*) are now an obvious feature

of modern, educated Malay or Indonesian. However, the two, *pun* and *-lah,* no longer are used together to mark the topic-event relationship, the core of the classical figure.[30]

2. The other major difference is that many of the deictic connectives that established textual coherence are no longer used, except in very formal situations in which an archaic flavor is important. *Maka* no longer marks sentences. Temporal and causal coherence are much more "modern" strategies than the system of deictic densities described previously.

Time words appear more frequently within the verb phrase now, and causal connections are marked (in modern Malay or Indonesian) in dependent clauses with rather free ordering (the order I + II + III of the Classical Malay sentence was fixed). And so the boundary between section I (deictic connectives) and section II (the *pun, -lah* core) is lost, too.

The figure a sentence makes is a strategy of interpretation filling in subjectivity, temporality, referentiality, and intersubjectivity, which, tied to a specific cultural era, helps the people it is used by to understand and to feel coherent in their worlds. It is just as much a cultural artifact as a calendar, a genre of music, or a mode of painting.

ACKNOWLEDGMENTS

I must acknowledge the aid of several people: Danielo C. Ajamiseba, Liberty Sihombing, Ramli Salleh, Nangsari Achmad, Stephanus Djawanai, and all the advanced students of Bahasa Indonesia and Bahasa Malayu at Michigan, especially Patricia Henry and Jeffrey Dreyfuss, for imaginative commentary on these ideas. Deepest gratitude to Talmy Givón, David Levy, and Deborah Tannen for detailed commentary on the draft. I only regret that I could not make all the changes you suggest, since I do not yet know enough to be able to do it. I have also drawn on extensive discussions with Fred Lupke, Aram Yengoyan, John Verhaar, William Foley, and George Lakoff, whose paper, "Linguistic Gestalts," set me to thinking about prototypical sentences. But the debt is greatest to Kenneth L. Pike, who threw me all the right challenges, including the challenge of a linguistics of particularity, a basis for modern philology.

NOTES

1. It might be clearer to use the term *rhetorical sentence,* a structure quite different from a clause, but the term suggests that there are nonrhetorical sentences, whereas I wish to suggest, rather, that sentences are the interface of syntactic relations and rhetorical relations, including tropes, defined separately for each language.
2. Mukarovsky (1977:15) wrote, "The central element of narrative language is the sentence, the component mediating between the language and the theme, the lowest dynamic (realized in time) semantic unit, a miniature model of the entire semantic structuring of the discourse."
3. See Ricoeur (1971:530–37), which this sentence attempts to summarize.
4. Translators, philologists, and tagmemicists, among others, have not had to relearn this. Tagmemic grammars have for many years now included major sections on discourse constraints. See Pike (1975:17–18). For further bibliography, see Joseph Grimes (1975).
5. For a discussion of the relation of hermeneutics and linguistics, see especially Ricoeur (1976).
6. My thanks to Benedict Anderson for pushing me to investigate the notion of power sources in language, particularly Anderson (1976).
7. The original quotation from Frost (1949) is: "The Figure a poem makes. It begins in delight and ends in wisdom. The figure is the same as for love . . ."
8. This sentence, from Hussain (1964:34), begins a section and is followed by these sentences.

   > Sa-genap batu ia berbaring, sa-genap pohon kayu ia dudok di-bawah-nya dengan leteh lesu rasa tuboh-nya. Maka bulan pun terbit-lah terlalu terang. Maka awan pun sunyi rupa-nya saperti menyuloh orang berjalan. Maka . . .

9. I am grateful for this identification of the source, and for a discussion of its contents, to Bpk. Minarno of the Akademi Seni Karawitan Indonesia in Solo, Indonesia.
10. The considerable deviance of modern Malay (and Indonesian) from other Austronesian languages is described in Foley (1974). The notion is further developed in Becker and Wirasno (1976).

11. This was a major point of discussion at the Second Eastern Conference on Austronesian Linguistics, Ann Arbor, 1974.
12. This point is discussed thoroughly and demonstrated for Tagalog, another Austronesian language, in Foley and Van Valin (1977).
13. For further discussion of the Greek origins of our basic linguistic categories, see Benveniste (1973).
14. See Foley (1974) and Becker and Wirasno (1976).
15. The terminology in this table is chosen to indicate that sentences display rhetorical relations and clauses, syntactic relations (see note 2). Further details about these structures are found in Ajamiseba (1973). Ajamiseba also describes several other kinds of Malay sentences (as rhetorical figures).
16. Written Classical Malay appears to have no "standard" dialect, and texts vary widely, as one can observe by reading even short passages of the *Hikayat Pandawa Lima,* the *Hikayat Rama,* and the *Hikayat Abdullah.* One can still, I think, recognize a direction of change that includes, among other things, the loss of the *pun, -lah* structure and closer syntactic resemblance with Indo-European languages. One of the focal points in this history is the *Hikayat Abdullah,* an autobiography by Raffles' Malay teacher and translator, who was not a native speaker of Malay. Aspects of the language of the *Hikayat Abdullah,* including major differences from the text under consideration here, are well described in Hopper 1979.

    There is as yet no adequate "outsider's" grammar of Classical or modern Malay (including Bahasa Indonesia). There are several excellent works in Malay and Bahasa Indonesia.

    The meaning of these affixes remains problematic, though it is by now clear that they are not easily describable in Western grammatical terminology. Up to now grammarians have only been able to illustrate the range of their functions, which my own labels have tried to suggest. I think that a major source of the difficulty in describing these affixes has been that discourse strategies have changed rapidly in the past few hundred years of the history of Malay—and with them the semantics of the verb-affix systems (see note 10).
17. The notion of stereotypic scripts comes from Schank (1975). See also the notion of plot in Young, Becker, and Pike (1970).
18. See Longacre (1976), especially chapter 5, on plots.
19. Javanese aesthetic notions are described in Zoetmulder (1974), particularly pages 172–73. The word for aesthetics, *kalangwan,* can describe both art and nature. It is an inflexion of a root *langö,* which describes (p. 173):

    the quality by which an object appeals to the aesthetic sense. It does so not by the clarity and immediacy of its beauty, but, on the contrary, because it seems distant, half hidden and apparently inaccessible; because it is suggestive, but does not reveal itself fully; because it allures, hitting at as yet unrevealed riches, so that the seeker after beauty is consumed by longing and the desire to reach it.

20. Reverse deixis (making the hearer the reference point) is a characteristic of politeness systems of many Southeast Asian languages. It would reverse speaker and hearer in this cline. I have added *location* as the pole opposite *person*, so that the progression is from figure to ground.

21. For Kawi, see Becker and Oka (1977). For Malagassy, see Rajaona (1971, 1972).

22. This notion has also been central in the work of John Robert Ross, in many recent articles, including Cooper and Ross (1975), and in the work of Talmy Givón, particularly in Givón (1976).

23. See Verhaar (1977).

24. See Jeffrey Dreyfuss (1977) for a more elaborate description of this "stative" prefix and its syntactic functions.

25. The presence of the Malay form *mentelah* indicates that *te-* (from *ter-*, which loses *-r* before *l-*) is a prefix; if it were clearly part of the root, the form would be *menelah*. Of course, the etymology may be more complex, e.g., the converging of two roots, *la'ah* and *telah*.

26. This notion of "heaviness" came up first in a discussion of the *Hikayat Pandawa Lima* with R. Anderson Sutton. For its relevance to both calendars and music, see J. Becker (1979), A. Becker (1979), and Geertz (1973).

27. For etymology as a strategy in Javanese theater, see A. Becker (1979). An excellent study of etymology as a strategy in linguistics is Malkiel (1975).

28. Density of context is a distinctive feature of Southeast Asian music, painting, and shadow puppetry. The tropical forest, as a source of generative power, is probably a model for them all; i.e., all are iconic of a particular kind of nature with multiply simultaneous seasons (e.g., trees, our stable natural calendars in the north, in a tropical forest lose their leaves at different times, in different length cycles, some years long) rather than the more nearly unified cycle of the northern forest. Without getting too reductionist about it, dominant ecosystems could not help having an influence on what we think "natural" in symbolic systems underlying wayangs, calendars, and music: in one dimension—the dimension of "naturalness"—is the perceived image of the tropical and subtropical ecology. My thanks to Derek Brereton for his paper on this idea. See also A. Becker (1979), J. Becker (1979), and Geertz (1973), which all imply this notion, I think.

29. Many more figures—i.e., sentences as rhetorical strategies—remain to be studied before we can begin to understand a *text*, with *understanding*

defined as 'the imagination of deep context', what Clifford Geertz calls 'thick description', here applied to linguistics: sentence by sentence, text by text, a grammar emerges. Some of the other figures are described in the works of Shelley Errington (1974, 1975, 1976), which led many of us into a deeper understanding of Malay texts—a truer reading, as she taught us to reconstruct a segment of the Classical Malay world.

30. Hopper (1979) describes very well a later stage of Malay in the work most usually mentioned as the beginning of modern Malay, the *Hikayat Abdullah*. The date of the *Hikayat Abdullah* is mid–nineteenth century. The date of the *Hikayat Pandawa Lima* is "kira2 pada pertengahan kurun Masehi ke XV" [Syed Nasir bin Ismail, Kata Pengantar, *Hikayat Pandawa Lima*—see Hussain (1964)]: approximately in the middle of the fifteenth century A.D. The great grammatico-rhetorical variety in Classical Malay texts is not only to be explained by change over time but must also be explained by a variety of literary dialects, if not individual styles, I suspect.

REFERENCES

Ajamiseba, Danielo C. (1973) *A Classical Malay Text Grammar: Insights into a Non-Western Text Tradition*. Doctoral dissertation. University of Michigan.

Anderson, Benedict (1976) "A Time of Darkness and a Time of Light: Transposition in Early Indonesian Nationalist Thought." Paper presented at the Congress of Human Sciences, August.

Becker, A. L. (1979) "Text-building, Epistemology, and Aesthetics in the Javanese Shadow Theatre." In A. Becker and A. Yengoyan, eds., *The Imagination of Reality*. Ablex, Norwood, New Jersey.

Becker, A. L., and I Gusti Ngurah Oka (1974) "Person in Kawi: Exploration of an Elementary Semantic Dimension." In *Proceedings of the First International Conference of Austronesian Comparative Linguistics*. Honolulu, Hawaii.

Becker, A. L., and Umar Wirasno (1976) "On the Nature of Syntactic Change in Bahasa Indonesia." Paper presented to the Second Eastern Conference on Austronesian Languages, Ann Arbor, Michigan.

Becker, Judith O. (1979) "Time and Tune in Java," in Becker and Yengoyan, eds., *The Imagination of Reality*.

Benveniste, Emil (1973) "Categories of Thought and Categories of Language." In *Problems in General Linguistics*. University of Miami Press, Coral Gables, Florida.

Cooper, W., and John Robert Ross (1975) "World Order." Unpublished manuscript.

Dreyfuss, Jeffrey (1977) "Verb Morphology and Semantic Case Role Information." Paper presented at the Austronesian Symposium, Honolulu, Hawaii.

Errington, Shelley (1974) "A Disengagement: Notes on the Structure of Narrative in a Classical Malay Text." In *Papers from the Conference on Indonesian and Malay Literature*. Madison, Wisconsin.

Errington, Shelley (1975) *A Study of Genre: Form and Meaning in the Malay Hikayat Hang Tuah*. Doctoral dissertation, Cornell University.

Errington, Shelley (1976) "Some Comments on Style in the Meanings of the Past." Paper presented at the Conference on Southeast Asian Perceptions of the Past, Australian National University, Canberra.

Foley, William (1974) "Whatever Happened to Malay?" Paper presented to the First International Conference on Austronesian Linguistics, Honolulu, Hawaii.

Foley, William (1976) "Inherent Referentiality and Language Typology." Unpublished manuscript.

Foley, William, and Robert D. Van Valin, Jr. (1977) "On the Viability of the Notion of 'Subject' in Universal Grammar." In *Proceedings of the Third Annual Meeting of the Berkeley Linguistics Society*, Berkeley, California.

Frost, Robert (1949) "The Figure a Poem Makes." In *Complete Poems of Robert Frost, 1949*. Holt, New York.

Gass, William H. (1973) Introduction to *The Geographical History of America*, by Gertrude Stein. Vintage Books, New York.

Geertz, Clifford (1973) "Person, Time and Conduct in Bali," chapter 14 of *The Interpretation of Cultures*. Basic Books, New York.

Givón, Talmy (1978) *On Understanding Grammar*. Academic Press, New York.

Grimes, Joseph (1975) *The Thread of Discourse*. Mouton, The Hague.

Hawkinson, Ann, and Larry Hyman (1974) "Hierarchies of Natural Topic in Shona," *Studies in African Linguistics* 5, 147–70.

Hopper, Paul J. (1979). "Aspect and Foregrounding in Discourse." In Talmy Givón, ed., *Discourse and Semantics (Syntax and Semantics 12)*. Academic Press, New York.

Hussain, Khalid, ed. (1964) *Hikayat Pandawa Lima* (Siri Sastera DBP. Bil. 18). Dewan Bahasa dan Pustaka, Kuala Lumpur.

Longacre, Robert (1976) *An Anatomy of Speech Notions*. Peter de Ridder, Lisse.

Malkiel, Yakov (1975) "Etymology and Modern Linguistics," *Lingua* 36, 101–20.

Meyerowitz, Patricia (1975) Introduction to *How to Write*. Dover, New York.

Mukarovsky, Jan (1977) In *The Work and Verbal Art*, John Burbank and Peter Steiner, eds. Yale University Press, New Haven.

Pike, Kenneth L. (1975) *On Describing Languages*. Peter de Ridder, Lisse.

Rajaona, Simeon (1971) *Problème de morphologie malagache*. Rev Perc Zucclto, Ambozontany, Fianarantsoa.

Rajaona, Simeon (1972) *Structure du malagache, étude des formes predicatives.* Ambozontany, Fianarantsoa.

Ricoeur, Paul (1971) "The Model of the Text: Meaningful Action Considered as Text," *Social Research* 38, 529–62.

Ricoeur, Paul (1976) *Interpretation Theory: Discourse and the Surplus of Meaning.* Texas Christian University Press, Fort Worth.

Shank, Roger C. (1975) "SAM—A Story Understander." Yale Artificial Intelligence Project, Research Report 43, Yale University, New Haven.

Silverstein, Michael (1977) "Hierarchy of Features and Ergativity." In Dixon, ed., *Grammatical Categories in Australian Languages,* 112–71. Australian Institute of Aboriginal Studies, Canberra.

Stein, Gertrude (1975 [1931]) *How to Write.* Dover, New York.

Verhaar, John (1977) "On Speech and Thought." In William McCormack and Stephen A. Wurm, eds., *Language and Thought, Anthropological Issues.* Mouton, The Hague.

Wittgenstein, Ludwig (1958) *Philosophical Investigations.* Macmillan, New York.

Young, Richard, Alton L. Becker, and Kenneth L. Pike (1970) *Rhetoric: Discovery and Change.* Harcourt, Brace, and World, New York.

Zoetmulder, P. J. (1974) *Kalangwan.* Martinus Nijhoff, The Hague.

Silence Across Languages

It has long seemed to me that the experience of writing an essay and the experience of learning a new language in situ have much in common. In the rhetoric book I wrote years ago with Richard Young and Kenneth Pike, field-work was very much in our minds—the work of discovery and emerging understanding within a strange and distant language. When we finished Rhetoric: Discovery and Change *in 1969, I was in Java, trying to reattune myself to a strange wordscape. Here, in 1985, I was in Malaysia, beginning once again.*

The difference was the framing: just as learning Javanese was framed by my experience in Burma, so learning Malay was framed by my experience in Java. Each time the earlier experience began to make sense later.

❖   ❖   ❖

Exotic Wordscapes

I have just returned once again from an episode of fieldwork, five months in Malaysia where I was living again in a very different culture, speaking a very different language, feeling my identity eroding and reshaping once again, as it had before in Burma and Java—each time no less painfully. This last time, in fact, I was not there in Malaysia to gather information or to seek instruction but rather just to have this experience once again.

I was teaching semantics in Malay at a Malaysian university, and so I had a forum, my class, in which reflections on the experience of entering a new language were appropriate. In Malaysia a lot of things happened to me just because I could understand Malay pretty well, even though I expressed myself very awkwardly. But few of the people I met during long weekend walks through the country-side knew that I could understand them: they would say things to each other on the assumption that I could not understand, and some of the things they said they would be far too polite to say if they thought I could understand. For instance, I would sometimes be referred to by children as Mat Salleh, a common Malay name frequently used in colonial times to refer indirectly to an Englishman. It sounds like "mad sailor," for only a mad dog, Englishman, or drunk would walk around so fast in the noonday sun, but I am not sure where the name comes from. They wouldn't have used that name if they thought I could understand it. It triggered elaborate verbal play and a flurry of jokes among children, as I walked by not letting on I understood—but taking it all back to class as the raw material for studying semantics.

Gradually, as one becomes more and more attuned to the unfamiliar wordscape, a context different from the context of English emerges. Some very exotic things, like food and dress, for instance, become familiar rather rapidly—even rotten fish (Burma) and bare bellies (Bali)—and very familiar things become more and more exotic—like modes of verification or courtesy. When we confront a distant language, we are compelled to give full attention to the fact that saying, for instance, "I am" is something we do with words in English, for in that distant language there is no *I* like our *I*, and no *am* at all. To put one's speaking self into words in Burmese, Javanese, or Malay is to make claims of status (high or low) that alienate our very selves, an in none of those languages is there either a verb like *be* (a copula) or a distinction between present and past tense.

And so, in these exotic wordscapes, there is always an exuberance of meaning that comes of reading English into the wordscape (seeing *I*, and *being*, and *present tense* in the world not in my language). And there is a simultaneous deficiency of meaning that comes of not bringing the distinctions of Burmese, Javanese, or Malay into play. Fieldwork is where these things get sorted out, slowly, over generations.

Silences

At the center of fieldwork one confronts silence—a silence beyond language. The great Spanish philologist, José Ortega y Gasset, described it clearly and succinctly when he wrote, "The stupendous reality that is language cannot be understood unless we begin by observing that speech consists above all in silences. . . ." We think first of the little pauses between words and sentences—the silences between sounds—but Ortega means something more basic. He continues, "A being who could not renounce saying many things would be incapable of speaking. . . ."

Such is clearly the case for us all, even in monolingual settings, but Ortega carries the idea further, to the interaction across languages, to translation.

> And each language represents a different equation between manifestations and silences. Each people leaves some things unsaid *in order to* be able to say others. Because *everything* would be unsayable. Hence the immense difficulty of translation: translation is a matter of saying in a language precisely what that language tends to pass over in silence. A "theory of saying, of languages," would also have to be a theory of the particular silences observed by different peoples.

Prior Text

Let's think about these silences across languages. Silence is more than the fact that in Malay or Burmese there isn't a word for something (like *I*), and silence is also not just about having or not having a grammatical distinction (like tense) or having or not having a syntactic figure (like the copula figures); silence is something far more pervasive and difficult to cope with than these—the silence of memory. My hearing of Malay, reinforced by many grammars and many dictionaries, is almost entirely one-dimensional. I do not know, when I hear something in Malay, whether it is an original utterance, or a cliché, or a proverb. Suppose I said to you, "Seek and ye shall find," and you took that sentence as an original act of language shaping by me. In just that way, I often did not know whether a Malay was saying something new and original or old and well known. It was the same a few years ago when my written account of the power and originality of the Javanese shadow play struck my

Javanese friends as we might be struck if someone said the obvious, like "The interesting thing about TV is the way stories are inter-rupted by commercials." What was fresh for me was obvious for them.

When one considers that everything anyone says or writes both speaks the past (says something old) and speaks the present (says something new), to use Maurice Bloch's terms, then the importance of not being able to tell old from new and past from present gets serious.

In my failure to recognize quotations or clichés, I began to sense the pervasiveness of a kind of indirect quotation in all of our languaging. *Everything* anyone says has a history and hence is, in part, a quotation. *Everything* anyone says is also partly new, too, and part of anyone's ability in a language is the ability to tell the difference between the new and the old. But when you speak a foreign lan-guage, everything is contemporary, for outsiders have very little mem-ory in that new language and its past is silent. It seems to me that grammars and dictionaries are attempts to remedy this deficiency of memory.

One can have a similar experience in one's own language, experi-encing lingual exclusion nearer to home. I once found myself, a small-town Midwesterner, at a rather prestigious East Coast institution. At lunch, I was repeatedly intimidated by the power and originality of the conversation, so much so that I stopped having lunch at all after a few weeks, for I felt my confidence as a teacher and writer slipping away, and that seemed, just then, more essential than good food. A friendly local native finally told me that the problem was only a defi-ciency of prior text, which could be overcome if every morning I read, as they did, the "agenda," the *New York Times*. I did, and it worked. I now shared with them a daily prior text, an aggregate of memories, and I heard now the pervasiveness of prior text in all they said. They were not intimidating, and I could speak, now, with confidence and originality. Language intimidates until, like Dorothy with the Wizard, you find out how it all works.

All that we know has an agenda, an aggregate of remembered and half-remembered prior texts, which are there to be evoked. And most of what we say about sports, politics, war, science, philosophy, health, law—in fact, almost everything—has come to us from prior texts. It comes to us already in words, already languaged. When we speak, we adjust this old language to new situations, but our originality, of social necessity, is minimal. In Malay, I had no memory to speak from. What prior texts Malay evoked for me were all English, except for a very few literary texts: the *Hikayat Hang Tuah*, the *Sejarah Melayu*, a few Malay poems by a friend, and a few Malay proverbs I had memorized once from a book. Essentially Malay was and remains one-dimensional to me.

I believe that it is this one-dimensionality, the absence of memory, that creates the basic need for grammars and dictionaries. In the absence of a lingual memory to draw upon in Malay, I try to formulate tactical generalizations about how to shape utterances in Malay and to establish equivalences between Malay and English words. This is, of course, not something I do alone, for it is part of a long, historical process begun when the first unknown Anglophone met the first unknown Malayophone. They probably met in mutual fear and it was an act of bravery for the one who first spoke of herself or himself as *I* or *aku* in the other's language.

The only way I can verify any of this is to point to these experiences, tell these stories, and hope that they evoke resonant memories in you, for there is no human Language of Truth beyond individual human languages. If there were a Language of Truth (Sanskrit? Latin? Arabic? English? Malay?), I could describe Malay in it for you and you would see that what I say is true or false. But there is no Language of Truth—only many languages in which people try to tell the truth, and these languages are very different. Each language is a different equation between manifestation and silence. If these deep differences between languages are not real, then there is no reason, as too many now believe, not to strive for a world in which only English remains. But I doubt that any Malay or Burmese or Javanese wants that, for it entails a loss of all but English memories. One senses that the important battles of the twenty-first century will be over the noosphere, the realm in which we shape, store, retrieve, and communicate our knowledge.

The silence of the fieldworker is a silence of memory. Silence here is a negative thing: something is missing. Prior text. It is worth noting, I think, that there is this same silence in all structural linguistics—an absence of time, of memory. The dominant metaphor in most current linguistics sees language as a timeless code, encoding timeless, universal "thought" or "concepts" in different ways. An alternative to this is to think of languaging as an endless social process of orienting and reorienting ourselves and each other to a constantly changing environment. The Javanese call this process *jarwa dhosok*, pressing old texts into the present situation. Here we do well to replace the word *language*, as an accomplished system or structure, with the word *languaging* as the performance of a repertoire of games or *orientations*, à la Wittgenstein, or Goffman, or Maturana (e.g., greetings, lectures, last words, messages on answering machines, little signs in the rear windows of cars, etc.), all of them changing over time, driven by their own pasts. Language in this view is not denotational but orientational; in other words, languaging is one means by which we continually attune ourselves to context. In a distant language, we have to relearn to attune ourselves, which means primarily building new memories.

A fieldworker learns, it seems to me, that we have a common language to the extent we have common prior texts.

That Reminds Me of a Story

On the first day of the semantics class in Malaysia, I told a story, translating it unrehearsed from English to Malay. I wanted to make a point about stories, shifting the focus of these advanced Malay students of linguistics away from words and sentences examined out of context toward stories in context. "Storying-in-context" is a basic way people understand things and hence the appropriate basis for this course in semantics I was to teach there. Thinking about stories this way—as "orienting" people, not denoting "concepts"—was something I had first learned from the work of Gregory Bateson, and so I felt it was appropriate to begin the study of semantics in Malaysia with homage to him. Telling this story of his would, in my plan, lead into discussion of Bateson and his way of thinking. And, also, one learns in Southeast Asia that it is far better to speak the past in statements concerning basic truths than it is to speak the present. It is a matter of both politeness and verification. It is seemly to praise one's teachers, and it lends validity to what one says.

Here is Gregory Bateson's little story about stories, in his words.

There is a story which I have used before and shall use again: A man wanted to know about mind, not in nature, but in his private large computer. He asked it (no doubt in his best Fortran), "Do you compute that you will ever think like a human being?" The machine then set to work to analyze its own computational habits. Finally, the machine printed its answer on a piece of paper, as such machines do. The man ran to get the answer and found, neatly typed, the words:

THAT REMINDS ME OF A STORY

In the silence that followed my retelling of this story in Malay, I finally laughed, out of the awkward self-consciousness of speaking a new language. Nobody in the class understood the story. It struck me that my Malay was completely inadequate, and so, in a panic that I hoped was concealed, I asked a Malay professor, Dr. Azhar Simin, who had finished his Ph.D. in linguistics at Michigan and had read Bateson, if he would tell the story. He agreed, and as I listened to his Malay it seemed beautifully lucid. But still, nobody in the class laughed, nobody understood. And so we tried to explain, Dr. Simin and I, and it all got more and more complex. Trying to translate that story into Malay consumed the class period and left it tangled like knotted string.

That night I tried to put my finger on why it had been so difficult to explain Gregory's little story. It was not that my Malay students didn't know computers, for there was a room full of computers down the hall and I had seen these students working there. They knew what the words meant, even *Fortran*. It was the silences that gave them trouble. Why did the man want to know about mind? they had asked, and why did it remind the computer of a story? And I had answered that it didn't matter why the man wanted to know, only that he was the kind who might—and it dawned on me that one never said in Malay, "That reminds me of a story." That sentence, translated into Malay, evoked no memory. If you haven't heard that sentence many, many times, Gregory's story has no point, for it rests on the ordinariness, the vernacularity, of "That reminds me of a story." The point of the story is the way the answer to the man's question *demonstrates* the computer's understanding. It takes real effort for us to see how much prior text that story rests upon.

In my room that night in Malaysia I tried to list the silences a Malay might face in understanding that story—the prior texts it requires to be both funny (a joke) and serious (an insight) at the same time. The next day I would check my list with the class. I would use the story as an example of silence across languages, and I got out my Ortega, another voice from the past I wanted to share. Then it occurred to me that I couldn't think of a Malay word for silence. How would I talk about the English word *silence* in Malay?

I got out some dictionaries, but there was no Malay word for silence that didn't also entail too many other things, like loneliness or motionlessness. For the rest of my stay in Malaysia I asked the help of poets and scholars, but we found no useful Malay word for the English word *silence*. And even if we had found one in the end, the difficulty of the search suggests that the word would have evoked little memory in my undergraduates.

Now, it is very important that you, the reader, not see this as a description of any inadequacy of Malay or Malays. I fear to tell these stories because they are so often taken as instances of cross-cultural condescension, particularly English-language condescension to Malay. Every human language must appear deficient from the point of view of another language. Every human language is a way that people have developed of orienting themselves to each other and to nature, and each is a different equation, in Ortega's terms, between utterance and silence. There is no competition between English and Malay to eliminate all silences, and I leave it to others to point out all the silences of English. It just seemed to be a fortuitous coincidence that Malay should be silent about silence.

And I hope the reader is careful in the way a fieldworker must be, reminding ourselves continually that *silence* is not a transcendental, universal concept but a word in our language with a history. And the difficulty of translation I experienced did not uncover a hole in Malay but rather a hint of a significant difference between the languages. Each language, from the point of view of another, appears full of holes. Forgive me for repeating this point, but it is crucial—and for a fieldworker who has returned home and reentered Plato's Cave, it is a persistent point of misunderstanding.

Fieldwork and Writing

Before going any further with these reflections of a semantics teacher in Malaysia, I want to turn to some of the reasons I think that these matters are relevant to someone writing an essay.

The silences we all face in writing are very much like those I confronted in Malaysia. Our differences of memory are just as troublesome right at home as they are across the world in Southeast Asia. I can only guess, reader, what prior texts these words and stories evoke for you. I count on enough similarity so that you can recognize what I am trying to do and enough charity that you will help in supplying the similarities from your own repertoire of stories. A writer counts on that in a reader. But the difficulty of writing, like the difficulty of reading, is that across two different minds there is so much exuberance and so much deficiency in the understanding of each. Contemplating the experiences of fieldwork, you come to see this not as a special problem but as the normal situation of languaging. Ortega called these two conditions (*exuberance* and *deficiency*) the first two axioms of modern philology. Everything anyone says or writes is always, to another, both exuberant (i.e., says more than it plans) and deficient (i.e., says less than it intended). Across distant cultures or between husband and wife, these can be and frequently are intolerable.

In return for the reader's filling in of silences, a writer promises useful or at least amusing stories.

Another Story: You Can't Ask Questions Like That

Here is another story about Ortega's kind of silence. (I am convinced that if I tell the right story the right way you will believe me.) This story, too, is about absence of prior text. It is from the *New York Times* (i.e., the "agenda"), Sunday, November 13, 1977; it is titled "They Call Him the Baryshnikov of Bali." The article is written by Allen Hughes, paraphrased and condensed here by me.

The Baryshnikov of Bali was Wayan Pasek Yusabawa, a young Balinese dancer in a troupe touring in the West who was evoking very laudatory reviews in the London and New York press. He was called "a boy prodigy," a "star." Mr. Hughes interviewed him in New York via a translator.

> The first question was, "How old are you?" Wayan looked perplexed. The translator explained that the matter of age in years has little meaning in Bali.
>
> Wayan's passport says 17, which is clearly impossible, and a recent press release mentioned 12. Somebody at the interview said he was 13, which seemed not unreasonable since he is in the equivalent of our first year of junior high school.
>
> That was only the beginning of all those questions about age and time.
>
> "How old were you when you began to dance?" Shoulder shrug and doubtful look. "Ten?" The answer was something of a question.
>
> "And how long have you studied dance?" Answer: "Study?"
>
> The company administrator says not more than six months, adding, "In Bali, six months can be too long for a child."
>
> Then, "Do you practice dance every day?" Answer: "Every day? Why would anyone do that? No, only when we have to dance somewhere."

There are many more exchanges in Mr. Hughes's very perceptive story of this interview, but I will quote just one more, near the end.

"What do you want to be when you are an adult? A dancer?"
Silence.
Translator: "You can't ask Indonesians questions like that."

What the translator meant, I think, in explaining the silence of the Baryshnikov of Bali was not just that it is impolite to ask an Indonesian questions like that but that you are putting the boy in real jeopardy if you expect him to make an utterance only a god could utter. Not every being can utter every *I*.

It is not just that a particular story, like Gregory's computer story, may never have been told in another language but also that what you do with words in one language is not the same as what you do with words in another. The language games are different—not all but most. What do you do in an interview? What do you not do?

The silences across languages involve not only things one is not able to say but also things one *should* not say, or *must* not say, for one reason or another. An act of languaging, a language game, has a past, but it also has some essential silences: things you do not do with words without changing the game. Howsoever the Balinese translator might describe what happened to evoke that boy's silence, he declared the question outside the game of interviewing.

Putting an Edge on It

So far this essay has been a string of stories (walking roads in Malaysia, teaching semantics there, reading the *New York Times*, telling Gregory's story about the computer, the Baryshnikov of Bali, among others) oriented around silence. I have served you if you find any of them retellable—reoriented to your own memories. To give them a point, I have added commentary and some quotations, with the hope that these also are useful. But there is something more, something elusive. I think maybe it is restrained aggression. Anger, maybe. Against what? Disrespect for silence. Each people—and each person—leaves some things unsaid in order to be able to say others. Each language—and each person—represents a different equation between manifestations and silences.

And *anger* is a word for a rhetorical motive, a reason for doing something with words. With anger, the breath gets a little rough and strong. Try to breathe in and out heavily and speak at the same time. You will sound angry. Why would anyone want to sound like that? Silence. Discretion suggests keeping silent what should be kept silent, but I would like to have an edge of anger to push these words a little harder, a little anger like a barely perceived motion, seen out of the corner of the eye, alongside a road in Malaysia.

ACKNOWLEDGMENTS

The references to Ortega are primarily to chapter 11 ("What People Say: Language. Toward a New Linguistics") in *Man and People*, translated by Willard R. Trask (New York: Norton, 1957). The references to Bateson are to the introduction of *Mind and Nature: A Necessary Unity* (New York: Dutton, 1979). The references to Wittgenstein are to *Philosophical Investigations* (New York: Macmillan, 1953). References to Goffman are to his last book, *Forms of Talk* (Philadelphia: University of Pennsylvania Press, 1981). References to Maturana are to *The Tree of Knowledge: The Biological Roots of Human Understanding* (Boston: New Science Library, 1987). The references to Bloch are to "Symbols, Song, Dance and Features of Articulation" (*European Journal of Sociology* 15, 1974); and to the introduction to his *Political Language and Oratory in Traditional Society* (New York: Academic Press, 1975).

On silence, see particularly Bernard P. Dauenhauer, *Silence: The Phenomenon and Its Ontological Significance* (Bloomington: Indiana University Press, 1980); and Deborah Tannen and Muriel Saville-Troike, eds., *Perspectives on Silence* (Norwood, N.J.: Ablex, 1985).

I must also acknowledge the help of my students and colleagues in Malaysia and Indonesia, particularly Mohd. haji Salleh, Azhar Simin, Ariel Heryanto, and Bambang Kaswanti Purwo. In America, I am grateful to the English Department of Carnegie Mellon University, particularly Richard Young; the Law and Culture Club, particularly James B. White, Kenneth DeWoskin, and Joseph Vining; and the English Composition Board, University of Michigan, particularly Barbra Morris, for useful reactions to previous versions of this essay.

PART 4
TRANSLATING EMERSON INTO OLD JAVANESE

Beyond Translation:
Esthetics and
Language Description

For many years I have tried, without success, to write an essay called "Going Out and Coming Back" in which I want to argue that translating into one's own language is a profoundly different process, at all levels, from translating out of it. Enrichment versus impoverishment, gain versus loss.

Here is the other half of the process—an attempt to take a well-known sentence of Emerson's out of English and into Old Javanese with the help of many Javanese and Balinese friends. It proved to be one of the most pleasant episodes of fieldwork I have ever undertaken. Up to now I have pontificated on the problems of translating into English, and here I turn the other way and come to realize the loss translation entails, for which restitution is necessary.

In this essay, too, I began to spell aesthetics *as* esthetics, *as John Dewey spelled it, for in Dewey's* Art as Experience *I found, finally, a useful approach to considerations of beauty, power, and emotion in languaging. Before reading Dewey, I had been searching for a way to talk about esthetic matters: with Dewey's work I found it. And so I follow his spelling of the word.*

Furthermore, I found in American pragmatism, in the work of Emerson, Charles Peirce, William James, Gertrude Stein, and Dewey particularly, a philosophy of language I could feel at home in.

❖   ❖   ❖

Art and the equipment to grasp it are made in the same shop.
—Clifford Geertz

This essay is put together as a main plot plus several asides, meant to give some support to the main plot. The main plot is an answer to the question: How does one describe a language in order not to exclude esthetic—one might even say moral—values?

297

Language as Paradox

In the fifties, the Spanish Heideggerian philologist, José Ortega y Gasset (1959), began a seminar on Plato's *Symposium* with a discussion of "the difficulty of reading." To read a distant text—distant in space, time, or conceptual world—is a utopian task, he wrote, a task whose "initial intention cannot be fulfilled in the development of its activity and which has to be satisfied with approximations essentially contradictory to the purpose which had started it" (1959:1). In that sense, the activity of language is in many particular ways utopian: one can never convey just what one wants to convey, for others will interpret what they hear, and their interpretation will be both exuberant and deficient. As Ortega (p. 2) put it:

1. Every utterance is deficient—it says less than it wishes to say.
2. Every utterance is exuberant—it says more than it plans.

He called these "Axioms for a New Philology." (I think we can substitute *linguistics* for *philology*, since Ortega himself appears to use the terms interchangeably.)[1] It may seem strange to found something on a paradox—the successful resolution of which is utopian—yet Ortega is not the first to find matters lingual in some basic way paradoxical. Bateson (1972:271–78) gave us the notion of the double bind as a condition necessary for higher learning. A double bind is a situation in which one receives two simultaneous and contradictory messages plus the further condition that one may not or cannot leave the situation. Such a bind impels one to examine the context of the whole situation and, in some way or other, try to correct or reshape it. Scollon (1981:344–45) has argued that "all communication must . . . depend on some form of double bind."

> In any communication, the participants are faced with the dilemma of respecting the other's right to be left alone (negative face) and the other's right to be accepted as a participating member of society (positive face). . . . I believe the temporal bond of

ensemble completes the picture . . . it is ensemble which holds participants together in a mutual attention to the ongoing situation, and it is the polarity of positive and negative face that forces the attention to the communication of relationship. These in consort produce a double bind which is the mechanism by which conversants learn to learn.

And so conversation, like philology, is a matter of continual self-correction between exuberance (i.e., friendliness: you are like me) and deficiency (i.e., respect: you are not like me). In reading a text from Java or Burma, my understanding is exuberant because of all that I read into the text and deficient because of all that I am blind to.

Of course, this is true, too, between even the closest of friends. However, across great lingual distance one can seldom distinguish cultural stereotype from personal deviation. The hardest thing for me to do in Southeast Asia is to hear, authentically, the individual voice. The differences of culture, in their freshness and strangeness, cannot at first be—as they are to an insider—part of the background. Across distant languages, the hardest thing to hear is the individual voice, i.e., the deviation from stereotypes. A deviation is the way prior text is shaped to the situation at hand.

Everything I observed about Javanese puppet theater—which made me aware of new possibilities for drama—was heard by Javanese friends with an ultrapolite version of "So what else is new?" My esthetic enjoyment in coming to terms with Javanese theater was at the level of the genre itself: I never heard the individual voices until I was able to background the newness of the whole tradition (Becker 1979).

Perhaps this can be made clear with a story about birds. There are several varieties of white-crowned sparrows. Those in Ann Arbor sound slightly different from those in Berkeley or Princeton, though the major contours of the song are recognizable. The bird book (Peterson 1961:237) gives it this way.[2]

Voice:—song begins with a clear plaintive whistle . . . but ends with a husky trilled whistle.

However, that is not all that there is to a white-crowned sparrow song. The general contours are constrained by the species—white-crowned universals, maybe; some variation is dialectical, but part of what a white-crowned is singing is his own song, his own deviations—so that other birds know not only that there is a white-crowned over there, but that it is the same white-crowned who was there yesterday. Each song is to some extent shaped by the particularity of the living being and the environment.

Language, too, can be seen as a hierarchy of constraints, from the species-wide constraints on all humans (and perhaps birds and whales, too) to the particular constraints that make me sound like me (and work out of my memory, shape as I shape, relate to others as I do, and live in my world with some kind of coherence). One can study this continuum at any level, but language is not reducible to just one level. Certain phenomena—like esthetic understanding—appear only at the level of the particular. If we are interested in language in full context—real language—we must take care not to exclude the individual voice, which is the only place where self-correction, that is, change, happens—where the living organism interacts with the environment.

Dewey's Vernacular Esthetics

In order to see what we miss if we exclude esthetic values in studying a language, we must first confront that difficult term, *esthetics*. As a term it is laden with problems—mainly from an exuberance of prior context.[3] One way to cut through all that context is to follow John Dewey and vernacularize the term: bring it back to everyday experience.[4]

> The sights that hold the crowd—the fire engine rushing by . . . the men perched high in the air on girders, throwing and catching red-hot bolts. The sources of art in human experience will be learned by him who sees how the tense grace of the ball player infects the onlooking crowd. (Dewey 1934:5)

In all these experiences, one does not remain a cold spectator, but—in Ricoeur's terms (1981:182)—we are "appropriated" by an event, integrated with it. In a famous passage, Dewey (1934:16) says that experience:

> comes from nature and man interacting with each other. In this interaction, human energy gathers, is released, dammed up, frustrated and victorious. There are rhythmic beats of want and fulfillment, pulses of doing and being withheld from doing.

As he says, repeatedly, a live being recurrently loses and reestablishes equilibrium with his surroundings. Imagine walking in the woods and suddenly realizing you are lost. Emotion, says Dewey, is the conscious sign of a break—actual or impending—in the equilibrium of a person with his or her surroundings. But the break—realizing you are lost—"induces reflection" as well as emotion. One forms an idea of where one is, and as the idea is acted upon one may come gradually to feel it is correct, and a new integration with the world seems more and more possible, and emotion more and more intense. As Dewey (p. 17) writes, "the moment of passage from disturbance into harmony is that of intensest life." At that moment an idea—a plan to find one's way in the forest—becomes incorporated in the world. This is a successful experience, for Dewey "art in germ."

"The thinker," writes Dewey (p. 16), "has his esthetic moment when his ideas cease to be mere ideas and become corporate meanings of objects."

There is a difference—no matter how difficult it may be to place it—between being lost in the woods and seeing a new play. The difference does not lie so much in the experiences themselves as in the cultural frames in which we think about them, as ethnologists and conceptual artists have taught us. It is a game in forest-service training to be left in the woods, with a compass and a map, and no food. The task is called *orienteering*. Here the artifice—the make-believe (Walton 1978)—is only in the circumstances leading up to being lost and the human safety net they insure. One is intentionally lost, like a philologist with a new text.

Successful interaction with the environment—nowadays we would say context—is mediated for humans (and cetaceans? and birds?) by language. And because there is language constantly between us and the world (except, I am told, after long meditation) we lose our animal grace, our unselfconsciousness. Language gives rise to lying, deceit, and self-deception (Bateson 1972:128). Or, at least, it adds a whole new dimension to these sins. Make-believe—for good or bad, or both at once—becomes possible. In a language-encrusted world, the situation at hand is hard to get at.

The problem is not only that there is language but that it is so complex. Using language involves doing several things at once, any one of which can go wrong. That is, in using language I am making sounds (or inscribing them), shaping structures, interacting with people, remembering and evoking prior text, and referring to the world—all at once.[5] Successful interaction with one's context involves harmonizing constraints from all those sources.

Successfully making sounds (or inscribing them)

Successfully building structures

Successfully evoking prior text (or scripts)

Successfully interacting with other people

Successfully referring to a world

Of course, one may be unsuccessful in any of these ways, too, and language can get pathological, because of, say,

A speech impediment

Structural confusion

Unshared prior text

Interpersonal animosity

Lying about the world

These are potential varieties of unsuccessful language experience, ways by which a person can lose integration with context. Successful language experiences imply the successful integration of all these acts involved in uttering. It is at best an unstable integration. Sometimes and with some people we are fluent, sometimes utterly clumsy and inarticulate.

An esthetic experience, then, in this Deweyan sense, is one that begins in disequilibrium (or call it noise or incoherence) and moves toward equilibrium (or harmony or coherence). In art, a special kind of esthetic experience, the disequilibrium—the *ostranenie* ('defamiliar-ization')—is intentional, and there is make-believe in one of the dimensions of meaning.

In another language—distant or close—one has to learn (by self-correction) new ways of interacting in all five dimensions.

New ways of sounding (and new ways to make your face look as you sound)

New ways of shaping words, phrases, sentences, discourse

New ways of interacting—new speech acts

New traditions of prior texts (new scripts)

New perceived, natural worlds

Biography of a Sentence

To illustrate these things, I would like to think about a sentence I have liked for a long time. Dewey (1934:28) quotes it as an example of the intense emotion of the integration of a live being and its context. It is by Emerson, from his long essay, "Nature" (in which he examines all the different ways a person can relate to nature).

Crossing a bare common in snow puddles at twilight under a clouded sky, without having in my thought any occurrence of special good fortune, I have enjoyed a perfect exhilaration.

The first thing to do when studying a sentence like that is to memorize it, just as a pianist studying someone else's music begins by memorizing it and then comes slowly to understand it. One experiences the sentence by slow self-correction of the exuberance and deficiency with which one begins. (One such exuberance in reading Emerson—an exuberance that makes his writing difficult, even painful, to many of my friends—is the speed at which you read him. He must be read slowly, and sounded. He wrote slowly, with a quill pen, for the lecture hall. In order to be appropriated by the work, one must read slowly.)

As you repeat the sentence, bleached, backgrounded things come to the foreground. For instance, it takes a while to hear the sentence, and when one does hear it, to see pattern in the sounding. There are sound metaphors, vocal gestures that enact part of the meaning. I think that what will stand out, in repeating the Emerson sentence, is the k–s sequence, the lingual motion from the back to the front of the mouth. It is there, at the beginning and ending, and repeated in the key words:

> Crossing . . . common . . . snow . . . clouded sky . . . occurrence of special . . . exhilaration

There appears a kind of dimly perceived, submorphemic meaning in articulation itself, including the way one's face looks when making the sounds. In order to see and feel the gestural metaphor of k–s (i.e., motion outward) more clearly, reverse it and sound a list of s–k words (i.e., motion inward).[6]

The correspondence of the sound metaphor and the other meanings of the sentence create what Peirce called iconicity: motion outward and feeling integrated with the world outside. Someone is sure to ask, could Emerson have known all this? The answer, I think, is yes. He did not know it as we have known it just now, but surely the sounds of key words echo through a sentence in the process of composing it, and they are a source of coherence in that sentence, and sometimes something more, a sound metaphor, there in the words. (In this way, words seem more culturally determined and a priori than sentences, which are more shapable to context; that is, the sequence k–s was there in *crossing* before Emerson wrote, but probably not the sequence from *crossing* to *exhilaration*.) We might now define an *iconicity* as an 'integration' across two or more of the multiple acts of using language. In this case it was an integration between sounding and referring.

There is another powerful integration, in this second case, across syntactic shaping and referring. We would all probably divide the sentence into two parts, between *fortune* and *I*. Something rather strange happens at that point in the sentence—as a Javanese linguist put it, it is like a shift in the flow of electricity. Up to *I*, the phrases one by one seem to relate backward (i.e., leftward) to the verb, *crossing*. They contextualize *crossing*, i.e., crossing what? (a bare common), what kind of common? (in snow puddles), when? (at twilight under a clouded sky) how? (without having in my thought any occurrence of special good fortune). The subject of *crossing* is not given, which creates the dependency of this participial phrase on the second part of the sentence. Its nonfiniteness creates a further dependency. But, with the finite main clause (I have enjoyed a perfect exhilaration), all those backward-looking phrases reverse polarity, and all become context for the experience of enjoying perfect exhilaration.

This reversal of polarity gives each of the phrases something new to relate to. We might play with the sentence in order to see this more clearly. First, I number the parts.

1. Crossing a bare common
2. in snow puddles
3. at twilight
4. under a clouded sky
5. without having in my thought any occurrence of special good fortune
6. I have enjoyed a perfect exhilaration

Try any combination of numbers—say 162534. For my taste, every combination seems possible. However, the change of polarity is lost if 1 is not first and 6 last.

A parsing problem arises over whether we treat 2–5 as modifiers of 1, each more distant, and the whole 1–5 as a modifier of 6 (I saw it that way at first), or, on the other hand, consider that the structure is tight up to the *I* and then the modification shifts and the phrases relate separately to 6, as the separate conditions of *exhilaration*. My feeling is that the sentence is dynamic, and that its structure changes. That change of polarity is what gives it rhetorical power, what Gertrude Stein (1931) called its "emotion"—the grammatical ground on which *exhilaration* means.

These are but two ways that the sentence performs what it says. Crudely put, the sounding enacts "motion outward" and the syntactic shaping says something like, "reorient things." These are two instances of particular iconicity.[7]

I am unclear what prior text Emerson's sentence evokes—perhaps a sermon—but the language act he performs is clear. Burke (1966:5) has called it *pontification*.

> pontificate; that is, to "make a bridge." Viewed as sheerly terministic, or symbolic, function, that's what transcendence is: the building of a *terministic bridge* whereby one realm is *transcended* by being viewed in terms of a realm "beyond" it.

Having got about that far in thinking about the sentence and using it a while (and wondering about things like the odd deviation of *in snow puddles*—was that use of *in* a norm for Emerson?), I got a notion to try to translate that sentence into Kawi, an ancient written literary language of Java, still alive in Bali. In the process I learned a great deal more about how the sentence is integrated to a context. There are many things that won't translate. The *k–s* sequence wouldn't work. The change of syntactic polarity was not possible either. In fact, as a rhetorical figure (a language game, a coherence system) this sentence was not possible. Since I had thought some of the meanings of the sentence might appeal to them, I sent a copy of it, in English, to several Kawi scholars in Indonesia. Then, while I was there for ten weeks, working on something else, I talked with each of them about how to translate it into Kawi. The oddest thing about the experience was that none of my friends thought it was at all odd to translate from Old American to Old Javanese.[8]

By the kind of double coincidence one learns to expect in Java and Bali, two of my friends were working on dictionaries going from modern Indonesian to Old Javanese (Kawi). It would be like a dictionary from modern American English to Anglo-Saxon. Everyone had told these lexicographers that such a dictionary was useless. But no. For my task it was useful. Word by word we went from English to Bahasa Indonesia to Kawi. The result was a bizarre English sentence with Kawi words. And, of course, the untranslatable words were little words, like *I, have, a, of*—the little words that supply cohesion within a sentence. Each requires pages of interpretation—for example, a whole set of choices about *I*, which is not relevant to us in English.

In Java, another of my friends began the translation by imagining he was a shadow puppeteer, and he asked, where in a shadow play might that statement (Emerson's) appear, and who could say it? Until that was decided there was no basis for grammatical choices. "Who is speaking?" I was asked, "Is it the puppeteer himself? Impossible, the play is not ever about him. Is it the audience? Impossible, no reason to utter that sentence. If it is in the play, who? to whom? Only a wise god, like Siva or Krishna, talking to other gods, could be so personal. The pronoun must be *nghulun*" (see Becker and Oka 1974). At that point, lexical and grammatical choices were constrained. Already, in the single term 'I' there is a Javanese exuberance, an unavoidable excess of meaning.

Notice here that there are two modes of translation, lexical and pragmatic (or rhetorical). Another friend approached the task a third way. He searched old texts for a similar figure. He found parts of it but no figure like the Emerson sentence. However, by trial and error we all came to a consensus translation.

Lumampah ta   nghulun i harahara asepi
walk   (topic) I   at field   empty/lonely

Ikang sangku ringkā liniputing hima
that pool   there covered   snow

ri wayah ning sandyākāla
at time of   evening

   kasongan ikang ākāsa sök denikang nīlajalada
   under   the sky full of the   blue clouds

 tanpangen ta   nghulun ri wr̥tta ning waralabha
 not-recall (topic) I   at event of   good fortune

paripūrna suka   ta   manah ni nghulun
perfect   liking (topic) heart of I

There is a great deal more exuberance to the Old Javanese sentence
and, at the same time, great deficiencies; for example, there is no
equivalent of the English "*have*" strategies in Kawi. But, when I asked
my friends if the Kawi version of Emerson were a good sentence, if it
were beautiful in Kawi, they all said no. How could such a strange
sentence be beautiful? It is unique. There is no Javanese context for it
to be a part of, no family for it to have resemblance to.

To make a point, I have been going backward—translating out of
English instead of into it—defamiliarizing Emerson to show how far
the Kawi experience is from Emerson, at the most backgrounded or
unselfconscious of levels. If "art and the equipment to grasp it are
made in the same shop" (Geertz 1976:1497), then how can esthetic
values—the successful integration of person and context—be understood across cultures and languages? We are back to the original question, how does one describe a language in order not to exclude those
esthetic values?

Description as Self-Correction

The experience of the Kawi figure, in all its multiple modes of meaning, is different from the Emerson sentence. We usually experience it
the other way around, when literature, music, mythology, grammar,
or any other cultural artifact is brought into English and appears too
exotic in some ways, too bland in others; but we interact with it and
get meaning, seldom bothering to look too closely at the sources of
that meaning. But mostly those distant texts seem like the distant god

that the Javanese first personal pronoun evoked: far from the vernacular, particular world we know. My point is not just the impossibility of translation—which we all know and immediately forget about—but rather its incompleteness as a source of understanding another language, as a particular means by which an individual interacts with his environment, as a possible form of life. It seems to me an interesting task for a linguist to try, in description, to go beyond translation. That is, I think we can use translation as a starting point and—by cutting back exuberances and filling in deficiencies in all dimensions of meaning—move back toward the original. And as the original emerges, like a slowly developing photograph—there is an esthetic experience very special to the philologist—a newly achieved integration within a new world.

But there is an immediate protest. This task is utopian. How can we ever exhaust the manifold exuberances and deficiencies of even a single sentence, to say nothing of a whole literary work? The answer, it seems to me, is that constraints on description are rhetorical and not logical, or as Grimes put it (1975:257–58), "the speaker quits elaborating what he has to say at the point where he has reason to believe that the hearer knows what he is talking about."

Imagine a grammar that begins with a detailed description of a single rich utterance (i.e., a *lebensform*, an episteme, a language game, a coherence system)—minimally a sentence, since that is the smallest lingual unit for which all the modes of meaning are staged (see Ricoeur 1981a). We might think of it as a biography of a sentence, a particular sentence. What the reader might see from that is how to make important corrections of exuberance and deficiency in approaching that language. Translation is the beginning point, necessarily, and the end point is when the particularity of the sentence slowly emerges, enough so that it evokes an authentic environment, a context. Dewey (1934:15–16) put it, somewhat cryptically, this way: "The thinker has his esthetic moment when his ideas cease to be mere ideas and become the corporate meanings of objects." That means, I think, when a "plan" to find one's way out of the woods becomes a successful "way" to get out of woods, or when an interpretation of a distant text makes it appear a successful means of being in the world.[9]

I am not attempting to replace those in linguistics who seek formal representations of a speaker's abstract lingual competence but rather to suggest that not all we need to know about languages can be seen that way, and that our methodology in seeking generalization has its own exuberance and deficiency and needs the self-correction of understanding in a new mode of particularity, new language games, new ways of being in the world, successfully. In fact, I am merely elaborating on Wittgenstein's (1958:81) somewhat puzzling statement "To understand a sentence means to understand a language." To understand a sentence is to hear it or see it in a situation where all of its relations to context—all of its meanings—are active and somehow interacting. At the heart of esthetics is that complex interaction. Bateson and others have explored its disharmonies—those pathological effects of contradictory messages in different "channels" of meaning (for example, saying "I love you" but conveying a metamessage of annoyance, even hatred). Is the opposite of contradictory messages—the harmony or coherence of meanings our understanding seeks—just a lack of contradiction, or something more: a kind of moiré effect across systems, like the exhilaration Emerson experienced?

Summary

Several friends have suggested that a summary of the argument in this essay would be helpful, although the assumption that an essay (unlike an article) is coherent around an argument need not always hold since an essay is predominantly a genre of description and exploration, of describing and exploring a particularity rather than supporting a generality. Yet one might shape a general argument here, as follows.

1. Esthetics, in a Deweyan sense, is about emergent attunement of a live being with its context.
2. Particular language—as a mode of being in the world (à la Wittgenstein or Heidegger)—is attuned to context in at least

five different ways, depending on the mode of context: medium, interpersonal use, lingual structure, evoked prior text, and the extralingual world (Nature) that the text presupposes.

3. In any of these modes, esthetic attunement (or lack of attunement) is possible, giving rise to different definitions of esthetics (see note 3).

4. Attunements across modes (i.e., homologies between medium, use, structure, prior text, and Nature) give a text a kind of esthetic depth that is quite particular.

5. Esthetic depth is in most cases impossible to translate, so that fuller understanding of a distant text requires a step beyond translation, a deconstruction of the translation and a reconstruction of the context of its source, mode by mode, so as to describe and explore its particularity.

ACKNOWLEDGMENTS

Several people have helped me in articulating these thoughts: D. Tannen, J. Becker, S. Tyma, D. Tyma, J. Verhaar, T. Givón, H. Byrnes, C. Geertz, and R. Isaac; and, in Indonesia, I Gusti Ngurah Oka, Soewojo Wojowasito, L. Mardiwarsito, H. Bambang Kaswanti Purwo, and I Gusti Ngurah Bagus. Special thanks are due Anneliese Kramer for helping me to see that language description is also esthetic.

NOTES

1. In several places in his work (1950, 1957, 1959), Ortega mentions his "principios de una Nueva Filología." The earliest such mention I know of is in his *Papeles sobre Velázquez y Goya* (1950).

> Dos leyes de apariencia antagónica, que se complen en toda enunciación. Una suena así: «Todo decir es deficiente»–esto es, nunca logramos decir plenamente lo que nos proponemos decir. La otra ley, de aspecto inverso, declara: «Todo decir es exuberantes» esto es, que nuestro decir manifesta siempre muchas más casas de las que nos proponemos e incluso no pocas que queremos silenciar.

Later, in *Man and People* (1957:242) he writes:

> precisely the splendid intellectual achievement represented by lin-
> guistics as it is constituted today obliges it (noblesse oblige) to attain
> a second and more precise and forceful approximation in its knowl-
> edge of the reality, "language." And this it can do only if it studies
> language not as an accomplished fact, as a thing made and finished,
> but as in the process of being made, hence *in statu nascendi*, in the
> very roots that engender it.

Here and elsewhere, Ortega projects a comparative phenomenology of
language that he calls "una Nueva Filología." As far as I know, he did not
go beyond the two axioms quoted here before he died in 1955.

2. Charles Pyle once remarked on how interesting a metalanguage for
sounds one finds in bird books. Why is the whistle "plaintive," then
"husky"? Here is a purely metaphoric metalanguage, in which birds are
quite usefully humanized.

3. One can describe the history of esthetics as a shifting emphasis on one or
more of the various ways in which a symbolic system relates to a context.
For instance, emphasis on part-whole relations in a hierarchy (structure)
leads to an esthetics of proportion—the relation of parts to each other
(e.g., the *congruentia partium* of Augustine or the elegance of mathemati-
cians and formalists). Emphasis on interpersonal relations leads to an
esthetics of emotion or powerful feeling: pity, fear, eros, the sublime, or
the *rasas* of Indic esthetics. Emphasis on prior text leads to an esthetics or
recognition or the reenactment of Jungian archetypes, or perhaps the
working out of a genre, e.g., the novel or the sonata allegro form. Emphasis on the medium leads to an esthetics of sound itself (in language or
music), or "the line," or the human voice. (For a study of the Chinese
philosophy of sound, see DeWoskin 1982.) Emphasis on the world leads
to an esthetics of imitation or mimesis—the imitation or representation of
"reality" (from Aristotle to Marx). One can see the shifting emphases on
these different perspectives, and their combination, in a work like Beardsley (1966) (see also Philipson 1961). The advantage of an approach like
Dewey's (1934) is that it encourages a multiple view in which all these
sources of esthetic experience are possible.

4. I am using the term *vernacular* in the sense recently developed by Illich
(1980:41).

> *Vernacular* comes from an Indo-Germanic root that implies 'rooted-
> ness' and 'abode'. *Vernaculum* as a Latin word was used for whatever
> was homebred, homespun, homegrown, homemade, as opposed to
> what was obtained in formal exchange. . . . *Vernacular* was used in

this general sense from preclassical times down to the technical formulations found in the *Codex of Theodosius*. It was Varro who picked the term to introduce the same distinction in language. For him, *vernacular speech* is made up of the words and patterns grown on the speaker's own ground, as opposed to what is grown elsewhere and then transported. And since Varro's authority was widely recognized, his definition stuck. He was the librarian of both Caesar and Augustus and the first Roman to attempt a thorough and critical study of the Latin language.

In his very enlightening article (now, I am told, a book) Illich describes the first attempt in Europe to grammaticize the vernacular as a mode of political control, with the *Gramática Castellana* of Elio Antonio de Nebrija, in 1492.

5. For the general notion of language as interlocking actions, I am indebted to Pike (although he formulates it somewhat differently, as in Pike 1978). If one defines meaning as relation to context, then these acts can be considered five epistemologically different contexts in which a text has meaning. Coherence, then, is possible between a text and one source of meaning (e.g., a sentence and its structural context—the larger discourse of which it is a part) or between one kind of context and another (e.g., between structural and interpersonal context, or between prior text and present reference, etc.). These latter coherences are what Peirce termed "iconicities." For an earlier version of this approach, see Becker (1979). Cf. Ricoeur (1981) for a different formulation of context.

6. The notion of "sound metaphor," along with the term, is taken from Fonagy (1971), which includes a bibliography of earlier work.

7. One of the more intriguing questions that occurs to one studying iconicities (or coherence across two or more dimensions of meaning) is whether there may not be some resultant phenomenon (or epiphenomenon), like the moiré effect, a kind of Peircean "third."

8. It must be pointed out, however, that in Java, and particularly Bali, Kawi, or Old Javanese, is still alive. Kawi is reshaped in the shadow theater. Almost everyone has heard it sounded and understands a bit. Consequently, it is not so much a prior stage of language as a specialized current register. Furthermore, each of my informants knows at least five languages, and is quite accustomed to regular code-switching.

9. The connection between esthetic experience and morality for Dewey is that both involve, in a rather Buddhist way, harmony with the situation at hand. Dewey writes (1972:94): "What, then, is moral theory? It is all one with moral *insight*, and moral insight is the recognition of the relationships at hand. This is a very tame and prosaic conception."

For the development of Dewey's conception as the basis for a critique of the social sciences (which is quite applicable to current linguistics), see Rorty (1981). One might substitute *linguistics* for *social sciences* in the passage: "What we hope from the social sciences is that they will act as interpreters for those with whom we have difficulty in talking" (Rorty 1981). See also Rorty (1978) for a detailed argument against the rationalist foundations of much current linguistics.

REFERENCES

Bateson, Gregory. 1972. Style, grace, and information in primitive art. In: Steps to an ecology of mind. New York: Ballantine.

Beardsley, Monroe C. 1966. Aesthetics from Classical Greece to the present. New York: Macmillan.

Becker, A. L. 1979. Text-building, epistemology, and aesthetics in Javanese shadow theatre. In: The imagination of reality: Essays in Southeast Asian coherence systems. Edited by A. L. Becker and Aram A. Yengoyan. Norwood, N.J.: Ablex.

Becker, A. L., and I Gusti Ngurah Oka. 1974. Person in Kawi: Exploration of an elementary semantic dimension. Oceanic Linguistics XIII.229–55.

Burke, Kenneth. 1966. I, eye, aye—Emerson's early essay "Nature": Thoughts on the machinery of transcendence. In: Transcendentalism and its legacy. Edited by Myron Simon and Thornton H. Parsons. Ann Arbor: University of Michigan Press.

Dewey, John. 1934. Art as experience. New York: Minton Balch.

Dewey, John. 1972. Moral theory and practice. In: Early works of John Dewey. Vol. 3. Carbondale: Southern Illinois University Press.

DeWoskin, Kenneth. 1982. A song for one or two: Music and the concept of art in early China. Ann Arbor: Center for Chinese Studies, University of Michigan.

Fonagy, Ivan. 1971. Double coding in speech. Semiotica III.189–222.

Geertz, Clifford. 1976. Art as a cultural system. MLN 91.1473–99.

Grimes, Joseph. 1975. The thread of discourse. The Hague: Mouton.

Illich, Ivan. 1980. Vernacular values. The Co-Evolution Quarterly. Summer. 22–49.

Ortega y Gasset, José. 1950. Papeles sobre Velázquez y Goya. Madrid: Revista de Occidente.

Ortega y Gasset, José. 1959. The difficulty of reading. Diogenes 28.1–17.

Peterson, Roger Tory. 1961. A field guide to the birds. Boston: Houghton Mifflin.

Philipson, Morris, ed. 1961. Aesthetics today. New York: Meridan.

Pike, Kenneth L. 1978. Here we stand—creative observers of language. In: Approches du langage: Actes du colloque interdisciplinaire tenu à Paris. Sorbonne, Serie "Etudes" 16.9–45.

Ricoeur, Paul. 1981. The model of the text: Meaningful action considered as a text. In: Hermeneutics and the human sciences. Edited by John B. Thompson. New York: Cambridge University Press.

Rorty, Richard. 1978. Philosophy and the mirror of nature. Princeton: Princeton University Press.

Rorty, Richard. 1981. Method and morality. In: Values and the social sciences. Edited by N. Hahn, R. Bellah, and P. Rabinow.

Scollon, Ron. 1981. The rhythmic integration of ordinary talk. In: Georgetown University Round Table on Languages and Linguistics 1981. Edited by Deborah Tannen. Washington, D.C.: Georgetown University Press.

Stein, Gertrude. 1975 [1931]. How to write. New York: Dover.

Walton, Kendall. 1978. Fearing fictions. Journal of Philosophy LXXV.5–27.

Wittgenstein, Ludwig. 1958. Philosophical investigations. Trans. by G. E. N. Anscombe. New York: Macmillan.

On Emerson on Language

This essay continues themes found in the previous one, the search for opacity in one's own tradition, one's own philology, and the emerging recognition of a native ancestry of thought about language in American pragmatism, the tradition from Emerson, William James, Charles Sanders Peirce, Gertrude Stein (a student of William James), and John Dewey up to the present in the modern Emersonians and Deweyans. At a time when some of us in linguistics (a very small some, it seemed) were seeking a way out of the impasses of structuralism, this body of interlinked prior texts has proved inspiring and useful.

But here, in this essay, the process was just beginning for me, and it was driven more by Foucault than by pragmatism at this point—a looking back in one's own tradition to find the same kinds of opacity that one finds in a distant language. Emerson's writing on language seemed to me naive and vague until I learned to reattune myself to his distant episteme with the same charity and openness that the languages of Southeast Asia had called for. In that process I discovered some of Emerson's usefulness in the present.

❖   ❖   ❖

Emerson wrote by sentences or phrases rather than by logical sequence. . . . The unity of one sentence inspires the unity of the whole—though its physique is as ragged as the Dolomites.
—Charles Ives

The maker of a sentence . . . launches out into the infinite and builds a road into Chaos and old Night, and is followed by those who hear him with something of wild, creative delight.
—R. W. Emerson

Comparative Noetics

For a philologist, the task is to build a road across time to an old text, or across space to a distant one, and to try to understand it. It is a utopian task but nonetheless essential, at least to the extent that such understanding of distant texts is crucial in an age of rapidly growing, increasingly powerful systems of communication, and diminishing resources. What does it mean that Balinese watch *Star Trek* on television, followed by a propaganda film on the American space program, and mix the two? There are few more difficult questions right now. Is there something like noetic pollution, a spoiling of the noosphere by some cancerous overgrowth? And where might we be—American linguists—in the sweep of the noetic history we are just beginning to write?

The term *noetic* is an old word in English; its turbulent history is traced in the *Oxford English Dictionary*. Coleridge used it to designate a science of the intellect, drawing on the Kantian philosophers of Germany. Emerson knew Coleridge's work well, and visited him on his first visit to England in 1833. In Emerson's early work, the mental realm—the noetic sphere, or, as Pierre Teilhard de Chardin called it, the noosphere—is called Spirit or Thought. Walter Ong has given currency to the old word *noetic*. (In Javanese, the term for reviving old words is *jarwa dhosok*, forcing—literally 'pushing'—old language into the present.) In his essay on the drum languages of Africa, Ong (1977) defines *noetics* as the study of the shaping, storing, retrieving, and communicating of knowledge. He has also laid the groundwork for a new kind of study: comparative and historical noetics, or looking out in space to other cultures and back in time, even within our own, at others' ways of shaping, storing, retrieving, and communicating knowledge. Surely the whole process is language-ful, which is what Benjamin Lee Whorf has had such a hard time trying to tell us: that language is involved in the whole process of shaping, storing, retrieving, and communicating knowledge.

In the histories of particular noetic traditions, there appear to be a very few powerful laws, among them a one-way sequence of changes from orality, to writing, to printing, to secondary orality (this latter is Ong's term for the print-based, electronic orality of our American present). Each stage in this continuum seems to recontextualize the prior stage, so that certain kinds of knowledge remain in the medium of the past: most prayers are still spoken (or thought), many personal letters are still appropriately handwritten, and most books are still printed, though photocopy would allow mass circulation of manuscripts. As Ong and others have shown us, each of these media entails its own noetic economy, its own power and authority: the power of the voice, of the signed document, of print, and of television. Furthermore, major changes in noetic systems seem to happen initially in a few places and then spread to other places, across language boundaries. That is to say, noetic changes for most people in the world have involved language contact, within which a noetically more powerful language exports the secret of its power to the weaker. What increases over time appears to be the scope of central control, as a language adds media. In making these statements, one is forced to hedge, with terms like *appear* and *seem*, in acknowledgment that a new myth of history is being shaped, and like most myths it is to some extent self-serving. As Sartre (1964) wrote: "Progress, that long, steep path which leads to me."

Yet the myth has its power in helping one interpret changes one sees going on. For instance, imagine a village, small, in the hills, where knowledge is stored in the cultivated memories of a few old people, often blind, often women. They sit in special places in trials and other village meetings and tell who is related to whom, and who did what, and who owns what bit of land, and what the last ruler said. And now imagine what happens to them when a young person who can read and write the new national language returns, after a few years of schooling, to the village. The old blind people enter their own new dark ages. This is a dramatic, but oft repeated, instance of noetic change.

Or imagine what happens when a foreign colonial language, always more powerful noetically, replaces—as a source of knowledge—important functions of the local language. Sometimes a voice across time and space lets us share a feeling of noetic change. A Javanese poet writes, in a world in which understanding of the present was shaped by Dutch, in the late nineteenth century:

Anglakoni zaman edan
Ewuh aya ing pambudi

'(We) walk in an unstable world
Not at home, struggling against our own imagination'

I have written elsewhere about this remarkable poem, and the difficulties we have in reading it and understanding it; the English meanings at the deepest levels we must abandon, even as we encounter new ones, meanings of tense and person as background cohesion, and the presence of elaborate focus and deixis—to mention only a few of the more obvious grammatical differences one encounters.

The paradox of philology, to paraphrase Ortega (1959), is that distant texts are always both exuberant and deficient at the same time. I read too much in, and I am unperceptive of what is there, and so I understand only through successive approximation, by giving up—unexpectedly—various etic aspects of English and slowly getting attuned to new emic possibilities of language. Noetic exploration into terra incognita is, of necessity, a very slow and very difficult process of abduction.

Pontification

But one can go back into one's own language, too, as Michel Foucault has done in French, to another episteme, another noetic era. Many years ago I began a lingual biography of Emerson. He left us an abundant record of letters, journals, lectures, and essays from throughout his life—plenty of data, and the primary philology has been done very well. It is all laid out chronologically, well annotated. Furthermore, Emerson was self-conscious about language itself and was keenly interested in the ideas and books the New England ships brought back from India. His European correspondents kept him in touch with the exploration of Sanskrit. For many generations of academics his "The American Scholar" has provided our own version of the Hippocratic oath. However, the task of understanding Emerson on language is not unlike other philological excursions: it is slow and difficult.

Emerson's own language changes noticeably when he leaves America on Christmas Day, 1832. He was very sick, his nineteen-year-old wife had died, and he had resigned his prestigious Unitarian pulpit in Boston, agitated with religious doubt. He was sailing to Italy in search of health. Up until then, his writing was quite conventional.

When he arrived in Italy, well and energetic, the voice we recognize as Emerson's has emerged, and one begins to read him as the words quoted earlier suggest, "with something of wild, creative delight." Just one sample: he writes his brother William from Messina: "The fault of travellers is like that of American farmers, both lay out too much ground & so slur, one the insight the other the cultivation of every part. Aetna I have not ascended" (Rusk 1939:364).

Writers in different times and places innovate at various levels of language, some at the levels of sentences, like Emerson. (The reader is invited to parse the sentence just quoted, in whatever methodology seems comportable.) Some writers innovate at the level of words, like James Joyce. Some innovate in drawing on new sources of prior text, like the Irish mythology that Yeats both shaped and drew from. Some innovate in the language act they perform, like the opening of the inner newsreel in Virginia Woolf or, again, Joyce. It is very Emersonian to ask: what are the ways people can innovate in language? In what different ways can we deviate from the norms we inherit? Emerson, like his literary descendant, Gertrude Stein, is an innovator in sentences.

His sources vary, and he sometimes uses odd words, but the language act he performs is constant. Kenneth Burke (1966:5) has called it pontification: "pontificate; that is, to 'make a bridge'. Viewed as a sheerly terministic, or symbolic, function, that's what transcendence is: the building of a *terministic bridge* whereby one realm is *transcended* by being viewed in terms of a realm 'beyond' it." As a writer of sentences, Emerson slows us way down. We academics have come to expect innovation at higher levels and a certain "stereotypicity" at the level of the figure of a sentence. We can read rapidly only if the lower figures are regular. Some see our field of linguistics as one big text we are all engaged in writing, and of necessity we must agree, therefore, to certain conventions and still our individual voices. In what language acts do personal constraints matter? If there is one idea popularly associated with Emerson, it is his celebration, like Gertrude Stein's, of the individual voice shaping sentences: "The maker of a sentence . . . launches out into the infinite and builds a road into Chaos and old Night, and is followed by those who hear him with something of wild, creative delight."

Norm and Deviation: The Individual Voice

The most difficult task of the philologist is to hear the individual voice. In reading an Old Javanese text, I have very little sense of what is stereotypic and what is innovative, what is norm and what is deviation. That means that an essential feature of aesthetic response, deviation (however so slight it may be in a traditional genre), is inaccessible. More often than not, in a new language one sees everything as unfamiliar innovation. A few years ago, when I wrote about constraints on the creation of a Javanese shadow play (Becker 1979)—where etymologizing is an opportunity for innovation, where stories have no climax, where several languages are used simultaneously—the repeated response of my Javanese friends was "What's so new about that?" Their stereotypes were innovations for me, and therein lies the odd aesthetic excitement of philology.

Emerson saw the American scholar as a deviation from the European norm. A new context brought new meanings, a new relationship with the world. But before he presented his well-known lecture, "The American Scholar," he published a small book called *Nature*, in which there is a section called "Language." If we read it as one must an Old Javanese text, not as something to agree or disagree with but rather first as something to understand, it makes an interesting noetic journey for a linguist, back to our own chirographic age, as it is preserved in print. In his own day, as many people heard Emerson as read him, even as far off as Kalamazoo or Ann Arbor. Though the book *Nature* was prepared for printing, Emerson's sentences were hand-shaped, first, in his letters and journals. The journals became sources for lectures, the lectures sources for essays. The essays are talks to be read, meant to be heard, with the voice in them, shaped by handwriting. The best way to enjoy Emerson is to read him aloud, slowly. I suspect it may be impossible to read him fast.

Nature as a Source of Constraints

Nature, Emerson writes, is "all that is separate from us, all which philosophy distinguishes as the *not me*." The aim of science, he says, is "to find a theory of nature."[1] He lists those aspects of nature not only unexplained but previously thought inexplicable: sleep, madness, dreams, beasts, sex, and language. Central to the essay, then, is the image of I and Other, a particular ego and its context. How does an "I" relate to its context? Emerson lists four ways.

I use nature as a commodity

I use nature as a source of beauty

I use nature as a source of language

I use nature as a source of discipline

Note the order in the list. I relate to the world as first subject to my will and finally as subjecting me to its discipline, with aesthetics and language in between.

The section on language explores the nonarbitrariness (or iconicity) of the relations between language, nature, and thought. For Emerson, language consists of signs for Nature (as he defined it, the "*not me*"), while Nature in turn is symbolic for what he calls Spirit, but which we might call, after Bateson (1979:89–128), *mind*, what phenomenologists call *noema*.[2]

Iconicity and Double Metaphors

One sentence from the section on language of Emerson's *Nature* first struck me a few years ago when I was trying to understand the root metaphors behind the Burmese system of classifiers (Becker 1975): "Parts of speech are metaphors because the whole of nature is a metaphor of the human mind" (p. 18).

This is a puzzling statement. It seems to require some adjustment in our thinking in order to make it appear true. It is not self-evidently true.

There is some prior text. In a lecture entitled "The Uses of Natural History," given in 1833, Emerson expressed a similar idea (Whicher, Spiller, and Williams 1959:24).

The strongest distinction of which we have an idea is that between thought and matter. The very existence of thought and speech supposes and is a new nature totally distinct from the material world; yet we find it impossible to speak of it and its laws in any other language than that borrowed from our experience in the material world. We not only speak in continual metaphors of the *morn*, the *noon* and the *evening* of life, of dark and bright thought, of sweet and bitter moments, of the healthy mind and the fading memory, but all our most literal and direct modes of speech—as right and wrong, form and substance, honest and dishonest . . . are, when hunted up to their original signification, found to be metaphors also. And this, because the whole of Nature is a metaphor or image of the human mind.

The deeply metaphoric nature of one's own language is most clearly seen across cultures, in that "passage to India" that motivates the philologist-linguist. Emerson had a mistaken opinion about the language of "savages": he thought it was like the language of children (Sealts and Ferguson 1969:15). It remained for his student, Henry Thoreau, to begin to understand the language of "savages" by living close to them and listening. Yet Emerson's notion that parts of speech are metaphors is strongly confirmed in the work of the comparative philologist, for whom even nouns and verbs lose their iconicity, as does the notion of grammar itself. Languages seem to select from nature one or another pattern—a set of regularities to build coherence around: temporal sequences, perspectives from the speaker or from the hearer, the basic dramatis personae of case, the distinctions of the sexes, or the division between changing actions and stable things—all the etic icons that cohesion may be built around. These regularities perceived in nature are all, in a sense, available in nature—in the relation of person and context—to build language around. The deepest regularities are the most backgrounded features of language—the most iconic. (By *iconic* I mean felt by the observer—culturally defined—to be the most natural—as ordinary speakers of English feel tense to be a natural fact, not a lingual metaphor, or as Burmese speakers feel their classifiers to be in nature, mirrored in language.) To learn a new, distant language is, in Emerson's terms, to develop a new relationship with nature, a new set of iconicities, at least in part. "Parts of speech are meta-phors because the whole of nature is a metaphor of the human mind." Or, as Gregory Bateson (1979:17) put it, "contextual shaping is only another term for grammar."

A Figure for Defamiliarization

"Parts of speech are metaphors because the whole of nature is a metaphor of the human mind." This is a favorite Emersonian figure, the strategy of the double metaphor. It dominates this section of his essay, where about 75 percent of the sentences are equative strate-gies, simple and complex. A figure is a sentence or larger unit conceived of as a substitution frame, in which certain points are more open to substitution than others, for example, the figure of a recent riddle, "How many ——— does it take to change a light-bulb?" in which one substitutes a name of a human category, such as a nationality, a profession, a religion, etc. The answers evoke the stereotypes of each category. (A new point of substitution, and a new impact, came later, when someone substituted *government* for *lightbulb*.) All language can be conceived of as sets of partially remembered figures.[3]

The general shape of Emerson's figure might be rendered as: "X is Y because the A of B is a Y of C." It is a complex equative or identificational strategy, the figure of definition and of metaphor, of overlays. For Emerson and others in the Kantian tradition, metaphor is a strategy of reason, which, as readers of philosophy know, meant just the opposite then of its normal present meaning: it meant intuition—direct apprehension, "first thought." Part of the difficulty in moving into another episteme (in time or space) is learning not only new words but new meanings for old ones, a variety of what has been called *ostranenije* 'defamiliarization' or even 'alienization', mak-ing things strange,[4] or what Burke (1964) calls "perspective by incon-gruity." Defamiliarization is essentially a metaphoric process: seeing the familiar in a new way. Javanese makes one see English in a new way: it defamiliarizes it. Javanese is a metaphor of English, and vice versa.

Within the metaphoric figure that recurs in the text, Emerson plays with three classes of terms: terms for language, terms for nature, and terms for what he calls Spirit or *mind*. What are the relations of language, nature, and thought? The central proportion, expressed in the sentence we are considering, is that "Language is to Nature as Nature is to Thought". "Parts of speech are metaphors because the whole of nature is a metaphor of the human mind."

Linguistics of Particularity

There have been hundreds of books and articles written about this one essay by Emerson, but only Kenneth Burke penetrates below the macrostructure to the kinds of microstrategies Emerson uses in order to make possible higher-level meanings. Is there not artistic and philosophical creation at the level of sentences, a play of figures and lexical classes at a level below that usually noticed by the literary scholars, and a bit above that usually studied by linguists, a level where, as Isidore of Seville wrote, "grammar is joined to the art of rhetoric" (quoted in Murphy 1974)? It is here that we encounter what Kenneth Pike has called the *linguistics of particularity,* and Paul Ricoeur calls *discourse.* For Ricoeur (1971:529–62), discourse differs from language (i.e., Saussurian *langue*) in that discourse has a particular writer or speaker, a particular reader or hearer, a particular time, and a particular world. I would add, any discourse also evokes a particular set of prior texts for the participants. A discourse can be understood only in its particularity.

For the study of particular discourse, we need techniques of textual parsing that include all the kinds of discourse variables that constrain its particularity—that help shape it. Such techniques will have to allow us to move across levels of discourse and discern the different kinds of constraints operating at various levels: word, phrase, clause, sentence, paragraph, monologue, exchange.

One of the reasons why I never found local grammars of Southeast Asian languages, although I looked hard for them, was that Southeast Asians do not customarily view language, I recently realized, at the level of the clause and the sentence. In Java, for instance, people have a rich vocabulary (much richer than ours) for what they call *unda usuk,* that is, the choices of words or phrases in given positions within figures. (*Unda usuk* means literally 'the parallel wooden strips on a pitched roof on which one hangs ceramic tiles'.) This set of terms represents a conventional understanding of paradigmatic choices. One might imagine a traditional Javanese student of language beginning his or her study of English with a description of the difference between "Close the door" and "Shut the door." That is, the Javanese would begin with paradigmatics rather than with syntagmatics, with constraints on substitution rather than immediate constituents.

Returning to Emerson's figure—X is Y because the A of B is a Y of C—one notices that it includes two equative clauses, although rhetorically they might better be called identificational clauses. In general, identificational strategies operate at the noun-phrase level, and—as is well known—many languages have no equivalent of an identificational copula; in those languages, equational clauses are structurally identical with noun phrases. Without a copula, the copula strategies are awkward to express. In the West, copula strategies characterize some of our most important figures: definitions, syllogisms, generics, even passives—all our most evaluative figures. In pontification (i.e., writing the moral essay) copula strategies dominate. (It is interesting to think of the essay as the reverse of narration, to some extent: in narration, narrative strategies dominate, and are evaluated by, among other figures, generic copula strategies; while in the moral essay, copula strategies dominate, and are evaluated by, short bits of exemplary narrative.)

Within copula strategies, Emerson relates three sets of terms to one another over and over again, offering evaluative instances: terms for language, terms for nature, terms for spirit or mind. A double metaphor is established, in which language is metaphoric of nature, and nature—now considered as text—is metaphoric of mind. The essay establishes terministic depth via a sequence of overlays. Each time a term for nature, mind, or language reappears, it has acquired more context. "Parts of speech are metaphors because the whole of nature is a metaphor of the human mind."

This sentence, like the fragment of a hologram, projects an image of the whole essay, "Nature."[5] This double metaphor is at the heart of transcendentalism, where grammar, rhetoric, and epistemology meet, in a figure "as ragged as the Dolomites" (Ives 1970:23). To understand it means to be reshaped by it, to let it defamiliarize one's world. It means to think and write for a moment like Emerson, who concludes his section on language with these words.

> "Every scripture is to be interpreted in the same spirit which gave it forth," is the fundamental law of criticism. A life in harmony with Nature, the love of truth and virtue, will purge the eye to understand her text. By degrees we may come to know the primitive sense of the permanent objects of nature, so that the world shall be to us an open book and every form significant of its hidden life and final cause.
>
> A new interest surprises us whilst, under the view now suggested, we contemplate the fearful extent and multitude of objects, since "every object rightly seen unlocks a new faculty of the soul." That which was unconscious truth becomes, when interpreted and defined in an object, a part of the domain of knowledge,—a new amount in the magazine of power. (pp. 18–19)

The goal of this short excursion into a few lines of Emerson's "Language" has been to think about another episteme, another conceptual world, another noema, another mind. Our difficulty on so many levels—including the grammatical—in reading Emerson's words as currently relevant knowledge tells us much about ourselves and the distance—even within our own culture, within our own language, and within our own field of study—of the conceptual world of 1836. The task requires, I think, that we change ourselves as readers, moving from an etic to an emic understanding, by imagining a world in which those words could be true: "Every scripture is to be interpreted in the same spirit which gave it forth"— words Emerson quotes from George Fox—might also be the fundamental law of modern philology, and hence a discipline for one important approach to the study of text.

ACKNOWLEDGMENTS

Dedicated to Marvin Felheim, 1914–79. Thanks for critical readings of a prior draft to J. Becker, A. Yengoyan, and D. Tannen.

NOTES

1. Quotations from Emerson's *Nature* are from Sealts and Ferguson (1969). These passages are from page 5. Page references for later quotations will be cited in the text.
2. For an overall view of phenomenological methodology, see Ihde (1977). *Noesis* and *noema* are discussed on pages 43–54.
3. Most medieval rhetorics and grammars included discussion of figures, or common deviations from ordinary language. The number of figures varied, but it was common to distinguish forty-five figures of diction and nineteen figures of thought. Ten of the figures of diction were called tropes. Later writers described up to two hundred figures. For details, see Murphy (1974). I use the term *figure* here to designate a minimal text strategy.
4. This term is fully explicated in Stacy (1977). The term was first used by the Russian critic Viktor Shklovsky.
5. The hologram has given rise to a new sense of wholeness. See Bortoft (1971:43–73).

REFERENCES

Bateson, Gregory. 1979. Criteria of mental process. In: Mind and nature. New York: E. P. Dutton. 89–128.

Becker, Alton L. 1975. A linguistic image of nature: The Burmese numerative classifier system. International Journal of the Sociology of Language 5.109–21.

Becker, Alton L. 1979. Text-building, epistemology, and aesthetics in Javanese shadow theatre. In: The imagination of reality: Essays in Southeast Asian coherence systems. Edited by A. L. Becker and Aram Yengoyan. Norwood, N.J.: Ablex.

Becker, Alton L. (1982) The poetics and noetics of a Javanese poem. In: Spoken and written language: Exploring orality and literacy. Edited by Deborah Tannen. Norwood, N.J.: Ablex.

Bortoft, Henri. 1971. The whole: Counterfeit and authentic. Systematics 9.2:43–73.

Burke, Kenneth. 1964. Perspectives by incongruity. Bloomington: Indiana University Press.

Burke, Kenneth. 1966. I, eye, ay—Emerson's early essay "Nature": Thoughts on the machinery of transcendence. In: Transcendentalism and its legacy. Edited by Myron Simon and Thornton H. Parsons. Ann Arbor: University of Michigan Press.

Ihde, Don. 1977. Experimental phenomenology: An introduction. New York: Capricorn Books.

Ives, Charles. 1970. Emerson. In: Essays before a sonata. Edited by Howard Boatwright. New York: Norton.

Murphy, James J. 1974. Rhetoric in the Middle Ages. Berkeley: University of California Press.

Ong, Walter J. 1977. African talking drums and oral noetics. In: Interfaces of the word: Studies in the evolution of consciousness and culture. Ithaca: Cornell University Press.

Ortega y Gasset, José. 1959. The difficulty of reading. Diogenes 28.1–17.

Ricoeur, Paul. 1971. The model of the text: Meaningful action considered as text. Social Research 38.529–62.

Rusk, Ralph L., ed. 1939. The letters of Ralph Waldo Emerson. Vol. 1. New York: Columbia University Press.

Sartre, Jean-Paul. 1964. The words. Greenwich, Conn.: Fawcett.

Sealts, Merton M., Jr., and Alfred R. Ferguson, eds. 1969. Emerson's Nature: Origin, growth, meaning. Carbondale: Southern Illinois University Press.

Stacy, R. H. 1977. Defamiliarization in language and literature. Syracuse: Syracuse University Press.

Whicher, Stephen E., Robert E. Spiller, and Wallace E. Williams, eds. 1959. The early lectures of Ralph Waldo Emerson. Vol. 1. Cambridge, Mass.: Harvard University Press.

PART 5
MUSIC AND LANGUAGE:
LANGUAGE AND MUSIC

Translating the Art of Music

Having a wife who is a musicologist, who plays the Burmese harp, the Javanese rebab, and most of the other instruments of the gamelan, and who tests one's pontifications in the context of the texts and prior texts of music, means that one has a nearby, persistent critic in addition to a beloved companion. I tend to think of music as a kind of simplified languaging; she thinks of language as a kind of simplified music—which makes for a thick, dialogic marriage. The two essays that follow are both results of that situation.

The first is a preface to the second volume of Judith O. Becker's three-volume work, Karawitan: Source Readings in Javanese Gamelan and Vocal Music, *which is a collection of translations of Javanese writings on music. The preface was written as a reminder to English readers of how much lingual music is missing in the translations. In place of supplying a single translation of a poem in a calendar picture (fig. 13), I try to push the reader to make his or her own translation—somewhat like using a menu in a Chinese restaurant: one from column A, one from column B, one from column C. I call this* paradigmatic *translation, and I hope it allows more of the multiple possibilities of the Javanese original to show through.*

Please look at the picture for a while, as we did, before reading the essay.

◆　◆　◆

Look at the picture for a while, if you will, even if you cannot read the Javanese writing on it. It is a picture on a calendar for the months of November and December 1978. I remember Judith and I were talking then about the likeness between the structure of Javanese music, the way plots of shadow plays are put together, and the way calendars work. In them all, to put it very abstractly, simultaneous cycles regularly coincide, sometimes all at once, sometimes in partial coincidences. This single principle seemed to make these various things (music, text building, and time reckoning) resemble each other. It seemed then that this is the way cultural coherence works: a few deep

Fig. 13. Picture on a Javanese calendar. (Artist unknown, original in color.)

metaphors bind various things together, make them resonate and mutually reinforce each other, and make the world seem orderly, reasonable, and harmonious.

The picture on the calendar for the months of November and December 1978 was opaque for us then. We could sound out the writing and recognize some words, but we did not know what it was a picture of or what the language meant. At the bottom was written, "*cuplikan*, SASTRA GENDHING, 'quoted from *The Art of Music.*' "

Most of the words turned out to be some fairly well-known verses about music and musicians from the *Serat Centhini*, the great, early-nineteenth-century work of philosophical poetry attributed to Sultan Paku Buwana V.[1] This essay is about translating those verses, as they are shaped and framed in the picture, with an eye to revealing some of the problems of translating Javanese writing.

There are two major ways of translating poetry from a distant language: looking up the words in dictionaries, and asking people for whom the poetry is transparent to explain it. Both seem to be necessary in that they correct each other: dictionaries are often too abstract, while people are often too particular. Both methods are used in figure 14. In that figure, beneath the words from the calendar, which have been transliterated in Roman letters (itself a major kind of translation),[2] I have listed some of the definitions of these words given in various Dutch, English, German, and French dictionaries. Also included are the explanations of several knowledgeable Javanese scholars, given to us informally when we asked about this particular picture. As is common when one defines words informally, they frequently used similes to sharpen their definitions. (See, for example, in fig. 14, the explanation for one of the first words, "[It is] like a kite on a long string, out of control.") Dictionaries, on the other hand, seldom use similes at all. Similes are very helpful in that they connect words to *particular* contexts. I hope the similes and other personal glossings included in the figure will be useful to the reader, to whom I am going to present the raw materials for a translation rather than the translation itself. I hope you will see many possible English poems emerging from the Javanese words written on our calendar.

Line 1 (eight syllables, *u* vowel)

KODHENG	ANDHENDHENG	GUMENDHUNG
wall-eyed, bewildered	*stubborn, obstinate*	"conceited"
	"follows own wishes"	*to boast*
"lost memory"		
	grand, étendu	"show off"
niet (meer) weten wat er van te denken, er niets van begrijpen	"like a kite on a long string, out of control"	*mal, ijdel grootspreken*
"lost mind"	*zich in de lengte uitstrekken, en traag, langwijlig, voortmaken*	

Line 2 (eight syllables, *i* vowel)

KANG	DEN	ÈDHÈNG-ÈDHÈNG	MUNG	GENDHING
that which	do	"in the open"	only	"gamelan music"
		voor ieder zichtbaar vertoond		"striking metal"
		"boldly"		*une manière d'éxecuter le gamellan*
		ridderlijk voor de waarheid uitkomen		

Line 3 (eight syllables, *a* vowel)

SARTA	GINANDÈNGAN		GENDHANG
and	"like people going hand-in-hand"		"sound" (*Stimme laut, klar*)
	connected, related		"singing" *zich gedurig laten horen*

Line 4 (eight syllables, *i* vowel)

TINONDHÉ   TANPA   TANDHING
"be compared"   without   "comparison"
wedergade   *matched [against]*
"balanced"

Line 5 (eight syllables, *a* vowel)

TAN   DUWÉ   ÉLING   SAMENDHANG
not   have   "awareness"   "like a rice husk"
               to remember, bear in *broken-up, discarded rice husks;*
               mind   *figuratively, trivial, insignificant*
               "self-possession"
                                       un atome, un grain de poussière

Line 6 (eight syllables, *i* vowel)

KANG   SINANDANG   KANG   SINANDHING
that which   "be clothed"   that which   "be very close"
                s'habiller; souffrir, endurer   *close by, next to*

Fig. 14.   Poetic paradigm of the first *kinanthi* (See p. 338 for explanation.)

The first verse is found in the box at the top of the picture, with double-tailed *cakra* arrows on each side. The verse is in a Javanese poetic form called *kinanthi*, but even to call it a poetic form must give us pause. In modern English, highly serious, important things (such as science, philosophy, history, and the news) are presented in prose, a prose in which much of the potential aesthetic impact has been intentionally restrained. Further, it is not a prose that the reader is expected to memorize verbatim, and hence to hear as well as to see. In most of Southeast Asia, on the other hand, learning until recently was first of all memorizing, and scholars were also poets in the everyday sense of the word: they expressed themselves with skill in well-known poetic forms. Indeed, a basic test of the validity of a notion, I

often was told, was its suitability for shaping in a traditional poetic
form. Until it was so shaped, it was not knowledge. One glimpses
here the tremendous political power implicit in traditional forms of
language.

The traditional form of language called a *kinanthi* is six lines long;
each line, in principle, is eight syllables long. Each line must end with
a syllable that contains a certain vowel sound: the first line must end
with a syllable containing the vowel *u*, the second with *i*, the third
with *a*, the fourth with *i* again, the fifth with *a*, and the sixth with
another *i*. As one hears *kinanthi* over and over, one comes to recognize
the sound of it: *u,i,a,i,a,i*, . . . *u,i,a,i,a,i*, . . . *u,i,a,i,a,i*. Because traditional Javanese verse is meant to be sung, several melodies also are
associated with the *kinanthi* form.[3]

Figure 14 is a poetic paradigm of the *kinanthi* at the top of the
calendar picture. Dictionary definitions of problematic words are rendered in italics; personal glosses by Javanese readers are in quotation
marks.[4]

I hope the reader is able to bear with the slow pace of reading this
poetic paradigm. Most words in any language are more like symbols
than signs, more like metaphors than names, and a translator wants to
savor the whole range of resonances that a word evokes. That is a great
part of the power of a word—to evoke its own past in the varied word-
memories of its readers. Words are multidimensional, and one would
like to retain more than one dimension in a translation. The trouble is
that the metaphors Javanese words make are seldom the metaphors English words make, and the memories they evoke are not our memories.

One of the first things an English reader notices about the stanza
of *kinanthi* examined above is that it is comprised almost entirely of
predicates and connectives. There are no subjects, so sentence boundaries are hard to determine. The few nouns that do occur are the
objects of predicates: *instrumental music* (*gendhing*), *singing* (*gendhang*),
rice husk (*samendhang*). As in much Southeast Asian discourse, the
subject (who or what the text is about) is to be supplied by the hearer
or reader, identified either from the context of performance or from
memory. The connective words (*tanpa, sarta, kang,* and *mung*) and the

morphology of the predicates (the affixes *ang-*, *a-*, *-um-*, *-in-*, and *ka-*) serve to sort out who does what in the action of the poem. This sorting is difficult to discuss, since there are no widely known English terms that can describe the things Javanese connective words do. We usually find rough English equivalents (such as *without, and, that, which,* and *only*), and then we quickly forget just how rough they are.

It is tedious—more tedious than reading poetic paradigms—to try to explain the details of Javanese predicate morphology, but perhaps describing it in a simile can make its aesthetic possibilities clearer. The simile is that grammar is like drama. It is a widespread figure, found in many languages, Javanese as well as English. In Javanese, for instance, *adegan* names both 'a scene from a play' and 'a punctuated unit of discourse', combined in the metaphor of a 'door' or 'gate'. In English terminology, the entities missing from our *kinanthi* are the actors. The verb morphology helps us to understand how those unnamed actors are related to the rest of the scene, and how one scene is related to another. The actor is not named, but his or her role is.

In the poem, the predicates mark one of five roles, whose English glossings might be given as follows.

having or experiencing (*ka-* prefix)

doing[1] (*aN-* prefix)

doing[2] (*-um-* infix)

being (*a-* prefix)

done to (*-in-* infix)

Note that when the *a* vowel of an affix meets a *u* vowel in a stem, the combination becomes *o*, as in the word *kodheng* (line 1); when an *a* vowel meets an *i* vowel, the combination becomes *e*, as in *éling* (line 5). In cases such as this the affixes have become frozen, as philologists say, to the stem. Note further that there is no consensus among philologists about the difference between what I have called here *doing[1]* and *doing[2]*. For both, the role of the unnamed actor is what philologists describe as *agentive*. One interpretation is that, when they occur together, *doing*² is background to *doing*¹, indicating the relation of one predicate to another rather than the relation of an actor to a predicate.

The dramatic movement of a discourse can be observed in the sequence of roles (somewhat like the sequence of tenses in English). In our *kinanthi*, that movement might be described as *experiencing, doing*¹*, doing*²*, being, done to, done to, having, being, done to, done to*. A pattern emerges from this parsing, that is, the repetition of *being, done to, done to*. Part of the aesthetic of Javanese verse—what makes it interesting—lies here, in what seems to a foreigner like following the trace of an invisible actor through shifting roles. This is the movement my description is trying to simulate. By leaving actors unnamed (unnamed from an English perspective) text building in Javanese opens up aesthetic potentialities that are possible but very highly marked in English, in which text building is far more dependent on the sequence of tenses and on repeated, explicit subjects.

So far, then, the first *kinanthi* on our calendar has been treated as a sequence of words (few of them corresponding to English in form or meaning), on which are marked the shifting roles of an unnamed actor. The close reader will have noticed already the internal sound-play, called *purwakanthi sastra* in Javanese. Most obvious is the play with the syllable *dh——ng: dhèng, dhèng, dhung, dhèng, dhèng, dhing, dhang, dhing, dhang, dhing*. Not only do we see in it the vowel pattern of the *kinanthi* (*u,i,a,i,a,i*), but these syllables are also the mnemonics assigned to musical pitches in Javanese. Below is one version for a five-note scale. The numbers refer to gamelan pitches, with the mnemonic syllables listed below.

note:	1	2	3	5	6
syllable:	dhing	dhong	dhèng	dhung	dhang

This syllabification of musical notes is similar to our assignment of the syllables *do, re, mi, fa, sol, la,* and *ti* to pitches in Western music. What the author of the *kinanthi* has done is compose a poem in which the syllables *dhing, dhong, dhèng,* and so on play a kind of "tune" within the words of the verse. It is not an identifiable tune, but it does suggest an excess of music, which is the theme of the poem.

Visually, too, there is a great deal happening. The last line of the *kinanthi* in the box at the top of the calendar page is split by the image of a crown. If you look closely you will see that the two sides of that divided line, on either side of the crown, are mirror images of one another (the way the letters *b* and *d* are mirror images in Roman script). This is a second kind of self-reflexivity (the first being the musical notes in a poem about music). The two predicates on either side of the crown, *sinandang* and *sinandhing*, make an interesting contrast in meaning as well as in form. The first, *sinandang*, might be interpreted to say that the unnamed actor is covered by something, clothed by it, as a husk clothes a grain of rice. The second predicate, *sinandhing*, leads one to think of that same actor as being surrounded by something. In other words, the unknown actor pays no attention to either appearance or surroundings. He or she has neither the awareness nor the presence of mind of a rice husk about his or her appearance or about other people.

Could anyone include all of this in a translation? Better, perhaps, to describe it and let the reader imagine a poem, rich in sound and shape, about a bewildered, strung-out, show-off who displays his self-righteous obsession with gamelan music, values it more than anything, and at the same time disvalues religion, personal appearance, and other people.

The second verse in the calendar picture, written within the circle in the center, is also a *kinanthi*. It is filled with the same play of musical *dhong-dhing*, the same lexical richness, as the prior verse. Here, too, words are resonant in interesting and enjoyable ways. I will make another poetic paradigm (fig. 15) in the hope that poetic paradigms are useful, at least for those who would explore calendars.

Please look again for a moment at the circle in the calendar picture. Do you see the drum and the small pot-gong? Also, the final word, *gendhing* 'music', is shaped like hands, which are crushing the rest of the final line of this second *kinanthi*. The whole verse is shaped like a hanging gong.

Here again the definitions from dictionaries and the explanations by Javanese scholars are meant to suggest the resonance of words and

Line 1 (eight syllables, *u* vowel)

MUNG GENDHING DEN UNDHUNG-UNDHUNG
only music do *to amass in abundance*

"like he is buried in stones"

opstapeling, ophoping

"heaped up"

Line 2 (eight syllables, *i* vowel)

KEKENDHANGAN NORA DHONG-DHING
drumming not (the mnemonic syllables
discussed above)

"follow the notes"

the facts about something

"follow the rules"

Line 3 (eight syllables, *a* vowel)

RINA WENGI ANGADHANG-ADHANG
day and night *to wait somewhere for
people/things to go past*

"like waiting for a train"

*venir a l'encontre,
venir contre quelqu'un*

"wait with hope"

Line 4 (eight syllables, *i* vowel)

WONG ANANGGAP GENDHING
person "ask for" music
"arrange"

Line 5 (eight syllables, *a* vowel)

MRING   AGAMA   NORA   DHANGAN
about   religion   not   *willing to help*

                          "happy with"

                          licht, gemakkelijk
                          (z'n werk doen, iets aanvatten enz)

                          "like one recovered from an illness"

                          n'être arrêté par rien, n'avoir aucune
                          objection; être exempt de toute
                          difficulte; n'avoir aucune chagrin

Line 6 (eight syllables, *i* vowel)

KATENDHANG   TUNDHUNG   ING   GENDHING
"kicked like a soccer ball"   "tossed"   in   music

schoppen met het onderste plat   *to send someone off*
van de voet

"crushed"

"both words [*katendhang* and *tundhung*] are
meaningless sounds trying to find the *dhong-*
dhing"

Fig. 15.   Poetic paradigm of the second *kinanthi*

to open the possibility of many translations, rich in sound and shape, in which the unnamed actor is buried in music improperly performed, the drums not following the rules, waiting for another gig, forgetting religion, crushed in music. . . . But that is to make it too transparent, for the lines are thick with an overlay of poetic activity. The aesthetic here, as in gamelan music, as in batik, as in shadow plays, is an aesthetic of overlays. Sound is superimposed on sound, design on design, event on event.

Jaap Kunst translated this stanza, prosaically, as follows: "He glorifies only music. He lives in a disorderly atmosphere; night and

day he waits for people to call him to come and play. He has no
religious inclination, owing to the power that music has over him."[5]

In the *Serat Centhini*, after many similar stanzas, the speaker turns
to the opposite view—that music can aid spiritual insight by creating
an inner harmony and tranquility, although we must not stop there,
he warns, but go beyond and trace sound back to its source. The
calendar, on the other hand, quotes only two verses of *kinanthi* from
the *Serat Centhini*, but it adds, in a kind of pedestal across the bottom,
two lines of prose.

SANADYAN	WURU	YEN	WURU	WURUKING	NGÈLMU
let be	drunk	if	drunk	teachings	wisdom
			(with)	of	

INGULIHKEN	SWARA	MRING	KANG	DUWÉ	SWARA
be brought back	sound	with	what	has	sound

These last lines stimulated a great deal of discussion in Java. No
one identified their source. Each new reading was accepted as an
enrichment of the last, not a correction of it: "You might also say
that." There was no effort to come to a single correct reading.

One of the scholars we consulted was the noted musician and
teacher, Sastrapustaka. He described the three sections of the calendar
picture (the top square, the central circle, and the two lines at the bottom) as, respectively, *cipta* 'idea', or the way of thought, for the square
at the top (which he said was probably meant to be a page of a palm-
leaf book); *rasa* 'feeling', or the way of the heart, for the *kinanthi* in the
central circle; and *karsa* 'action', or the way of the future, for the final
two prose lines at the bottom. He suggested that the three—thought,
feeling, and action—together create a symbol for the whole person.
He also said that the colors are symbolic: white for purity, black for
torment, red for carnal desire, and yellow for other hopes and desires.
In this reading of the colors another dimension of meaning emerges,
for he noted the particular importance of the fact that in the last line
only the central word, *mring* 'with', appears on a white background.

ingulihken swara mring kang duwé swara
let the sound be brought back with the source of sound

This suggests that the point of balance, *mring*, is associated with purity—a special foregrounding with color of a word that would remain unstressed and in the background in an English translation.

When we next asked Javanese scholars how we should think about the figures on the sides of the picture, and about the things inscribed there, no one was very confident. A few said that there are two poison serpents, one on each side, facing outward. The interpretation that seemed most resonant with the rest of the poem was that the verses are flanked by two grains of rice, with elaborated husks, recalling the end of the first stanza.

Slowly, over time, and with a great deal of help, we began to understand the calendar. We have come nowhere near mastering or explaining it, but it has lost some of its opacity.

The calendar takes meaning from many sources: from shapes, from colors, from sounds, from the world of gamelaning it evokes, from its metaphors (the rice husk), from the genre *kinanthi*, from its lexical parallelism and grammatical coherence, from its author (Sultan Paku Buwana V of Mataram, everyone said), and from you, a modern reader, imagining a reality to be seen through it. This short essay has exhausted none of these sources of meaning. The letters in the corners remain unexplained, as do the *cakra* arrows with the split tails. The didactic intent of the calendar is not clear either—except for the admonition to combine morality and knowledge, which is the common assumption of writings. To take that admonition seriously is to become another, slower kind of reader, and, *ungulihken swara mring kang duwé swara*.

ACKNOWLEDGMENTS

The author gratefully acknowledges the aid of many people who have suggested translations, interpretations, and sources: Bambang Kaswanti Purwo,

Rama Kuntara Wiryamartana, Benedictus Yusuf Harjamulya Sastrapustaka, R. Anderson Sutton, Soewojo Wojowasito, Mukidi Adisunarto, Harold S. Powers, R. M. Soedarsono, Margaret Kartomi, Patricia Henry, and, for detailed criticism and advice, Alan Feinstein. None, I suspect, would agree with everything written in this essay.

NOTES

1. The *Serat Centhini* (*Serat Tjentini*) was published in four volumes by the Bataviaasch Genootschap van Kunsten en Wetenschappen in Batavia in 1912–15. The verses discussed here appear in the fourth volume, page 203 (canto 276, verses 43 and 44). They are translated and discussed in Jaap Kunst's *Music in Java* (1973, 267–69). See also Pigeaud's *Literature of Java* (1967, 1:228–29), and R. M. Ng. Poerbatjaraka's *Kapustakan Djawi* (1952).
2. For a discussion of the ways meaning changes under transliteration, see Becker (1983).
3. See, e.g., Prawiradihardja (1939, 11); *Tembang Djawa* (1943, 14.78); Tjitrosomo (1949, 89); Hardjasubrata (1951, 21, 22); Wignosoeworo (1957, 7); and Kodiron (1968, 5).
4. The dictionaries used are: for English, Elinor Clark Horne, *Javanese-English Dictionary* (1974); for Dutch, Th. Pigeaud, *Javaans-Nederlands Handwoordenboek* (1938), and J. T. C. Gericke and T. Roorda, *Javaansch-Nederlandsch Handwoordenboek* (1901); for French, Pierre Etienne Lazare Favre, *Dictionnaire javanais français* (1870); and for German, Hans Herrfurth, *Djawanisch-deutches Wörterbuch* (1972). I am grateful to Alan Feinstein for providing most of the dictionary references.
5. See Jaap Kunst, *Music in Java* (1973, 268).

REFERENCES

Becker, A. L. 1983. "Literacy and Cultural Change." In Richard W. Bailey and Robin Melanie Fosheim, eds., *Literacy for Life: The Demand for Reading and Writing*. New York: Modern Language Association of America.
Favre, Pierre Etienne Lazare. 1870. *Dictionnaire javanais français*. Vienna: Imprimerie Impériale et Royale.
Gericke, J. T. C., and T. Roorda. 1901. *Javaansch-Nederlandsch Handwoordenboek*. Ed. A. C. Vreede. 2 vols. Amsterdam: Muller; Leiden: E. J. Brill.
Hardjasubrata, R. C. 1951. *Serat Tuntunan Aku Bisa Nembang*. Jakarta: Ministry of Education and Culture.

Herrfurth, Hans. 1972. *Djawanisch-deutches Wörterbuch.* Leipzig: Verlag Enzyklopädie.

Horne, Elinor C. 1974. *Javanese-English Dictionary.* New Haven, CT: Yale University Press.

Kodiron. 1968. *Sinau Tembang Djawa.* Solo: Toko Buku Pelajar.

Kunst, Jaap. 1973 [1934]. *Music in Java: Its History and Its Technique.* 2 vols. The Hague: Martinus Nijhoff.

Pigeaud, Th. 1938. *Javaans-Nederlands Handwoordenboek.* Batavia and Groningen: J. B. Wolters.

Pigeaud, Th. 1967–70. *Literature of Java: Catalogue Raisonné of Javanese Manuscripts in the Library of the University of Leiden and Other Public Collections in the Netherlands.* 3 vols. The Hague: Martinus Nijhoff.

Poerbatjaraka, R. Ng. 1952. *Kapustakan Djawi.* Jakarta: Djambatan.

Prawiradihardja, R. 1939. *Serat Mardi-Laras.* Surakarta: Privately Published.

Serat Tjentini: Babon Asli Saking Kita Leiden ing Negari Nederland. 1912–15. Ed. R. Ng. Soeradipoera, R. Poerwasoewignja, and R. Wirawangsa. 8 parts in 4 vols. Batavia: Ruygrof.

Tembang Djawa. 1943. Djakarta: Djawa Gunseikanbu.

Tjitrosomo, A. S. 1949. *Poenarbawa,* vol. 1. Djakarta, Batavia: J. B. Wolters.

Wignosoeworo, Bonokamsi R. M. P. 1957. *Sekar Matjapat, Tengahan dan Sekar Ageng.* Solo: R. Ng. Prodjosoejitno.

A Musical Icon:
Power and Meaning in Javanese Gamelan Music

with Judith Becker

This essay was jointly authored (with Judith Becker) for the International Conference on the Semiotics of Art, held in Ann Arbor in 1978. From the tradition of American pragmatism, more particularly from Charles Peirce, we borrow the term iconicity *and argue that it is often in homologies between musical text-building strategies and other cultural forms that musical power is expressed. The point is developed in descriptions of an array of Javanese musical compositions of increasing length and complexity, all built around a single, iconic strategy of elaboration.*

❖   ❖   ❖

For several years, we have studied from many different perspectives the traditional music and literature of Java and Bali—traditions as old, rich, varied, and subtle as the European and American traditions we grew up with, though strikingly different from them: different in structure, different in meaning, different in what might be called *writtenness*—that is, the degree to which and the ways in which a written text or score constrains a performance. Recently a friend asked what in these traditions were and are the sources of power—what made and continues to make a particular kind of music or literature "powerful" (or "true," or "beautiful," or "natural," to suggest some other terms for the compellingness or evocativeness of musical and literary types). We would like to suggest an answer here: that the major source of power of a kind of music or literature is associated with the iconicity, or "naturalness," of the coherence system that informs that music or literature. This essay will explain that answer and show how it helps describe the power of Javanese gamelan music.

We might call *iconicity* the nonarbitrariness of any metaphor. Metaphors gain power—and even cease being taken as metaphors— as they gain iconicity or "naturalness." Consider a term like *orbit* and the power with which that term informs our concepts of nature, from the smallest particles to the spheres themselves, as well as our concepts of political and personal power.

One way to describe what happens to make terms like *orbit* powerful is to say that they operate across epistemologies, from one kind of reality to another kind of reality. Based on the referentiality of human languages, there seem to be four basic kinds of reality we talk about: nature, human relations, language itself, and the supernatural. These categories of referentiality are described clearly by Kenneth Burke. In *The Rhetoric of Religion: Studies in Logology* (1961) he develops an interesting notion of referentiality. In his words,

> There are four realms to which words may refer:
> First, there are words for the natural. This order of terms would comprise the words for things, for material operations, physiological conditions, animality, and the like. Words like "tree," "sun," "dog," "hunger," "change," and "growth." These words name the sorts of things and conditions and motions there would be in the universe even if all ability to use words (or symbols generally) were eliminated from existence.
>
> Second, there are words for the socio-political realm. Here are all the words for social relations, laws, right, wrong, rule and the like. Here belong such terms as "good," "justice," "American," "monarchy," "out-of-bounds," "property rights," "moral obligations," "matrimony," "patrimony."
>
> Third, there are words about words. Here is the realm of dictionaries, grammar, etymology, philology, literary criticism, rhetoric, poetics, dialectics—all that we like to think of as coming to a head in the discipline we would want to call "Logology."
>
> These three orders of terms should be broad enough to cover the world of everyday experience, the empirical realm for which words are preeminently suited. But to say as much is to realize that we must also have a fourth order: words for the "supernatu-

ral." For even a person who does not believe in the supernatural will recognize that, so far as the purely empirical facts of language are concerned, languages do have *words* for the supernatural. (Burke 1961:14–15)

Burke develops this notion in great detail in his examination of theological logology—words about the supernatural. Whether or not Burke's four realms prove to be the proper number, and no matter how many subclassifications and indeterminacies may be necessary in comparing one culture with another, this scheme suggests several interesting things about languages and musics.

1. That the epistemology appropriate for discussing things is different for each realm: i.e., a stone is "real" in a different way than a friend is "real" or divine grace is "real." Sounds made by birds or instruments are "real" in a different way than a dominant seventh chord is "real," and both are "real" in different ways than the music of the spheres or the hum of the void (*Om*) is "real."
2. In a given culture, at a given point in history, one "realm" may be given priority, in the sense that discourse is most convincing if it can be put in terms of one particular realm.

In our culture, Electronic America, we have tended to favor explanations strongly rooted in nature. Things in the other realms are "real" (i.e., convincing) to the extent that they can be seen as iconic with nature. Phonological rules are natural to the extent that they can be shown to be based on physiology. Musical systems are natural, or nonarbitrary, to the extent that they can be shown to be based on acoustics. To see an alternative view, one need only move back in American culture to Emerson, who believed that the whole of nature is a metaphor of the human mind—Emerson is our own radical constructivist. Another way to an alternative view is to move conceptually into another culture, which is often a movement to a new "reality" in which Burke's realms of referentiality are valued differently.

For example, in most dominant languages/cultures in Southeast

Asia, what we label *language* is called by some variant of the Sanskrit term *bhasa*. What is a *bhasa*? A *bhasa* could be defined as a language that resembles Sanskrit, the language that the gods speak.[1] To "resemble" here means to have word roots close in form to Sanskrit roots, and to thereby be a proper vehicle for translating Sanskrit knowledge—the *sastras* and mantras. Thus, etymologizing, or tracing roots, became a major way of gaining knowledge—etymologizing across language families, such as from Javanese to Sanskrit, and tracing Javanese roots back to Sanskrit so that Javanese becomes a *bhasa*. This is a frequent strategy in Javanese/Balinese shadow puppetry, what the Javanese call *jarwa dhosok*—the forced interpretation of old words or a kind of carrying new words to the past and bringing old words to the present— finding in Javanese words the shapes of Sanskrit and, later, Arabic, Dutch, or English words, and vice versa. In these cultures, truth and legitimacy were features of *bhasa*. (There are true names for things; if you want to understand the thing, you must know its proper name.) History[2] is an account of the state of *bhasa*—that is, an account of major events in the *third realm*. The pure kingdom becomes more corrupt each time its ruler utters a lie. The history of the decline of the kingdom is the history of the succession of lies uttered by its rulers. (In a logocentric culture, lies are the major source of evil.) Note, now, that the meaning of a Javanese word or a text must entail the way Javanese think words mean—Javanese ideas of referentiality itself. Do stars "follow" calendars or calendars "follow" stars? It's a chicken-or-egg question probably, but you meet the former notion (stars "follow" calendars) far more often, and it is more seriously held in Java and Bali than in Michigan.

3. Iconicity can be defined using Burke's categories as finding the image of something in another realm, for example, finding kinship (realm 2) in nature (realm 1): plants belong to "families"; finding ecological "truths" (realm 1) in human relations (realm 2): intellectual "flowering," an "arid" theory, the "organic" growth of the university; finding features of language (realm 3) in nature (realm 1): the "syntax" of DNA, or structuralism, a linguistic model of how things are.

Among the most iconic features of language, for us in the West, are probably things like tense, location, and being itself. We see these categories as categories of nature rather than categories of language. The past versus the future, in front of versus behind, and whether or not something *is* or *is not* are ordinarily taken to be *facts* about nature (realm 1) rather than about language (realm 3), until we meet tenseless languages, languages in which deixis is reversed ("here" is near the hearer), and languages without a copula (the verb *to be*). Note, however, that translating from a tenseless, hearer-centered, copulaless language (like Javanese or Classical Malay) into English would *require* adding things like tense, English locationals, the copula (all our most iconic features of language) and omitting things like intricate interpersonal levels, particular sound symbolisms, hearer deixis, classifiers, degree of intentionality for each act, etc., as nonessential. Good English is bad Javanese—to the extent that they differ in the way words mean.

One illustration: a few years ago a graduate student of ours was given the task of translating a passage on the origin of music in Java into *good* English. He did. We passed the translation on to a bilingual Javanese friend, whose reaction was troubled and honest: it sounded strange, deeply non-Javanese. It took time and patience to find the problem: *good* English entailed narrative order unless otherwise marked;[3] the Javanese text was a series of overlays and simultaneous actions in which a word has multiple and simultaneous etymologies, an event has multiple and simultaneous motives.

The fact that we highly value narrative-causal structures in our texts—in our chronological histories, our linear time, our narrative requirement in courtroom testimony, our novels, our life histories—is probably related in large part to the fact that we speak a language inflected for tense and use tense as our predominant mode of textual coherence. It seems safe to say that a language/culture's predominant mode of textual coherence would be what is perceived to be one of the more iconic features of that language/culture.

When we translate a text from an unrelated language we add our systems of coherence in order to make sense out of what we are translating. In so doing we alter to some degree the basic iconicity of the text. It seems clear we do the same with music; we search out and find the most iconic elements of our own "music" and judge coherence in terms of our own coherence. Westerners have been known to assign keys to Javanese gamelan music, and Ravi Shankar assigns ragas to all the world's music.

We are making the claim that the most prominent feature of iconic power in Javanese or Balinese music is coincidence—small coincidence and large coincidence—small coincidings and large coincidings of cycling sounds, all iconic with the cycles of calendars and cosmos, and thus, for the Javanese, completely "natural."

The basic unit of all Javanese gamelan music is an entity called a *gongan,* a melodic cycle that can be repeated as many times as one wishes and whose beginning (marked by a stroke on the largest gong) is simultaneously its ending. A gongan can be as short as two beats (*Sampak*) or as long as 1,024 beats (*Minggah, kethuk* 16, *Irama* III). Javanese cyclic systems in whatever cognitive realm—music, calendars, planets—are multiple; more than one cycle is turning within one system. Moreover, these different cycles are not all turning at the same rate. Or, if turning at the same rate, they may be of different sizes or lengths. The primary subcycle of the gongan is a unit called a *kenongan,* named for the *kenong,* a set of large horizontal pot-gongs. The kenong plays either two or four times per gong, marking either the halfway point and gong point of the cycle, or marking the four quarters of the cycle (see fig. 16).

In many Javanese gamelan compositions, particularly the most archaic pieces, a gongan is simply the sequence of two or four kenongan whose full-cycle return to the beginning is marked by a gong. These are the simplest kind of gongan, in which the second half is a mirror image of the first, and the gong marks the return to the beginning (see fig. 17). The coincidence of the kenong with the gong marks the return, the point of stasis and stability. In more complex pieces, many other instruments play melodic sequences that are more or less independent of each other, producing a rich polyphonic texture. Even with their relative independence of each other, these melodic sequences must all conclude at the stroke of each kenong, and on the same pitch as the kenong. Or, the endings

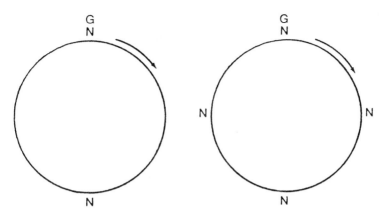

Fig. 16.   Gong (G) and kenong (N)

of all melodic sequences *coincide* with and play the same note as the kenong.

The word *kenong* comes from the root *kena*, which means 'to strike', 'to touch', and also 'to coincide', 'to come together'. A *kenongan* is the section of the gongan whose end point is marked by a stroke on the kenong, and also that point where melodic sequences come together and coincide on the same pitch.

The multiple cycles of gamelan music, the multiple melodies coinciding at predictable points in the music system, seem related in underlying concept to a similar system of Javanese calendrical cycles. The notion of coincidence and the meanings, the beauty, and the power it generates operate across different kinds of reality. The word *kenong* itself may in Javanese have formerly referred to the coincidence of a particular constellation with the moon, which was the beginning of the agricultural cycle. At least that is the case today in North Sumatra where the seasons are regulated by the conjunction of the constellation Scorpio with the moon and the divisions between two such encounters, called *keunong* periods.[4]

In Java, a day is reckoned by describing its position within a number of simultaneous cyclic systems, all moving at a different rate or all of different lengths. For us, it suffices to say that today is, for example,

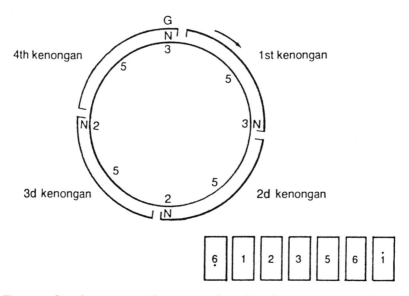

Fig. 17.   Simple gongan with saron pitches. (Numbers represent pitches played by a bronze xylophone-type instrument called a *saron*.)

1. Wednesday = fourth day of seven-day cycle
2. April 5   = fifth day of fourth month of twelve-month cycle
3. 1978   = noncyclic, linear reckoning of the number of complete twelve-month cycles

To designate the same day within the Javanese calendrical system one would have to include the following information.

1. Rebo   = the fourth day of a seven-day cycle
2. Kliwon   = the first day of a five-day cycle
3. Pahang   = the sixteenth week of a thirty-week cycle (each year has 210 days within this cycle)
4. Kasepuluh = the tenth month of a twelve-month cycle (each of the twelve months varies in length with a total of 360 days per year)
5. Panglong = the descending half of the lunar-month cycle

6. 1910   = linear reckoning of years according to the Caka era, a Hindu system introduced into Java in the seventh century A.D.

The meanings of the different coincidings of calendrical cycles in the life of an individual are complex, sometimes arcane, and constitute a recognized field of study and expertise. Each year, almanacs called *primbon* are published to aid individuals in charting their life course so as to avoid certain activities on days of hazardous coincidence and to take advantage of beneficial coincidings. While not different in concept from Western astrology, Javanese calendrical reckonings differ both in their complexity and in the degree of respect that they command.

It can be argued that musical coincidings constitute a different experience than calendrical coincidings. A musical coincidence is a coming together of simultaneous sounds, which may then echo (meaninglessly?) after the moment has passed. Gongs and kenongs are audible and can be *felt* in one's skin, or brain, or heart in a way that calendrical coincidings cannot. Calendars depend upon numerology and can only be linked metaphorically with musical simultaneities. But metaphoric linkage is one of the most important ways in which artistic forms mean. The iconicity of sounding gongs with calendars (and other systems within the culture) is one of the devices whereby they resonate with import beyond themselves. Coincidence, or simultaneous occurrence, is a central source of both meaning and power in traditional Javanese culture. Coincidings in calendars and in music both represent events to be analyzed and scrutinized because of the importance of the concept that lies behind both. *Kebetulan*[5] 'coincidence' in Indonesian and *kebeneran* in Javanese both derive from root words meaning 'truth' (*betul/bener*). As pitches coincide at important structural points in gamelan music, so certain days coincide to mark important moments in one's personal life. One might say that gamelan music is an idea made audible and tactile (one hears with one's skin as well as one's ears). Tonal coincidings are no more random than calendrical coincidings, but occur at the severely constrained cycle subdivisions marked by *kenong*, the word itself suggesting its musical import.

As calendrical cycles ultimately relate to the realm of nature (days and seasons) and the cycling heavens, so gamelan music draws power from its iconicity with the same realm—"the sorts of things and conditions and motions there would be in the universe even if all ability to use words (or symbols generally) were eliminated from existence" (Burke 1961:14).

Given a cyclic musical system whose meaning and significance are centrally tied to the concept of coincidence, it follows then that the major source of innovation and change in gamelan music has been to add more cycles, thus adding richer possibilities of coincidence. Musically this means adding more melodic sequences coinciding at kenong and gong and also providing more possible points of coincidence within the gongan. With a very short gongan, it is hardly possible to add more cycles; there isn't room. But if the cycle is expanded, both the number of coinciding cycles and the points of coincidence can be increased.

An example of a more extended cycle than the previous example is the piece called *Puspa Warna*. In this type of gongan, all instruments and voices coincide on the same pitch at each stroke of the kenong (the first subdivision of the gongan), many instruments coincide on the same pitch at the midpoint of each kenongan (the second subdivision of the gongan), and some instruments further coincide at the third subdivision of the gongan, or at each one-eighth gongan. The ciphers on the inside of the circle in figure 18 indicate the *saron* notes played at each one-eighth subdivision. On the outside of the circle are the notes of an instrument called *bonang*, which in this type of piece coincides with each stroke of the *saron* as well as with the kenong and gong.

With such an expanded structure, more instruments can play, more different sequences are heard, and subdivisions of the kenongan as well as the gongan become opportunities for coincidences. In the history of the development of the gamelan genre, the expansion process has occurred repeatedly, until one finds kenongan and gongan of astonishing length and as many as ten layers of melody coinciding at kenong.

In how many ways are these musical coincidences iconic? To

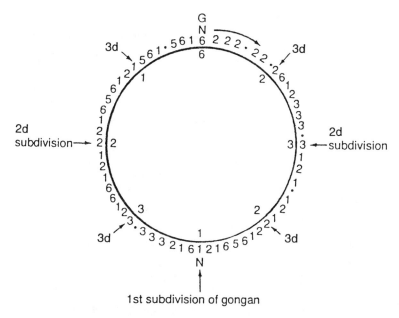

Fig. 18. Structure of *Puspa Warna*

repeat our definition of iconicity: iconicity is finding the image of something in another realm. We believe that musical coincidences are iconic with at least one other realm in Java besides the cosmic/calendrical realm, that is, the realm of dramatic plot—Burke's sociopolitical realm—the realm of human relationships. To extract richer meanings from the coincidence of calendrical cycles one adds more cycles. In setting a date for an important event such as a wedding the couple will consult an astrologer to find the day with as full a coincidence of positive days (such as birthdays of the bride and groom in various cycles) as can be expected within a reasonable time.

The plots of the shadow-puppet plays reflect the same overlay of cycles: Sanskrit-speaking gods work their huge plots over slow time; Old Javanese–speaking heroes search for their birthrights; low Javanese–speaking natural demons of all sorts and sizes follow their blinder drives; and modern Indonesian–speaking clowns try to make it all a rustic picnic in the present, like wide-awake men in a dream world.[6] These and other creatures from other times follow simultaneous but separate plots—in different times and different languages—which at some points partially and at one point totally coincide; the structure of the shadow play, like that of the music, is built on cycles and their coincidences, not around a unified causal sequence of actions that reach some climax.[7]

The assertion that longer gongan cycles with more concurrent cycles are "powerful" can be illustrated by the types of gongan and kenongan that accompany persons and events in the shadow-puppet theater. Longer kenongan, with more instruments, more simultaneous melodies, and more coincidences accompany the spiritually refined heroes (pieces like *Puspa Warna*). The less refined the character, the shorter the kenongan, with demons accompanied by the short, fast pieces like *Bendrong*. Likewise, the accompaniment for actions follows the same paradigm. Meditation is accompanied by longer kenongan with more concurrent cycles and more possibilities of meaning. Fights, situations with all options gone but one, are accompanied by the shortest possible kenongan with the fewest possible coincidences (*Sampak*, with the gongan only two beats long).

We began this essay as a search for the naturalness of artistic forms. We have claimed here that this naturalness, which is an essential part of aesthetic experience, grows, at least in part, from the system of coherence that binds together units in that form. The naturalness—that is, nonarbitrariness/iconicity—of that coherence system varies from culture to culture and over time within a culture. As cultures come into sustained contact with other cultures, systems of coherence rise and fall, changing among other things language and music. There is time for only a brief look at the way gamelan music has changed over its history and is continuing to change.

The coherences, or iconicities, we have been describing for music and calendars inform the symbolic realm of traditional Java. That realm united people, nature, language, and the cosmos, each an icon for the other. From an outside perspective, it is a remarkably integrated worldview. In Java today, this kind of coherence of overlaid cycles and their coincidences competes with equally powerful systems, mostly coherence systems from *our* world. Subtle shifts of emphasis and the restructuring and reinterpreting of symbolic forms happen daily. There are indications of deep change in the coherence system of gamelan music. Modern gamelan compositions are often based upon a song, in which the sung melody is the most prominent feature and the gamelan becomes an accompanying ensemble. In these pieces, the kenong and gong almost entirely lose their function as markers of coincidence and instead become punctuation for a verse, essentially no different from commas and periods (*Suara Suling* or *Aku Ngimpi*). The gongan cycle with its rich system of coincidences becomes no more than a strophic verse form.

Deciphering a change in coherence systems, a change in iconicity, comes not only in observing what is being performed. Equally significant is what genres are not being performed, what genres have fallen into disuse, or, to use a metaphor from the realm of nature, what forms are "dying out."

There is a category of very long gamelan pieces, called "great" pieces, which are rarely played in Java today. The reason usually given is that they are "too difficult." But they are not intrinsically more difficult than much shorter pieces, and in some ways they are simpler: the melodic patterns are often more stereotyped than those of shorter pieces. What makes these pieces inaccessible to a modern audience and to modern musicians, we believe, is their absolute resistance to melodic interpretation and their insistence on coincidence as the only thing happening. Within our concept of music as primarily melodic, they are "boring." They are a kind of ultimate realization of coincidence as the primary source of musical meaning and power, the starkest manifestation of a former system of coherence in Javanese music, a kind of iconicity that seems to be losing its power in Javanese symbolic forms.

In figure 19, the outside circle represents the first gongan of the piece *Kiyanggong*. The ciphers represent the points of coincidence, where all instruments play the same note together. For comparison, the gongan cycles of *Bendrong* and *Puspa Warna* are inserted inside the gongan of *Kiyanggong*. In this piece, unlike *Puspa Warna* (and most other pieces in the gamelan repertoire), the other instruments do not play melodic patterns but simple, predictable formulas leading to the

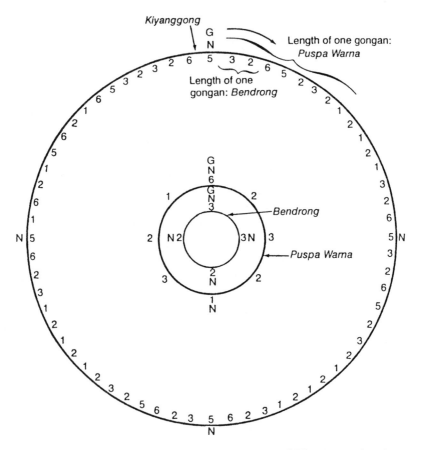

Fig. 19. Comparison of *Bendrong, Puspa Warna,* and *Kiyanggong* showing points of coincidence

coincidence tone, for example, a formula with the upper neighbor alternating with the coincidence tone

(2121   3232)
        1   2

The effect of a large ensemble playing slow, repetitive, predict-able patterns leading to a note that they all play simultaneously, and playing a piece of great length, is either excruciatingly boring or over-whelmingly powerful, depending upon one's musical epistemology. The idea of beauty, or expressiveness, or meaning resides in the relationship between a piece of music and its context.

In conclusion, we wish to reiterate the points made earlier. (1) Systems of musical coherence differ greatly from culture to culture. Cyclicity and coincidence are of low value and low priority in establishing coherence in Western music. On the other hand, the coherence system of harmonic relationships/tonality proves worse than useless in the analysis of gamelan music. (2) Coherence systems in language and music seem natural to their users. A Javanese musician who has studied Western music for over a decade still finds it nearly impossible to compose music (Western or Javanese) that doesn't have a gongan structure. In spite of his years of acculturation, he says of his own nongongan pieces, "They almost don't seem like music." (3) To the extent that the coherence system of Javanese gamelan music is felt to be natural, it is iconic with Javanese conceptions of the workings of time. Musical systems or languages are always more than organized sounds, vocabularies, and syntaxes. They are instances of the way a specific people understand and relate to the phenomenal world.

ACKNOWLEDGMENTS

We are indebted to several people who have helped us in the course of this study: Madhav Deshpande, Susan Walton, Shelley Errington, Harjo Susilo, and particularly Benedict O'G. Anderson for his initial questions about power in the arts. The original concept of the isomorphism of music drama and calendars came to us after reading Soebardi (1965:53).

NOTES

1. We are indebted to Professor Madhav Deshpande for these insights into the concept *bhasa* (see Deshpande 1979). He is currently completing a monograph on sociolinguistics in ancient India in which these notions will be developed more fully.

2. This notion of history first came to our attention in the work of Shelley Errington, particularly her dissertation (1975).
3. Support for this notion is found in the work of William Labov on natural (i.e., nonliterary) narrative, particularly Labov (1972).
4. We are indebted to Professor James Siegel of Cornell University who suggested we look at the entries under *keunong* in R. A. Dr. Hoesein Djajadiningrat (1934).
5. L. F. Brakel first pointed out to us the importance of this etymology.
6. Old Javanese, or Kawi, is the name of the language of various modes of discourse written in Java from about the ninth to the fourteenth centuries. It is still alive as a literary and ritual language in Bali. Low Javanese, or *ngoko*, is a style of modern, colloquial Javanese, which gives no special status to the hearer.
7. During the youth of a now elderly gamelan teacher in Yogyakarta, Bapak Sastrapustaka, when an honored guest would come to the sultan's palace, three ensembles would play at once, each with its own piece. A *pelog* gamelan would play Ladrang *Raja Manggala*, a *slendro* gamelan would play Ladrang *Prabu Mataram*, and a Western band would play the Dutch anthem (called "Lagu Raja Wilhelm"), a striking example of the use of simultaneity to honor as well as to invoke power.

REFERENCES

Burke, Kenneth. 1961. *The Rhetoric of Religion: Studies in Logology.* Berkeley: University of California Press.
Deshpande, Madhav. 1979. *Sociolinguistic Attitudes in India: An Historical Reconstruction.* Ann Arbor, Mich: Karoma Publishers.
Djajadiningrat, R. A. Dr. Hoesein. 1934. *Atjehsch-Nederlandsch Woordenboek.* Batavia: Landsdrukkerij.
Errington, Shelley. 1975. "A Study of Genre: Form and Meaning in the Malay Hikayat Hang Tuah." Ph.D. dissertation, Cornell University.
Labov, William. 1972. "Transformation of Experience in Narrative Syntax." *Language in the Inner City: Studies in the Black English Vernacular.* Philadelphia: University of Pennsylvania Press, 354–96.
Soebardi. 1965. "Calendrical Traditions in Indonesia." *Madjalah Ilmu Sastra Indonesia* 3(1): 49–61.

PART 6
A PLACE FOR PARTICULARITY

A Place for Particularity

The lecture and the essay—as forms of languaging—have a long association. All of the essays in this book took shape first as talks and lectures, repeated over and over in classrooms and larger halls, in many parts of the world and in several languages, until some reason for writing them came up. These two final works are much closer to being "raw" lectures than the earlier ones— indeed, the last one, "Language in Particular," is a touched-up transcript of a recording of a talk delivered at Georgetown University to a large audience of linguists. It was not read but delivered from notes. It was a precious moment for me—a chance to address my peers, fellow linguists, in an open lecture without any topical pressure. It was also a chance, by means of a game, to involve them directly in the points I wanted to make. Here the particular responses in the game form the texts to be examined. Particularity demonstrates itself. It had best remain a lecture.

The first work in this section, "Attunement: An Essay on Philology and Logophilia," is more "written," less spontaneous. It was first delivered at UCLA as one of the 1984 Harry Hoijer Lectures. It was also the centenary of Edward Sapir's birth. Again, and for these reasons, it was for me a precious moment. In this lecture many of the themes and stories already presented in this book are to be found once again. Here, however, I take more care to trace them to their sources—to the work of Kenneth Burke, José Ortega y Gasset, John Dewey, Alfred Kroeber, August Schleicher, and many, many others— from which I have "quoted boldly," as Emerson encouraged us to do. It makes the point, again, that everything said has a past and all languaging is at its core jarwa dhosok, *the pushing of prior texts into attunement with new contexts.*

Attunement: An Essay on Philology and Logophilia

Ever since I was wounded I've had a hard time understanding and identifying things in my environment. What's more, when I see or imagine things in my mind . . . I still can't think of the words for these right away. And vice versa—when I hear a sound or a word I can't remember right off what it means. . . . Two ideas keep running through my head: I keep telling myself my life is over, that I'm of no use to anyone but will stay this way until I die. . . . On the other hand, something keeps insisting I have to live, that time can heal everything, that maybe all I need is the right medicine and enough time to recover.
—A. R. Luria

Any endeavor is always in need of self-correction. Self-correction is the heart of any skill, from the very subtle adjustments of a violinist's fingers, attuning ear and muscle, to the fine coordination of the steering wheel, eye, and gas pedal that constrain the everyday contests of driving. As skill grows, these self-corrections fall to the background of awareness, and so become themselves very hard to correct. Self-correction itself is constrained in two major ways: by the need for internal coherence and in response to the requirements of the environment.[1] One has a plan and one "comes up against" nature. Given enough power, the plan can force nature into its dimensions, or nature may force the abandonment of the plan—or an interaction may happen, a coevolution in which one thing attunes to another.

In self-correction there is always a degree of overcorrection: avoiding a car on the left but hitting a fence on the right; hearing sharp and playing slightly flat. One seeks a kind of balance—an ideal state that is constantly unstable, constantly requiring more and more adjustment. Conversation—indeed, any kind of lingual exchange—is a skill

369

based on many self-corrections, including the constant paradoxical imperative: be friendly but don't impose. That ideal state between friendliness (or courtesy) and imposition (or aggression) sometimes takes lifetimes to establish. Between strangers—from different cultures, speaking different languages—that ideal state itself may be differently conceived, and a compromise must be negotiated. The paradox of cross-cultural communication is but a magnification of the one we encounter in everyday conversation: I am like you/I am not like you.[2]

The task of the philologist has always been to make communication easier across cultures, or across time within one culture: to help us understand texts distant in time and space, spoken or written. This, too, is a species of self-correction, since reading that distant text in a reasonably authentic way requires that one adjust oneself in many subtle ways to make the text coherent and, in some way, true. The paradox of philology has been neatly stated by José Ortega y Gasset (1959).

> Every utterance is deficient—it says less
> than it wishes to say.
> Every utterance is exuberant—it conveys more
> than it plans.

We "read into" a text things that the author has not meant to say, and at the same time there remains an illegible residue. Ortega continues:

> This may seem strange, but it cannot appear questionable; in order to understand what someone wished to say (meant), we need to know much more than he wished to say and to know about the author much more than he himself knew. . . . The work is laborious; it requires diverse techniques and very complicated theories, some general, others particular. . . . The ensemble of these efforts, some technical, others the result of spontaneous perspicacity, is called "interpretation" . . . to read is to interpret and not anything else.

Ortega wrote these words in preparation for a university seminar on Plato's *Symposium*. He was long concerned in his writings
with the conditions that make language possible, not just once historically in some unimaginable prelingual past, but now, each time
someone "utters."

The most powerful condition, he writes, is silence—the possibility of silence: "the most powerful condition for anyone to succeed in
saying something is that he be capable of observing profound silence
about everything else." Some things are ineffable, like the particular
shade of the Princeton sky as this is being written. Its precise shade is
ineffable—not because it is complicated, sublime, or divine but because language cannot have different words for every particular state
of affairs one encounters. The ineffable bounds all language. At the
same time, in Ortega's words, "each society practices a different selection from the enormous mass of what might be said in order to succeed in saying some things . . . language from the beginning is an
amputation of saying." Ortega imagines superimposing languages on
each other and observing graphically

> their coincidence and divergences in declaring and in being si-
> lent. Each one is modeled by a different selective spirit which acts
> upon the vocabulary, on the morphology, on the syntax, on the
> structure of the phrase and period.

Besides this "frontier of ineffability" there is another condition
that makes language possible, another kind of silence: "all that which
language could say but which every language passes over in silence
because it expects that the hearer can and should himself suppose it
or add it." Here is a true "tacit dimension." There is a distinction
between what language says and what we say with it and do not say
with it. When one approaches a distant text, what can or should one
suppose or add to it? How does one interpret the unspoken? As
Ortega says, the work is laborious.

In reading a distant text, one tries to project oneself not into
another mind—at least at first—but into another language, which
held grip on that other mind, that other person, who inherited with

his language, choicelessly, the greater part of the ideas by which and from which he or she lives, without thinking about them at all. One lives intellectually on the credit of one's society, without questioning most of it.

It is this, the unquestioned frame for experience, that makes experience seem coherent and allows one to develop the skills of self-correction. One thinks one is engaging with the world, yet these inherited ideas about what things are, what other people are, what one is oneself, frame all our understanding. As Ludwig Wittgenstein (1958) wrote, "One thinks one is tracing the outline of the thing's nature over and over again, and one is merely tracing round the frame through which we look at it." Philology is the study of other frames.

❖   ❖   ❖

Philology is always a secondary language act: language about language, or—as some call it—*metalanguage*. It might be better called *logology*, following Kenneth Burke (1961) who defines *logology* simply as 'words about words'.

Burke writes of four "realms to which words may refer," the third of which is logological. First, there are words about nature.

> This order of terms would comprise the words for things, for material operation, physiological conditions, animality, and the like. Words like "tree," "sun," "dog," "hunger," "change," "growth." These words name the sorts of things and conditions and motions there would be in the universe even if all ability to use words (or symbols generally) were eliminated from existence.

Burke is not arguing metaphysics or ontology here but simply describing a rather basic lingual ordering of things.[3]

Second, Burke distinguishes words for the sociopolitical realm.

> Here are all the words for social relations, laws, right, wrong, rule and the like. Here belong such terms as "good," "justice,"

"American," "monarchy," "out of bounds," "property rights," "moral obligations," "matrimony," "patrimony."

These terms contrast with those in the first realm as "constitutive" facts contrast with "raw" facts in recent discussions of language acts. One does not use the same kinds of arguments and proofs to verify a tree that one uses to verify a friendship. (Of course one can use terms metaphorically, e.g., tree diagrams for genealogies or sentences: metaphors cross realms.) There seem to be epistemological differences between these kinds of referring.

Burke goes on to describe a third realm to which words refer, words about words: "Here is the realm of dictionaries, grammar, etymology, philology, literary criticism, rhetoric, poetics, dialectics—all that I would want to call 'logology.' " Here is yet a third epistemology. If *tree* is epistemologically different from *friend* as a term, then *noun* or *sonnet* stands in contrast to both. In this essay, I will use the old term *philology* to refer to what Burke calls *logology*. This is to restore to the older term some of its breadth, which it lost when linguistics, literary criticism, and rhetoric split away from philology in the nineteenth century. This split will be discussed in a moment. At present we must finish Burke's scheme.

There is a fourth realm that terms refer to: words for the supernatural. Even if one does not believe in the supernatural, it seems empirically evident that languages do have terms for the supernatural.[4] Furthermore, even if one assumes the realm of the supernatural to be beyond question, it seems empirically evident that words for the supernatural are necessarily borrowed by analogy from the other three realms (i.e., words for nature, society, or language). The supernatural is, by definition, the ineffable, and words for the ineffable must, therefore, be drawn from the effable orders of terms. Hence *God*—the word *God*—seems to be traceable, via historic etymology, to a verb, close to the Sanskrit past participle *huta,* meaning 'to beseech', 'to implore'. To speak of God as "The Word" is to draw analogy with language; as "father" is to evoke a social relation; and as a "powerful arm" is to use a physical analogy.

Of course, analogy works not only in the realm of the supernatural but across all realms. In a totemic system, categories of nature are analogous to social relations, and, just as often animals are given interpersonal names, like referring to tigers in Sumatra as "grandfather." Much of what we do in explanations is apply metaphors from one realm to another. When we speak of "subjective" and "objective" phenomena, note that we are, among other things, applying terms for language to the social and natural realms. Most terms have been "metaphorized" at least once.

Logology is the study of how terms move back and forth across realms of reference. The word *grace*, for instance, began in the secular, social world, in its Latin form, with meanings like 'favor, esteem, friendship, partiality, service, obligation, thanks, recompense, purpose'. In Burke's words,

> Thus *gratiis* or *gratis* meant: for nothing, without pay, through sheer kindness, etc. The Pagan Roman could also say "thank God" (*dis gratia*)—and doubtless such early usage contributed to the term's later availability for specifically theological doctrine. But in any case, once the word was translated from the realm of social relationships into the supernaturally tinged realm of relationships between "God" and man, the etymological conditions were set for a reverse process whereby the theological term could in effect be aestheticized, as we came to look for "grace" in a literary style, or in the purely secular behavior of a hostess.

Terms like *grace* (or *spirit*) take part in a constant dialectic or term-drama. As words move from realm to realm, they clearly bring something with them. *Grace* brings its social past into the theological realm, and something of both into the logological realm. And so, "there is a sense in which language is not just 'natural' but really does add a 'new dimension' to the things of nature" (an observation that would be the logological equivalent of the theological statement that grace perfects nature).

Logology is thus a kind of etymology, a concern with the evolution of words (and, by implication, of larger units of language, too), both historically, across centuries, and within each text. A word does not usually mean the same thing at the end of a text that it does at the beginning. Following a word (or a set of words) through the dialectic of a text, through the "discourse processes," as they have become clinically known, is another perspective on philology.

❖   ❖   ❖

In both Burke and Ortega, the word is the thing studied, within the constraints of the whole text and within a history beyond the text, both before and after it. The word was also the thing at the center of the split between philology (as a holistic study of texts) and linguistics as it was first conceived in Germany in the early nineteenth century: the study of the morphology of the word. John Arbuckle (1971) has examined carefully the central role of August Schleicher in this split.[5] Since the goal here is to reunite philology and linguistics, it is important to look in some detail at the reasons for the split. Though many wrote of it, Schleicher's work was most explicit and revealing of the issues behind it.

First of all, argues Schleicher (1850), in *Die Sprachen Europas*, philology is historical, while linguistics has nothing to do directly with the history of man. In his view, only where there is a written record is philology possible. Philology preserves and interprets this inscribed past. (Sometimes, in the history of the term, *philology* refers to the body of canonic or classical texts, commentaries, grammars and dictionaries itself, not just the study of it, a view to be discussed in the next section, on the philology of the anthropologist Alfred Kroeber.)

Second, Schleicher sees history, and hence philology, as the "sphere of operation of human free will" and linguistics, or those aspects of language properly studied by the new field of linguistics, as not within the reach of human free will but rather in nature and hence subject to "nature's unalterable laws."[6] That part of language in which nature's laws, not human will, holds sway was accidence—the way a root appears as adjective, noun, verb, etc., or in a certain case, tense, mood, etc. Accidence was the shaping or morphology of words. (Syntax, more dependent on free will, remained for many years part of philology, as did style.) In modern academic political terminology, philology remained in the humanities, while linguistics became a natural science (within the major constraint on a nineteenth-century natural science: universality). (Many linguists today define their prime goal as exceptionless, universally valid statements about "language.")

Languages were seen to be analogous with natural organisms, for which the central metaphor in nineteenth-century study was the "chain of being," culminating in Darwin's theory of evolution, "temporalizing the great chain of being," as Lovejoy describes it. Languages, too, were believed to evolve and form a chain of being, each higher state of a language preserving within it all previous, lower stages. The linguist, via accidence, studied this evolution in general, while the philologist studied one particular language or "family" of languages (taking "family" in the biological rather than the social sense). Linguistics is more abstract, more general, more universal than philology.

It is universal because it was felt to reflect thought—concepts and relations—and these, according to Schleicher, are universal. He felt that some languages reflect the concepts and relations of thought better or more completely than others. Roots of words express basic concepts of meanings, but the whole word includes relations, too: "Relation and meaning together yield the word, since it is on this oral expression of both that the construction of the word depends, and from that the sentence and the whole character of the language."

Schleicher builds a system of language classification around this notion of meaning and relations (or root and accidence). Languages are classified according to the way the relational elements accompany the meaningful elements. First, relations may be unexpressed, in which case roots carry meanings and simultaneously imply relationships. Word types are not formally distinguished. One unit of thought is equivalent to one unit of sound. This is the monosyllabic stage, in Schleicher's terminology. The natural analogy is the crystal. (Crystallography was another of the morphological natural sciences, along with botany, anatomy, and linguistics, all concerned, in Goethe's scheme, with a shape, its distinctions, its foundation, and its transformation.)[7]

Going up the evolutionary ladder one step, one finds languages (called agglutinating) in which roots carrying meaning are accompanied rather loosely by relational roots, which have acquired general meaning, or—as modern terminology puts it—have been "bleached." Gradually, in this evolutionary chain in which one type merges into another, the bleached relational bits get bound onto roots, though they are still clearly distinguishable. Words of this sort were thought to resemble plants.

Finally, the two elements—meaning and relation—merge again, giving the truest reflection of the processes of thought, a version of Hegel's dialectic: from unity of meaning and relation, to their separation, and then to their reunification—a new synthesis in this dialectic of unity and differentiation. The inflectional languages thereby stand at the highest point of lingual evolution. In their union of multiple parts (*Einheit in der Mannigfaltigkeit der Gleider*) they correspond to the animal in biological evolution.

All of this evolution, however, was seen as prehistoric, having taken place in a primitive golden age of language building. Then comes history and writing, and the decay of language.

In the sharp opposition of mind and matter, or Spirit and Nature, or Freedom and Necessity, philology and linguistics split, reflecting the apparent certainties of dialectical idealism. Language seemed to fit the system. A new science was needed to "assign languages to their proper place in the new Hegelian great chain of being, according to the organic complexity of their phonic units; to discover evidence of the earlier stage in the later; and to find the specific laws of decomposition. . . . So linguistics (*Linguistik*) was born," a natural, morphological science, absolutely rooted in phonics—that part of language that lies beyond human will (Arbuckle 1970:27).

Saussure extended the search for universal laws into the realm of symbols, and later syntax, too, became part of the new science, and more recently discourse and even stylistics.

Yet, as Arbuckle concludes, we are still left with the question, "What is the nature of the constraint language puts its speaker?" Does the Spirit-Matter dichotomy upon which Schleicher's scheme rested still satisfy us? We now recognize that the Hegelian stages of language evolution, as well as the accidence-syntax distinction, are ethnocentric and false. Is there any basis for, or any need to maintain, the philology-linguistics split?

❖   ❖   ❖

As a cultural activity, as A. Kroeber saw it, philology has had an ancient and unique function. At some time in the "growth" of a culture (we are still within the organic metaphor) it becomes important to keep certain old texts alive for the knowledge they embody. In the framework of poetry, these texts were memorized and passed on but simultaneously reshaped to the contemporary world.[8] But sounds changed, old words got replaced where possible (not usually, for example, at rhymes), and new information was inserted. Keeping the text alive was an important, time-consuming activity. The old text was always the frame for new knowledge. Even today, one cannot speak the present without also speaking to some degree the past: each of us has in memory a deep bed of past stories and schemes on which we build present understanding, a kind of personal philology.

If they are written, these old texts are harder to lose but also progressively harder to read, since almost unconscious oral reshaping and "correcting" are now missing, and the frozen, archaic language gets harder and harder to understand. Another kind of self-correction became necessary: philology—as Kroeber understood it. As an activity it appeared after writing: the activity of making grammars and dictionaries and other devices for keeping old texts alive. Many today would find Kroeber's image too "graphocentric." Self-consciousness (and self-correction) of our graphocentrism has been, however, a very recent lesson. Where writing is concerned, most of us are still quite Schleicherian in our assumptions about the stages of medial development: oral, to written, to printed language, governed by necessity.[9]

Kroeber (1944) also states, "it is probable that no people, except as borrowed a philological technique ready-made from others to apply it to their own speech, ever discovered grammar until after they had a literature the text of which was canonical or classical." The desire for textual purification and for standardized versions led to textual commentary, and "only after this had been in vogue for some time did interest in grammar for its own sake, as a problem of the discovery of forms, awaken." In this same way, "medicine, or attempts at medicine, preceded physiology; and counting, measuring, and reckoning, mathematics for its own sake."

Philology is a secondary language act. But once established, grammar seems to be given an important place in education, "for its supposed practical and applied value, which is probably insignificant for all except the professional scholar." Kroeber adds a hedge: "On the other hand, there is of course a very real intellectual discipline in learning to deal with abstracted form; and this value of grammar has been and still is for the most part overlooked in popular estimation." In this hedge we get a glimpse of grammar as a framework for other studies, a notion emphasized to the present in the great Sanskritic philological tradition.[10]

The development of philology, as Kroeber sees it, is "a struggle to substitute conscious recognition of structure for unconscious use of it."

❖   ❖   ❖

Each of these writers, Ortega, Burke, Schleicher, and Kroeber, give us a perspective on the problems of understanding distant texts, distant because we can't read them without persistent self-correction. Ortega focused on the exuberances and deficiencies of meaning, Burke on the dialectic of terms, Schleicher on the modes of word shaping, Kroeber on social activity. What is needed is not so much another alternative to the study of distant texts but rather a vocabulary that attempts to join and sustain the truths of all these—and several more—positions. I would like to suggest such a vocabulary: one that can accommodate prior insights yet remain open enough to allow the self-correction necessary to lingual exploring. First some terms, then some exploring.

The vocabulary has roots in a tradition that might be called American naturalism, a tradition with some coherence back to Emerson, and later successes in Thoreau, in William James, in Charles Peirce, and, in the generation before ours, in John Dewey, who examines most completely the notion, which the others share, that meaning is to be observed in the relations of an organism with its particular environment. Not that meaning was "in" things, waiting to be discovered, nor that it was in the mind, to be projected, but rather in the interaction of a living thing with its context—a "co-evolution" in Paul Ehrlich's term. (One could, of course, come to this view by other roads, via Wittgenstein, via Heidegger, to name only two other, European guides.)

For Dewey, the experiences in which we interact with our contexts divide themselves into "strands," with beginnings and endings, and all kinds of interdependencies ("histories"), which are difficult to sort out. In a well-known passage from *Art as Experience*, Dewey (1934) writes:

> Direct experience comes from nature and man interacting with each other. In this interaction, human energy gathers, is released, dammed up, frustrated and victorious. There are rhythmic beats of want and fulfillment, pulses of doing and being withheld from doing.

Sometimes these experiences are successful, sometimes not. Sometimes the organism loses integration with the environment. Dewey sees emotion as the sign of an actual or an impending break in this integration—like a breakdown in a conversation where the mutually established interaction goes wrong. At this point there is need for conscious self-correction: we all do it constantly, intelligently sometimes, not so intelligently sometimes, too.

In the case of language, the interaction is complex, less direct than picking up an apple and consuming it, for instance. With language one relates to the environment in several ways simultaneously. (At this point I am no longer reporting Dewey, but developing an elaboration for which Dewey bears no responsibility.) To state it differently, the organism interacts with several environments that are very different from each other. When one experiences language successfully, there is no need for self-consciousness about these different environments. With breakdowns—or across the gulf of distant languages (where one starts with "breakdown")—one becomes conscious that there is more than one environment, as in the following exchange between A and B.

1. A: "What's the matter?"
   B: "Well, what you say about the apple is right, but I don't like your tone of voice."
2. A: "I'm just saying what the teacher said."
   B: "Well, I don't see how it follows from what you said before."
3. A: "Let me diagram it on the blackboard."

This imaginary dialogue begins after an imaginary breakdown and reflects attempts at correction in several very different contexts (or *environments*, in Dewey's language). In (1), B says the problem is not in what A says but in the way it's said. The area of correction is identified as interpersonal not referential. In (2), A refers the problem to prior text (the teacher's), while B sees it now as a problem of coherence within A's language. In (3), A shifts to a different medium on the assumption that it will correct the breakdown. The appeals for correction make reference to five different kinds of context.

1. Interpersonal relations (e.g., in the dialogue above, "your tone of voice")
2. Referential relations ("what you say")
3. Intertextual relations ("I'm saying what the teacher said")
4. Intratextual relations ("I don't see how it follows")
5. Intermedial relations ("Let me diagram it")

The experience of language seems to me to involve all five of these contexts, plus silence as a ground.

There is no a priori reason that there should be five categories or sources of meaning, nor is this analysis of context unique: others might combine categories, or split them (Becker 1979b, 1984). But, to develop a vocabulary, one must select, in Ortega's terms, "from the enormous mass of what might be said in order to succeed in saying some things." Each of these contexts is relational. That is, each marks out a ground for interaction and, hence, a potential basis for self-correction. In a way, these five contexts sort out the ways a text can mean, with *meaning* defined as the interaction of something with its contexts.

Interpersonal Relations

These can be considered in at least three ways—ways that correspond with what is a prime candidate for a language universal: the lingual marking of "I," "you," and "other" (or first person, second person, and third person).[11] This is the area of what has been called *pragmatics*, or, more interactionally, the *cline of person*, the continuum from me to it. The relations, shown in figure 20, are minimally triadic. Of course, in a more complex situation (e.g., a character speaking in a novel) there may be multiple framing of this simple triad. Imagine a writer (1) who writes through a persona (1b) who is quoting another character in the story (1c). He is also speaking simultaneously to a parallel nesting array of 2's: Figure 21 displays but one possible array of persons.[12]

Cross-culturally, the potential arrays of person seem far greater than one would first expect, given an elementary set of just three variables. One thing that leads to complexity, besides the embedding displayed in figure 21, is the great number of ways a language community can elaborate 1, 2, and 3: by age, birth, sex, number, distance, rank, relation to an action, caste, religion, authority, and many other kinds of socially relevant differentiation, in the case of 1 and 2, and by the manifold schemes of nominal classification—for example, humans, animals, and many many "things"—in the case of 3.

Referential Relations

These are a bit different from just "what can be talked about," since anything can be talked about, including 1 and 2. There is nothing that

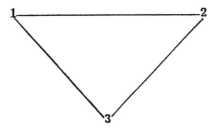

Fig. 20.   Simple relations of person

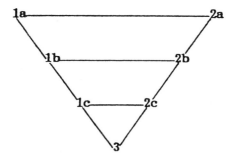

Fig. 21.   Multiple framing of person

limits language from being self-referential, maddening and pathologi-cal as it can become. No, the referential realm is the realm the words of a language "project" as being beyond language, the world a speaker believes, in Burke's terms, "would be in the universe even if all ability to use words (or symbols generally) were eliminated from existence" (Burke's realm of nature). Nature is what Emerson saw as our strongest discipline, that which puts limits on our fantasies.

This is not meant to be an ontological argument but merely a way of referring to the world that all languages presuppose the existence of, but that is not identical from language to language. It is, hence, a totally metaphoric realm, as Emerson noted when he wrote, "The whole of nature is a metaphor of the human mind"—that is, a product of the interaction of a language-ful organism and its environment.[13]

Intertextual Relations

Very little of what one says or writes is new. One can see this clearly with words. Few people in modern English feel compelled to invent new words. Word building is not a conventional mode of invention now, as it was, for instance, at certain stages in the history of Sanskrit. Some invent new "turns of phrase" or sentence figures—new usages—but most people most of the time are "speaking the past." Most of our language is imposed on us. As Ortega (1957) put it, "Our mother tongue socializes our innermost being." Everyone belongs choicelessly to a language, from which only a few willingly flee.[14]

And when we speak or write we evoke—overtly or only by suggestion—prior language, prior text. A conversation today will draw upon prior conversations. A cowboy movie is about prior cowboy movies much more than it is about whatever may have happened in the American West in the second half of the nineteenth century. There are genres, everyday ones as well as literary ones—language games with histories. Some of these "games" are quite intimate, like the repeated exchanges of a husband and wife, and some very public, like polite greetings or play-by-play reports of baseball games. All are, to a great extent, repetitions of past language, prior texts.

In none of these cases is a prior text being identically repeated. That is impossible. Even seeing a movie twice is not a repetition, since the viewer of the first is not the viewer of the second because the viewer of the second showing has already seen the first.

And so, every language experience speaks both the past and the present.[15] It is impossible to do just one or the other. Texts vary greatly as to how much they are repeating and how much they are deviating. A completely deviant, "private" language would not be a language, as Wittgenstein has argued so convincingly.

One of the most difficult things to know in studying a distant text is when, or to what extent, someone is speaking (or writing) the past, and when, or to what extent, deviating from it.

Intratextual Relations

This is the structural realm, the relations of parts to each other, hierarchically, in a whole of some sort (although the notion of lingual "whole" must be separated carefully from organic, social, and material wholes). This is the field of structural cohesion—the way words (or other units) interrelate in phrases, phrases in clauses, clauses in sentences, sentences in paragraphs, and so on up the hierarchy to entire monologues (or "monographs") and exchanges. At each level, successful interaction requires at least an illusion of cohesion.[16] To understand a distant text, one must often deal with new modes of cohesion and discard inappropriate ones.

Intermedial Relations

We are becoming more and more sensitive to this "environment"— this aspect of our context—as we explore our own "graphocentrism." How does spoken language differ from written, printing from handwriting, syllabic from alphabetic writing, etc.? Each seems to have its own "economy," its own *noetics* (to use a term with its own interesting history in English, from Coleridge to Walter Ong). *Noetics* refers, in Ong, to the whole process of shaping, storing, retrieving, and communicating knowledge. We are becoming more and more aware of noetic differences across languages and cultures—how the medium, in popular terms, is the message.

Much older philology saw the first task of the philologist as putting a distant text into modern Roman print, in order to build a Kroeberian philology, often for a distant colonial language community, uninvited. The second traditional task was textual criticism: establishing textual authority entirely from a set of values grounded in printed language wherein a text must be fixed and variation strongly constrained. Any discussion of medium seems to lead to questions of authority.[17]

The separateness of these different sources of meaning can indeed be debated, for certainly there is overlap—an overlap that makes interaction between them possible. Yet each seems to be a radically different kind of context and so a different source of constraints on any text. Some will say that the view of language that encompasses all five contexts (plus silence) is too diffuse or too broad, yet, as we shall see, to understand breakdowns and successes—pathology and beauty—requires all of them, since these phenomena themselves involve two or more of the contexts, and are, hence, invisible in a narrower view of language. It is their interactions that create the conditions of languaging.[18]

A vocabulary for modern philology, then, must minimally consider these things, since the wholeness and coherence of one's interaction with a distant text depend on skillful self-correction in all these ways.

❖   ❖   ❖

To leave out in our picture of language one or more of these sources of constraints is to make the kind of error theologians have called a heresy. It is an interesting notion, a verbal strategy in Burke's sense, which one can extend to identify, for instance, ecological heresy (leaving out ecological constraints so that, e.g., prior experience with insecticides, which renders some insects immune—ecological prior text—is neglected) or philological heresy. Heresy has to do with misinterpretations based on overemphasizing one part of a doctrine to the exclusion of other parts. To shift metaphors radically, it is like eating in Burma: as Daw Mi Mi Khaing explains, foreigners foolishly eat what they like at Burmese meals, unaware that in proper Burmese meals one dish balances another, and so to eat the one without the other is to risk illness. No wonder foreigners get sick so often.[19]

Logophilia is a perversion of philology. The term comes to me from a book by Michel Pierssens: *The Power of Babel: A Study of Logophilia* (1980). Pierssens describes some classic cases—Mallarmé, Saussure, Roussel, Wolfson, and Brisset. In each case the pathology is an obsession with one dimension of language, a search for the "key" to language in sound symbolism, puns, or the decomposition of words into basic elements that reveal their "true" meanings. Cross-culturally, logophilia is the assumption that one or more of the six sources of constraints on language remains identical as we cross from one language to another, and that this identity provides a grounding for our understanding of that language. This grounding encourages us to define an abstraction ("Language") apart from languages.

For the philologist confronting a distant text, there is need for correcting exuberances and deficiencies of interpretation in all those ways a text can mean, in all the ways it relates to context: in the ways the parts relate to each other, in the ways it evokes prior text, in the ways people relate to each other with it, in the ways a medium shapes it, in the ways it shapes a world that those who use it believe exists beyond language, and in the ways silence surrounds it. All of these six are potential sources of philological errors. In order to illustrate the kinds of self-correction a philologist must make to attain what Pike was first to call an *emic* understanding, I would like to list briefly some of my own errors in each of these six sources of contextual constraints.

One thing shared by anthropologists and philologists is the absolutely essential experience of fieldwork—the experience of learning a language in context, by trial and error, by making mistakes and learning—by necessity—that the only way to learn anything is by making mistakes. Here, then, is a catalog of my own biggest mistakes (self-selected). My only authority for writing all of this rests on my having made these mistakes—and later recognizing them as mistakes and trying to correct them.

The earliest mistake is the one it took longest to become aware of as a mistake. We enter other languages with a strong phonemic bias.[20] To come in from the outside requires that we confront a distant language either as writing (the archaeological door) or sounding. In the 1950s during my first trip into a distant language in Burma, my linguist friends were not interested in Burmese writing. Even today graphology gets minuscule attention compared with phonology. Furthermore, colonial philology, as a preliminary act, transliterated Southeast Asian texts into the Roman alphabet.[21] This, of course, is a mode of phonemicization, since phonemic writing is a rationalized version

of the Roman alphabet. To phonemicize a language is to reduce it to
our language, a process full of exuberance and deficiency. I have
written elsewhere (Becker 1984) about how this happened for me.

> On arriving in Burma in 1958, I began to learn Burmese from a very
> kind and patient old teacher, U San Htwe. As I had been taught to
> do, I would ask him words for things and then write them down.
> He watched me writing for a while and then said, "That's not how
> you write it," and he wrote the word in Burmese script. For the
> word evoked by English "speak," I wrote /Pγɔ/ and he wrote ၆ၛၥ.
> I insisted it made no difference. He insisted it did and told me I was
> hurting his language. And so I began, somewhat reluctantly, to
> learn to write Burmese: /p-/ was a central ပ and /-y-/ wrapped
> around the ပ to make ၛ and the vowel /၆——ɔ/ fit before and
> after it: ၆ၛၥ.

This difference in medial representation made a great difference,
on at least two levels. For one thing, I could not segment the Burmese
syllable into a linear sequence, as I could / Pγɔ /, as one can see clearly
by studying the two representations. But segmentation into linear
sequence is a prerequisite for doing linguistics as most of us have
been taught it: normally, sounds string together to make morphemes
and words, and words string together to make phrases, and so on. We
analyze strings, with analog phenomena relegated to super- or sub-
segmental status. To write my kind of grammar I had to violate his
writing.
    At first it seemed to me a small price to pay, to phonemicize his
language. But over the years—particularly twenty years later, in Java
and Bali—I learned how that kind of written figure (a center and
marks above, below, before, and after it—the figure of the Burmese
and Javanese and Balinese syllable) was for many Southeast Asians a
mnemonic frame: everything in the encyclopedic repertoire of terms
was ordered that way: directions (the compass rose), diseases, gods,
colors, social roles, foods—everything.[22] It was the natural shape of
remembered knowledge, a basic icon.
    As Zurbuchen (1981) has shown us, this notion of the syllable is

the ground even of the gods: it is evoked at the beginning of every Balinese shadow play. Even though the shadow play is taught and performed orally, it begins with an invocation of the written symbol as a source of power.

> Just as the boundaries of awareness become perceptible
> There is perfect tranquility, undisturbed by any threat,
> And even the utterance of the gods subside.
> It is none other which forms the beginning of my obeisance to
>   the Divine.
> Greatly may I be forgiven for my intention to call forth a story.
> And where dwells the story?
> There is a god unsupported by the divine mother earth,
> Unsheltered by the sky.
> Unilluminated by the sun, moon, stars, or constellations.
> Yes, Lord, you dwell in the void, and are situated thus:
> You reside in a golden jewel,
> Regaled on a golden palanquin,
> Umbrellaed by a floating lotus.
> There approached in audience by all the gods of the
>   cardinal directions . . .

These last lines, after locating the written symbol outside of time and space, describe metaphorically the shaping of the written symbol as a focal point for natural order. Zurbuchen's translation continues, describing the implements of writing.

> There, there are the young palm leaves, the one lontar,
> Which, when taken and split apart, carefully measured are the
>   lengths and widths.
> It is this which is brought to life with *hasta, gangga, uwira, tanu.*
> And what are the things so named?
> *Hasta* means "hand"
> *Gangga* means "water"
> *Uwira* means "writing instrument"
> *Taru* means "ink"

What is that which is called "ink"?
That is the name for
And none other than
The smoke of the oil lamp,
Collected on the bark of the kepuh-tree,
On a base of copper leaf.
"Written symbol" is its name,
Of one substance and different soundings . . .

The translation, which I have taken the liberty of arranging in lines (mainly to slow down the reader), goes on slowly to evolve the story from the written symbol.

My point, however, is not to explore this image further, or to retell Mary Zurbuchen's fascinating stories, but to try to understand why U San Htwe had insisted on my learning Burmese this way. I think it was that the traditional learning was organized around that shape, that it was a root metaphor, the stuff that holds learning together—just as our sequential writing lines up so well with our sequential tense system and our notions of causality and history. That is a great deal to ask anyone to give up—the metaphoric power of his writing system. And I had tried to argue with that wise old man that it did not matter.

One of the most subtle forces of colonialism, ancient or modern, is the undermining of not just the substance but the framework of someone's learning. As Gregory Bateson put it, in his oft-quoted letter to the other regents of the University of California, "Break the pattern which connects the items of learning and you necessarily destroy all quality." I see now that what I had been suggesting to my teacher, though neither of us could articulate it, was that we break the pattern that connects the items of his learning. When methodology and language conflict, it is the methodology that should give way first.[23]

My error, calling my phonemicization of Burmese sounding a notational variation of Burmese writing, was in my view the most profound error I made—the basis for all the others. It was the philological heresy on which the others rested. As Wittgenstein wrote, "A picture held us captive. And we could not get outside it, for it lay in our language and language seemed to repeat it to us inexorably." I will never forget the moment—in East Java this time—when a student in my class went to the blackboard, pointed to the last letter in a word I had written, and said, "Here, at the front of the word . . ."

❖   ❖   ❖

The exuberances and deficiencies of my structural understanding of Southeast Asian languages—the structural mistakes I am aware of—are very numerous. I imagined that tense, number, articles, the verb *to be*, third-person inanimate pronouns—all the basic stuff of my language, the "glue" that holds words and clauses together—were understood, like shadow limbs on amputees. I had not yet learned Ortega's lessons about silence: that "speech consists above all in silences" and that "each language represents a different equation between manifestations and silence." It has taken many years to just face the fact that those things just aren't there, and that to put them in is to interpret their language in terms of mine, and to that extent nonemically. This was the exuberance. Not using tense for textual coherence the way we do, for instance, means that events/acts/plots have been conceived in different ways—equally compelling—in Burmese or Javanese. My claims that this is an exuberance of interpretation—reading-in "shadow" tense—has been widely misunderstood. Western scholars of Southeast Asian languages have said things like, "That cannot be. Do you mean to say that if a Malay were on a plane he wouldn't know that he got on before he gets off?" And Southeast Asian linguists have told me, "You think our languages are deficient, don't you? Still primitive." And they go on to argue that some lingual phenomenon or other shows understanding of temporal order. Both these reactions seem to me to miss the point: that coherence in texts is not marked by tense because there is none, and that this makes a profound difference.

The profound difference is hard to imagine in English, since it is not just that something is missing but also that something else is there, doing the work of binding language. It won't do to try to speak English with no tenses, like pretending to be blind by walking around with a blindfold on all day, since that corrects the exuberance but doesn't fill in the deficiency. The deficiency in English is our lack, from a Southeast Asian perspective, of the things they use to build coherence, for example, focus devices in Malay, Javanese, and Tagalog. These small grammatical facts have large rhetorical consequences. I have described this elsewhere, too (Becker 1979a), and so a brief example may suffice here.

There is a common rhetorical figure in Classical Malay that might be called a *pun -lah* figure. Here is an example.

sa-telah demikian maka Sang	*Bimanyu pun*	*berjalan-lah*
	Bimanyu	walk

sambil	*mencium*	*bau*	*bunga-bunga-an*	*menghiborkan*
while	sniff	smell	flowers	entertain

hati-nya itu,	*naik*	*bukit*	*turun*	*bukit*	*berapa*
heart	ascend	hill	descend	hill	many

gunong	*dan*	*jurang*	*dilalui.*
mountain	and	valley	pass-over

In this figure, after a three-word pre-core (*sa-telah demikian maka*), which is untranslatable (except very awkwardly as 'having gone over-thus-then'), and which relates the figure to the larger textual context, there is the core of the figure (*Sang Bimanyu pun berjalan-lah*) in which the topic is introduced by *pun* and the general action (the verb-topic) by *-lah*. After that, until the end, there is an elaboration of the core, a string of verb phrases marking the role and focus of the unrepeated topic (*Bimanyu*). In the verb prefixes there is a progression from agentive role in focus (*men-* and *meng-*) to agentive role out of focus (*di-*). There is no assumption that these actions happened in any particular temporal order. The movement out of focus marks the closure of the figure. I hope that in this brief example the reader can see something of the rhetorical power of the Malay focus system, which can bind clauses with all the complexity of our tense system.[24]

Let me shift again to Burmese. To give coherent directions (to someone passing my house, for instance) in Burmese meant not imagining "shadow" tense but learning to meet the problem in new ways, for example, chaining one sentence to another by repeating the nucleus of the predicate of the previous sentence. And I learned that the word I thought "meant" past tense (*pyi:* 'finish')—a word I overused to the utter confusion of many Burmese (although some were used to "foreigner talk," a colonial attunement)—was what linguists call *inchoative:* to say what in English I thought meant 'come + past' (*la + pyi:*) usually meant something more like 'already begun coming'.[25] One can imagine the chaos generated by a speaker who makes that error constantly.

Mistakes in medium, mistakes in understanding structural relations—these were minor in immediate impact when compared with mistakes in interaction, the interpersonal context. There is, for instance, a principle that John Ross calls *me first*—the constraint that makes us say "here and there" rather than "there and here" and "that and this." However, speaking in Southeast Asia seems constrained by a principle one might call *you first,* so that they do say in Indonesia "there and here" (*sana sini*) and "that and this" (*itu ini*), and this deictic reversal extends throughout the language. As Clifford Geertz (1960) wrote:

> Politeness is something one directs towards others; one surrounds the other with a wall of behavioral (*lair*) formality which protects the stability of his inner life (*batin*). Etiquette is a wall built around one's inner feelings, but it is, paradoxically, always a wall someone else builds.

In most of Southeast Asia, one relies on being supported by others, and one reciprocally gives that support to others. Even the mildest forms of self-assertion are very hard, since they suggest inattention or lassitude on the part of others. And so, indirect (from our perspective) forms of communication are common, including multiple grammatical forms of what is often mislabeled "passive" in Austronesian languages. Self-expression itself, in these circumstances, becomes a common form of logophilia.

Of all the different kinds of mistakes a philologist must make in attuning to a new lingual world, the most difficult to overcome are mistakes of prior text. Prior text (or lingual memory) builds over a lifetime, giving resonance to things people say or hear. The hardest thing for an outsider to know is what is new and what is common—when people are speaking the past, when they are speaking the present. A lot of the more romantic exuberances of the ethnologist or philologist have their roots here. My own discussion of the basic "features" of Javanese theater (Becker 1979b) has been received by Javanese the way we might receive from someone the statement, "On television, stories are interrupted by commercials." What's original and exciting to me was old hat to others.

Kenneth Pike used to make the point, I now recall, in just those terms—the prior text from which "old hat" came just a moment ago. In a gently sexist way (since in the 1940s and 1950s it was not uncommon to laugh about women's hats), Pike used to say that if we were to describe all the women's hats we saw on the street as carefully as we could, we would still leave out one thing every woman saw: which ones were the latest fashion and which were slightly out of fashion. That's what "old hat" evokes for me—reinforcing a sexist stereotype with it (i.e., that women are the slaves of fashion). But the point is still important. Every utterance is to some extent speaking the past and to some extent deviating from it (the lingual analogs of embryology and evolution). To speak a cliché is not to make a clever remark, but an outsider can't tell them apart, since his or her store of remembered prior text is very meager. Subtle language play is nearly impossible in such conditions, and so is an emic aesthetic sense.[26] The real a priori of language is not a set of underlying logical propositions but rather remembered old language, the *philology of a group* (to extend Kroeber's sense of the term beyond just writing to include all evokable prior text, what people in artificial intelligence have lately called *scripts*). As Sapir once said, "Our culture in all its most frozen aspects has been created by its literalization of anterior tropes." Logophilia here might be called *culture troping*—framing another's words with one's own prior texts.[27]

The fifth distinct source of constraints on a text is the world that everyone believes, in some sense, exists outside or beyond language.

Here, above all, one is conscious that one is speaking in metaphors. For instance, in the previous sentence, the words *source, outside,* and *beyond* are self-evidently metaphors: what is language such that something can be said to be outside it? In what sense is it inside anything, or is anything beyond it? Is it any more or less meaningful to say referential meaning is located outside rather than inside language? To speak at all is to use metaphors. At this level there are no metaphor-free languages, nor is one possible. As Nietzsche (1873) wrote a good while ago: "to be truthful means using the customary metaphors—in moral terms: the obligation to lie according to fixed convention, to lie herd-like in a style obligatory for all."[28] Language is in this sense a tangle of metaphors we are *thrown* (to use Heidegger's term) into. One can remain quite unconscious of these metaphors. Here, too, there is profound exuberance and deficiency.

There are people of intelligence and goodwill who find the landscape quite familiar in other languages, and there are those bilinguals in unrelated languages who do not feel the depth of difference between them that I tell them I feel. For me, Burmese and English—or Indonesian and English, or Burmese and Indonesian—"project" strikingly different worlds, while to others I seem to be romanticizing an experience in which most of the landscape is quite familiar, so that in Burmese, or English, or Indonesian water is water, eyes are eyes, and oranges are round.

I continue to believe these friends (and the philosophers they read) are living in (or under?) an illusion, that they are unmindful of the deeply metaphoric nature of language—unmindful that even the "is" of "water is water" is metaphoric. This is a prime example of, in Sapir's words, "a literalization of an anterior trope." *Being,* in that sense, is a literalized trope, which one sees when one enters a language with no verb *to be.* It is one of the metaphors, in Nietzsche's sense, by which we tell the truth.

I suspect that my friends who think languages are basically alike too easily substitute foreign terms for English ones, make many unconscious grammatical adjustments, and leave the deepest metaphors intact. To ask anyone to do more than that may be asking too much, although something like that—the conscious recognition of the illusory power of language—is just what one of the major Southeast Asian religions, Buddhism, does ask of its congregations. If a language can be thought of as a repertoire of prior texts, then to enter a language spoken, and shaped, and transmitted by Buddhists is to take on the picture of language in those texts, along with the sounds, words, and grammatical conventions. In this Buddhist picture, language as a whole is basically pathological if one is not mindful of its illusory nature. In sharp contrast to this picture of language is the Sanskritic idea, widely held in Bali and parts of Java, that while nature is illusory some language is not: the pure Vedic Sanskrit spoken by the gods, which exists like Platonic forms. Madhav Deshpande (1979) has written about this.

> The status of Sanskrit in classical and medieval times resembles that of the world of Platonic Ideas. This is clearly reflected in the linguistic speculations of the Sanskrit grammarians, ritualists, and logicians. Therefore, the process of Sanskritization of non-Sanskrit languages continued to dominate the Indian linguistic scene and remained a very significant way of increasing the prestige of those languages. . . . In later times, the Persian and English compete with Sanskrit in this regard.

It is not my point here to argue one picture of language or another (impermanent or permanent) but rather to open up the difficulty a philologist faces in describing the exuberances and deficiencies of referential meaning. That "language *reflects* the world" is a metaphor. That "language constitutes the world" is another. There is no way out. As Sapir said, "the real world is to a large extent unconsciously built up on the language habits of the group."[29] We may argue about how large "a large extent" is, but, in any case, to make conscious that extent is to threaten images of self and world in painful ways. Logophilia here becomes a two-edged sword: it can mean to become so highly self-conscious about one's own language as a metaphor, or "lie," that one is somehow incapacitated from using it, since one must act as if one believes in something in order to speak at all. To live in the constant irony of this Nietzschian awareness makes one a constant threat to healthy conversation, the kind of talk that gets beyond these ironies. It is pathological not to forget sometimes about language and just be thrown into it and use it—in order to build friendships and seek truth.

On the other hand—it is the plague and virtue of professors always to see the other hand—there is a logophilia in failing to grant someone else the full validity of his or her lingual world—particularly if one is, as it were, a guest there. Again, one must seek to be thrown likewise into it and use it—in order to build friendships and seek truth. Relativism of this sort seems essential: not that anything goes, but that in a multilingual world many things do.[30]

We come, thereby, to the moral edge of this all. "A definition of language," Raymond Williams wrote, "is always, implicitly or explicitly, a definition of human beings in the world."[31] As such, it makes a difference when a language is lost—as it will when the last elephant, or orangutan, or fox is gone. Each language is an attunement over time—a unique way of sounding, shaping, remembering, interacting, and referring, and its loss means that the world it constitutes is lost, too. If one believes that all languages represent the same world, using the same underlying means, then the loss of one or more makes no difference at all. In fact, having a single language in the world is then something to dream of.

Whose language?

(How about Sanskrit?)

❖   ❖   ❖

In this essay about self-correction I have said nothing much about silence.[32] As Ortega said, "one has to renounce saying some things to be able to say anything at all." And so there are gaps—in sentences, in whole texts. There is the unsaid for which one would like to be given credit. And the unsayable.

As I write this I'm watching two geese standing by a pond. They are both preening, each standing on one foot, heads reaching back to fluff up their feathers and straighten their wing feathers. As I watch, something emerges: the two geese are moving nearly in unison. One head swings left and, after a second, the other follows. Sometimes one leads, sometimes the other. In the silent emergent attunement, we recognize mind. It is a love story, but even the cruelest, most bitter drama rests on that silent ground.

This lapse into silence is an awkward groping toward an authentic biological context for language, from which one might build toward language from something as basic as the earth's magnetic field, in relation to which those geese, they say, learn to orient themselves and build a consensual domain.

Philology might now be defined as the study of the consensual domain our languaging shapes.[33]

❖   ❖   ❖

And logophilia? Like Luria's man with a shattered world, maybe all we need is the right medicine and enough time to recover.

ACKNOWLEDGMENT

This essay was written while the author was a member of the Institute for Advanced Study, Princeton, New Jersey. I am grateful to the Institute for providing ideal conditions in which to write: silence, birch trees, a blue sky, geese, and sharp critics.

NOTES

1. That is, in a biological perspective, embryology and evolution.
2. The expression of the paradox built on the silent rhythm discussed below derives ultimately from the work of Gregory Bateson, elaborated in the studies of dialogue by Deborah Tannen (1984), Ronald Scollon (1981), and Frederick Erickson (1981).
3. I would feel more comfortable if Burke had written, "These words name the sorts of things and conditions and motions *we believe* there would be in the universe. . ." No matter what the ontology, to speak a language entails believing in a world beyond or outside language.
4. It was pointed out to me by Aram Yengoyan that in other languages (e.g.,

Australian languages), the natural and supernatural worlds are reversed. In these cases, a dream world is not metaphoric.

5. I draw heavily here on Arbuckle (1970). More recent work by Aarsleff further illuminates this period in the history of language study (see Aarsleff 1982). For an overall view of traditional philology, see the classic, U. von Wilamowitz-Moellendorff (1982 [1921]).

6. The quotations from Schleicher are in Arbuckle (1970).

7. For a detailed description of Goethe's organization of the morphological sciences, see Vietor (1950:20).

8. The process is well described in Bloch (1974).

9. For a serious challenge to this noetic myth, see Brandt (1981).

10. This tradition is described in Deshpande (1979).

11. For a detailed comparative study of person, see Forchheimer (1953).

12. This array is further broken down in Goffman (1981:124).

13. This is explored in part, for English, by Lakoff and Johnson (1980).

14. One of the few is Louis Wolfson whose interesting story is discussed in Pierssens (1980).

15. I owe this notion to Maurice Bloch (see Bloch 1974).

16. Weizenbaum (1967) remains one of the best descriptions of this illusion.

17. Two recent works explore this relationship of medium and authority: Anderson (1983), and Illich (1981).

18. Further insight into the conditions of languaging, sought, as we have seen above, by Ortega, is found in Bateson (1972).

19. For a pioneering study of the anthropology of food, see Mi Mi Khaing (1962, chap. 7).

20. Harris (1980) discusses this in detail.

21. One such tradition is described and criticized in van der Molen (1983).

22. These mnemonic sets are described in detail in Zurbuchen (1981:75).

23. This passage is quoted from Becker (1984:143–45).

24. Other modes of binding clauses into sentences are described in Foley and Van Valin (1984) particularly in chapter 6.

25. It is described as "change of state" in Wheatley (1982).

26. The notion of an emic aesthetic sense is explored in Becker (1982).

27. Culture troping is described from two points of view in Becker and Mannheim (1984).

28. From Nietzsche (1873), quoted in McDermott and Taylor (1983).

29. See Sapir (1929:209).

30. This kind of relativism is discussed in Geertz (1983).

31. Williams's neo-Marxist position (see, e.g., Williams 1977) bears a family resemblance to the position developed here.

32. Some recent explorations of silence are found in Tannen and Saville-Troike (1985).

33. The notion of consensual domain derives from the work of the biologists Humberto Maturana and Francisco Varela. In many long discussions we compared our disciplines (see Maturana 1974, 1976; and Varela 1979).

REFERENCES

Aarsleff, Hans
    1982   *From Locke to Saussure: Essays on the Study of Language and Intellectual History.* Minneapolis: University of Minnesota Press.
Anderson, Benedict
    1983   *Imagined Communities: Reflections on the Origin and Spread of Nationalism.* London: Verso.
Arbuckle, J.
    1970   August Schleicher and the Linguistics/Philology Dichotomy: A Chapter in the History of Linguistics. *Word* 26:17–331.
Bateson, Gregory
    1972   The Cybernetics of Self: A Theory of Alcoholism. In *Steps to an Ecology of Mind.* New York: Ballantine Books.
Becker, A. L.
    1979a   The Figure a Sentence Makes: An Interpretation of a Classical Malay Sentence. In *Syntax and Semantics 12: Discourse and Syntax,* ed. by T. Givón. New York: Academic Press.
    1979b   Text-building, Epistemology, and Aesthetics in Javanese Shadow Theatre. In *The Imagination of Reality,* ed. by A. L. Becker and A. Yengoyan. Norwood, N.J.: Ablex.
    1982   Beyond Translation: Esthetics and Language Description. In *Georgetown University Round Table on Language and Linguistics, 1982,* ed. by Heidi Byrnes. Washington, D.C.: Georgetown University Press.
    1984   Biography of a Sentence: A Burmese Proverb. In *Text, Play, and Story.* Proceedings of the American Ethnological Society, ed. by Edward M. Bruner. Washington, D.C.: American Ethnological Society.
Becker, A. L., and Bruce Mannheim
    1984   Culture Troping. Paper presented at the Symposium on "The Dialogic Emergence of Culture," American Anthropological Association, Denver, Colorado.
Bloch, Maurice
    1974   Symbols, Song, Dance, and Features of Articulation. *European Journal of Sociology* 15:55–81.
Brandt, Elizabeth A.
    1981   Native American Attitudes Toward Literacy and Recording in the

Southwest. *Journal of the Linguistics Association of the Southwest* 4:185–95.

Burke, Kenneth
  1961   *The Rhetoric of Religion: Studies in Logology.* Boston: Beacon Press.
Deshpande, Madhav
  1979   *Sociolinguistic Attitudes in India: An Historical Reconstruction.* Ann Arbor: Karoma.
Dewey, John
  1934   *Art as Experience.* New York: G. P. Putnam's Sons.
Emerson, Ralph Waldo
  1836   Language. In *Nature.* Boston: James Munroe and Co.
Erickson, Frederick
  1981   Timing and Context in Everyday Discourse. In *Children's Oral Communications,* ed. by O. W. Dickson. New York: Academic Press.
Foley, William, and Robert D. Van Valin, Jr.
  1984   *Functional Syntax and Universal Grammar.* London: Cambridge University Press.
Forchheimer, Paul
  1953   *The Category of Person in Language.* Berlin: Walter de Gruyter and Co.
Geertz, Clifford
  1960   *The Religion of Java.* New York: The Free Press.
  1983   The Way We Think Now: Toward an Ethnography of Modern Thought. In *Local Knowledge: Further Essays in Interpretive Anthropology,* New York: Basic Books.
Goffman, Erving
  1981   Footing. In *Forms of Talk.* Philadelphia: University of Pennsylvania Press.
Harris, Roy
  1980   *The Language Makers.* Ithaca: Cornell University Press.
Illich, Ivan
  1981   *Shadow Work.* London: Marion Boyars, Inc.
Kroeber, A. L.
  1944   *Configurations of Cultural Growth.* Berkeley: University of California Press.
Lakoff, George, and Mark Johnson
  1980   *Metaphors We Live By.* Chicago: University of Chicago Press.
Luria, A. R.
  1972   *The Man with a Shattered World: The History of a Brain Wound,* translated by Lynn Solotaroff. New York: Basic Books.
Maturana, Humberto R.
  1974   Cognitive Strategies (Strategies Cognitives). In *L'unite de l'homme,* ed. by E. Morin. Paris: Editions du seuil.

1976   Biology of Language: The Epistemology of Reality. In *The Neuro-psychology of Language*, ed. by R. W. Rieber. New York: Plenum Press.

McDermott, R. P., and Henry Taylor
1983   On the Necessity of Collusion in Conversation. Text 3.

Mi Mi Khaing
1962   *Burmese Family*. Bloomington: Indiana University Press.

Nietzsche, Frederick
1873   On Truth and Lies in an Extra-Moral Sense. In *The Portable Nietz-sche*, ed. by F. Kaufmann. New York: Viking Press.

Ortega y Gasset, José
1957   What People Say: Toward a New Linguistics. In *Man and People*, translated by Willard R. Trask. New York: W. W. Norton and Co.
1959   The Difficulty of Reading. *Diogenes* 28.

Pierssens, Michel
1980   *The Power of Babel: A Study of Logophilia*. London: Routledge and Kegan Paul.

Sapir, Edward
1929   The Status of Linguistics as a Science. *Language* 5:207–14.

Schleicher, August
1850   *Die Sprachen Europas in Systematischer Uebersicht*. Bonn: H. B. Konig.

Scollon, Ronald
1981   The Rhythmic Integration of Ordinary Talk. In *Georgetown University Round Table on Language and Linguistics, 1981*. Washington, D.C.: Georgetown University Press.

Tannen, Deborah
1984   *Conversational Style: Analyzing Talk among Friends*. Norwood, N.J.: Ablex.

Tannen, Deborah, and Muriel Saville-Troike
1985   *Perspectives on Silence*. Norwood, N.J.: Ablex.

Tedlock, Dennis
1983   *The Spoken Word and the Work of Interpretation*. Philadelphia: University of Pennsylvania Press.

van der Molen, Willem
1983   *Javanese Tekstkritiek: Een Overzicht en een Nieuwe Benardering Geillustreerd aan de Kunjarakarna*. Leiden: Royal Institute of Linguistics and Anthropology.

Varela, Francisco G.
1979   *Principles of Biological Autonomy*. New York: Elsevier/North-Holland.

Vietor, Karl
1950   *Goethe the Thinker*. London: Cambridge.

von Wilamowitz-Moellendorff, U.
  1982   *History of Classical Scholarship.* Baltimore: Johns Hopkins University
  [1921]   Press.
Weizenbaum, Joseph
  1967   Contextual Understanding by Computers. *Communications of the Association for Computing Machinery* 10, no. 8.
Wheatley, Julian K.
  1982   Burmese: A Grammatical Sketch. Unpublished Ph.D. dissertation, University of California, Berkeley.
Williams, Raymond
  1977   Language. In *Marxism and Literature.* New York: Oxford University Press.
Wittgenstein, Ludwig
  1958   *Philosophical Investigations.* New York: Macmillan.
Zurbuchen, Mary S.
  1987   *The Language of Balinese Shadow Theater.* Princeton, N.J.: Princeton University Press.

Language in Particular: A Lecture

The point of this talk might also be stated as, "If there is a linguistics in the humanities, if there is a humanities, what might it be and how might we do it and why would we want to do it in the first place?" In the title as it is given, the notion of the "particular" has been my road to a kind of linguistics in the humanities. It is a road that was first laid out by a very great teacher whom you heard last week, Kenneth L. Pike. It was Pike who said to me when he left Michigan, "What you should really work on is particularity. What is linguistics when it focuses on particularity?" It was a nice challenge, although I really had no idea what he meant. It was one of many challenges Pike gave me as a teacher. One thing we all do as linguists—or nearly all of us—is teach at one time or another. It is an important part of our activity as linguists and Pike has been one of the very best.

But there are many paths to the kind of linguistics that we might locate in the humanities, and many of you will already be further along, on other paths than mine. There will be some paths that you have already rejected. There are paths from Heidegger (1971), which carry one through such great rhetoricians as Ernesto Grassi (1980) from Italy and José Ortega y Gasset (1957, 1959) from Spain, both students of Heidegger. They had to leave Germany in 1931, disturbed by the "basic 'Germanic' characteristic of Heidegger," as Grassi writes in his book, *Rhetoric as Philosophy: The Humanist Tradition.* But they carried the lessons back and applied them in very interesting ways in their own cultures, as do, in our time, people like Hans-Georg Gadamer (1976) and Paul Ricoeur (1981) and, closer yet to us, Clifford Geertz (1983). I think there is a Heideggerian tradition of thought about language that these names represent.

There is another path. It's a path from Wittgenstein (1958), which brings us closest to home with people like Erving Goffman (1981), who took the notion of language games and turned it into those beautiful investigations and explorations that he spent his too short life describing, showing us the variety and particularity of the games that we play with language. Many of Erving's students are here tonight.

There is also, I believe, a tradition that is less well known, an American tradition, which, on the eve of the Fourth of July, seems appropriate to talk about, a little academic patriotism. This tradition starts for me with Ralph Waldo Emerson (1836) and his essays on language, which, I think, still have a lot to teach us if we can relearn how to read them. For one thing, it takes a lot of slowing down to read someone like Emerson, who wrote with pen and ink, not with a word processor; the kinds of things he wrote then took longer to write, and hence to read, than the kinds of things we write and read now. So when I recommend Emerson to my linguist friends, they often have difficulty, mainly because they try to read too fast. But you can go along and join this tradition wherever it gets easy, with any of the people who developed it, people like William James and Charles Peirce, and closer to our times, John Dewey, who as a language philosopher has been neglected. He sat in Peirce's classes at Johns Hopkins and tried to figure out the obscurity of that strange man, Peirce. At the celebration of his ninety-second birthday in New York, someone asked Dewey if he could sum up what he'd learned of importance in all those years, and he said something Emerson could have said, "Democracy begins in conversation" (Lamont 1959:58).

And there is one student of William James who is not usually recognized as a student of William James, though she is recognized as one of the most subtle explorers of everyday conversation. I'm talking about Gertrude Stein. I would like to play for you, in her own voice, an excerpt from *The Making of Americans*. It's a voice from the past, and so this is a little bit of what the Javanese call *jarwa dhosok*, taking old language, old voices, and trying to make them speak to us in the present. This is the traditional task of the philologist: trying to make old or distant language speak to us in the present. *Jarwa dhosok* in Javanese means, literally, taking old language (*jarwa*) and forcing it, pushing it (*dhosok*), right into the present. It takes several kinds of effort. But I think Gertrude Stein's voice is part of the Emersonian tradition I am talking about (see, for example, Stein 1974). (Pike's is, too.) She had one of the great lingual imaginations. She was one of those who can look at a particular bit of language and just play with it and see things in it of great richness. If you read any of her works, again slowly, like Emerson's, you will know what I am talking about. So I'd like to make her, with your permission, Patron Saint of Humanistic Linguistics, and I'd like to play a bit of her voice reading from *The Making of Americans*, talking about repeating ("repeating then is in every one"), and ending with the statement, "That was all there was then of discussing."

[A tape recording of Gertrude Stein reading the following passages]

Repeating then is in every one, in every one their being and their feeling and their way of realising everything and every one comes out of them in repeating. More and more then every one comes to be clear to some one.

Slowly every one in continuous repeating, to their minutest variation, comes to be clearer to some one. Every one who ever was or is or will be living sometimes will be clearly realized by some one. Sometime there will be an ordered history of every one. Slowly every kind of one comes into ordered recognition. More and more then it is wonderful in living the subtle variations coming clear into ordered recognition, coming to make every one a part of some kind of them, some kind of men and women. Repeating then is in every one, every one then comes sometime to be clearer to some one, sometime there will be then an orderly history of every one who ever was or is or will be living.

. . .

It happens very often that a man has it in him, that a man does something, that he does it very often that he does many things, when he is a young man when he is an old man, when he is an older man. . . . One of such of these kind of them had a little boy and this one, the little son wanted to make a collection of butterflies and beetles and it was all exciting to him and it was all arranged then and then the father said to the son you are certain this is not a cruel thing that you are wanting to be doing, killing things to make collections of them, and the son was very disturbed then and they talked about it together the two of them and more and more they talked about it then and then at last the boy was convinced it was a cruel thing and he said he would not do it and his father said the little boy was a noble boy to give up pleasure when it was a cruel one. The boy went to bed then and then the father when he got up in the early morning saw a wonderfully beautiful moth in the room and he caught him and he killed him and he pinned him and he woke up his son then and showed it to him and he said to him 'see what a good father I am to have caught and killed this one,' the boy was all mixed up inside him and then he said he would go on with his collecting and that was all there was then of discussing and this is a little description of something that happened once and it is very interesting. (Stein 1966:284, 489–90)

So if you had any doubts about Gertrude Stein as an ancestor, I hope that this passage has erased them, because there is such a great deal in these words about the kinds of things we are trying to study and understand today. What makes there be an end of discussing? Or, as William Labov (1982) asked here a few years ago, what makes fights in bars? Or on the Mediterranean?

That's all fine and interesting, you may say, but why a linguistics in the humanities? What's wrong with the linguistics we have now? The answer is, probably nothing. It's just that there is a lot of other work to be doing that involves a close look at languaging, and other ways to be doing it, and I would like to present some thoughts on this linguistics in the humanities that these ancestors have opened up for us. I speak not in opposition to another kind of linguistics but rather to identify a kind of work that needs doing. I don't want to replace scientific linguistics with anything else. I want to look at something that I think is important to do but that can't be handled within scientific linguistics.

Others will object, and say, "Didn't it take years for every linguistics department to drive out the humanists, often called *philologists?* What possible reason could there be for asking them back?" Let me say right away that the reason is not to restore some genteel and elitist kind of great thoughts or great books program in linguistics, a kind of old philology or new humanism. It's not a matter of old books, and old manners, and things like that, but of something quite different and new. I think the job to do is simply the one Paul Friedrich asked of us last night, to put the observer into our work. Put the observer back into our knowledge. Put the knower back into the known. In simplest words, I think, that is what linguistics in the humanities is all about. Years ago Kenneth Pike (1978) called it *emic analysis.* It took a long time to understand what he was talking about and what it meant. Questions come up about what things are in our analysis because of the observer. What parts of our analyses are observer parts? Can we separate these things out? Can we say, "this is language and that is the observation of language"? I think not.

In our seminar here this week we did an experiment that demonstrates these things more clearly than talking about them will. It's one of the quickest ways to demonstrate what I would like to talk about. By doing a short experiment I can evoke an experience that we all share, and that will save many words—something worth doing in the beautiful Georgetown twilight. (In Burmese this time of day is called "ugly-things become beautiful-time.") I'm going to ask you to write a sentence for me. I'm going to ask you to write a sentence, which can be as long as you like—as many clauses, compoundings, and embeddings as you feel inclined to—in which you describe the simple action that I'm going to do. The only constraint is that it be a single sentence. Then I'm going to look at some of these sentences and use that personal experience of writing that you will have had as the particularity we will focus on. In a linguistics of particularity, you have to have a particularity to start with (that's where the discipline or rigor comes from!) and the particularity is what you are making right now. So I'll say "start" and then I'll say "stop" and that episode between those words is what I want you to describe.

"Start . . . [the speaker performs a simple act, walking up the steps to the podium] . . . Stop."

[There is a long pause while the audience writes.]

There are slow writers and fast writers, just like there are slow speakers and fast speakers, and slow readers and fast readers. Some of you will have already written the first page of your novels.

What I'd like to do now is hear some of these sentences. If we did this in a smaller group we would stop with each one and we would talk about it and parse it and describe it and then compare it with the previous ones and think about what was different about them. What are the dimensions of the differences? What are the kinds of differences appearing between these sentences? At this point the experiment gets a little unwieldy because of your numbers, so, in the interest of saving time, I would like for you to read what you wrote in a loud clear voice, and we won't make much comment on each one but rather hear a bunch of them and then come back and try to summarize the dimensions of difference. I'll work a little less inductively because of the size of the crowd and the time constraint, but even in a seminar it can take weeks.

Fred Erickson, would you start?

"He walked up the steps across the stage to the podium, and slapped the book down on it as he arrived there."

Thanks. Ray McDermott?

"Repeating himself, he walked up a well-traveled path in this shrine of knowledge and took a place at the podium, where, repeating himself . . . [laughter]."

Wow! I said we weren't going to comment but you can see why this takes a long time when you are doing it in a seminar, because of the differences you see in each one. But let's go on. Deborah?

"You stepped onto the stage holding a book, walked to the podium, and put the book on the podium."

Rosalia?

"He walked slowly toward the podium, placed the book he was carrying on it, and looked at us."

Haj?

"Pete walked up the three steps to the stage carefully, continued carefully, watching his feet, stepping over the tangle of wires, came up to the podium, raised his arms, opening them wide to grasp both sides for it was wide, slowly raised his head and eyes to look at us gravely."

Wow! Gertrude Stein took, I see.

Let's continue. Would you read yours?

"He was walking up the steps to the podium being careful not to trip."

The next one?

"The man with the small paperback book in his hand who was standing at the edge of the stage began to walk up the steps onto the stage and then crossed the small semicircular platform to the podium where he put the book down onto the surface of the podium."

Very careful! Next one, please?

"Under the curious watchful eye of the assembled group, A. L. Becker engaged in a simple act in hopes to illustrate particularity."

That's what happens when someone does it twice in one week. She's in the seminar. Let's go on.

"He climbed the stage with a book in his hand and was approaching the podium where he put the book in front of the microphone."

Good. He got there, I think. Do you have one?

"The man walked to the place where he said 'start' and then to the place where he said 'stop.' "

No nonsense about that. How long is it going to take us to get to the back of the room? We'll probably never get to the back of the room but we have to do a few more.

"Calmly and deliberately, he climbed the stairs, watching the podium, set his book on the podium, and looked at his audience."

"The linguist, though he had removed his spectacles, walked up the stairs without tripping."

The major accomplishment of the evening. Anyone else? Yes, please?

"The knower being entirely the known walked across the stage to the lectern."

Emersonian! Yes, Andy Pawley.

"A vertical figure moved across a [noise] field, then it ceased to move, its lower part obscured by a square object."

There's a Martian in every audience, isn't there?

That was the voice from the etic side!

You see how this thing sets you up and you know you could go on for a whole week, and there's nothing else you'd have to do except this. The thing we haven't done is talk about the ways these sentences differ. But I would like first to make a general comment about them. The one thing that you have noticed from the start was that there were no two alike. And if we went through the whole hall, even if there were five hundred people, there would be no two alike. If there were two alike, we would be surprised, and suspicious. It hasn't yet happened to me in the twelve or so years I've been doing this experiment that there were ever two alike. What does that mean? What does that say about what is happening here, about what languaging does, about how languaging works?

On the other hand, I could have set up the experiment so that there would have been more than two alike. There is a very easy way to do it, and I have tried it that way. That would be to ask you not to write your sentences down but to just speak out your sentences from aural memory. As you might guess, after about five or six, people start saying, "Well I said just what he said." The inventiveness of new versions, of new "takes" on this situation seems to dry up under the pressure of the oral situation. This is fascinating, and it means that one of the things important in shaping these sentences you wrote is the fact that I asked you to write them, and the writing itself, the medium itself, is part of what shapes them. It is a basic part, which we don't have a real contrast for here because all of you read them. [Points to someone.] Except you, and yours was very short. It says interesting things about living within societies in which writing is common, and those where it isn't, and how deeply different these can be. One of those "inevitabilities" that everyone believes in right now is the notion that going from orality, to writing, to printing, to postprinting is a natural law of human cultures. And that we are getting a better and better noetic sphere to live in—that we are getting better at shaping, and remembering, and communicating knowledge. It is something that large parts of the human population are not quite sure about yet. It has to do with the pollution of the noosphere, if you want a nice political name for it.[1]

Well, we could make a list of the differences between your sentences. We could see that interaction between you [points to one] and me was different from that between you [points to another] and me. You used my name, you said "he," and you used "the man." These are a set of variants, and they specify a dimension of variation, the interpersonal dimension.

Some of your sentences sounded like the beginning of poems, or novels, or short aphorisms, or metacomments, or newspaper stories, or police reports. We had many different language games going on here. Each of you reached back in memory to prior texts and made this one, the one you wrote, a variant of those prior texts. We recognized them as we went along, as they evoked memories of sentences we had heard before. Each of those sentences has a past, a history. I do not believe that they were generated by rules, but rather they were drawn from lingual memory and reshaped to present circumstances. We are thrown into language, says Heidegger, we don't create it. *Jarwa dhosok*, say the Javanese.

And, of course, the structure was different in your sentences, the grammar was different. The way the clauses were put together was different. Here linguists have a fine and subtle language, describing the hierarchy of part-whole relations we call *structure*.

In order to use language, it must have transparency, so that if I say, "Look at Haj over there," I want you to look at Haj, not my words. In order to use language, we all have to believe in a world beyond language, although the world beyond one language is not the same as the world beyond another. The things you observed in the world here, the things that were seen happening up here, were different. Some of them weren't mentioned, some of them were not even seen by everyone. If I were to ask you now a question like, "What really happened?" or "Who among you was right?" or "Which one of these sentences was most correct, which of them gave the truest explanation of what happened?"—are these possible questions anymore? Can we still say that truth value is correspondence of language with an event? What event? Was there an event apart from all of these "takes"? Is there a true event that makes the other "takes" fictional? In this sense, as many have said, language does not represent the world or reflect it. Describing it creates it. Our language pushes us into those very biased ways of saying things. Ours is a world experienced in the act of interacting with it lingually, in the act of languaging it. As Gadamer (1976) wrote, "Being that can be understood is language."[2]

All of you had not to say many things in order to be able to say some things. What was unsaid is one of the major differences between your sentences. It is a minor difference here compared to what happens with other languages. Ortega (1957) has a nice comment about that in his essay on the difficulty of translation.

> The stupendous reality that is language cannot be understood unless we begin by observing that speech consists above all in silences. A being who could not renounce saying many things would be incapable of speaking. And each language represents a different equation between manifestations and silences. Each people leaves some things unsaid in order to be able to say others. Because everything would be unsayable. Hence the immense difficulty of translation: translation is a matter of saying in a language precisely what that language tends to pass over in silence.[3]

So there is a dimension of the said and the unsaid in your sentences. Each one of those dimensions I have sketched is a dimension of difference.

1. negotiating interpersonal relationships
2. shaping the medium
3. making a grammatical sentence
4. looking through language to a believed world
5. evoking prior language
6. leaving many things unsaid, some of them unsayable

All of those things come together to shape the events that were happening when each of you was languaging about what I did. You will notice that I shift from the word *language* to the word *languaging*. That is one of the easiest ways I know to make the shift from an idea of language as something accomplished, apart from this activity we have shared, to the idea of languaging as an ongoing process. That, too, is something that those thinkers I mentioned earlier were all pressing: a movement away from language as something accomplished, as something apart from time and history, to language as something that is being done and reshaped constantly. That is why we can never run out of new sentences for that little episode that just happened here. We can never run out because old language (prior text) is always being reshaped to present needs. It's always being created.

So how do our various *fictions*, as Wittgenstein called them, our various "takes" on that episode differ? In all the ways that language can mean, they differ. The checklist I just gave you of six dimensions of difference is only a personal one. And the question of what "really" happened? Well, we could negotiate a joint statement. But in negotiating that statement, which we all might vote on, then, as being the most accurate negotiated description for some purpose, the negotiated statement itself would be subject to all the particular constraints that I just mentioned above and would not be a way of escaping them. So the observer is part of the observed. The observer is more than part of the observed. The observer is shaping the observed just as the observed is shaping the observer. They are interlocked.

The movement across languages, philology, is one of going to a place like Burma, or Java, or Bali and spending one's lifetime trying to converse with the people there in ways that make sense and ways that also allow them to preserve their worlds, allow them their descriptions of what is happening. I've done that little experiment in several of those countries when I was teaching there. It's amazing the things they say and do not say. In Java they would very often say things like "The teacher seems very annoyed with us today." With a Japanese audience I recall almost everyone in the audience referred to the size of the steps, with medium-sized steps or small steps or long steps— they didn't agree, except that steps were important.

What we are doing here is all in English. When we get to those other languages the differences are in the same dimensions I listed above—the interpersonal relationships, the prior texts, the reference to a world believed beyond language, and all the others—making sentences, breaking silence, shaping a medium. All of these things we did together are also the dimensions that can be different from one language to another. None of them is unchanged from language to language. Every one of those dimensions changes as we go into another language and we can often not predict how they will change: in the dimension of structure, the coherence of things, the ways things are put together. In the dimension of prior texts. The hardest thing to do in Burma, or Java, or any place foreign is to know when something somebody has told you is original with that person or has a past in that culture that everyone there would recognize. Prior text is the real a priori of language, not some logical deep structure or anything like that. Prior text is the real source, the real a priori of speaking, in the view that I'm trying to develop here.

And that great difference between languages, between ways of languaging, that profound difference is also one of the themes that those ancestors I claimed earlier share.

But the recognition of this variety and diversity in different languages leaves us with several demons. There are fears about where this kind of thinking can lead us, and those demons are very real ones and they are very scary ones. Learning to cope with demons is a lot of what living in certain parts of Southeast Asia is about. In many places, perhaps all places, the world beyond the world that language shapes is full of demons. And so I'm going to tell a demon story, mainly because I want to refer to it again in a minute, and now I've just mentioned demons, so it's relevant and timely. If I tell a story, you will recognize that I'm doing what humans do in *human linguistics,* as Haj calls it. One of Gregory Bateson's favorite stories was about the guy who asked the computer, in his best computerese, "Will you ever think like a human?" They put that into the computer, and it whirred and clicked for a while and out came a slip of paper that said, "That reminds me of a story."

Mentioning demons reminds me of a story, but that's not quite honest either. It says right here in my notes, "Tell the demon story." Erving Goffman (1981) was on to tricks like this, and he taught us to be sure that all of these little stories and asides we happen to remember are the most planned and rehearsed parts of any lecture.

In Bali they give shadow plays and readings of old texts and things when there are a lot of demons around, when someone dies, or someone is suffering, or something chaotic is happening. A puppeteer or a reading club comes to the place of difficulty and begins to perform nonstop until the corpse is cremated or some other imbalance has been brought back to balance. I watched the shadow plays, and fell asleep many nights to the voices reading and translating Old Javanese texts, and finally asked a Balinese friend:

"How does it work? You know how DDT kills bugs and then the malaria doesn't come. How does a story work? What goes on? How does a story get rid of a demon?"

And he said, "It's like doors."

"Like doors?"

"Yes." He acted as if I should be satisfied with that, or maybe it was just that in Bali you have to prod a story along more than we are used to prodding, so I said,

"Like doors? Okay. What do you mean 'like doors'?"

"You know how our doors are, around our homes and our temples. You have a wall. You have a gap in the wall and behind the gap you have a slab of wall a little wider than the gap. To enter, you have to go right or left around the slab. That's the first door. Then there is another wall with a gap backed by a slab, and this second door is not right across from the first door but offset a little. Do you understand how these doors work?"

"I never thought about it," I said. "I thought they were there so you could get privacy in your house so no one could see you. . . . You could sit in there relaxed."

And he didn't know what I was talking about, I suspect, for he said,

"Why would anyone want to do that?"

He returned to the topic, "It's to keep out demons."

"How does it work?"

He said, "Demons can only move in straight lines. It's people move in curves, they move around like this." And he demonstrated the way a lot of Balinese move on the street, around in curves all the time, nothing in straight lines. "Demons can't get in the doors because they bounce off the slabs. Humans just move around them. If a demon by luck gets through the first door, it just bounces off the next wall. So if you build a series of concentric walls with offset doors, you're safe from demons."

That made real sense. "But what about stories?"

"Demons think in straight lines, too. Our stories, you know how they are all so tangled and thick, one story inside another . . . or our music, with many things happening at once in different rhythms."

"Yes," I said, prodding.

"Humans love that. Demons can't stand it."

And thus I was taught one of the big lessons, that tangles should be welcomed as good news—they keep out demons.

There are demons in the air with this talk about observers and fictions and some of the other things we have been talking about this evening, this collection of experiences. The recognition of the immense variety of language games leaves one at the end of a Goffman essay with an almost oceanic feeling. It's the same at the end of reading Wittgenstein's later works. The variety of kinds of things that we can do with language defeats cataloguing, except at the most general levels. And at those general levels the particularities that we're concerned with here, the things that make you different from you, and you different from you, these particularities wash out. If we are interested in those differences, if we're interested in getting across those differences to talk to another person, then those things that wash out at higher levels of generality are just the things we need and just the things we can't afford to wash out. And that's why Wittgenstein talks about particularity: the things that make your sentences different, or that make English different from Balinese.

This kind of thought often is called subjectivism. There seem to be no constraints on one's fantasy in interpreting what other people say. One demon is fantasy.

Another demon of particularity is that it seems to shut out generalization. If we are not generalizing, if we are not capturing generalities, then what are we doing? It's what we get rewarded for, seizing on generalizations. If we turn toward particularity, one of the demons says, then that's all over. That's no longer something we do. Isn't that too much to give up?

Clifford Geertz (1983) has some interesting things to say about this matter of particularity and its demons as it applies to the social sciences. I think what he says applies to linguistics as well. He distinguishes two ways of approaching the work of the social sciences. One he calls "rules and instances" and the other "cases and interpretations." In the rules-and-instances approach, the rigor comes with the setting up of a body of rules, which instances illustrate. Instances come and go. If, when you are setting up a rule, your example doesn't fit, get a better example. It would be silly to use a bad example. The rules are the main source of discipline and examples come and go. In the cases-and-interpretations approach, the examples sit there. They don't go away. You spend twenty years trying to figure out a Burmese sentence. (See, for example, Becker 1984.) You go over a text the way Manny Schegloff did so beautifully on Monday night, over and over and over one passage for six months, eight months, a year, and then you begin to see the particularity of it. Particularity is not something we begin with; particularity is something we arrive at, by repeating. Particularity is something we learn. We don't distinguish birds until we learn their names and hear their songs. Up to that point we hear "birds" around us and then we begin to pick up their particularity along with the language. Particularity is something we achieve.

Our discipline and our rigor in humanistic linguistics come right there, from the particularity of the text-in-context not from the rigor of the rules. By *context* I mean the six sources of constraints I laid out a few minutes ago. For one working on interpreting a text-in-context, you pick up all the new theories that come along in linguistics, all the thirty million theories of grammar that Jim McCawley (1982) writes so well about—they come along, and you take them and apply them to your text-in-context, and they each show you something you didn't notice before, often something beautiful. But then you cast them aside because there's another one coming along that is going to show you something else. The discipline of the philologist comes not from theory but from a language—the texts and conversations he or she is trying to understand.

So you can see that there is a kind of reverse behavior for these two approaches Geertz identifies. The one working with a particular text grabs the theories as they come by and celebrates them by applying them and learning their lessons. But the discipline is not in the theories. The discipline is in the particularity of the text-in-context. One is grateful to the theories. Again, I'm not trying to replace anything in linguistics but to describe a kind of linguistics I call *philology*, the historic matrix from which linguistics was abstracted.

I want to say one more thing about particularity. Notice that all of the constraints that I talked about earlier—structural, interpersonal, generic, referential, medial, and silential—the sources of constraints on the unique sentences you wrote earlier about my walking up on the stage: all of those different constraints, which were working on each of you in different ways, can only be seen and can only come together in particularity. They don't come together at more general levels. They come together in the particularity of the sentences you wrote. Holding on to the experiences that we just shared is our discipline. That's what is going to keep us talking about the same thing, not necessarily the logic or lack of it in the superstructure.

There is one more demon. Relativism. This all sounds like relativism, and the conversation goes off into aspects of morality. Aren't we just loosening up morals? Are there no standards anymore? Is this the 1960s all over again? (No, I assure you it's the 1940s talking, the decade of Einstein and Gertrude Stein.) Relativism is one of the demons some people conjure up, but I think that they get it wrong. A relativist like me doesn't think anything goes. A relativist does think, however, that many things go, and that many different languages and their cultures around the world have learned, over thousands and thousands of years, to attune themselves to their worlds in much better ways than other people tell them they must or should. Relativism doesn't mean anything goes but it means that the world the Balinese live in, and that they shape into understanding with their language, is a valid, real, true, good world to be in and doesn't have to be destroyed and replaced. So relativism does not seem to be a real demon for us either, unless we insist on thinking in straight lines.

If the demons of relativity and particularity are at least at bay, there remains subjectivism. There was something we might call *the personal* in the sentences you wrote tonight, something very close to particularity: your own voices sounding out of your own memory, shaping old texts coherently to new situations. This personal part is not best described, as it often is, as characteristic choices among varying possibilities, but something much less intentional. You must examine yourselves in this. I am not planning the sentences I speak to you or choosing from a grammatical/lexical menu. I am not reading, but, as we all do as teachers, just speaking from notes, old language shaped to the present situation—*jarwa dhosok.* I can look back at what I said and parse it or explain it in different ways, but one thing I cannot do, and I assume you can't either, is parse and speak a new sentence at the same time. I can do a lot of other things simultaneously to speaking—like wave to a passing friend or wonder if my shirt is hanging out in back—but I can't parse as I speak. This, too, is something Wittgenstein and Goffman liked to talk about, the deep difference between speaking and an analysis of speaking.

There is a huge personal dimension in languaging that makes each of your sentences different, and that's just what I want to get at. Most of the languaging we do most of the time is not conversation but rather that inner newsreel that goes on all the time, replaying today's events and trying to make ourselves come out more heroically by adjusting all sorts of things and getting our replay fictions right, or rehearsing an upcoming task. Buddhist teachers sometimes call it gossip. That continual personal play of language within us is probably where we spend most of our time. I'd bet a goodly number of you are there right now. This is not to say that conversation is not essential in order to learn languaging. I'm aware of Wittgenstein's arguments against the possibility of a private language, but the language that we are thrown into becomes a part of our consciousness—how great a part we are only now beginning to realize. This is hard to discuss, the huge personal dimension of language, this thing we are thrown into and that we experience at such a personal level.

The problem many of us have with science is that it does not touch the personal and particular. Doing science means making sentences that meet certain criteria, one of which is that the sentences be impersonal. The criteria for scientific statements include explanatory hypotheses, which will give mechanisms for generating whatever you are observing, and which will then lead to deductions and predictions about other things, and include actual tests that you can carry out to demonstrate what you are talking about. Can we do that? In the world that I am talking about, is it possible? If we study the particular, the differences between each one of your "takes," can we meet all of the criteria for scientific statements? I think the answer is no.

I do not think we should worry that the answer is no. There are other ways of making true and useful statements; there are other disciplines, just as rigorous, just as important, and just as necessary as scientific statements are—if our study is of particularity. By adopting scientific constraints on the statements we make, we move away from the very thing we want to study. This seems to me to be one of the major points of Wittgenstein's *Philosophical Investigations* (1958). The nonuniversality of scientific statements, their cultural embeddedness, is clear to many anthropologists—one thinks immediately of the work of Gregory Bateson (1972), and Clifford Geertz (1983), and Stephen Tyler (1978)—and to many philosophers, from John Dewey (1934) to Richard Rorty (1986).

What, then, must we do? What do we do that is different than what we did before? Our goal, following Wittgenstein, is description, as careful and self-conscious as we can make it. And why describe languages—that is, languaging in different societies? I think the answer, as Geertz often puts it, is to learn to converse with those we have difficulty conversing with. Whether they are our own neighbors and family or people halfway around the world, the same kinds of differences are involved, I think, and learning about one teaches about the other. Recognizing the dramatic differences I confront in speaking to a Balinese prepares me to recognize the more subtle differences I confront in speaking to my wife or my children, and it teaches me to respect them, not out of some abstract moral principle but as the practical first step in having my own differences respected. I know as a lifelong language teacher that this is very difficult to do, particularly with people who believe in the myths about the universality of logic and emotion.

All of this is clearly reflected in the ways we write. What we do as scholars is determined mostly by the final product we anticipate, the kind of statements we will be making and the criteria with which it seems proper to evaluate them. There are many things humanist linguists do. Sometimes we describe words. (People like Raymond Williams [1977], and Gaston Bachelard [1969], and others have done brilliantly with that.) We describe language games and how they work, different plots and rhetorical figures in different languages, all with the goal of helping us to better converse with those we have difficulty conversing with.

One of the main things we do, one of the central activities of the modern philologist, is translating. We often make translating the focus of our work, the way parsing is the center for a linguist. I am often asked, by deans and such, what it is every linguist must know, humanistic linguist, or scientific linguist, or linguist of any kind, and I think that the answer is clearly "parsing"—detailed, rich, and subtle parsing. But for the philologist parsing is subordinate to the greater discipline of translating. Parsing is still essential, but it is not the goal. Translating is. I mean here the process of translating as a method of analysis and exploration, going back and forth and forth and back from source text to translation and translation to source.

In that process, back and forth, what we are doing, in the words of Ortega (1959), is learning what our exuberances and deficiencies of interpretation are. What is happening in this process of translating is that the observer is changing. We put before us a line of Javanese and then we put beside it an English translation, any English translation, from a linguist's glosses to a poet's well-wrought figure; it doesn't matter which. And then we look at all the things in the English that are not in the Javanese: the exuberances. We find almost always that exuberances account for more than half of the stuff in the English translation. (Given our experiment tonight, I'm sure you can believe that.) Then we look at the Javanese and we see all the things in the Javanese that didn't get across into the English because there is nothing in English that can be a counterpart of those things. These are the deficiencies, and they almost always account for more than half of the stuff in the Javanese text we are translating from. The exuberances are those things in your translation that are there only because your language demands them, and the deficiencies are the things in the original language that don't get across.

In too many articles by linguists what is being parsed is the exuberant and deficient translation, often in the form of a set of glosses that evoke English prior texts. And that is why parsing, I think, must be subordinate to translating.

I think the point about exuberances and deficiencies is clear without an example. I invite you to try it on your own turf. At all linguistic levels there are these exuberances and deficiencies, from the tiniest grammatical "facts" to the largest rhetorical ones.

The products of this exploration are not scientific articles, not statements that meet the criteria of science I mentioned earlier, but essays. Essays are disciplined by particularity. They are exercises in correcting the exuberances and deficiencies of an observer—with the goal of helping us to converse with those people we have difficulty conversing with, attuning ourselves to another language, another person's languaging, and keeping his or her philology, his or her world, intact (or nearly so) in doing it. It's a necessary kind of work, I think. It's an important kind of work, if Dewey was right—and I think he was—that democracy begins in conversation.

It is also very tough, because particular texts are unmerciful disciplinarians. Like doors. And like clocks. So, I'll stop.

ACKNOWLEDGMENTS

This text was transcribed and edited from a tape recording. I would like to thank Deborah Tannen, Haj Ross, Andrew Pawley, John Lawler, and J. O. Becker for useful comments and Carolyn Leilich for making the transcription.

NOTES

1. The term *noosphere* is from Pierre Teilhard de Chardin. Walter Ong talks of the "noetic sphere" with, I think, the same sense. Inscribed over the door to the hall where this lecture was held, there were these apt words of Teilhard's: "The age of nations is past. It remains for us now if we don't wish to perish, to set aside the ancient prejudices and build the earth." That a major part of these ancient prejudices are right down there in our language is also something shared by the thinkers invoked at the beginning of the lecture. In Wittgenstein's (1958:114) clear phrasing: "One thinks that one is tracing the outline of the thing's nature over and over again, and one is merely tracing round the frame through which we look at it."

2. This phrase appears often in Gadamer's writings. See the essay "Aesthetics and Hermeneutics" in *Philosophical Hermeneutics.*

3. The quotation is from the chapter, "What People Say: Language. Toward a New Linguistics" in *Man and People.* This chapter is also the source of my use of the term *philology.* What is translated into English as "a new linguistics" is in Spanish "una nueva filología."

REFERENCES

Bachelard, Gaston. 1969. The poetics of space. Boston: Beacon Press. (See especially the introduction, in which he discusses the differences between the philosophy of science and that of the humanities.)

Bateson, Gregory. 1972. Steps to an ecology of mind. New York: Ballantine. (See especially the essay: Style, grace, and information in primitive art.)

Becker, A. L. 1984. Biography of a sentence: A Burmese proverb. Text, play, and story: The construction and reconstruction of self and society, ed. by Edward Bruner, 135–55. Washington, D.C.: American Ethnological Society.

Dewey, John. 1934. Art as experience. New York: Putnam.

Emerson, Ralph Waldo. 1836. Nature. Boston: Munroe. (See especially chapter IV: Language.)

Gadamer, Hans-Georg. 1976. Philosophical hermeneutics. Berkeley: University of California Press. (See especially chapter 4: Man and language.)

Geertz, Clifford. 1983. Local knowledge. New York: Basic Books. (See especially chapter 1: Blurred genres; and chapter 7: The way we think now: Toward an ethnography of modern thought.)

Goffman, Erving. 1981. Forms of talk. Philadelphia: University of Pennsylvania Press.

Grassi, Ernesto. 1980. Rhetoric as philosophy: The humanist tradition. University Park: Pennsylvania State University Press.

Heidegger, Martin. 1971. On the way to language. New York: Harper and Row.

Labov, William. 1982. Speech actions and reactions in personal narrative. Analyzing discourse: Text and talk. Georgetown University Round Table on Languages and Linguistics, 1981, ed. by Deborah Tannen, 219–47. Washington, D.C.: Georgetown University Press.

Lamont, Corliss (ed.). 1959. Dialogue on John Dewey. New York: Horizon.

McCawley, James. 1982. Thirty million theories of grammar. Chicago: University of Chicago Press.

Ortega y Gasset, José. 1957. Man and people. New York: Norton. (See especially chapter 11: What people say: Language. Toward a new linguistics.)

Ortega y Gasset, José. 1959. The difficulty of reading. Diogenes 28.1–17.

Pike, Kenneth L. 1978. Here we stand—Creative observers of language. Approches du langage: Actes du colloque interdisciplinaire tenu à Paris. Sorbonne, Serie 'Etudes' 16.

Ricoeur, Paul. 1981. Hermeneutics and the human sciences. Cambridge: Cambridge University Press.

Rorty, Richard. 1986. Method and morality. Values and the social sciences, ed. by Robert Bellah and Paul Rabinow. (See also, more recently, The contingency of language, London Review of Books, 17 April 1986.)

Ross, Haj. 1982. Human linguistics. Contemporary perceptions of language: Interdisciplinary dimensions. Georgetown University Round Table on Languages and Linguistics, 1982, ed. by Heidi Byrnes, 1–30. Washington, D.C.: Georgetown University Press.

Ross Haj. 1986. Languages as poems. Languages and linguistics: The interdependence of theory, data, and application. Georgetown University Round Table on Languages and Linguistics, 1985, ed. by Deborah Tannen and James E. Alatis, 180–204. Washington, D.C.: Georgetown University Press.

Stein, Gertrude. 1966. The making of Americans. New York: Something Else Press.

Stein, Gertrude. 1974. How writing is written. Los Angeles: Black Sparrow Press.

Tyler, Stephen. 1978. The said and the unsaid: Mind, meaning, and culture. New York: Academic Press.

Williams, Raymond. 1977. Marxism and literature. Oxford: Oxford University Press.

Wittgenstein, Ludwig. 1958. Philosophical investigations. New York: Macmillan (see especially paragraphs 109, 114, and 115).

PART 7
AFTERWORD

An Afterword: Apologia for the Essay

In the prefaces, and in some of the essays themselves, I've mentioned how important it is that these works be taken as essays. In these few final words I want to say a little more about the essay itself, for it seems to me that what distinguishes philology from linguistics is not so much theory and technique as it is the goal each discipline aims toward, the kinds of posttexts each would shape. More simply, linguists tend to write articles, philologists, at least of the sort I have in mind, essays.

A great deal of misunderstanding starts there. The writer of linguistic articles wonders where the rigor is in an essay, why the hypothesis is not clearly stated, and how reliable the evidence is. The writer of essays deplores the impoverishment of the "data" in an article and condemns the scientific jargon, the formalism, and the pose that it is all impersonal. But, rather than condemn one or the other, it makes sense to recognize them as different genres, each with its own uses and disciplines.

I often have heard from my friends in linguistics a reaction to my work that is something like "That's all very interesting, but it's not linguistics." I argued for years that it is, or ought to be, linguistics, but then I came to agree with them. It is something else—and the old term, *philology,* seemed available, after its having been gradually cast out of linguistics over the period of more than a century, since the days of August Schleicher and Goethe and the rise of the morphological sciences. Most (not all) academic departments of linguistics got rid of their last philologists some time ago, and professional journals in linguistics don't, as a matter of course, print essays.

There are two prime analytic acts in linguistics: glossing and parsing. Linguists tend to be highly skilled and sophisticated about the latter, parsing, but clumsy and crude about the former, glossing. Glossing is a rough kind of translation based on the premise that a word can have, in isolation, a neutral or "central" meaning. In the linguist's articles, foreign texts, usually contextless sentences, have written under each word an English "equivalent." Scholars quibble about the accuracy of the *glosses,* as they are called, but very rarely over their very presence, their possibility, their ontology—because on close examination almost every gloss seems wildly exuberant and deficient.

Furthermore, the parsing, in which the glossed words are assigned to grammatical categories, has seemed to me to be preordained by the glossing itself; once the foreign word became an English word its grammatical categories were, for the most part, already determined. It seemed clearer and clearer to me over the decades of studying Southeast Asian texts that, whatever the benefits might be (and they are considerable) of describing a foreign language in the categories and terms of English (or Dutch, or Sanskrit, or some other Indo-European language), it is just as aggressive and appropriative as any other "colonial" act.

Further still, after performing appropriative glossing and parsing, to then claim, as some linguists do, that all human languages look basically alike seems now a more political than scientific assertion. Is there a universal grammar, language-neutral, operating in the minds of all humans (as most linguists still believe), or do we not, with our exuberant and deficient glossings and parsings, merely describe one language in terms of another? The latter possibility has at least, in Dewey's words, "warranted assertability," which is about as close as a pragmatist can come to "truth."

The question remains open. My bias is clear. And so, I hope, is the ethics it grows from.

The kind of philology I am sketching is thus a comparative discipline, and, because of the ethics of it, it is also a rhetorical one (if one accepts the old description of rhetoric as the ethical study of language).

At the center of this new philology, as with the old one, is translation. The aim here, however, is not to achieve more and more accurate translations of everything into English. Rather, the goal is reciprocity, or, in Derrida's unfairly maligned term, *deconstruction* of a translation, a movement toward the source, which entails further deconstruction of the source into its many sources. As the Javanese poem (see page 344, above) puts it, *ungulihken swara mring kang duwe swara*, or, in all its exuberance and deficiency, 'Let the sound go back to the source'.

The philologist has traditionally done this work in footnotes, commentaries on translations, and so the philological essay might well be considered an expanded, elaborated footnote on a translation. The particular translation provides the exigency or occasion for the essay. It is also the source of discipline and rigor for the essay beyond translation.

In an essay called "Blurred Genres" (often quoted in these pages) Clifford Geertz distinguishes between, in his words, "a law and instances ideal of explanation" and "a cases and interpretations one." In the former, which I would associate with the writing of academic articles, the discipline and rigor reside explicitly in the theory, in the system of axioms and laws of which one's hypotheses are a part. The "instances" are selected to help support or "prove" the hypotheses. One does not choose a bad example. The rigor is to be found in the formal consistency of the laws not in the particularity of the instances. Laws are meant to hold firm while instances come and go. Instances are adjusted, simplified of irrelevant details.

In contrast, in a cases-and-interpretations ideal of explanation, the discipline comes from the cases, the particular cases. For a philologist, the texts to be translated are the cases. Many different, even contradictory, modes of interpretation are adopted, and then cast aside if they are not useful, to help one understand the cases. New theories provide new insights into the case at hand, the text, whose disciplinary rigor comes from its particularity. To the question of where the rigor in their work comes from, writers of articles and writers of essays have very different answers.

Philological essays, like footnotes to a translation, grow from the particularities of translation and take their rigor from them. They are self-consciously comparative, one language described in terms of another, and they have an overriding rhetorical aim: cross-lingual restitution, beyond translation.

Index